The Early Settlement of North America

The Early Settlement of North America is an examination of the first recognizable culture in the New World: the Clovis complex. Gary Haynes begins his analysis with a discussion of the archeology of Clovis fluted points in North America and a review of the history of the research on the topic. He presents and evaluates all the evidence that is now available on the artifacts, the human populations of the time, and the environment, and he examines the adaptation of the early human settlers in North America to the simultaneous disappearance of the mammoths and mastodonts.

Haynes offers a compelling reappraisal of our current state of knowledge about the peopling of this continent and provides a significant new contribution to the debate with his own integrated theory of Clovis, which incorporates vital new biological, ecological, behavioral and archeological data.

GARY HAYNES is Professor and Chair of the Department of Anthropology at the University of Nevada, Reno. He is internationally renowned for his research on the ecology of extinct mammoths and mastodonts as well as southern African paleoecology and prehistory. He is the author of *Mammoths, Mastodonts, and Elephants: Biology, Behavior, and the Fossil Record* (Cambridge, 1991), and a member of the Society for American Archaeology, the American Quaternary Association, the Society of Africanist Archaeologists, and the Zimbabwe Scientific Association.

The
Early Settlement of North America

The Clovis Era

GARY HAYNES

University of Nevada, Reno

CAMBRIDGE
UNIVERSITY PRESS

PUBLISHED BY THE PRESS SYNDICATE OF THE UNIVERSITY OF CAMBRIDGE
The Pitt Building, Trumpington Street, Cambridge, United Kingdom

CAMBRIDGE UNIVERSITY PRESS
The Edinburgh Building, Cambridge CB2 2RU, UK
40 West 20th Street, New York NY 10011-4211, USA
477 Williamstown Road, Port Melbourne, VIC 3207, Australia
Ruiz de Alarcón 13, 28014 Madrid, Spain
Dock House, The Waterfront, Cape Town 8001, South Africa

http://www.cambridge.org

First published 2002

Printed in the United Kingdom at the University Press, Cambridge

Typeface Quadraat in 9.5/12pt.   *System* LaTeX 2$_\varepsilon$ [TB]

A catalogue record for this book is available from the British Library

ISBN 0 521 81900 8 hardback
ISBN 0 521 52463 6 paperback

Contents

Figures

Tables

Preface

The ancient hunting-gathering people who made Clovis fluted points throughout North America created an archeological watershed. On the far side of the dated Clovis presence is a continent where earlier sites and artifacts are difficult if not impossible to find, implying a landscape virtually empty of human beings. But on the near side is a continent-wide occupation by people whose artifacts, settlements, and technology are everywhere similar enough to suggest either close and continuous social interactions by low-density foragers, or a rapid dispersal by a single culture into previously unoccupied territory.

I begin this book with a quick review of the long debate about the first people to colonize North America. Some archeologists think the peoples who made Clovis projectile points were the first to enter the continent, but others have disagreed for decades. I then interpret patterns in what I see as human adaptations to North American habitats during the time interval when fluted points were being made. I also review the information at hand about the dramatic environmental changes that occurred at the same time the fluted-point-makers were so widely distributed. The focus is on the resources available for people to use in different ecozones of the continent, particularly the largest mammals.

North America's last populations of megamammals – those weighing over 1,000 kg, namely mammoths and mastodons – died out completely during the same narrow time interval when the fluted-point-makers were widely dispersing. Some prehistorians do not think there is a chronological correlation between first appearances of big-game-hunting human groups (Clovis) and the last appearances of large mammals (Grayson 1989, 1991; Meltzer 1995), but the radiocarbon record does indeed show that both "events" converged at 11,000 rcybp.

This book's chapters re-examine archeological interpretations of fluted-point assemblages and sites, including my own interpretations, and also provide new information about mammoth and mastodon bone assemblages. In addition to being a survey of the traditional anthropological theories and principles that can be applied to understanding migration and foraging, the chapters re-examining archeological materials offer an explicitly ecological perspective on population dispersals and movements. I aim to appraise ideas currently in circulation about fluted-point-makers, plus introduce previously unpublished facts and ideas related to the late Ice Age and fluted-point peoples in North America. This book is a critical review of the available data about the time period when Clovis existed.

The archeological "culture" named Clovis is identifiably distinct, and appears as a short-lived horizon in much of unglaciated North America. It is fascinating and unique. Its life is so short, its dispersal so rapid and far-reaching, its effects on natural ecosystems perhaps so extraordinary that an exceptional and original body of theory is needed to explain it. As in a natural science such as physics, a set of interrelated but extremely complex phenomena require a complex set of explanatory principles and concepts, a sort of "unified" of "superunification" theory. Such a unified theory – in this case about Clovis and the peopling of the New World – would refer to diverse aspects of the peopling process, such as the genetics of the first colonizers, the DNA comparisons between Old and New World populations, historical-linguistic comparisons, lithic analyses (encompassing both historical-typological studies and technological processes of manufacture and use), migration theory, climate change dynamics, foraging theory, archeological data, and so forth. A unified theory would allow us to understand and explain the relationships between cultural traditions and the forces of nature.

A theory of Clovis would explain the two most mysterious archeological problems, the ones we can not seem to find the answers to – where did Clovis come from, and how did it spread? I do think such a body of theory will be formulated, based on the fine and thoughtful work done by archeologists up to this time. In this book I have tried to synthesize and set the stage for such theory rather than describe everything known or invented about the last millennia of the Pleistocene. For some readers, the journey through this book may seem as long and migratory as the trek made by the first North American people thousands of years ago, but there really is a goal at the end of all the pages. In the rest of this book I explore and map out the intersecting facts, educated guesses, and hypotheses leading to the conclusion that the time period when Clovis and Clovis-like projectile points were made was one of exploration by people who spread through the continent not by slow diffusion but by rapid dispersal. These dispersing people were broad-spectrum foragers, of course, who chose to narrow their range of preferred food items during a very specific time interval of the late Pleistocene. It is this time period I describe and try to understand here.

Acknowledgments

This book would not have been written without the help of many colleagues and friends. I thank them all for discussing their ideas, assisting me in examining museum collections, and providing copies of papers and articles. Special thanks go to Ted Goebel (University of Nevada, Reno), who not only read part of the manuscript but also rode to the rescue at a late stage of manuscript preparation with some critical maps and artifact drawings. Paul Martin (University of Arizona) read the entire manuscript and as always was a patient source of new ideas and useful suggestions about how to improve the writing. He is a true gentleman of science, and a pleasure to know.

C. Vance Haynes (University of Arizona) is not related to me but is like family in another way, which is his generosity and willingness to keep on teaching and talking about Clovis. I cannot thank him enough. Also like family (at least in the way I look at it) is the inimitable Jeff Saunders (Illinois State Museum), who knows more about mammoths and mastodonts than I do. Dennis Stanford (Smithsonian Institution) was kind to me early in my career, and I have never done enough to thank him, but he is still kind anyway. I thank him for allowing me to look at and photograph the Smithsonian Institution's Paleoindian materials.

Joaquín Arroyo Cabrales, Eduardo Corona M., and Oscar Polaca (all at the Instituto Nacional de Antropología e Historia, Mexico) were very considerate hosts during an enjoyable visit to Mexico. I am especially thankful to Eduardo and Oscar for a wonderful long field trip outside Mexico City, and to Joaquín for a personalized look at the Tocuila mammoth site.

I thank Antoni Milewski (Percy Fitzpatrick Institute, University of Cape Town) for an invaluable education in animal biology, and also for his sustained interest in my research. Antoni read part of one chapter and helped improve the content and the presentation. Also in South Africa, Anusuya Chinsamy-Turan (University of Cape Town and South African Museum) and Norman Owen-Smith (Witwatersrand University) were excellent sources of information and inspiration.

My studies in Zimbabwe have been both very rewarding and very difficult for a variety of reasons, the most recent of which is the economic and political buckling of the country. Still, I must thank the Department of National Parks and Wild Life Management for nearly twenty years of cooperation and (usually) encouragement. I also thank David and Meg Cumming for support and a dear friendship in Zimbabwe. Valuable assistance in the Zimbabwe fieldwork came from Peter Ngwenya and the late Million Malifa, the late Felix Banda, and the late Fibion Ndiweni.

Back in the USA, I want to thank Russ Graham (Denver Museum of Nature and Science), Mike Jacobs (Arizona State Museum), Kevin Moodie (University of Arizona), and Ted Daeschler (Philadelphia Academy of Sciences) for generously leading me through various bone collections. Richard Laub (Buffalo Museum of Science) and Calvin Smith (Strecker Museum, Baylor University) not only led me through their own collections but also took personal care of me in their cities, for which a feeble "thank you" is offered here.

Tom Stafford (Stafford Research Labs) has been a very helpful friend when it comes to explaining data, dates, and interpretations. Another friend, Larry Agenbroad (Northern Arizona University), is not only kindhearted and gracious but a bottomless well of knowledge and notions about mammoths of the late Pleistocene.

I thank Stuart Fiedel (Louis Berger Associates) for his extremely detailed comments on a complete draft of the manuscript, and also for providing me with many new (and necessary) references, unpublished papers, and ideas. Alan Turner (Liverpool John Moores University) likewise provided editorial encouragement along the way. Laura Niven (Tübingen University) was generous with her time in Germany and helped me understand the Upper Paleolithic in new ways, as did Piotr Wojtal (Polish Academy of Sciences).

Many other people may be passed over unthanked here because I cannot remember them all, and I hope they forgive me. I do remember to thank the big grey cat who forced me to stay at my computer almost all winter by sleeping in my lap.

My biggest and best thanks go to Janis Klimowicz (University of Nevada, Reno), who is a special favorite.

All the errors and weaknesses in this book are mine alone.

I Fluted points and the peopling of the Americas

> When a thing ceases to be a subject of controversy, it ceases to be a subject of interest. William Hazlitt (Flesch 1957:48)

1.1 Introduction

The beginning of prehistory in the Americas is a moving target. The bull's-eye on this target contains three missing pieces of crucial information: the date when the very first colonists arrived, the homeland where the first immigrants originated, and the subsistence behavior of the first people. But the target doesn't stand still – with each new discovery, the earliest dates keep changing, the possible homeland moves from Asia to Europe and back again, and the foraging behavior of the first migrants is lost in a fog of debate.

One hypothesis that has been around for a long time is that a single earliest founding population entered North America about 12,000 radiocarbon years ago (rcybp), which is approximately equal to 14,000 calendar years ago (see Appendix 1 for calibrated equivalencies of radiocarbon and calendar years). The hypothesis was inspired by the discovery that the earliest archeological materials in just about every geographic zone in North America were similar stone tools datable radiometrically or typologically to the same relatively brief time interval, 11,500 to 10,500 years ago. The trademark tool is a unique kind of stone spearpoint (Fig. 1.1) given the type name "Clovis," after a town in New Mexico near which early discoveries were made. These artifacts were manufactured by widely separated prehistoric people at almost the same time throughout North America, south of the great ice sheets that covered half of the continent. The fluted points from Nova Scotia are much the same as those from California. They are not identical, but the similarities outweigh the minor differences. Not only are the spearpoints similar across most of the continent, but there are other significant stone-tool classes and aspects of culture in general that seem to be equally widespread (Storck 1988). It legitimately can be said about almost every sampled locale in North America that Clovis is the "basal stratum from which other cultural groups descend[ed]" (quoted from Morrow 2000a:86, describing mid-continent finds).

But very occasionally an archeologist samples a locale where cultural materials underlie Clovis artifacts, or apparently pre-date the Clovis time interval. And increasingly, linguists and physical anthropologists find their interpretations of variability in Native American languages and biology hard to reconcile with models of basal Clovis migration. The dynamic interplay of data and opinions from different scientific disciplines is reshaping the debate about America's earliest people.

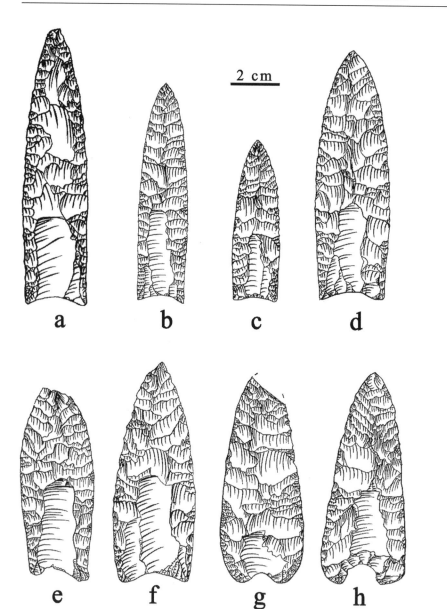

2 cm

Fig. 1.1 Clovis points: (a) and (b) are from Blackwater Locality No. 1 (New Mexico); (c) is from Domebo (Oklahoma); (d) is from Lehner (Arizona); (e) is from Murray Springs (Arizona); (f) is from Dent (Colorado); (g) and (h) are from Colby (Wyoming) (drawings by Ted Goebel).

1.2   *Fin de siècle* paradigm-busting, or, what's at stake in the debate about the colonizing of North America?

> We have reached a point where further proof is superfluous, and where the weight of disproof lies upon those who deny . . . One feels that the stage of investigation is passed, and that of religious construction is overdue.
>
> Arthur Conan Doyle 1918:94, 95

When twentieth-century discoveries were made of fluted spearpoints, archeologists began to ask why people living in different habitats and ecozones throughout the continent would have manufactured stone tools that were so similar. One answer offered in earlier archeological literature was that the fluted

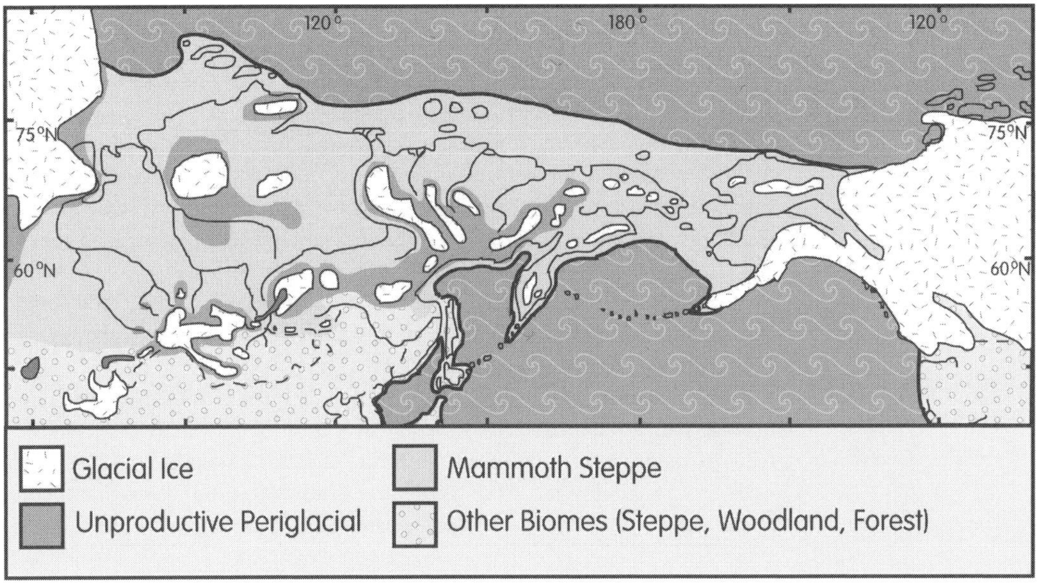
120°
180°
120°
75°N
75°N
60°N
60°N
Glacial Ice
Mammoth Steppe
Unproductive Periglacial
Other Biomes (Steppe, Woodland, Forest)

Fig. 1.2 Beringia and the land bridge connection between North America and northeast Asia, showing glacial coverage and shorelines during the Last Glacial Maximum about 18,000 rcybp (from a map drawn by Ted Goebel).

points were emblematic of a single culture carrying a coherent technology with them and spreading quickly into lands unoccupied by other people. A related answer was that the points were specialized for killing large animals, and they were such efficient killing tools that they contributed to the extinction of big-game species such as mammoths and mastodonts. When the large mammals died out during a period of rapid climate change, the Clovis way of life came to an end, the fluted spearpoints were replaced by other tools, and subregional cultural traditions replaced Clovis culture throughout the continent (Anderson and Faught 2000:512).

But not everyone agreed with this picture of the settlement of the New World. Among others, Alex Krieger declared that it was impossible to believe America was unoccupied before the appearance of fluted points (Krieger 1962, commenting on Mason 1962), because so many pre-Clovis sites were known to him. For decades, sites and artifacts had been discovered with artifacts (or *possible* artifacts) that may have been much older than the Clovis fluted points (for readable histories of over a century of controversy, see Meltzer 1991 or 1993b). Some of the sites contained simple-looking stone tools whose simplicity seemed to equate with "older," and some sites contained only very old bones thought to have been cutmarked and broken by humans. The sites that lacked stone tools altogether, it was suggested, had been created by people who could find no suitable stone at hand or who made tools out of only bone, antler, and wood because they had "lost the art of stone-flaking while [migrating] through the vast stretches of boreal forest and across the alluviated Bering land bridge" (Bryan 1969:345–6) (Fig. 1.2). Numerous summaries of putative very early materials appeared almost regularly, starting late in the nineteenth-century (for example, Wright 1892) and leading up to a late-twentieth-century flurry including (alphabetically) Bryan (1969), Krieger (1957, 1964), MacNeish (1976), Payen (1982), Stanford (1982, 1983), Waters (1985), and others.

As well, some linguists analyzed Native American languages and insisted that there had to be more than 12,000 years of language separation in the present-day continent. Up to (or over) 40,000 years of separation was proposed, based on the language diversity. And some physical anthropologists also claimed that the few earliest pre-Columbian skeletons from North America showed too many morphological and genetic differences from Asian skeletons to be explained by a mere 12,000 years of separation.

Thus two opposing factions became clearly defined in the study of the peopling of the New World. The two factions unwittingly unfolded their debate in terms of "stereotypes in opposition" (Sherratt 1997), which seems fairly typical whenever discourse develops in major scientific issues (see Oreskes 1999, for example). In the case of the Clovis issue, the factions were those prehistorians who favored an early entry of the first American settlers (pre-dating the Clovis projectile points) versus those who favored a late arrival (in which Clovis-point-makers were the first settlers) (Bonnichsen and Schneider 1999).

The "early-entry" (pre-Clovis) faction tried to adopt into its cause each new discovery of a potential pre-Clovis-age site or artifact; but the "late-arrival" (Clovis-first) faction scrutinized the earlier sites with skeptical coldness. The early-entry faction was suffering cognitive dissonance; the Clovis-first faction could argue that the early-arrival advocates wanted so much to believe in pre-Clovis that they blocked out the arguments showing the weaknesses of their case. On the other hand, the pre-Clovis faction could accuse the late-arrival advocates of condescension every time they uttered pre-Clovis judgments, which were sometimes along the lines of Sherlock Holmes's lofty remark to Watson about the giant rat of Sumatra – it's a tale for which the world is not yet prepared (Conan Doyle 1924).

The serious ill-feelings resulting from the disagreement gave a permanent gravitas to the study of the peopling process. When an announcement was made about a pre-Clovis site that contained unusual artifacts, it was often soundly trashed by the group of archeologists favoring late arrival. The faction supporting an early entry argued that the standards for accepting archeological evidence from pre-Clovis finds were much more exacting or limiting than the standards for Clovis-age or later sites (Bryan 1991). This claim is identical to one made by a faction of paleontologists during the acrimonious 1980s debates about whether a meteorite impact caused dinosaur extinctions 65 million years ago; the standards demanded to prove the new theory were said to be "far higher than is normal in science" (Raup 1994:151). All uncertainty had to be removed from a huge range of topics if the new theory was to become acceptable. The Freudian psychiatrist Wilhelm Reich also echoed this sentiment in 1956 – just before going to jail – after the Federal Drug Administration refused to allow his "Orgone Energy Accumulator" box to be manufactured or distributed: technically, he said, he'd lost to "an incomprehensible procedure treadmill" although in a historical sense his good fight would be long remembered (Heard 2000:193–4).

It has been written that the stakes were much lower in the Clovis versus pre-Clovis debate (Meltzer 1995) than they were in other scientific arguments, such as the fierce forty-year fight over continental drift, in which one antagonist complained that if the new theory were true, geologists would have to "forget everything which has been learned in the last 70 years and start all over again" (R. Chamberlin in 1928, quoted in Oreskes 1999:313). The outcome of pre-Clovis debates will have much less effect on American prehistory, even after models of migration and subsistence are rethought. The existence of a pre-Clovis human presence may stretch the timeline yet it does not restructure mainstream archeological methods, end the prevalence of inductive reasoning, or replace foundational ideas such as the law of superposition and uniformitarianism.

But the stakes really are sky-high in the scramble for the spotlight by individual participants, because career visibility goes up when the fighting starts. To be recognized as an iconoclast or revolutionary is to be assured a voice and a forum. To be quoted at length in a popular news magazine or to be featured in a major television program is exhilarating and attracts supporters (and ultimately funding). Thus combative and self-assertive archeologists have everything to gain from participating in the debate while the field itself will change very little.

As the pre-Clovis arguments developed in the 1960s through the late 1990s, the early-entry faction in the debate inevitably came to speak of themselves as an embattled minority treated unfairly by the highly respected and imperious specialists who shaped public opinion. The skeptical authorities were deemed small-minded people, like "humorless pedants [of the variety] who correct grammatical errors in love letters" (Sokal and Bricmont 1999:ix). In one case, a criticized early-entry advocate seemed to brandish his critic's skepticism "as though this were a criminal attitude in science" (Fiedel 2000b). Why did the early-entry minority feel so oppressed?

Scientific scrutiny – especially the dissection of claims that lie out of mainstream thinking in any discipline – is harsh and uncompromising. This is because archeologists know that every archeological find is destroyed when it is discovered. An excavated site cannot be pieced together again except on paper, which means that data can be submerged, hidden, or altered. In fact it is relatively simple to pull off a hoax with an archeological find; for example, in November 2000 "one of Japan's best-known archaeologists confessed . . . to having falsified important finds by secretly burying items and then 'discovering' them" at two sites claimed to be up to 700,000 years old " (Joyce 2000; see also Anon. [Japan Times] 2000; Anon. [Mainichi News] 2000; Bleed 2000; Keally 2000). The entire sequence of the Japanese Early and Middle Paleolithic "has sunk into the mire of scandal" (Keally 2000); as a consequence, it has been suggested that Japan may have no Middle or Early Paleolithic sites at all! Another possible example of a hoax is the unusual Sandia point type that some people believe was planted in Sandia Cave (NM) and other sites and did not belong in the early stratigraphic levels where it was reported (Preston 1995). The most famous example is the Piltdown hoax of the early twentieth century (Spencer 1990a, 1990b).

Even when hoaxing is not deliberate, archeological interpretations that are hasty, intuitive, or unsubstantiated can lead to blunders or oversights. During the 1970s the Old Crow collecting localities in Yukon yielded a broken caribou tibia that appeared modified by human hands to make a defleshing tool (although some archeologists disputed whether the toothed working end of the implement really had been deliberately created by human actions [Lee 1975:23; Payen 1982:362–3]). A fraction of the bone (in fact half of it was sacrificed to provide enough inorganic carbon for the date) was radiocarbon dated to about 27,000 rcybp (Irving and Harrington 1973). Surely this was universally indisputable proof of a pre-Clovis human presence in the Americas? Only a few professionals doubted the artifactual origin of this specimen, but the early date did surprise archeologists. Numerous broken bones also had been recovered from the stretch of the Old Crow river where the defleshing tool was found, and many bone fragments were claimed as artifactual debris left by people who flaked tools out of large bones instead of stone. However, a few years after the initial discovery, the tibia deflesher was sampled again for dating – this time using improved methods that needed a small part of the remaining organic carbon – and and the tool's age was exposed as late Holocene (Nelson, Morlan, Vogel, Southern, and Harrington 1986). Later research also revealed that the associated broken bone "artifacts" recovered from the river's beaches and bars could have been fragmented by noncultural processes, which no one had adequately studied at the time of the original interpretations. The scientific method of scrutiny, skepticism, and testing was therefore a success in that it forestalled an automatic (but naïve) acceptance of dubious materials. The devoted advocates of pre-Clovis found themselves dragging more and more of this sort of burden behind them like Marley's chain.

Developments in the search for North America's first inhabitants were decidedly different from the same kind of archeological search going on in Australia in the late twentieth century. There, between 1960 and 1970, on a continent about the same size as unglaciated North America, a true revolution took place in the dating of the earliest human arrivals (Jones 1979). In 1961, the oldest "acceptable" human occupation of any site was early Holocene in age; but within a year a site with a terminal Pleistocene date was soon joined by more and more, at the rate of about two discoveries per year, until dozens of acceptable sites had joined the record. None of these older and older discoveries had been set ablaze as if they were Trojan horses, which is how American archeologists seemed to think of each pre-Clovis announcement. Why would Australia's prehistory be rewritten so swiftly and almost instantaneously, when North America's was proving to be so contested and unchanging?

Australia had remained an archeological blank well into the middle of the twentieth century, accounting for the missing information about deep prehistory. But once the archeologists began exploring and digging they succeeded in finding the earlier and earlier sites, and they succeeded in convincing colleagues. And once the reports and publications finally hit the streets, Australian archeologists sensibly reordered their research goals and strategies to take advantage of the emerging knowledge. But North America has been examined and surveyed for much longer, by a larger population of amateur and professional archeologists with an ever-expanding number of journals and periodicals for publications to appear in, and still the conventional wisdom placed the first human arrivals at not much earlier than 11,500 rcybp. Thus it would seem that maybe North America did not possess the same kind of reservoir of undiscovered ancient sites that Australia had, or if it did, the sites were somehow being passively censored.

The last two decades of the debate in North America may have been even more heated than the decades before, because frustrated Americanists could see the Australians burrowing deeper and deeper in time, slowly moving beyond 20,000 years, then quickly to 35,000 and 40,000 years, and beyond. Recent studies (Miller, Magee, Johnson, Fogel, Spooner, McCulloch, and Ayliffe 1999; Roberts, Flannery, Ayliffe, Yoshida, Olley, Prideaux, Laslett, Baynes, Smith, Jones, and Smith 2001) attribute the massive megafaunal extinctions in Australia to human colonists entering around 46,400 rcybp. Meanwhile, in the New World the arguments still raged about sites dated to a mere 12,500 rcybp.

By the early 1980s, the two most important "doyens of American archaeology" (Fiedel 2000a:43), Gordon R. Willey and Jesse Jennings, who wrote influential textbooks and commentary on North American prehistory (Jennings 1974, 1983; Willey 1966, 1974), were eagerly convinced that more and better archeological evidence would be found to prove humans had been in the New World for at least 25,000 years. Their support clearly shows – as Fiedel (2000a:43) notes in his review of the debate – that "the scientific 'establishment' has not been predisposed to crush such claims." Still, some posturing archeologists insisted that pre-Clovis colleagues feared for their reputations and funding because of their involvement in early-site research. These alarmed colleagues were rarely (if ever) named (see Morell 1990). Geographer George Carter, after one of his papers was rejected by the journal *Science* in 1960, wrote to the editor: "I have a correspondent whose name I cannot use, for though he thinks I am right [that humans lived in California 90,000–80,000 years ago], he could lose his job for saying so. I have another anonymous correspondent who as a graduate student found evidence that would tend to prove me right [but] he and his fellow student buried the evidence. They were certain that to bring it in would cost them their chance for their Ph.D.'s." Carter went on in that vein to refer to other (unnamed) professionals afraid of losing their jobs (Lee 1977:4).

In 1999, *Newsweek* magazine ran an article that mentioned mysterious (but also unnamed) "mandarins of American Anthropology" who had held archeology "in a stranglehold" before a critical moment of acceptance (see below – the Monte Verde pronunciamento), and who had been capable of banishing pre-Clovis finds. These mythical deities allowed "no deviation . . . from the party line" that Clovis was the very first culture in the New World (Begley and Murr 1999). Of course mandarins do not exist in archeology, and if they did they never would have agreed on anything. But the real lesson of this attitudinizing is that the force of the majority opinion clearly had been perceived as nothing short of oppressive and conspiratorial.

Ironically, even some non-archeological anti-evolutionists welcomed the archeologists' long history of resistance to pre-Clovis – particularly to the site in Chile named Monte Verde – because it supported their claims that "powerful forces in the academic world have suppressed research and publication" out of long habits of "prejudice and oppression" which these forces could perfect against creationism. The creationists now yearn for their own "Monte Verde milestone" (Jones 1999), referring to the appearance of a series of publications from prominent archeologists declaring one pre-Clovis site to be acceptable, after all. Cremo and Thompson (1998 [orig. 1993]) echo these sentiments, asking readers to question professional archeologists who steadfastly resist claims for very early people in the New World; Cremo and Thompson (1998:26) speak of a "shroud of silence" placed over unwanted findings, which soon fade into obscurity and disappear from all but the "moldering pages of old scientific journals." The anomalous evidence for very early people in the New World, doomed to the unseen depths, and supposedly suppressed by archeologists, includes a 505 million-year-old "shoeprint" from Utah (Cremo and Thompson 1998:810–13) and a 600 million-year-old metallic "vase" from Massachusetts (Cremo and Thompson 1998:798–9).

Over the last "two decades of acrimony" (a journalist's term – see Wilford 1998), in spite of what they publicly claimed was unsparing skepticism towards them, bordering on persecution – the early-entry advocates apparently won what they think is the right to represent the consensus in New World studies (Adovasio and Pedler 1997; Meltzer 1997; Meltzer, Grayson, Ardila, Barker, Dincauze, Haynes, Mena, Nuñez, and Stanford 1997). At the beginning of the twenty-first century, archeologists prefer thinking that long before 12,000 years ago "multiple origins and numerous migrations" (the quote is from David Hurst Thomas's *Skull Wars* [Thomas 2000:171]) had created a continent full of regionally separated people, who had different technologies, ate different foods, spoke different languages, and looked very different from each other. The implication? America has always been an ethnic melting pot (Dillehay 2000), from the very earliest days of Pleistocene human colonization.

This theory of New World colonization has had several variants, and even the most popular versions have been decomposed "into elements that enjoy different levels of acceptance," a common enough occurrence in science (Clemens 1994:endnote 3.9). Yet the underlying linking idea of a pre-Clovis human presence is widely accepted by mainstream archeologists. Why are the claims for pre-Clovis migrations accepted by so many prehistorians who once rejected them?

Sometimes just the sheer weight of repetition in a science has a telling effect, as when one side repeats its claim often enough that people begin believing it. Shipman (2000:491–4) has suggested other reasons why scientists gradually replace their skepticism with belief – sometimes the evidence itself seems better and stronger over time, or famous experts sign on to the teams making the discoveries, thus enhancing credibility. And skepticism itself earns a bad name when rejected discoveries are later substantiated. "Skepticism is a cheap stance to adopt," Shipman (2000:494) writes, "for it is easier to cast doubt than to substantiate, especially if new techniques and new paradigms must be forged along the way." Skeptics are viewed as spoil-sports and wet blankets, while the new and unusual discoveries are welcomed with open arms.

Over the past century of archeological study of the peopling of the New World, a variety of larger social, political, or philosophical attitudes behind the scenes probably helped to shape the favored interpretations of the peopling process. The various interpretations can be seen as narratives that have storylines behind them, reflecting popular trends in the way we view human behavior. The Clovis-first (late-arrival) storyline, which imagines Clovis people to have been specialized big-game-hunters who spread rapidly into an unoccupied continent, is a great story to archeologists because it is so familiar – in fact, its appeal goes right back to the historically pervasive notion of the American frontier. Anthropologist John Alsoszatai-Petheo (1986:20) and journalist Roger Downey (2000:78–9) viewed the Clovis-first model as an updated variant of Frederick Turner's influential visions of the waves of pioneers entering the "wild" American frontier in the last century, "discovering" and then conquering it. The resident Native Americans occupying the frontier were treated as merely a difficulty to be overcome in the westward march of American settlement. Much of American life today, from political rhetoric to adventure movies, was influenced by this frontier obsession, according to Downey, providing a "richly provocative (if unconscious) template for thought" that still appeals to archeologists. The Clovis-first and Clovis-fast model was accepted and stuck around so long in the literature possibly because it is an exciting story white Americans like to tell over and over again about this continent. The story appealed to archeologists at the same time as it once again validated the western world's ideals of dominion over nature (Alsoszatai-Petheo 1986:20), relentless expansion and exploitation, American exceptionalism, and the supremacy of technology. The possibility that Clovis hunters extinguished America's largest mammals – mammoths, mastodonts, horses, camels, and dozens of other species – was also employed as an object lesson in human insensitivity and power negatively to transform the natural world.

The alternate interpretation of the peopling process, the Clovis-NOT-first model, approaches the big lesson to be learned from another angle altogether. Archeologist Tom Dillehay (2000:293) wrote: "The Americas of the late Pleistocene [may have been] one of the world's first real ethnic melting pot [sic] and multicultural society" that had "no true categories of race and ethnicity." This sort of directly opposite model emphasizes the successes of local subsistence patterns rather than continent-wide cultural blueprints, seeks evidence for the existence of distinct and recognizable migrating groups derived from geographically separate homelands, regards technology as strictly shaped and limited by unique sets of regional resources, and does not allow us to view any archeological culture as superior or first or faster or more successful. This model's storyline is fitting for the political and social sensibilities of the twenty-first century.

Thus stories about the past continue to change to fit the current trends in thinking. Plus, some scientists can argue a new theory better than others, gaining the upper hand in print. The sharpest archeological rhetoricians may establish a theory that is the result of a "selective search through the literature for corroborative evidence, ignoring most of the facts that are opposed to the idea, and ending in a state of auto-intoxication in which the subjective idea comes to be considered as an objective fact" (Sullivan 1991:15). Ironically, this remark was made by a paleontologist attacking the early theory of continental drift, which has turned out to be correct after all. Ulysses S. Grant (1885–6) once observed that it saves a lot of trouble to declare a victory instead of fighting for it.

Obviously the scientific rules for "discovering" the true facts about the peopling of the Americas are in perpetual states of change. The appropriateness of certain kinds of evidence seems to change, as does the potential meaning of the evidence. One reason for the shifting ground is that scientists' opinions sometimes carry more weight than the evidence at hand. If an eminent expert announces that she or he disbelieves a particular interpretation of a discovery in the field, such as a new site or new DNA study, then the thousands of interested onlookers who make up the archeological community may also follow the trend towards disbelief. Similarly, a handful of experts approving a new discovery can be the catalyst for community acceptance or the stimulus for a testy backlash. The most vocal and enshrined experts reserve the right to shape thought and policy in the study of the earliest peopling process, and expect the archeological community to follow them.

This points up a very non-scientific feature of this subfield concerned with the peopling of the New World. The subfield has always been a no-holds-barred, wide-open and almost separate specialty in American archeology, a science "frontier" as it were – defined as a "boundary or limiting zone" (Ashcroft, Griffiths, and Tiffen 1998:107) that distinguishes the well known from the unknown. As with other frontiers, the prehistorians who want to be players in this subfield communicate in a unique priestly jargon whose lexicon is rewritten

all the time (for example, the appellation "Clovis culture" is frequently rede-
fined). The players choose friends carefully, because certain individuals may be
disliked or disbelieved, and must prove themselves capable of mastering the
secrets and esoterica. The evidence needed or sufficient to support favored scenarios is discovered, discussed, and debated by the players. New classes of data
are introduced and allowed to be analyzed. Official chronologies are drawn and
redrawn or discarded. The qualifications of acceptability needed by an artifact
or a site are set. Adding publicity is like giving oxygen to a fire. The specialists
stand ready to fight it out on the streets and in the saloons (in conferences,
publications, backrooms), trying to agree on something that can be called the
truth, because the winners earn the power to define completely or invent the
very objects of their studies. An aggressive disrespect is displayed towards the
opposition, especially by those archeologists who want to be seen as original
thinkers and critics.

Announcements about new discoveries are often treated with open contempt
by adversaries who scoff at the evidence's insupportability. If the discoveries
do not fit into the conventional categories – such as specific kinds of stone
implements, or radiometric date ranges, or the sequence of deeply stratified
tools – then the discoverers and opponents battle for the discovery's right to any
kind of shelf-life. The well known and the unknown trade places daily in the
canon of knowledge.

The experts thus demarcate the boundaries and conventions of their own
study, and in so doing of course they establish themselves as distinct from the
many other kinds of archeologists. The leaders in this subfield are responsible for imperially setting the boundaries around the original colonizers of the
Americas. The experts define the ancestry of all Native Americans – they officially
determine the time when the first people arrived in the New World, they decide
upon the original homelands of the first peoples, and they make models to explain the behavior and adaptations of the founding settlers. For this reason, the
stories told by experts about the peopling of the New World are of critical interest
to Native Americans (for example, Deloria 1995) and post-modern archeologists
(Kehoe 1998), as well as philosophers of science, sociologists, and historians
concerned with changing patterns in scientific interpretations. Indeed, as suggested by Downey and Alsoszatai-Petheo, perhaps the archeological narratives
of the peopling process and related interpretations really are examples of "post
hoc objectification of Manifest Destiny" (the words are from Bruce Trigger's
[2000] review of Kehoe [1998]). Some Native American activists flatly reject
the archeological reconstructions (Deloria 1995, for example) because of conflicts with oral histories, legends, folklore, or religious beliefs. Deloria (1995)
finds a scientific belief in trans-Beringian migrations to be absurd and unacceptable; but the preferred alternative stories about Native American origins are
quite varied and unreconciled. The Hopi "speak of transoceanic migrations in
boats," while other people "speak of the experience of a [local? in situ?] creation."
"Some tribes," Deloria (1995:97) states, "even talk about migrations from other
planets." Deloria's point is that either Native Americans originated nowhere
else but in America, or they came to the continent far earlier than scientists
know is possible. The politically significant implication of such a disagreement
is easy to see – native people refuse to allow themselves to be defined as just
another migrant influx.

The dispute has been transformed from science into politics. Not only are lines drawn in the sand to separate factions, but the styles of quarreling also differ within each faction. On the one side are the "urban" scientists (Segerstråle 2000:263), who are sophisticated, well connected, politically minded and unafraid of arguing loudly in public, and who tend to be cynical as well. The urban scientists are intellectuals who look for answers in controlled experiments, and who theorize and invent scenarios to predict the archeological data they expect to find. On the other side of the dispute are the "country" scientists, the simpler and more straightforward sorts steeped in natural history, who look for answers in nature, who observe events and processes and then make *ad hoc* explanations for them. Both kinds understand the political implications of the different scenarios of the peopling process (see Segerstråle 2000:262–3, for a discussion of another heated scientific dispute, this one about sociobiology).

The study of the peopling process is charged with emotion. It is impossible to write a book about the first settlers in America without offending someone, be it an anti-scientist, a Native American whose beliefs about ancestry are not open to question, or a scientific archeologist with a different point of view about the evidence at hand. Now that a "new paradigm" (Dillehay 2000) has been proclaimed for studying the peopling process, independent thought and skepticism are going to be run through flash furnaces to eliminate impurities, once again, which is what the Clovis-first proponents were accused of doing. The new generation of experts do not want to argue anymore, and the honorable tradition of skepticism is unwelcome. Even the potentially useful parts of the old Clovis-first models are to be rejected in the spirit of reactionary nihilism, which is skepticism carried to an extreme. The new generation of archeologists in the peopling discourse are absolutists whose beliefs are no longer subject to debate.

This book is my entry into the debate while it is still open. I offer certain clear opinions and a purpose that is not ultimately to uphold any existing model; rather I hope to assess the competing models and find productive directions for further research, and also for further questioning. I begin with a review of approaches that have been used to address the largest unanswered questions in the discourse.

1.3   How do archeologists address the big unanswered questions about fluted-point-makers?

> The superior man does not set his mind either for anything or against anything.
>
> Confucius (Flesch 1957:197)

"Clovis" is the name of a projectile point type widely found in North America. Similar points can be found in Mexico, Central America, and South America. The time period is rather narrow when the classic Clovis type is thought to have existed. Table 1.1 lists sites with radiometric dates customarily accepted as "Clovis" in North America.

Several Clovis finds have been dated radiometrically well older than the ages listed in Table 1.1, and some well younger. For example, the Lewisville (TX) site yielded a Clovis point, one flake scraper, a hammerstone, and a flaked

TABLE 1.1 Generally accepted radiometric dates on Clovis or Clovis-like point sites (from Dent 1999; C. V. Haynes 1993; Holliday 2000a; Tankersley, Ford, McDonald, Genheimer, and Hendricks 1997; Tankersley and Redmond 1999; Taylor, Haynes, and Stuiver 1996). Note that some of these commonly cited dates have been questioned (for example, by Roosevelt, O'Donnell, Quinn, Kemp, Machado, Imazio de Siveira, and Lima da Costa 1998), because of unclear sample selection procedures or disparities between wood dates and bone dates from the same strata.

SITE	DATE(S)	MATERIAL(S) DATED
Anzick, MT	Average of 3 = 10,820 ± 60	Bone
Aubrey, TX	Average of 2 = 11,570 ± 70 (but wide range of other dates)	Charcoal
Big Eddy, MO	8 dates from "Early/Middle Paleoindian levels" range from 10,260 ± 85 to 11,900 ± 80	Charcoal (mostly)
Cactus Hill, VA	10,920 ± 250	Charcoal
Clovis type-site (Blackwater Locality No. 1, NM)	Average of 2 = 11,130 ± 290 Average of 3 = 11,300 ± 240, (but wide range)	Plant remains Plant remains
Colby, WY	11,200 ± 220 (RL-392) 10,864 ± 141 (SMU-264)	Bone collagen Bone apatite
Debert, Nova Scotia	Average of 13 = 10,590 ± 50	Charcoal
Dent, CO	Average of 5 = 10,690 ± 50 plus 11,200 ± 500 (I-622)	Bone Bone organic acids
Domebo, OK	Average of 2 = 10,820 ± 230 Other averages 11,040 ± 250 and 10,940 ± 180	Carbonized plants Bone collagen and gelatin Bone collagen and gelatin
Johnson, TN	10,700 ± 980 (?)	
Lange/Ferguson, SD	11,140 ± 140 (AA-905) and 10,730 ± 530 (I-13104)	Charcoal flecks Bone organic acids
Lehner, AZ	Average of 12 = 10,930 ± 40	Charcoal fragments
Murray Springs, AZ	Average of 8 = 10,900 ± 50	Charcoal
Paleo Crossing, OH	10,980 ± 110 (AA-8250-E) 10,800 ± 185 (AA-8250-D) 11,060 ± 120 (AA-8250-C) (3 other dates average 12,150 ± 75)	Charcoal granules from postmold
Shawnee Minisink, PA	Average of 2 = 10,640 ± 290 10,940 ± 90 10,900 ± 40	Charcoal Carbonized hawthorne plum seeds

TABLE 1.1 (cont.)

SITE	DATE(S)	MATERIAL(S) DATED
Sheriden Pit, OH	Range of 13 AMS dates on culture-bearing stratum = 10,470 ± 70 to 10,970 ± 70	Wood charcoal (NB: burnt and calcined animal bones from elsewhere in cave yielded AMS dates about 1,000 years older)
Templeton, CT	10,190 ± 300 (W-3931)	Charcoal
Vail, ME	7 dates, ranging from 11,120 ± 180 to 10,040 ± 390	All but one on charcoal; youngest date on humates
Whipple, NH	Average of 2 = 11,050 ± 300 (2 other parts of the site were dated 9,400 ± 500 to 10,430 ± 300)	Charcoal (charcoal)

pebble associated with hearths and Pleistocene animal bones, radiocarbon dated > 37,000 rcybp (Crook and Harris 1962) (later work at the site indicated that lignite, which is mostly ancient carbon, was burned in the hearths, accounting for the very old dates [Stanford 1983]). Another example is a Kentucky mammoth (Vesper and Tanner 1984, cited by Lepper 1999:369) with a possible Clovis-point association, radiocarbon dated 8,360 ± 310 (Beta lab number not reported). More examples can be found in the literature; several Holocene dates on mastodonts are cited in Byers (1962, commenting on Mason 1962; also see Stafford 1994). The dating spread can be partly explained by the nature of radiocarbon dating – "dates" are only a statistical probability of an object's age and not a simple fact – or by the potential for sites, sediments, and samples to be contaminated, or by inappropriate choices of materials to be dated, or by "associations" that are speculative rather than clearly demonstrated, and so forth. Different materials dated from the same stratigraphic layers may give disparate dates – for example, bone dates often seem to be several hundred years younger than associated wood-charcoal dates, as suggested by C. V. Haynes (1992). At least one-half of all radiocarbon dates returned over the past half-century probably have been rejected or suppressed because of suspected errors. This might make readers nervous that the *true* dates of Clovis could be quite different from the 11,500–10,500 radiocarbon years generally accepted. The possibility that Clovis sites are not correctly dated was raised (Roosevelt, Douglas, Brown, Quinn, Kemp, and Weld 1998 and Roosevelt, O'Donnell, Quinn, Kemp, Machado, Imazio de Siveira, and Lima da Costa 1998). However, when dating samples have been carefully collected and the lab protocols followed so that contamination is controlled or eliminated, sample selection is supportable, and different components of bone (such as collagen or non-collagenous proteins) are tested, the dating much more often produces results within the expected time interval (see Stafford 1988, 1994, 1999a; Stafford, Brendel, and Duhamel 1988; Stafford, Jull, Brendel, Duhamel, and Donahue 1987; Taylor 1991).

Over the last quarter-century, archeologists normally kept these cautions and qualifications in mind when addressing the big unanswered questions about the peopling of North America. Perhaps the biggest question was – and still is – this one:

(1)   When did the first colonizers arrive?

In 1989 David Meltzer asked, "Why don't we know when the first people came to North America?" His suggested answer was that pig-headedness and entrenched archeological arguing in general have not by themselves made a consensus answer impossible, as some archeologists insisted; instead, or so he proposed, a central and underlying assumption about the very nature of colonization may have been dead wrong. Meltzer suggested that the Pleistocene migrations of founding populations were not discrete waves of separate groups, but were continuous dribbles over long periods of time. He also suggested that cycles of pre-Clovis colonists may have established themselves in the continent temporarily, long before the terminal Pleistocene, but then disappeared (genetically, morphologically, technologically, etc.) (Meltzer 1989a).

More than a decade later we still do not know when the first people came to North America. In fact, now we seem to be even less able to produce a reasonably acceptable approximation of an answer. Not only has the archeological background changed since then, but now the supplemental information about possible human populations in the New World is coming in waves of contradictory or confusing suggestions. At the time of Meltzer's article, many archeologists believed in a three-pulse migration model that accommodated archeological, linguistic, and bioanthropological data (Greenberg, Turner, and Zegura 1986). The limited amount of analyzed genetic and immunoglobulin data did not contradict the implications of the three-pulse model – namely, current Native American populations could be fitted into three language families (Amerind, Na-Déné, Eskimo-Aleut), as well as three parallel dental and genetic groupings, and three accompanying technological and chronostratigraphic groupings of archeological finds, whose earliest time of arrival followed the Last Glacial Maximum.

Sites that contained artifacts which did not fit into the three technological groups were often considered to be dubiously dated or suspiciously interpreted. Yet the discovery and publication of early sites or assemblages proceeded throughout the next ten years, even though the earlier sites, if valid and correctly interpreted, would have fatally weakened the three-phase model. An even more serious weakening of the model occurred when competing genetic, linguistic, and bioanthropological studies began to pile up in the literature. The first widespread appearance of such studies may have been adversarially motivated, and specifically intended to attack and replace the three-pulse model of colonization.

LINGUISTS HAVE THEIR SAY

Linguists had early on joined the movement to revise the peopling timeline. Joseph Greenberg used a method of comparing large numbers of languages at one time and his results led him to propose that all indigenous American languages fall into only three genetic groups ("language families") of unequal size (Greenberg 1987a; Ruhlen 1991, 1994), each having an Asian origin (Greenberg

1987b, 1996). The spread of the largest language family, Amerind, "must have been . . . within one or two thousand years" (Greenberg 1996:531). Greenberg's thesis was criticized passionately by other linguists (for example, Goddard and Campbell 1994), some of whom may have been "extreme" empiricists who insisted on "getting all of the local facts first before saying anything general, that is, before saying anything that was at all interesting" (Sapir 1987:663; see also Darnell 1987:653, 656). As a result competing theories emerged about the sources of American native languages. Many of the unhappy linguists were "splitters" who scorned Greenberg's attempt at "deeper classification [of language] in the Americas" (Greenberg 1987b:666) because they saw no possibility of reconstructing direct ancestral connections among so many distinct languages. A "majority of linguists working on American Indian languages" believe in the existence of 100 to 200 pre-Columbian linguistic stocks lacking affinities (Greenberg 1996:532), as opposed to Greenberg's classification of all languages into either eleven stocks or six "branches" or aggregated stocks (Greenberg 1987a:60, 378) which were subsumed in three families.

The points of view of both Greenberg and his adversaries predisposed them to expect either a few or multiple migrations; Greenberg's adversaries expected to see many waves of different language-speakers entering the New World throughout longer spans of time than Greenberg had proposed based on his sweeping approach to language classification, his knowledge of the dated archeological finds, and the biological connections between Old and New World populations.

The linguist Johanna Nichols (1990), building on the earlier work of Austerlitz (1980), and based on what she believed to be a relatively high density of linguistic stocks in the New World, proposed that the separation of all indigenous American languages must date back at least 35,000 years to explain her linguistic model. Greenberg has suggested that part of the disagreement between him and Nichols (and other linguists) about the number of linguistic stocks in the New World is due to the use of the widely applied comparative method (which compares languages presumed to be related), rather than Greenberg's "mass" or "multilateral" comparisons (which examine broad arrays of languages in order to note "how they group genetically" [Greenberg 1996:535]).

In later publications, Nichols estimated that over the last 6,000 years, about 1.5 "language families" have separated out in each ancestral "language stock" in the northern hemisphere, and she used that figure and allowances for new migrations to predict that the New World's 140 language families separated out over at least 40,000 years (summarized in Gibbons 1998). However, if the number of language families is lower, as Greenberg's methods conclude, then the separation time also could have been much reduced.

Greenberg (1987a, 1987b:665) had pointed out that linguistic studies are very weak when trying to uncover absolute chronologies – such sequences of time cannot be reliably discovered. Thus, a linguistically inspired estimate of 35,000–40,000 years in the Americas is hardly a steadfast datum point. Nichols herself has cautioned that linguistic reconstructions of origins, movements, and language spread are not simple and easily proven; she noted (1997) that "the rate at which languages diverge . . . is not constant," and that "given present knowledge of language change and probability . . . descent and reconstruction will never be traceable beyond approximately 10,000 years." Languages change rapidly when in close contact with other languages. Linguistic density is highest in areas where autonomous small societies live in small territories with year-round and reliable food resources (Nettle 1998), and "neither time settled nor number of colonizations has any appreciable effect on genetic density, which is determined entirely by geography, population density, and economy." Therefore, it would seem that the only supportable test of an estimate of the time elapsed since language divergence is an age estimate in harmony with archeological or geological data (Nichols 1997). Because solidly dated archeological sites in the 40,000-year-old range are not generally available in North America – unless one accepts such finds as the mid-Pleistocene flaked stones at the Calico site in southern California (Budinger 2000; Leakey, Simpson, and Clements 1968; Patterson 1999; Simpson, Patterson, and Singer 1986) – the linguistics-based estimates of deep age must be viewed as untested (perhaps untestable) hypotheses about New World colonizers.

PHYSICAL ANTHROPOLOGISTS DO SOME MEASURING UP

A relatively small sample of fossil human skeletal material over 8,000 years old has been available from the Americas (Table 1.2). These remains are not uniform, but all of them are anatomically aligned exclusively with modern *Homo sapiens sapiens* (Steele and Powell 1994). Thus, based on the fossils, no suggestion of an earlier hominin population such as archaic *H. sapiens* in the New World has been taken seriously. Unfortunately, even as more and more studies are made of the skeletal sample's morphologies and genetics, several different scenarios and models still compete to explain how these individuals came to be in the Americas so long ago.

Jantz and Owsley (2001) could find no morphometric affinity between early Native American crania and recent Native Americans; instead the greatest (but still imperfect) affinity seemed to be with Europeans, Polynesians, and East Asians. The earliest skeletal samples from North America are not neatly assignable to any extant geographic or ethnic populations. Neves and Pucciarelli (1991), on the basis of craniometric studies, proposed that the first colonizers of the New World were from a generalized "non-Mongoloid" population. Either another wave of people characterized by "Mongoloid" cranial traits later contributed to the population, or the Mongoloid traits appeared by local evolu-tion (see also González-José, Dahinten, Luis, Hernandéz, and Pucciarelli 2001). Neves (2000; Neves and Pucciarelli 1991) concluded that the earliest South American founding populations had a "marked morphological affinity with present-day Africans and Australians," and show no resemblance to present Asian Mongoloid physical types or American Indians. Africans and Australians, it must be remembered, have been geographically separated for over 50,000 years. Chatters, Neves, and Blum (1999) interpreted the 7,900-radiocarbon-year-old Kennewick (WA) skeleton as similar to Polynesian or Ainu in size and shape, but not similar to Mongoloid, thus adding yet other possible source areas for Native American ancestry (although no Polynesians lived in the Pacific be-fore about 3,500 years ago). Thus the oldest known crania are not "Mongoloid," while those from the more recent Native Americans are.

Native Americans are physically and genetically variable, as are other people in the rest of the world. Compared with Asian populations, they are more genetically differentiated, their anthropometrics are more variable, and their mtDNA also

TABLE 1.2 Human skeletal finds older than 8,000 radiocarbon years.

LOCALITY (REFERENCE)	N	REMAINS	AGE (RCYBP)
Anzick, MT (1)	2	cranial fragments	8,620–10,500; later redated 11,500
Arlington Springs, CA (2)	12	femora	10,000 ± 310; collagen redated 10,960–11,500
Browns Valley, MN (3)	1	skeleton	8,700 ± 110
Buhl, ID (4)	1	skeleton	10,700
Fishbone Cave, NV (5)	1	postcranial fragments	10,900–11,200
Gordon Creek, CO (6)	1	skeleton	9,700 ± 250
Horn Shelter, TX (7)	2	skeletons	9,000–10,000
Kennewick, WA (8)	1	skeleton	8,410 ± 60
La Brea, CA (9)	1	skeleton	9,000 ± 80
Marmes, WA (10)	3	cranial fragments	10,000–11,000
Mostin, CA (11)	1	bone fragments	10,000–11,000
Pelican Rapids, MN (12)	1	skeleton	–
Sauk Valley, MN (13)	1	skeleton	–
Shifting Sands, TX (14)	1	tooth fragments	–
Spirit Cave, NV (15)	1	skeleton	9,400
Vero Beach, FL (16)	1	cranial fragments	–
Warm Mineral Springs, FL (17)	1	postcranial fragments	10,620 ± 190
Whitewater Draw, AZ (18)	2	skeletons	8,000–10,000
Wilson-Leonard, TX (19)	1	skeleton	9,000–11,000
Wizards Beach, NV (20)	1	skeleton	9,200

References

1 Stafford 1999a; Stafford, Jull, Brendel, Duhamel, and Donahue 1987, D. C. Taylor 1969
2 Orr 1962; Stafford 1999a   3 Jenks 1937
4 Green, Cochran, Fenton, Woods, Titmus, Tieszen, Davis, and Miller 1998
5 Orr 1956, 1974   6 Breternitz, Swedlund, and Anderson 1971
7 Young 1988   8 Chatters 1999   9 Berger 1975; Kroeber 1962
10 Fryxell, Bielicki, Daugherty, Gustafson, Irwin, and Keel 1968
11 Kaufman 1980; Taylor, Payen, Prior, Slota, Gillespie, Gowlett, Hedges, Jull, Zabel, Donahue, and Berger 1985
12 Jenks 1936   13 Jenks and Wilford 1938
14 D. G. Steele and Powell 1994, citing Owsley pers. comm.
15 Edgar 1997; Jantz and Owsley 1997; Tuohy and Dansie 1997
16 Stewart 1946   17 Clausen, Brooks, and Wesolowsky 1975
18 Waters 1986   19 Steele 1989; Weir 1985
20 Dansie 1997; Edgar 1997; Tuohy and Dansie 1997

shows more variability (but less variability than Europeans). Hence the question arises: how variable were the founding populations, to have allowed this much unusual variability now? Or did the variability derive from multiple migrations, or even from in situ evolution? The human fossils dated older than 8,000 years are at least as variable as modern samples from the same geographic area.

In 1991, Cavalli-Sforza described work that brought together genetic, archeological, and linguistic data (Cavalli-Sforza 1991, 1997) to reinterpret human evolution, and decided that the first human entry into the Americas most likely occurred between 15,000 and 35,000 years ago, somewhat encouraging a stretching of the earlier three-pulse model farther back in time. Wallace and Torroni (1992) proposed a view of "American Indian prehistory as written by mtDNA," in effect finding that one of the three linguistic groups proposed by Greenberg, namely Amerind, originated from two Asian migrations dated four times older than the Na-Déné migration. Thus, in this interpretation only two different migration waves populated the continent – the ancestors of Amerind and of Na-Déné.

A rush of exciting new DNA studies began to appear in the mid-1990s. By 1996 some genetic studies, particularly of mtDNA, seemed to indicate that either all New World native populations shared a single ancestry in Asia – one migration introduced all the mtDNA (Merriwether and Ferrell 1996; Merriwether, Hall, Vahlne, and Ferrell 1996; Merriwether, Rothhammer, and Ferrell 1994, 1995) – or they derived from only two pulses of migration (Torroni and Wallace 1995; the views are summarized in Gibbons 1993, 1996). Yet, while suggesting the three-pulse model was not correct, these studies could not find common agreement about the timing of this one-wave or the two-wave scenario, owing to the fact that the human bone samples analyzed did not possess significant antiquity and may have reflected relatively recent losses of genetic diversity or intermixing of older genetic lineages (O'Rourke, Hayes, and Carlyle 2000). Still, one group of researchers claimed that the genetic data indicated the first wave appeared 20,000 to 25,000 years ago (Gibbons 1996). Unfortunately, as geneticists were realising, "There are just too many different histories compatible with present-day patterns of genetic variation" (Goldstein 2000:62).

THE MONTE VERDE MOMENT

While these sorts of interesting but unreconciled studies were being read and debated, several archeologists were making a concerted push to persuade colleagues to accept the validity of pre-Clovis dating on materials from a site named Monte Verde in Chile (Adovasio and Pedler 1997; Fagan 1997; Grayson 1998; Meltzer 1997; Meltzer et al. 1997). By 1998 some of the so-called "revisionists" who wanted to rewrite the peopling scenarios were presenting their ideas at a meeting of the American Association for the Advancement of Science, a heavyweight organization indeed. These different views were termed "the culmination of a series of spectacular recent discoveries that have contradicted the accepted model and thrown the field of Paleo-Indian anthropology into turmoil" (McDonald 1998:A22).

According to McDonald, the "widespread acceptance" of the pre-Clovis dates from Monte Verde "lent credence to the authenticity of sites older than Monte Verde that had been bitterly contested by adherents of the traditional view of migration" (McDonald 1998:A22). The controversial sites in question had been dated to 12,000 to 20,000 years old, and in some cases even older. Up until the moment that leading archeologists announced that Monte Verde must be accepted as older than Clovis, the long lists of pre-Clovis localities were viewed as Elvis sightings, hardly taken seriously by many in the archeological community.

Monte Verde gained its widespread acceptance because of pronouncements made by a few prominent archeologists who had visited the site (Adovasio and Pedler 1997; Meltzer *et al.* 1997). However, at least one of the Monte Verde visitors later rejected his role as a *miraculé* cured of his Clovis-first affliction when he later reconfirmed his feelings of doubt (C. V. Haynes 1999a).

A more convincing source of authentication for all the other archeologists unable to visit the site should have been the huge published second volume (Dillehay 1997) detailing the Monte Verde site's findings and interpretations. This 1,100-page book was praised by reviewers (for example, Fagan 1997, who called the book brilliant; also Grayson 1998; Meltzer 1997) and won the Society for American Archaeology's 1998 book award. But Stuart Fiedel (1999b), like the ancient mariner, wrecked the three reviewers' celebration when he zeroed in on the book's numerous problems such as inadequately documented key finds and maps or tables that contradicted each other (see Rose 1999a). Dillehay and eighteen colleagues (Dillehay *et al.* 1999a) and other interested parties (Adovasio 1999; Collins 1999b; Meltzer 1999) responded to Fiedel's "hostile" remarks (Dillehay and six others 1999b), hoping to clarify or dismiss the criticisms as unimportant or understandable in view of the Monte Verde project's complexity. Dillehay and six colleagues also published a much longer and irritable website reply to Fiedel (Dillehay *et al.* 1999b), calling his comments "biased and error-ridden," and his questioning an "unscrupulous" challenge to the site, upon which Fiedel (2000b) returned to the as yet unresolved problems, and declared that the extremely important report about Monte Verde did "not rise to the modest standard of an average Phase II cultural resources report" (Fiedel 2000b). The fortissimo exchange of views had been pumped up to furioso very quickly, but it was allowed to diminuendo publicly (although not in the private backrooms) (Thomas 1999) through the years 2000 and 2001.

DEVELOPMENTS AFTER THE MONTE VERDE CONVERSION EVENT

While the Monte Verde quarrels raged, certain other prehistorians were elaborating the emerging hypothesis that the morphology of the earliest known American skeletons (mostly dated to the early Holocene and possibly late Pleistocene) reflected an early pulse of migration whose human populations died out completely and had little or no relation at all to later Amerind populations. One possible implication was that pre-Clovis migrations were not only early, but also unrelated to later migrations, and derived from very different regions of the Old World. Another alternative possibility was that small groups of people from different homeland areas entered the New World and lived separately from each other, sometimes scattering quite widely over the continent. Over time, genetic drift and natural selection occurred, changing gene frequencies and sometimes eliminating some DNA altogether. Later, Holocene gene flow from northeast Asia added a large input to the New World genetic reservoir to create the modern Amerind morphology and genome.

According to one popular writer, 1998 was the year that "the fall of the Clovis barrier" provoked excitement at the annual meeting of American archeologists in Seattle (Hall 1998). However, the apparently better-educated physical anthropologists, human biologists, and geneticists who had already "long inferred pre-Clovis entry of people into the Americas" (Hall 1998:13) showed far less excitability at their own annual meeting in Salt Lake City. What did emerge from the physical anthropology meetings were more seemingly incongruous suggestions about the timing, origins, and spread of the earliest American populations.

By early 1999, anthropological geneticists realized that DNA research could be interpreted in at least two different ways, depending on one's fundamental model of the human fossil record, and the two ways led to contradictory conclusions. In one model, analysts assume that DNA differences between populations arose almost exclusively after geographic isolation of those populations. The other model would have genetic variations arising from interbreeding of populations at very low levels in combination with random mutational changes or founder-effect. The two models have led to two views about human evolution: either all modern humans are descended from "founding" populations that originated in Africa after 200,000 years ago and began to migrate out about 60,000 years ago; or modern humans are descended from interbreeding regional populations around the world that were in place 100,000 to 200,000 years ago.

The annual meeting of American physical anthropologists in 1999 saw more conflicts in interpretations of the first peopling of the Americas. Some scholars favored two migration waves; but some did not. Some favored the idea of "continuity" of populations, meaning that microevolutionary changes within regions accounted for morphological differences over time; some favored "replacement" of populations, meaning that successive waves of immigrants added new genes swamping the old ones over time. Some favored a relatively "late entry" of populations, and some did not (see the summary in Hall 1999).

By the year 2000, craniometric studies by physical anthropologists continued to emphasize that the earliest known human remains from the Americas did not closely resemble modern Native Americans, although there were some similarities. The usual conclusion reached about the variability in American skulls was that, of the several geographically separate founding populations which migrated to the New World, the earliest had been the least similar to the modern native people. The first founders must have pre-dated the development of Mongoloid populations, to whom Native Americans are most closely similar. Gene flow was uninterrupted over time, however, and after Mongoloid microevolutionary development in Asia the New World populations continually received an input of Mongoloid genes and traits.

Of course, it must be remembered that shapes and measurements of prehistoric human skulls are not always clear reflections of ancestry. If fossil skulls do not match modern ones from the same locales, but do show similarities to skulls from more distant world areas, the differences need not result from ancestry alone. For example, 9,000-year-old skulls from the Elmenteita site in Kenya are more similar to Peruvians, Ainu, and Europeans than they are to modern Africans, a similarity that is not at all due to any temporally close relationship to those other ethnic groups (Howells 1995). The similarities are due to other factors such as sexual selection, genetic drift, or adaptation. Another example of how skulls may vary is the one "certified" precontact Peruvian skull which seems to be as European as it can be, in a study by W. W. Howells (1995). Yet this skull is from a Native American, *not* a Spaniard or another Caucasian living in pre-Columbian South America. Howells (1995:55) warns that "departures and wrong assignments" of skulls to ethnic groups is "to be expected in a small proportion of cases." Perhaps the sample of early American skulls is the proverbial small proportion of cases.

In the late 1990s, prehistorians still spoke of waves of colonization, but the meaning of the word "waves" had changed from the days of Greenberg, Turner, and Zegura (1986). Instead of referring to temporally and spatially discrete founding populations, the geneticists used the word waves to mean trickling expansions of one or more founding lineages coming from slightly different parts of the Old World. Initial migrations may have begun before the Last Glacial Maximum in eastern Siberia, from which one or more lineages dispersed eastward; later another circum-arctic set of lineages expanded after the glaciers melted. Studies of mitochondrial DNA provided support for this hypothesis.

Mitochondrial DNA (mtDNA) is maternally inherited, and is not fitness related, thus it does not change gene frequencies in response purely to natural selection as quickly as other DNA, although it does evolve rapidly. These characteristics make mtDNA useful to study because it may reflect ancestral relatedness much more than it reflects "adaptedness." MtDNA research showed that all modern Native Americans can be included in five different "matrilines" or haplotypes of mtDNA (labeled A, B, C, D, and X), and these also are found in lower frequencies in the Old World (Schurr 2000). Yet not all the haplotypes were found everywhere in the Old World at comparable frequencies, although larger sampling seems to indicate that they may cluster around parts of southern Siberia (Derenko, Grzybowski, Malyarchuk, Czarny, Miścicka-Śliwka, and Zakharov 2001). Are multiple source areas required for the New World's groups, or were all haplogroups once present everywhere in the Old World, and only recently did certain groups disappear? In all, four or five lineages (people whose genetic traits clustered) entered the New World in two or more "waves," separating 26,000–16,000 years ago from an ancestral population that also eventually gave rise to modern-day Mongoloid people (Stone 1997).

Schurr and Wallace (1999) suggested that certain lineages expanded into Siberia from their homeland to the west about 30,000–25,000 years ago, moving eastward into North America soon after, while other lineages expanded into North America only after 17,000 years ago. Another lineage may have entered the New World much later, perhaps 10,000–7,000 years ago. These dates are based on estimated mutation rates of mtDNA, about 2.2–2.9 percent per million years, itself based on the postulated date of the 2–4 percent divergence of humans and chimpanzees plus archeological dating of other language group divergence rates (Schurr and Wallace 1999).

Two possible scenarios may explain the mtDNA data: (1) one earliest wave of modern *Homo sapiens* brought all the existing modern haplotypes at one time, but the later addition of different mtDNA from more recent migrants completely changed proportions, or (2) different haplotypes came from people with different homelands, migrating over the course of many thousands of years. Either possibility seems acceptable based on the currently available information.

A new perspective on the timing of New World migrations based on DNA then emerged from genetic family trees; one international study of Y-chromosome variations was interpreted to mean that the most recent common male ancestor for all the world's people lived in Africa as recently as about 59,000 years ago, thus establishing the absolute earliest possible starting point for all modern human ancestry (Underhill, Shen, Lin, Jin, and seventeen others 2000; note that comments on the study by other researchers are divided, and the interpretations of dating and implications may change). Because modern *Homo sapiens* appeared in Europe no earlier than about 50,000 years ago (Klein 1999), which was 10,000 years after the earliest known modern male member of the species appeared in Africa, it may be fair to expect that the range-expansion of H. *sapiens* across Asia through the subarctic and arctic (and eventually into Beringia) would have taken thousands more years. A recently dated site in Russia's western arctic is about 40,000–35,000 radiocarbon years old, and may be the earliest human dispersal into the far north; nonetheless, the site's location is less climatically severe than the eastern arctic and subarctic, where no sites are yet known from this early time (Pavlov, Svendsen, and Indrelid 2001).

Of course, if a regional population of pre-modern humans ever existed in North America (for which evidence does not exist), it is possible that a trickle of gene flow from other evolving populations in Eurasia could have led to convergent development of an *in situ* population of modern *Homo sapiens* in the New World. If this unlikely possibility did occur, then continuous dribbles and spurts of migrations into North America by humans from Eurasia could have kept Amerind and Asian genes and skeletal morphology so similar.

One fundamental observation is important here. A relatively small population of modern *Homo sapiens* in Africa began dispersing into the rest of the world 100,000–50,000 years ago, not reaching northwest Asia until relatively late in the Pleistocene and thus putting brakes on the spiraling depth of time that many archeologists hoped to find in the Americas, especially South America.

BYPASSING BERINGIA?

However, and fortunately for the deep-time archeologists, other possible routes to the Americas have emerged to be taken seriously, therefore making unnecessary a very early Beringian migration – before 35,000 rcybp – which had to pre-date the late Pleistocene flooding of the land bridge, or pre-date the closure of an interior migration route lying between North America's continental glaciers. A North Atlantic crossing in skin boats from Europe later in the Pleistocene – within the last 30,000–15,000 years – has been proposed by several speculators, including E. F. Greenman (1963), who based his proposal on trait similarities between Northeast American Indians and certain Upper Paleolithic cultures. Amerind Y-chromosome haplotypes can be linked to European types, but the presence of intermediate types in southern Siberia suggests that the connection was overland through Asia.

Another casual proponent of intermittent transoceanic contact, Vine Deloria, Jr. (1995), suggested that occasional migrations from Europe had added diversity to the native population several times in prehistory, based on Native American folklore, his own belief that American Indians originated nowhere else except in America, and the occurrence of variability in Indian skeletal morphology and other physical traits.

Dennis Stanford and Bruce Bradley (Bradley 1999; Holden 1999; Stanford and Bradley 2000) have proposed European contact in the Pleistocene based on similarities in lithic technology between Clovis and the European Upper Paleolithic Solutréan. Another possible link is also somewhat hinted at by the geographic distribution of one mitochondrial DNA marker, haplotype X (traced to Europe, recently found in southern Siberia [Derenko *et al.* 2001]), and also present in Native Americans), and a putative physical resemblance between early Holocene American skeletons and Europeans (a resemblance that was proclaimed loudest in the popular press but which only a few physical anthropologists stated).

Straus (2000) has pointed out that Solutréan and Clovis technology and cultural patterns are far from identical, and solid evidence is lacking for a direct transplantation of Solutréan people and technology into the New World. Although the technological similarities between Clovis and Solutréan are multiple, most archeological researchers agree the "earliest settlement of the Americas must be seen as purely and simply an aspect of the earliest settlement of Beringia" (West 1996:540), meaning that the first Americans came only through Asia. However, archeological researchers probably secretly keep it in the back of their minds that a sea-borne journey almost 1,500 miles from western Europe across the north Atlantic might have been possible even as early as 18,000 rcybp, especially if the boats deliberately kept close to calving ice-fronts where open-water leads could be used to shelter from storms and high waves, and where sea-birds, sea-mammals, and fish might have been abundant. In 1976, English journalist Tim Severin (1978) and three companions made such a north Atlantic journey in a wooden latticework boat covered with ox-hides, thus demonstrating at least the plausibility of the sea-crossing hypothesis. "The Atlantic is not a barrier, even to the most primitive raft manned by a totally inexperienced crew," is how Santiago Genovés (1973:267) stated the case, after the Norwegian anthropologist Thor Heyerdahl's two Atlantic crossings on papyrus rafts named Ra I and Ra II (Genovés 1972; Heyerdahl 1971); "The raft [Ra II] went to America [from northwest Africa, about 10 degrees latitude south of Spain] whether the crew wanted it to or not" (Genovés (1973:267), "carried by wind and current."

Also proposed has been a sea-borne journey of colonists in watercraft on the *other* side of the continent, staying along the southern coast of Beringia and the Pacific coast of the Americas (Dixon 1993, 2001). Thor Heyerdahl (1953) had sailed a raft from Peru to Polynesia in 1947 (to prove South Americans could have colonized Pacific Islands), thus providing plausibility for the idea that the Pacific Ocean was crossable on simple watercraft.

Archeologists do not find concrete evidence of Pleistocene boats, seafaring technology and knowledge, or prehistoric navigation, and thus view the scenarios as interesting but unsupportable. Furthermore, the continental shelf where the earliest coastal sites would be located – the places where first landfalls would have been made – are under the sea now, and realistically cannot be surveyed or explored (although Fedje and Josenhans 2000 have shown that limited success may be possible in finding submerged early Holocene or late Pleistocene coastal sites on the Pacific side of the continent).

THE SEARCH FOR "FIRST PEOPLE"

It is frustrating to be constantly seeking an answer to simple questions about the first people in the Americas, but the truth is that the first peoples are chronically hard to identify in every continent. For example, Polynesia in the eastern Pacific Ocean was colonized only a few thousand years ago, yet where the first people came from is still debated, as are the speed and direction of migratory movement. Until recently the first humans in another Pacific realm, New Zealand, were thought to have arrived from Polynesia over 1,000 years ago and gradually colonized the islands while wiping out native moas. New Zealand is very rugged and mountainous, about 270,000 km² in area, and its colonization was thought to be relatively slow. But recently it has been confidently argued that the first people arrived no more than 800 years ago, promptly discovered all sources of toolstone, and killed all the moas within a few decades (Diamond 2000; Holdaway and Jacomb 2000; McGlone and Wilmshurst 1999). The first sites made by these swift colonizers are the large ones with mega-moa bones in them, not the once-proposed low-density scatter of nearly invisible sites created by people slowly establishing themselves. Perhaps the first Americans also immigrated quickly into an unoccupied continent, as did the first New Zealanders, and their earliest archeological sites also should be highly visible traces of megamammal kills.

Hence the first big question about peopling the Americas remains essentially unanswered, although a new generation of archeologists probably believes it is much closer to the true solution. New theories appear, the arguments rage, and a fully satisfying resolution has not been reached. The peopling yarn is still coming in installments, like the Pickwick Papers, without a plot or denouement.

Another big question about the issue also remains unanswered, partly because it is actually a set of interrelated questions.

(2)   How fast did the first migrants spread? Were the makers of fluted points actually "migrants" or were they members of pre-existing populations who adopted diffusing traits?

Interpretive fashions or intellectual preferences in the peopling-the-Americas debate change regularly. These changes sometimes come about relatively quickly, causing a reversal of opinion – a single new discovery can do that – but more often they involve a gradual veering away from the majority views. For example, over the last twenty years or so, readers of the archeologists' literature will have noticed an unmistakable trend towards revising or disagreeing with earlier ideas that Clovis populations entered a continent empty of other humans.

Archeologists' doctrines – their underlying beliefs – clearly affect how they evaluate prehistoric data, and how they go about making the data into evidence to support interpretations of the past. For example, the two main opposing models of the New World's peopling process, namely a fast-entry model versus a slow-entry model, are shaped by distinctive doctrines. These doctrines have little actual concrete proof or unequivocal support in the real world, but they seem to have been accepted by prehistorians as truths. The recent revisionist models assume Clovis-point-makers were not the first arrivals and that Clovis technology and economy spread among pre-existing human populations.

CLOVIS AS LATECOMER

In one model the Clovis-first idea has been replaced by an *earlier-entry* model. The newer model seems convincing to some prehistorians, but it may need an overhaul. When early-entry advocates attack what they call the "key propositions of the Clovis-First model" (Bonnichsen and Schneider 1999:507), objectivity is sacrificed for rhetoric. Bonnichsen and Schneider (1999:505–7) claim the four "predictive implications" of the Clovis-first model are weak and assailable. Their four "implications" are: (1) Clear evidence of a Clovis founding population should be found in Siberia – meaning Clovis points and identical technology, apparently – which of course will not occur, since Clovis is an American continental pattern. In fact, all that is really "needed" from Siberia is an Upper Paleolithic presence dating earlier than Clovis. (2) Clovis point distribution in the New World must have a temporal gradient from north to south – another unfair implication in light of the fact the very fine temporal resolution needed might not be possible to achieve. Besides, the time gradient could be in any direction, depending on Clovis technology's origins within the New World (it may be in Mexico or Maine, for all we know) and the rate of spread. (3) The similarities among Clovis assemblages are so minimal that Clovis cannot be a single "culture" – an expectation and conclusion the early-entry advocates argue from the perspective that human technology and learning are inflexible within social units. Apparently every site and assemblage made by any culture group must be identical or indistinguishable, and if they are not, then different culture groups must have made them. This is an unrealistic way of understanding the human capacity to adapt and deal with living day to day, but it is the criticism leveled by Bonnichsen and Schneider (1999:506) against the Clovis-first proponents. (4) Clovis is not the oldest cultural horizon in the New World, and therefore not the basal culture anywhere. "Evidence is now accumulating," early-entry advocates claim (Bonnichsen and Schneider 1999:507), that Clovis was just another variety of biface technology, and "may in fact be one of the later cultures." Such evidence has been accumulating for over a century, no argument there, but so have other kinds of evidence in the march of science, like the presence of a human face on the planet Mars (Carlotto 1997; Gardner 1985; Pozos 1986), the feasibility of creating cold fusion in a bottle (Close 1991; Huizenga 1992; Simon 1999; Taubes 1993), and the "out-of-Africa" model of modern human origins (Cann, Stoneking, and Wilson 1987; Stringer 1994). The out-of-Africa model has stood up fairly well to testing and nitpicking, and many scientists now accept this idea that was once considered peculiar, but the face on Mars and cold fusion are not doing so well. Deep accumulations of weak arguments and high towers of untested ideas are not always monuments to scientific truth.

In support of the Clovis-as-latecomer idea, Clovis ^{14}C dates are said to be incorrect owing to sampling error and unwitting contamination (Roosevelt, O'Donnell, Quinn, Kemp, Machado, Imazio da Silveira, and Lima da Costa 1998), and are said to show that Clovis points *post-date* the existence of other types of distinctive artifacts. The customarily accepted earliest radiometric dates on Clovis points (see Table 1.1) are said to be "exaggerated" (Roosevelt 2000) and Clovis is therefore no earlier than several other different cultures in the Americas. New arguments thus have been advanced that other "co-traditions" were contemporaneous with Clovis or pre-date it and possess even deeper roots in the Americas. The existence of these so-called "co-traditions" implies either separate ancestry (Bonnichsen 1997; Bryan and Tuohy 1999; Stanford 1997) or an early cultural divergence well before the appearance of Clovis. Was late Pleistocene North America home to many different cultures with many different adaptations during the Pleistocene–Holocene period, including at least two different cultures by Clovis times and three by Folsom (Stanford 1997)? "No one type of environment seems to have been colonized before others," writes Roosevelt (2000:77), "and people [at the time of Clovis] did not create one single style of artifact or survive on one particular kind of resource."

However, the evidence that these "co-traditions" existed is not stratigraphically supported everywhere. C. V. Haynes (1998) has shown that even when ^{14}C dates indicate the possible co-existence of different projectile points, the stratigraphy cannot be ignored if it contradicts the dates. Unsettled in the new models of Clovis are questions such as: Why is Clovis the first of a series at many sites, or simply alone at most? Is Clovis more or less widespread than the other co-traditions? What logically can explain the abrupt and huge spread of Clovis and the much more limited (abrupt) appearances of certain other "co-traditions"? This topic is taken up at some length in chapters 5 and 6.

Mitochondrial DNA age estimates of the human presence in North America may or may not continue to change as they have done recently, and therefore cannot be used as conclusive proof one way or another about co-traditions during the first peopling of the New World. Yet the age estimates based on studies have already inspired new scenarios of the peopling process. For example, Young and Bettinger (1995, 1997) suggested that North America was first populated well before Clovis appeared, and that increasing population density led to an abrupt visibility threshold, but only after 5,000 years of invisibility. Apparently some sort of critical density level was reached at Clovis times, but not before. Perhaps we should openly wonder why this would be so. Even if the human population in the Americas were increasing at an exponential rate after 16,000 BP, the increase would have been a continuous one of growth without abrupt jumps on the curve. Why would archeological visibility be effectively constrained from earlier times?

CLOVIS AS GENERALISTS

One other significant development in the literature of the 1980s and 1990s was a noticeable tendency for archeologists to interpret Clovis foragers as broad-spectrum generalists, incapable of (or unsuited for) hunting big mammals to extinction (Dent 1985; Meltzer 1988, 1993a, 1993b, 1995; Meltzer and Smith 1986). Such models were based partly on results from actualistic studies of African elephants, studies that revealed how easy it could be for foragers at certain times and in certain places to scavenge dead proboscideans, with no need to kill them (G. Haynes 1985, 1988a, 1988b, 1991), and partly on misperceived bodies of theory such as optimization or Optimal Foraging Theory (which I discuss in section 5.3 of this book). Archeologists also found other reasons to question "the received wisdom" about Clovis subsistence, such as Dent (1985:157) who began his rethinking after participating in the study of the Shawnee Minisink site (PA) where no large-mammal bones were found but

76+ seeds from ten plant genera were recovered in the Paleoindian levels (Dent and Kauffman 1985:table 5.2).

Unfortunately, the so-called received wisdom was often a jumble of clichés and muddled thinking. It was easier to reject bad parodies of Clovis foraging than the actual models advanced in the literature. One disdained vision of Clovis was of "relentless hunters of Pleistocene megafauna" in park–tundra biome (Dent 1985:155), which although making for dramatic magazine artwork had never been advanced in peer-reviewed publications. A new generation of sites such as Shawnee Minisink (McNett 1985) seemed to prove this dumbed-down scenario wrong without much trouble. Shawnee Minisink showed (1) the Clovis habitat was not park–tundra but transitional preboreal–boreal forest, and (2) there were no mastodont bones at the site, which, when taken together with radiocarbon dates on eastern mastodonts that were older than the site's Paleoindian component, indicated to Dent (1985:157) that all the mastodonts had died out before the fluted-point people arrived.

However, this revised view of Clovis turned out to be a house of cards. The missing mastodonts at Shawnee Minisink were mistakenly attributed to a lack of open grasslands – although mastodonts seem to have preferred transitional woodlands over grasslands (though grass phytoliths in mastodont fossil teeth imply that at least some grass featured in the diet in certain places [Gobetz and Bozarth 2001]). And further dating of mastodont sites throughout the eastern states has shown that mastodonts were still alive in preboreal–boreal forests at the same time as the fluted-point occupation occurred at Shawnee Minisink.

Dent (1985:157), like many others who argued against Clovis hunting of mega-mammals, started from a heavy emphasis on limited samples to make sweeping generalizations intended to set right our Clovis model. This urge to revise plus the interest in pre-Clovis sites or assemblages led to a synthesized re-vision of Clovis as *latecoming generalists*. Apparently the notion that Clovis was the de-scendant of earlier and very slowly dispersing cultures is linked in the minds of archeologists with another idea, that every forager tries to be an unfocused generalist. The propositions disguised as arguments about migrations were often advanced to make the case that foragers are cautious, slow dispersers, biologically unable to reproduce quickly, especially when migrating into new territory and learning how to forage for a wide range of diverse resources. This position is characterized by a degree of theoretical confusion and demographic guesswork, in the absence of facts and knowledge about migrations. Surovell (2000a) modeled the demographic potentials of mobile hunter-gatherers, and his study should go a long way towards correcting bias against the possibility of high mobility, high fertility, and wide-ranging exploration by foragers even with children in tow. !Kung San women in the Kalahari walk about 2,400 km a year (~1500 miles) during foraging trips, visits to relatives or friends, water-fetching treks, and so forth (Lee 1980), a staggering distance that should encourage a much less overstated view of the "impossibility" of the migration distances trav-eled by the first pioneers in North America. Individuals in foraging societies differ immensely in the distances they travel during their lifetimes (for example, see Hewlett, van de Koppel, and Cavalli-Sforza 1982).

Meltzer (1996:245) articulated the (mis-)perceived linkage between foraging and possible rates of human dispersal into new range. He argued there is no theoretical or empirical support that Clovis or any Paleoindians were "specialized or even primarily hunters," and more likely had to be generalized foragers. They faced "an empty continent . . . infinitely trackless," and "utterly unknown ecologically exotic landscapes"; hence they could not have known "which resources would kill them and which resources would cure them." For these reasons it is thought that the generalist pioneers moved very slowly into the new ranges. By implication, because Clovis appeared so rapidly over such a large geographic area, this model proposes that Clovis could not have been first in the New World nor could Clovis culture have been carried in by a rapidly dispersing population. In this view Clovis technology and perhaps other features therefore can best be explained as having spread by diffusion amongst pre-existing populations.

THE STATIONS OF THE CROSS?

This sort of interpretation of the pioneer settlement of the Americas takes on the character of the stations of the cross. The proposed faltering and the hesitation, the creeping rate of dispersal, the burden of exploration, are elements of the revisionist model that are no more proven and ethnographically supportable than are the elements of a competing rapid migration model.

Believers in the stations of the cross doctrine insist that human population movement between habitats and ecosystems is a lengthy, arduous journey. When people disperse or migrate from homelands into new ranges, they are constantly slowed down by obstacles or the unfamiliar and exotic encountered during the movement. Cultures encounter new plants, new animals, new climatic conditions. People presumably cannot quickly find their preferred lithic materials for tool-making. New parasites attack their bodies. Water sources cannot be predicted. Cultures hesitate, and then must stop to regroup perhaps for centuries or millennia. Behavior, technology, even language must slowly readapt to the strangeness of the new ranges. Every ecological, physiographic, or latitudinal change is a wall without open doors or windows. This model brings to mind pictures of stone age people migrating to Antarctica – step by step the bands barely move forward in the face of horribly alien landscapes. The people stumble and fall on the ice. They bleed from the bottoms of their feet; soon they have to eat the dogs. After a couple of thousand years someone invents skis. It takes ages to disperse away from the little warm hut and familiar fire.

THE ANDROMEDA STRAIN?

The "Andromeda strain" doctrine is very different, but it too is an important foundation of the hypothesized slow entry by broad-spectrum generalists into the Americas. This doctrine contains the belief that the fluted point and its associated stone toolkit (the scrapers, gravers, bifaces, for example) were simply technological innovations that spread very quickly amongst pre-existing human populations in the New World. In the minds of prehistorians who hold this viewpoint, no Paleolithic tribal group or coherent "people" could ever have spread so widely or so quickly into a new continent, which is the obvious possibility suggested by relatively close clustering of the dates on fluted-point assemblages. If prehistoric people with generalist economy could not possibly have migrated into new ranges so rapidly, then the artifacts (or the idea of making such artifacts) did the moving, spreading through fairly dispersed but already established (but invisible) human subpopulations that had earlier lived through the necessary millennia required to adapt to all the different regional and local habitats of North America. Fluted points can be viewed as a thought-virus that radiated out and affected the various (invisible) populations of the entire continent.

BOYZ 'N THE HOOD?

A third related doctrine underlying the revisionist ideas about Clovis is one that can be called Boyz'n the Hood, after a motion picture released in 1991. In this doctrine, fluted-point-makers are seen as one of several contemporaneous "gangs" in North America existing at the same time interval. During the late Pleistocene, according to those who hold this opinion, the fluted-point people lived in some parts of the continent, while there also were stemmed-point-makers in certain other regions of the continent, and the unfluted-point-makers living in yet other parts. These cultures may have used the same ranges sometimes, but foraged for numerous resources. As mentioned above, some prehistorians call this pattern in North America "co-traditions," a choice of words that implies different bifacial projectile point types were made by different people who lived in the same regions at the same time. No geochronological or stratigraphic evidence for co-existing traditions has been found in North America.

RAPID ENTRY DOCTRINES

Of course, adherents of the original rapid-entry hypothesis also hold on to identifiable assumptions, myths, or doctrines that are unproven, but that deeply underlie the presupposition that only rapid colonization by a single migrating culture can account for the wide distribution and narrow time-spread of fluted-points. Believers of the "Spring-break" doctrine, for example, see rapid dispersal into new ranges as normal population behavior when climatic conditions change from glacial to interglacial, which happened very swiftly in the late Pleistocene. Another canonical idea, which may be called the "Metastasis" doctrine, would have prehistorians uncritically believe that the fluted-point complexes must have spread so far and so fast (like tumors) by a process of lightning-fast human population growth, a result of unfettered access to resources in new ranges without competition, and Paleolithic cleverness and opportunism. In this doctrine, humans are seen as capable of ratcheting up their reproductive and dispersal rates whenever possible.

So far I have given no answers to the question of spread, only a listing of theories and claims. My opinions are much stronger about the next big unanswered question that has dominated archeological attention over the past quarter-century. This question has to do with Clovis subsistence and foraging in the late Pleistocene. Our uncertainty over the economies of early people in North America inspires endless questions, but my own version of the third question is this:

(3) Did Clovis fluted-point-makers preferentially kill big-game animals?

Among the new visions of earliest American colonization is the idea that foraging by Clovis-point-makers did not include the hunting and killing of big-game species such as mammoths. New models of the fluted-point-makers' subsistence are explicitly revisionist ideas rather than supplementary or additional to the classic Clovis models. These newer ideas have entered a rising cycle against what may be a declining interest in the classic Clovis model. Revisionists probably expect the "classic Clovis" model to be dying now from all the bullets fired at it over the last two decades.

The most serious questioning of the "hunting" model of fluted-point subsistence was mentioned above in the discussion of possible co-traditions existing with Clovis ("Clovis as latecoming generalists"). Much more attention will be given in chapters 5 and 6 to the questioning and the reinterpretations, but here I briefly review some trends in the original interpretive modeling.

The classic Clovis interpretations – that fluted-point-makers were Upper Paleolithic nomads who specialized in big-game hunting and who lived in small and mobile bands – first appeared in the 1930s, but took clearer shape during the 1940s and early 1950s. Clovis points at first (for example, the Dent [CO] discoveries in the mid-1930s, or those from the Miami [TX] site in the late 1930s) were considered to be variants of Folsom and unfluted leaf-shaped points (see Wormington 1957:38), but by the mid 1950s – the time of the discoveries at Lehner and Naco, Arizona – they were recognized as technologically distinctive and associated with different paleoenvironmental conditions (Haury 1953; Haury, Sayles, and Wasley 1959; Holliday 2000a; Sellards 1952). The excavations by Edgar Sellards (1952) at the original Clovis site (often called Blackwater Draw Locality 1), the increased application of radiometric dating in the 1960s (see Holliday 2000a), and the sedimentary and geomorphological studies by emerging experts, especially C. Vance Haynes (1964, 1967, 1970, 1984), clarified the chronostratigraphic relationships between Clovis and Folsom. What came to be called "Clovis Culture" was described in papers by C. V. Haynes and colleagues (for example, C. V. Haynes 1980), Stanford (1991, 1999b), and other archeologists.

THE LLANO COMPLEX

Before about 1985, some archeological experts preferred to keep the word Clovis reserved only for the projectile-point type, and called the collection of associated material remains the "Llano complex" (proposed by Sellards 1952) named after the llano estacado or "staked plains" of the southern High Plains, where Clovis points were found with megafaunal remains. Wormington (1957:21) considered Clovis to be one of several different "ways of life" found east of the Rocky Mountains (all of which were lumped together as Paleo-eastern traditions); yet, fluted points from the Pacific Northwest, California, Mexico, and the Great Basin also belonged in this tradition, along with examples from the High Plains and the eastern United States. Wormington distinguished the Paleo-eastern traditions from those found on the west side of the Rockies (hence, Paleo-western traditions) and in the north (Paleo-northern).

Jennings (1974:84) originally had been content to call all Clovis cultural complexes "The Llano Culture," but in the last edition of his influential textbook (Jennings 1989:82) he no longer mentioned the word Llano, and instead only carefully distinguished Eastern from Western Clovis cultures. Western Clovis was the classic kind of Paleoindian manifestation that involved mammoth kills (although not exclusively) where bones were preserved. Eastern Clovis, however, in Jennings's descriptions, included the even more numerous variants of fluted-point shapes and sizes associated very rarely with identifiable faunal remains. Thus, the operational definition of "Clovis Culture" had become no more than "the remains left behind by Clovis fluted-point-makers," whatever the variance that may have existed among the fluted points. (I supply my own definition of Clovis and other important terms later in the book.)

CLOVIS AND MEGAFAUNAL EXTINCTIONS

By 1980 the distinction between Clovis and later Paleoindian cultures in the western United States centered not only around technology and time period, but also around the main species of big game that was hunted. The possible Paleoindian connection with megafaunal extinction had been suggested long before, receiving a mixed reception (see Eiseley 1943, 1946), but was subsequently argued vigorously by biologist Paul Martin (1967, 1973, 1984; Mosimann and Martin 1975) and supported by models of mammoth-hunting that highlighted parallels between mammoths and modern elephants (Saunders 1980). The idea of megafaunal overkill by blitzkrieging Clovis foragers struck some archeologists as unlikely; and even the idea that Clovis deliberately and habitually hunted mammoths was downplayed. Willey (1966:38) perceptively noted that the existence of rather dramatic Clovis mammoth sites "over-emphasized" the degree of big-game hunting by Paleoindians, and that "their entire livelihood did not depend on the big Pleistocene animals." However, no sites provided nonnegligible evidence about what else their livelihood did involve. R. MacNeish (as cited in Meltzer 1996:245, although the reference has become a widely known one) remarked that if a Paleoindian ever did kill a single mammoth, he (or she) probably spent the rest of his/her life talking about it – and by implication never doing it again.

Doubts about whether or not Clovis people actually did kill mammoths worked their way into archeologists' consciousness in the 1970s, thus making the overkill hypothesis far less popular. At a symposium during the 1982 annual meeting of the Society for American Archeology in Minneapolis, co-organized by David Meltzer and Jim Mead, Paul Martin asked a packed audience of about 300 people how many of them believed in overkill, how many thought climate change had caused the terminal Pleistocene extinctions, and how many believed a combination of these two factors was responsible. I recall that perhaps a half-dozen people raised their hands to vote for overkill, while the rest of the audience voted overwhelmingly in favor of the combination of factors. Yet twenty years later, while archeologists still generally resist the idea of overkill, scientists in ecology and geology widely accept the late Pleistocene extinctions as probably human-caused or human-facilitated, distinguishing them from the earlier major waves of extinctions (see, for example, Alroy 1999, 2001; Brown and Lomolino 1998; Diamond 2000; Flannery 2001; Owen-Smith 1999; Roberts et al. 2001; Ward 1997).

CLOVIS ECOLOGY

Later rounds of research and opinion related to Clovis adaptations included Middle-Range models of hunting and processing events, and actualistic studies.

The new generation of research, following the data-gathering from Clovis excavations, included use-wear studies of Clovis tools (Kay 1986, 1996); taphonomic
studies of elephant-bone accumulations (such as G. Haynes 1988a, 1988b);
ethnographic observations of elephant-butchering (Crader 1983; J. Fisher
1987, 1992); and new attempts at chronostratigraphic scenarios that placed
Clovis in specific cultural-evolutionary contexts in different subregions of North
America (a leading example is W. Gardner 1974, 1975; also Frison 1978; Goodyear
1979).

Clovis "origins" studies (for example, C. V. Haynes 1987) were proceeding
in the 1970s and 1980s, relying on improved radiometric and distributional
analyses, and also encouraging the gathering of new data from additional sites,
assemblages, and private and public collections of artifacts. The Smithsonian
Institution's Paleo-Indian Program actively encouraged new research as well as
reanalyses of data from earlier studies (Stanford 1989).

During the 1980s and 1990s the focus on Clovis ecology supplemented but did
not replace an emphasis on Clovis typology, which has always been important in
fluted-point studies. Kelly and Todd (1988) proposed that the New World's first
human groups emphasized hunting for most of their dietary intake. However,
the relative instability of localized game populations at this time also forced a
frequent shifting of the hunters' ranges into unknown territories, further encouraging a heavier dependency on faunal foods, since the learning experiences
of hunting can be transferred more easily into a new habitat than those of plant
collecting. The frequently moving foragers were not very place-oriented: they
were residentially mobile, seldom returned many times to specific places, did
not store resources, often carried exotic stone tools made into bifacial forms
(which have a relatively long use-life, are easier to use in many different ways,
and are lightweight), and made use of a low diversity of local resources. The
sites of such foragers cannot be easily differentiated by function based on tool
inventories, since the same range of tool classes occurs in most sites. The main
point made by Kelly and Todd (1988) is that Clovis people explored for animals of
large body sizes, rather than for plants and small-game foods, because big game
is more readily located, does not necessarily vanish like edible plants in times
of drought, and can be tracked without the more arcane knowledge needed to
find and process non-toxic plants.

Advances in the ecological study of stone tools also complemented these sorts
of foraging studies in the 1980s and 1990s. Bleed (1986), Odell (1996), and others (see the imaginative papers in Ellis and Lothrop 1989, for example) made
direct and indirect contributions to Clovis research by providing a vocabulary
and a theoretical framework for modeling the ecology of stone-tool manufacture
and use. By the 1990s, Clovis tools came to be seen as "versatile," each having
many potential uses and needing little to no reshaping. The technology also was
"flexible," with multiple different uses possible for many tools through some
reworking. Early-stage bifaces, for example, could be shaped as needed into different final forms. In environments where resources are relatively unpredictable
and foraging for them must be tightly scheduled to optimize harvesting, high
reliability is needed in toolkits. Tools in "reliable" kits tend to be overengineered,
be better made than necessary, and have redundant components, all to ensure
that no failures occur (Bleed 1986). Such tools are probably intended for repeated
use, such as projectile points "counted on for more cycles of killing after the first
one" (Ahler and Geib 2000:811, referring to Folsom fluted points specifically).

Reliable tools are generally manufactured away from the use-locations in advance, in contrast to lighter, simpler, more easily maintainable tools made on-site to accommodate less tightly scheduled and less risky resource extraction. Yet even reliable tools may be manufactured to be "maintainable," meaning both that they are relatively easy to keep in use and also that if broken or dulled they can be effectively refurbished and modified to bring them back into full use (Ahler and Geib 2000:811).

Over the past quarter-century the lithic studies either strongly influenced our archeological views of Clovis subsistence, or they were themselves strongly influenced and shaped by hypotheses of big-game hunting – but either way, archeological thinking about stone technology seemed to accommodate the modeling of fluted-point-makers as highly mobile and highly efficient Pleistocene "hunters," whose "gathering" activities were very difficult to reconstruct from lithic assemblages.

THE TWENTY-FIRST-CENTURY VERSION OF CLOVIS

Yet a growing number of archeologists have found the big-game-hunting hypothesis unacceptable for different reasons, such as its male-centered framing of lifeways in the late Pleistocene, or its contrariness when viewed against the ethnographic record. Apparently archeologists writing about fluted-point subsistence are willing to concede that Western Clovis groups did hunt mammoths (once in a while, anyway), but do not believe eastern and midcontinental fluted-point-makers would have taken so many of their calories from big dead animals. Meltzer (1993a:303) remarked that "certainly there is evidence that a wide range of plant and animal species were exploited" by Clovis groups. But the evidence is so patchy that it deserves a hard look; I return to this point in chapter 5.

And so, presently, the third unanswered question about subsistence is not yet solidly answered, but I think I can say that opinions – configured more by social theory than by empirical data, apparently – have converged on generalized hunting and gathering as the Clovis way of subsisting.

Summary and current state of knowledge

> At any given moment, only a finite set of knowledge satisfies the reigning criteria for the formulation of scientific belief, and only this knowledge is eligible as truth.
>
> Oreskes 1999:6

As things stand today – probably just where they stood over most of the past century – "the probable, the possible and the provable aren't all the same where the earliest inhabitants of North America are concerned" (sub-headline attached to an article by Patrusky 1980:2). Goethe wrote, "Our proofs are only variations of our opinions" (from Flesch 1957:228), which is indeed the case when it comes to scenarios of Clovis and pre-Clovis colonization of the Americas. While opinions come fast and easy in the debate about the earliest peopling of the Americas, the true scientific proofs are extremely scarce.

The so-called "new paradigm" (Dillehay 2000) of American prehistory has been at least fifty years in the birthing. The first phase of its birth was a shadowy period when pre-Clovis sites were little more than campfire stories; dissenters from the Clovis-first model were considered lone gunmen or slightly dizzy, perhaps. For the last fifteen years of this phase, however, a subcycle could be detected in which a wider belief in pre-Clovis seemed to spread like wildfire only to fizzle out in the face of renewed skepticism. By the 1990s, archeological conspiracy theorists were openly speaking of a "Clovis mafia" or "police" acting to suppress pre-Clovis research. Such overinfluential professionals, if they ever existed, undoubtedly thought of themselves as gatekeepers or a border patrol of sorts, but the pre-Clovis advocates sneered at them as assassins and cover-up artists. By 1997, however, oracular statements appeared in leading scientific journals about the fall of the Clovis barrier. "Clovis-first" was dead, some said. In 1999, a Clovis (and "beyond") conference included a series of opinion papers that verbally lynched the most visible Clovis-first proponents, and in the year 2000 a consensus belief in early-entry (pre-Clovis) was clearly detectable among professional archeologists. But the knights of pre-Clovis themselves developed their own gatekeepers to examine dissent and independent thinking (for example, see passages in Dillehay 2000:15, 18, 217, 285 [endnote 2]).

"At the end of a century," in the words of Richard Dawkins (1989:50), "amid profound societal change and philosophical chaos . . . all the old unsinkable certitudes seem to be going the way of the *Titanic*."

However, whether or not the recent pre-Clovis consensus marks the beginning of a "new paradigm" in the sense of Kuhn (1962) is an arguable point. The "new paradigm" is certainly not a Kuhnian model of American prehistory incommensurable with the old model, or one that will transform the science of archeology. In fact, the "new paradigm" is nothing more than "new theories [that] grew naturally from the old" (Stenger 2000), which means that no actual paradigm shift is occurring, after all.

Interestingly enough, in the 1990s other sciences have also found themselves bombarded by claims of "new paradigms." "The number of grants and papers [in all sciences] invoking the term 'new paradigm' has been growing by leaps and bounds," said the premier journal *Science* (Cohen 1999:1,998). In 1998, "124 papers in leading journals invoked the term 'new paradigm' in their titles or abstracts." Yet "90 percent of new paradigm papers affected the research world very little indeed," since they were cited less often than were papers not using the term. Mere alternative hypotheses appeared all over science, and once the "new paradigm" moniker was attached to them, as in the pre-Clovis case, the term made a splash and was an attention-getter. But the term does not signal a radically different way prehistoric archeology will be carried out in the Americas. Archeology has always had tropisms towards the earliest and the unique, and the new acceptability of pre-Clovis means only that archeological minds will continue seeking to stretch the date of the New World's earliest peopling as far backwards as possible, but without changing the way the scientific work must be done.

And besides, all of the Clovis-first model may not be completely dead and buried. The early-entry advocates continue marshaling arguments for earlier and earlier immigrations, but the quality of some of their evidence is still shaky. However, to be fair here, the quality of the evidence behind many Clovis-first models also was wobbly. As in any debate involving stereotypes in opposition, whenever supplemental models were proposed by people prepared to believe in one or the other of the competing scenarios such as Clovis-first versus earlier-than-Clovis, an aura of enlightenment was attached to the details added to each model, even when clear supporting evidence was questionable (see Kaminer 1999 or Youngson 1998 for examples of dysfunctional debates). This trend continues in the current state of the discourse. Once the terminology and outline is developed for each competing model, and the basic principles behind them are set out for anyone to understand, the experts seem to feel free to elaborate elements of the models without worrying too much about discovering necessary new facts, explaining the data, or establishing the evidence.

Meanwhile, the archeological community is hungry for the news about the impending funeral of the Clovis-first model, much like the American crowds who desperately wanted to find out if Little Nell was dead yet when they mobbed the ships carrying the latest installment of Dickens's *The Old Curiosity Shop*. In fact, the Clovis-first funeral has been postponed, because there is no body, just tombstones.

I see the nature of the Clovis-first versus early-entry debate not as a deathwatch, but as a slow termite attack on a wooden house. The house – which is the Clovis-first edifice – was built over a century, with different individuals helping to design and hammer together the walls and floors. After moving into the house, the inhabitants discovered termites were invading and eating away the supports. Either the house would fall, inevitably, or the termites had to be exterminated and the supports repaired. Eventually we have discovered that the termites cannot be exterminated, yet miraculously enough the house has not completely fallen, since pre-Clovis evidence is still so strikingly scarce or questionable. In the meantime, as parts of the old house are being redesigned and rebuilt, the Clovis-first skeptics may be growing concerned that an "older-trumps-all" model will become acceptable, in which older and older sites are announced, fawned over, and willingly believed because skeptical replication has been eliminated from the cabinet of methods.

Are the lengthy debates over the peopling of the Americas examples of "pathological science" (Langmuir 1989; Rousseau 1992; Simon 1999), "non-science" (Gieryn 1983), or just bad science? Surely the vocal proponents of different competing models were not guilty of immoral or deceitful behavior. Most if not all claims were not deliberately fraudulent or even outrageous. But the bottom line is that most are not solidly proven. The signs of bad science in the debate have been around for at least fifty years – for example, some Clovis-first advocates attacked the pre-Clovis adversaries when disengagement would have been wiser, or stuck to unlikely explanations for anomalies (such as possible pre-Clovis-age sites) and put their reputations at stake defending a weakened position when the doubts increased. Bad science also could be seen when the pre-Clovis proponents discounted negative observations (specifically the lack of pre-Clovis discoveries in most of North America) as due to observer bias or inexperience. Rather than acknowledge the possibility that some pre-Clovis sites were merely false signals (in other words, not sites at all), some pre-Clovis advocates chose to argue that they had special roles as dicoverers of a totally new and unrecognized kind of human behavior. These new kinds of evidence had no established tests for their existence or correct interpretation, no "collectively acceptable definition or characterization of the phenomenon in question" (Simon 1999:92), so that replication was not a simple task following rules and guidelines every actor in the debate agreed upon (see Simon 1999 for an excellent analysis of

Fig. 1.3 The nine North American regions. The approximate positions of the continental glaciers are shown, but exposed continental shelves are not (base map after a North America shaded relief image at website www.nationalatlas.gov/shadedm.html).

bad science in action during the cold-fusion affair; also see Close 1991; Huizenga 1992; Taubes 1993). Errors in measurement and notation thus led to errors in meaning. For example, sharp incisions on pre-Clovis bones were often called butcher-marks made by otherwise archeologically near-invisible people; other kinds of "unnatural" features such as piled bones were called signs of human behavior. Radiometric dates on sediments were directly attributed to strange objects within the sediments, or wooden objects were called artifacts when in fact they were not distinct from naturally shaped wood, and so forth. So many apparent artifacts might have disappeared if cautious adjustments could have been made to the recording process.

The impossibility of "replicating" analytical results was an issue in these errors – different actors succeeded in finding "artifacts" and attaching meaning to them, but when other actors attempted replication they did not find the artifacts, because they disagreed about the criteria for recognition. The archeological evidence from the Clovis era therefore requires a sharp look and a critical re-evaluation, which I present in the next chapter of this book, so that the facts about the Clovis and pre-Clovis eras can be established.

In chapter 2 I summarize what is known and conjectured about Clovis-era archeological remains in North America, which I have operationally divided into nine regions (Fig. 1.3). The regions were selected and defined more by convenience than by any self-evident distinctions in geography, climate, biota, or archeology. The physical and cultural differences between regions are not especially great at their intersecting boundaries, but I follow regional experts in defining the differences based on either central tendencies or the most recognizably distinguishing features within each region. Meaningful physiographic/hydrologic regions do not neatly superimpose on the existing political boundaries of states or provinces, but because archeological reporting is state-based, these regions are here outlined by the political boundaries.

2

What is Clovis? The archeological record

See how many traces from which we may learn the [wood-]chopper's history. From this stump we may guess the sharpness of his axe, and, from the slope of the stroke, on which side he stood, and whether he cut down the tree without going round it or changing hands; and, from the flexure of the splinters, we may know which way it fell. This one chip contains inscribed on it the whole history of the wood-chopper and of the world.   H. D. Thoreau 1863:121

2.1   Introduction

Although archeologists say they study Clovis culture, the word "culture" is used very differently from the way modern ethnographers and sociologists use it. Clovis archeological culture does not include information about prehistoric language, religious beliefs, folklore, and other mental aspects of "culture" (see Kuper 1999 for a discussion of the concept of culture). In contrast to the richness of an ethnographically described culture, an archeological culture often is a set of typologically differentiated material remains such as stone-tool assemblages, and the associated patterning in site distributions and characteristics.

Megan Biesele (1993) wrote that a people's "technology" is much more than the tools they carry about; it is the knowledge and experience people bring to the manufacture and use of tools, and the principles that people understand about coping with the world. Technology is huge; tools are a very small part of technology.

Clovis archeologists study the froth of technology and material remains floating over an unplumbed depth of behavior and belief. They study the settlement and subsistence clues to Clovis foraging and social organization. They study the archeological footprints of Clovis people, or the resources and environments associated with Clovis foragers near the end of the Pleistocene.

In this chapter, I try to describe the froth found in different parts of the Clovis ranges, and I define Clovis footprints as the patterns of landscape use in separate regions of the continent. Ideally a list of regional footprints would include patterns in toolstone-acquisition strategies, diet, mobility, and site sizes and distribution. But it is sometimes impossible to find this information from all regions, or to compare and synthesize.

2.2   Clovis archeological footprints, region by region

Perhaps, after all, America has never been discovered. I myself would say that it had been merely detected.

Oscar Wilde (Flesch 1957:9)

Fig. 2.1 The Northeast region and several important sites. The Canadian component is not outlined because its changing boundaries are hard to define during the Clovis era.

(1) NORTHEAST

The Northeast as defined here (Fig. 2.1) is over 540,000 square kilometers in area. The region includes Nova Scotia, New Brunswick, Prince Edward Island, a deglaciated strip of Quebec, plus Maine, New Hampshire, Vermont, Massachusetts, Rhode Island, Connecticut, New York, New Jersey, and Pennsylvania. This region varies physiographically, with coastal plain on the Atlantic Ocean side, piedmont or ridge and valley physiography inland, relatively high mountains (the northern Appalachians), and upland plateau. Most of the vegetation after the Last Glacial Maximum was forest and parkland; the typical associates likely were woodland animals and plants – such as black bear, white-tailed deer, turkey, plus mammoths and mastodonts, *Cervalces* (a moose/deer), and woodland caribou north of Massachusetts. However, fossil records are scarce for many of the expected taxa – for example, white-tailed-deer records are known only from Pennsylvania and New York in the Late Glacial (9,500–15,500 rcybp [Faunmap Working Group 1994:25])

The possible existence of a pre-Clovis human population – most notably at Meadowcroft Rockshelter in western Pennsylvania (Adovasio 1983; Adovasio and colleagues 1975, 1977, 1978) – has been long questioned by some authorities (Dincauze 1981; C. V. Haynes 1977, 1980; Mead 1980) and long accepted as reality by others (Funk 1983; Jennings 1974, 1989; MacNeish 1982). The lowest levels at Meadowcroft contained lithic debitage and 123 tools dated between about 19,000 to 11,000 rcybp. The dating is disputed because biotic evidence such as

Fig. 2.2 A pentagonal (or triangular) projectile point from Cactus Hill (Virginia), very similar to other points from eastern sites such as Meadowcroft (Pennsylvania) (photographed from a cast in the collections of the Anthropology Department, National Museum of Natural History, courtesy of Dennis Stanford).

Late Glacial flora and fauna is absent. An unfluted Miller type projectile point was recovered from a level dated between 12,800 and 11,300 rcybp. The assemblage may share characteristics with Clovis-era assemblages as well as with earlier and later materials; for example, Meadowcroft's oldest layers yielded two fragments of a possible fluted-point thinning flake, plus blades, retouched flakes, gravers, and bifaces, reminding Adovasio (1983:8) of tools from (1) Clovis sites such as Shoop (PA), Debert (Nova Scotia), and Blackwater Locality No. 1 (NM), (2) post-Clovis sites such as Lindenmeier (CO), and (3) arguably pre-Clovis levels at sites such as Fort Rock Cave (OR) and Wilson Butte Cave (ID).

The Miller point from Meadowcroft and others from undated sites in Pennsylvania are similar to point forms found in other regions (see, for example, Fig. 2.2), but may pre-date them. Adovasio (1983:9) suggested that Miller lance-olate points could be "*locally* ancestral to the Clovis/eastern fluted point type" [italics in original]. However, no evidence can be found at Meadowcroft or anywhere else that shows the "evolution of fluting" (Adovasio 1983:9), so the relationship between Meadowcroft's earliest assemblages and Clovis is a mystery. Boldurian (1985) thought the Miller type similar to Plano, which is post-Clovis in the Plains. Adovasio (1983:10) professed it "impossible to believe" that pre-Clovis people "perished without genetic or technological issue or progeny," implying that Clovis sprung at least partly from the peoples who made Miller bifaces. But, as James Griffin (1983:22) remarked about another kind of impossibility, "It is . . . almost impossible for a large number of archaeologists to agree on any archaeological approach or interpretation of any prehistoric phenomenon," so the relationship of Miller to Clovis remains unresolved.

If the pre-Clovis levels at Meadowcroft are dated correctly, they were occupied during and just after the Last Glacial Maximum. Pine-dominated vegetation may have been growing in the eastern part of the region as far south as 30 degrees latitude at this time (S. Jackson, Webb, Anderson, Overpeck, Webb, Williams, and Hansen 2000). Cool-temperate conifers and hardwoods lived as far north as 34 degrees latitude, implying the glacial maximum was not as severely cold as previously believed (S. Jackson *et al.* 2000). Pre-Clovis foragers in this time would have had to adapt to the resources and climatic conditions of cold spruce-pine woodlands. By the time of the Clovis era, paleovegetation and climates had shifted considerably.

Most Clovis sites in the region are only plowzone occurrences, and many have been very well collected by amateur and professional archeologists. Over 1,400 fluted points are known from the region (Anderson and Faught 1998a), with the highest numbers coming from Massachusetts, New York, New Jersey, and Pennsylvania, in descending order. Many (perhaps most) fluted points are variants that may date to later in the Clovis era or afterwards.

Meltzer (1988; Lepper and Meltzer 1991) has proposed that there is a significant difference in the Clovis record between the northern and the central/ southern portions of this region. In Meltzer's proposal, he noted that isolated fluted points occur in much higher numbers in the central and south than in the north (Meltzer 1988:12; Lepper and Meltzer 1991:177). There are also relatively few sites in the south and central forests, perhaps reflecting different prehistoric land use and adaptation.

Meltzer (1988) modeled human responses to the two major biotic communities that existed in the east during the Clovis era – a parkland of spruce woods and tundra in the north, and to the south a forest of deciduous and boreal tree taxa. In the north, according to Meltzer, caribou could have been exploited by Clovis, while deer were available in the central and southern "species-rich forests" where Clovis people were generalists because resources were dispersed. In the southern subregion, Clovis activities such as nut-collecting would have left "little trace in the archaeological record" – for example, "readily observable food remains or tools to mark their former locations" – but caribou-hunting in the north left "a site record more conducive to discovery," according to Meltzer (1988:41–2; Lepper and Meltzer 1991:178).

My take on this prediction of archeological visibility is that it is the reverse of the foraging signatures logically expected from exploitation of plants and smaller game versus larger game. Generalists are small-scale patch users, and generalist foragers who depend on high-cost resources would manufacture the specialized types of tools and facilities necessary for extracting energy from them, creating high-visibility sites – because such tools and facilities are heavy duty and long lasting, and because resource patches are revisited regularly. Generalists probably would have left sites with reliable (but heavy) artifacts such as milling equipment, boiling facilities, roasting pits, and storage features. If Clovis people were generalists in the forest, their sites should contain the tool and feature assemblages that generalists expectedly create. Yet they do not.

On the other hand, big-game hunters are large-scale patch-users, creating lower visibility sites (unless large bone accumulations are preserved, which is rare in the eastern United States). Big-game hunters would have left flake tools and bifaces where animals were processed.

Meltzer (1988; Meltzer and Smith 1986) originally claimed that Clovis assemblages from the two different biotic regions are "quite distinct" (Meltzer 1993a:303) in such traits as "fluted point styles, assemblage characteristics, site structure, use of exotic . . . [toolstone], and apparent settlement mobility," but he later stated that probably more than just the two distinct Clovis patterns will be found to exist (Meltzer 1993a). In other words, Clovis patterns do not necessarily closely correlate with paleoenvironmental zones.

Dincauze (1993a, 1993b) and Curran (1999) proposed that the different kinds of archeological evidence – such as the numbers of fluted points in individual sites – suggest different phases of Clovis dispersal in the northeast. A first phase was the earliest exploration, which was followed by colonization and settling into optimal resource areas. The optimal areas are where the sites are largest, while the less appealing areas contain smaller and scattered sites. Curran (1999) suggested that a seriation of fluted-point measurements may allow a first-approximation temporal linking of small sites with large sites. Certain very large sites such as Bull Brook (MA) and Whipple (NH) may represent the first arrivals in New England who used the sites as residential loci from which to explore and forage far afield (Curran 1999; Dincauze 1993b). This proposed first stage of colonization, still undated, is sometimes referred to as the Bull Brook phase (Grimes, Eldridge, Grimes, Vaccaro, Vaccaro, Vaccaro,Vaccaro, and Orsini 1984: see Curran 1999 and references therein). Explorers traveled to the farther north of the region to forage for food and possibly also toolstone, but also regularly returned to the marshaling centers – which were usually but not always located in the southern reaches of the region – such as Nobles Pond (OH), Shoop (PA), and Debert (Nova Scotia) (see Curran 1999:table 1.1).

At Shoop in Pennsylvania (Carr 1988; Cox 1986; Holland and Dincauze 1999; Witthoft 1952), another very large site, suitable local raw materials were not used at all for making fluted points, in favor of exotic materials brought from outside the site locality. This selectivity by people who persisted in the use of exotics at a site having good local toolstone may indicate the Clovis-era people came from somewhere else – in other words, they were immigrants and not descendants of a pre-Clovis local population – and they brought preconceived ideas about what constituted proper lithic raw material; hence the Shoop site also may show that in some localities the Clovis-era people never developed plans to settle in or claim the place permanently.

(2)   MIDDLE ATLANTIC AND SOUTHEAST

This region (Fig. 2.3) is over twice the size of the Northeast, nearly 1,400,000 square kilometers in area. The states encompassed are Delaware, Maryland, West Virginia, and Virginia in the Middle Atlantic subregion; and Alabama, Florida, Georgia, Louisiana, Mississippi, North Carolina, South Carolina, Tennessee, Kentucky, and Arkansas in the Southeast subregion. The range of topography and physiography is similar to the Northeast region, but with a much wider coastal plain and piedmont extending west from the Atlantic ocean towards

Fig. 2.3 The Middle
Atlantic and Southeast
region.

the ridge and valley and plateau physiographic provinces. The deep Southeast
is "subtropical" in climate. Vegetation in both subregions was mainly mixed
hardwood and pine woods after the Last Glacial Maximum, and the region had
mostly the same animals as in the Northeast, without the caribou and moose.
Bison may have been available around the Gulf Coast (Lundelius, Graham,
Anderson, Guilday, Holman, Steadman, and Webb 1983) and central Florida
(Faunmap Working Group 1994:460).

Goodyear (1999a) pointed out that chronometric control is not especially
good in the southeastern states, and that most fluted points have been found
as isolates on ground surfaces. The region has yielded almost 5,500 fluted
points (D. G. Anderson and Faught 1998a), of which half or more are probably
variants that date to late in the Clovis era or afterwards. The highest counts
come from Alabama, Virginia, Tennessee, and Florida (in descending order).
Low tool densities and the frequent reuse of fluted-point localities by later
foraging groups has resulted in assemblage mixing. The highest densities of
fluted-point-associated materials are at toolstone quarry sources where the behavioral interpretations are slanted towards tool manufacturing processes. No
single stratified deposit contains a record of the southeast's culture sequence.

The Cactus Hill site is located 20 km south of the Williamson Clovis site
(both in southeastern Virginia), and contains possible pre-Clovis components –
dated about 17,000 to 15,000 rcybp – stratified in sand several inches below
a Clovis occupation that was dated 10,920 ± 250 rcybp, which itself is overlain by Archaic occupations (Johnson 1997; McAvoy 1997, 2000; McAvoy and

McAvoy 1997; Turner 2000). The pre-Clovis materials include prismatic blades made from prepared quartzite cores, and three small pentagonal bifaces (see Fig. 2.2) made of metavolcanics or chert and broken as if they had been used as projectile points (Kimball 2000). The pre-Clovis assemblage is interpreted as representing a population that occupied the site several thousand years before the Clovis era. However, as Fiedel (2000a) has noted, the pre-Clovis levels produce charcoal dates ranging from late Pleistocene to late Holocene, perhaps indicating past sediment mixing in the sandy substrate. The dated charcoal may have been derived from natural deposits already in the dune sand when the people arrived.

If Cactus Hill does contain pre-Clovis materials, the occupation was light and people did not return to the site for thousands of years until Clovis appeared, after which the site was then repeatedly used. The Clovis component, in other words, appears to be the actual initial "settlement" of the locality, as it also seems to be at the Williamson surface-site 20 km to the north.

The Topper site is another possible pre-Clovis occupation in the southeastern states. Situated on a hill over the Savannah river in South Carolina, the site contains Early Archaic materials overlying flaked implements technologically similar to Eastern Clovis, separated by sterile sediments from numerous small flakes, cores, and flake-"microtools," mostly microblades made of small local chert pebbles. The pre-Clovis levels yield an inventory of artifacts that is "light in number and small in size" (Goodyear 1999b). Thousands more pieces from the same levels appear naturally flaked, as if by heat. Excavations uncovered chert cobbles, possible quartz hammerstones, and an arc of possible post molds. The first dating attempts produced middle Holocene assays on the pre-Clovis level (Goodyear 1999b). But further chronometric work is underway. Goodyear's interpretation of the radiocarbon and optical luminescence dates from sediments below the pre-Clovis deposit is that they indicate windblown sands greater than 40,000 years old were covered by alluvium that is 20,000 years old or younger. The excavator, Al Goodyear, estimates the pre-Clovis artifacts are between 12,000 and 20,000 radiocarbon years old (Goodyear, Foss, and Wagner 1999; Rose 1999b). They are vertically and laterally diffuse in the sandy sediments, perhaps because of bioturbation or redeposition. Again, as at Cactus Hill, the Clovis occupation may have occurred several thousand years after the (putative) earlier people had been at the site, and if so Clovis seems to be the true beginning of colonization and settlement in the region, since the earlier foragers left no other consistent signs of their presence.

The Saltville Valley in southwestern Virginia is a rich late Pleistocene paleontological locale (McDonald 1984, 1985, 1986, 2000; Ray, Cooper, and Benninghoff 1967) that has produced fluted points (possibly late or post-Clovis [McCary 1986:fig. 2]) and possible cryptic signs of a pre-Clovis human population. In this valley's stratified alluvial, lacustrine, and paludal sediments are numerous vertebrate fossils and preserved pollen, plant macrofossils, and occasionally Pleistocene bone and antler pieces thought to be artifactually modified (McDonald 2000), although no solid proof is available. These bones may have been nonculturally modified.

Another very rich paleontological locality is Big Bone Lick (KY) (also written Bigbone Lick [Hay 1923] and originally called Big-Bone-swamp [Osborn 1936:135]), about 35 km southwest of Cincinnati (OH), where fluted points have been found but not in direct association with mastodont bones (Tankersley 1994a). Beginning in 1739, when local Indians gave fossil bones to a French military officer, mastodont bones and teeth from this locality were collected in "enormous quantities" (Hay 1923:401), filling up huge barrels and even entire wagons. In fact the mastodont bones discovered at this place inspired the birth of American paleontology, seizing the interest of international scientists such as Buffon, Blumenbach, Cuvier, and Linnaeus. But as at Saltville (VA), the evidence is either very slim or nonexistent for pre-Clovis or Clovis-era hunting of mastodonts, or of any of the locality's other fauna such as ground sloth, horse, musk-ox, caribou, bison, and mammoth.

The fluted-point occupation of the Middle Atlantic and Southeast subregions is much better studied than the pre-Clovis. In the Middle Atlantic subregion, Custer, Cavallo, and Stewart (1983) formulated a model explaining fluted-point settlement patterns; in their view, the distribution of lithic resources – particularly high-quality cryptocrystalline toolstone – shaped the distribution of sites as much as hunting and gathering tasks, a hypothesis supported by studies in the ridge-and-valley, piedmont, and coastal plain physiographic provinces. According to the model, Paleoindian and Early Archaic groups restricted their movements to "a catchment area of variable size with a radius up to 200 km centered around one or more cryptocrystalline lithic sources. The basis of this adaptation is a biface tool technology in which a curated biface represents a multi-purpose tool in and of itself as well as a core source for flakes which can be manufactured into more specialized tools" (Custer, Cavallo, and Stewart 1983:269; see also Callahan 1979).

D. G. Anderson (1996:37) proposed that the largest fluted-point concentrations found in the east were "settlement nuclei from which later Middle Paleoindian regional cultural traditions emerged" (see Fig. 2.17 below). Land areas between the denser concentrations were not entirely unvisited by Clovis and tended to be filled in by later people. By the time of the so-called Middle Paleoindian stage – after Clovis points were replaced by the Suwanee type in Florida, Redstone/Quad in Georgia and Alabama, Cumberland in Virginia and the Carolinas, and other variants elsewhere – only the Appalachians and the Gulf Coast remained sparsely peopled.

Clovis or the later variants are numerous in much of the southeast, but are relatively scarce south of latitude 33 degrees South, on the South Atlantic and Gulf coastal plains (Anderson 1990; Goodyear 1999a:437–8; Mason 1962). The Aucilla river region of Florida has yielded relatively more Clovis-like points than the lanceolate non-Clovis variants, and Goodyear (1999a:439) suggests this may have been the subregion where "an initial colonization of Clovis populations in the lower Southeast" was made.

Goodyear (1999a:443; Goodyear, Michie, and Charles 1989) speculated that if megamammals were extinct by 10,900 or 10,800 rcybp in the southeastern states, and if Clovis occupations did not begin in the southeast until after that time, no associations of Clovis foragers and megafauna will be found – and Clovis foraging in the southeast was therefore very different from foraging in the Plains and other parts of the American West.

However, the Kimmswick (MO) finds in the midcontinent, described below, do support the contemporaneity of humans and megamammals in some parts of the the southern United States (Graham, Haynes, Johnson, and Kay 1981).

As well, Florida finds of proboscidean ivory artifacts (for example, Dunbar 1991; Jenks and Simpson 1941; see Goodyear 1999a:444 for other references and discussion) that were probably worked when fresh and unweathered seem to indicate that Clovis people did indeed find megamammals alive when colonizing the farthest stretches of the region.

The Page-Ladsen site in a karstic part of Florida is a 10 m deep sinkhole located underwater within a slow freshwater stream, the Aucilla river. Contained within the site are peat, wood, bone, and stone artifacts from different time periods, starting from the late Pleistocene and continuing through the middle to late Holocene (Dunbar, Faught, and Webb 1988). One fluted point and several unfluted lanceolate points (Suwanee and Simpson types) as well as other lithics were found in the site or in nearby riverbank sediments, but none has been recovered *in situ* in association with the bones of extinct megafauna such as mastodont, mammoth, horse, camel, bison, ground sloth, and giant armadillo. Radiocarbon dates from the megafauna levels cluster around 12,300 rcybp (Dunbar, Faught, and Webb 1988).

Other underwater Florida sites such as Little Salt Spring (Clausen, Brooks, and Wesolowsky 1975) and Warm Mineral Springs yielded various taxa of extinct fauna. A large tortoise (*Geochelone crassiscutata*) at Little Salt Spring had a pointed wooden stake lying between its plastron and carapace, which was interpreted as a spear driven into the animal. Some of the animal's bones appeared carbonized and the tortoise may have been cooked, apparently with the spear/stake/stick still in it. However, the "spear" may not be a genuine artifact (Purdy 1991). The "spear" was radiometrically dated 12,030 ± 200 rcybp (Clausen, Cohen, Emiliani, Holman, and Stipp 1979), but a tortoise bone was dated 1,400 years older, so it seems that the association is not behavioral but only stratigraphic.

Several other cases of such possible but unproven Clovis associations have been found in Florida. Dunbar and Webb (1996) described modified bones recovered from underwater sediments without stratification. The specimens include scratched and broken proboscidean bones interpreted as a rasp, an anvil, a beamer, and a hoe; Bullen, Webb, and Waller (1970) described a fragmented mammoth vertebra they interpreted as butcher-marked, but the damage is not clearly the result of sensible carcass-processing action (see section 3.3).

These bone specimens have suffered noncultural modifications seen on Holocene, Pleistocene, and pre-Pleistocene fossil materials from collections made around the world. Thus, no firm association between people and extinct megafauna can be argued for the very part of Florida where Clovis points are the most densely distributed, based on the published literature (Goodyear 1999a:445), except for a broken (and typologically unidentifiable) chert projectile point embedded in the skull of an extinct *Bison antiquus* that may be Clovis-age (Webb, Milanich, Alexon, and Dunbar 1984).

Although the Clovis sites are not behavior rich in Florida, clever paleontological, archeological, and analytical work has wrested a fair amount of interesting information from the late Pleistocene materials. For example, while fossil bones and paleoenvironmental reconstructions indicate that American mastodonts were much more numerous in Florida than mammoths, analyses of worked ivory points recovered from the karstic portions of the state show that prehistoric people had a preference for mammoth over mastodont ivory (Herrera 1999;

Webb, Dunbar, and Waller 1990). This may have been because Clovis foragers repeatedly used certain favorable ecological settings such as shallow streams in grassy glades where mammoths outnumbered mastodonts, or possibly because mammoths were easier to kill than mastodonts.

During the Clovis era in Florida, sea levels were lower than today by an estimated 40 m (Dunbar, Webb, and Faught 1992; Faught 1996; Faught and Carter 1998). The modern sea level was reached in the middle Holocene. Thus, at 11,000 rcybp, the land area of peninsular Florida was much larger than it is now, because the gently sloping continental shelf was exposed for a distance of over 100 km in the Gulf of Mexico and up to 100 km on the Atlantic Ocean side (see map in Faught and Carter 1998). The streams, woodlands, grasslands, and biotic resources of this enlarged peninsula were much more abundant than they are on today's reduced land area. Foragers of the Clovis era could have explored and exploited landscapes that are now far offshore (Faught, Dunbar, and Webb 1992), as tantalisingly suggested by discoveries at the Ray Hole Spring site. This site is a freshwater sinkhole/spring in the Gulf of Mexico, about 32 km offshore and 11 m under the present sea level (Anuskiewicz 1988; Anuskiewicz, Gerrell, Dunbar, and Donoghue 1994). Dredge excavations at the site recovered lithic debitage around the spring. Firm dating to the Clovis era may not be possible.

The drier coastal lowlands around the Gulf of Mexico "appear to have been the least attractive for fluted point users of all the major [eastern] life zones or physiographic regions" (Dincauze 1993a:285). Clovis-era habitation sites are scarce. According to Dincauze (1993a:285), large numbers of fluted and unfluted lanceolate points discovered in certain locales may have deceptively inflated the intensity of the overall Clovis presence in the subregion.

The southern Florida peninsula probably supported vegetation and habitats similar to the western states' prairie and plains, with grasslands and scrubby woodlands, yet this part of the state lacks evidence of a Clovis occupation (Muniz 1998). The present-day Atlantic coast (which is relatively distant from the earlier Pleistocene coast flooded by sea level rise during deglaciation) shows a "very weak presence" of Clovis. The distribution of Clovis sites suggests that Clovis foragers focused on numerous different environmental settings, especially the borders of drainage basins where many more animal and plant resources were accessible. Muniz (1998) proposed that at least two distinct Clovis macrobands left separate artifact concentrations in the Florida panhandle and the Tampa Bay area.

The southeast has a good archeological record of post-Clovis and pre-Dalton (or pre-Early Archaic), thought to span the time interval of 10,900 to 10,500 rcybp. Some of the points from this time interval are fluted, including the Cumberland with its common full facial fluting that may reflect contemporaneity with Folsom on the Plains and Barnes in the center of the continent. The Cumberland type and others such as Redstone (an elongated triangle with full fluting) and the usually unfluted Suwanee and waisted Quad may be the natural results of "localization" and place-based differentiation by settled populations, who defined their identities through the localities they occupied or visited, and hence distinguished themselves ethnically and stylistically from neighboring populations (Goodyear 1999a).

Finding information useful to interpret Clovis foraging is difficult in most of the eastern United States. One reason may be that apparently very little sediment

Fig. 2.4 The Great Lakes and Midcontinent region. The portion of deglaciated Southern Ontario included in this region is not outlined.

was transported through erosion or deposition between 20,000 and 8,000 rcybp (Delcourt 1985), except on the southeastern floodplains where "energetic and rapid" sediment aggradation around 11,000 rcybp probably carried away most of the primary contextual information about Clovis behavior (Goodyear 1999a:470; see references therein). At the same time the aggradation deeply buried only a few examples of Clovis sites that may still await discovery. This aggradation may have taken place after the Clovis era in some places and before the Clovis occupations in others. The chances that Clovis camps were buried are rather slim in most alluvial settings, but Goodyear (1999a) has attempted to predict and anticipate the places where conditions are best for finding stratified, protected late Pleistocene assemblages – specifically in the floodplains in river valleys (many of which are now artificially flooded).

(3)   GREAT LAKES AND MIDCONTINENT

The Great Lakes and midcontinent region (Fig. 2.4) lies between the Allegheny mountains in the east and the High Plains in the west, and stretches from the Great Lakes in the north to the Ohio river drainage in the south. In area, the region is 1,158,000 square kilometers. Included are Ontario's southern-most landscapes, plus the states of Wisconsin, Minnesota, Missouri, Illinois, Indiana, Ohio, Michigan, and Iowa. The physiography is as varied as in the eastern regions. Over 2,600 fluted points have been recorded from the region (Anderson and Faught 1998a), but many may be post-Clovis-era variants.

I begin by describing and summarizing the Great Lakes subregion first, then move to the adjacent "midcontinent" subregion which includes the two states not bordering a great lake, namely Iowa and Missouri.

Lepper (1999:362, and see the references cited in this paper) describes this region in the late Pleistocene as a "dynamic mosaic ranging from ephemeral tundra and spruce parkland . . . [in the north] to a complex deciduous and coniferous forest in the south." The region includes both glaciated and unglaciated landscapes. The glaciated landscapes contain numerous postglacial lakes and bogs, plus rolling hills and outwash flatlands. During the Last Glacial Maximum around 18,000 rcybp, the continental ice front covered most of the basins which were later to become the Great Lakes; by 14,000 rcybp the ice was retreating, and "tundra-like" expanses of open ground existed in the north of this region, ringed by boreal forests and mixed deciduous and coniferous forests/woodlands (Lepper 1999 provides references for the paleoenvironmental interpretations).

Most of the animal taxa living in these habitats were the same as in the rest of the eastern United States. Because of the forested nature of the landscape, however, mastodonts probably outnumbered mammoths in the late Pleistocene. Overstreet and Stafford (1997) proposed that "mammoth and mastodon populations were not contemporaneous in the southwestern Lake Michigan basin, but were sequential inhabitants – mammoths were replaced by mastodons" between about 12,500 and 11,000 rcybp (Overstreet and Stafford 1997:70), and American mastodonts were extinct in southeastern Wisconsin by about 10,800 rcybp. Overstreet and Stafford also point out differences in bone ages between conventional radiocarbon dates and AMS measurements on highly purified chemical fractions, with conventional dating often far too young by 1,000 years or more.

Pre-Clovis in the midcontinent is a murky possibility, as it seems to be almost everywhere else. The Big Eddy site (MO) may contain pre-Clovis through Clovis in its strata (Lopinot, Ray, and Conner 2000, 1998; J. Ray, Lopinot, and Hajic 1998). The site is located along a rapidly collapsing bank of the Sac River, on the western edge of the Ozarks. One level of sediments at the site, from which a Gainey-like fluted point (see Table 2.2b below) was excavated, has been dated about 10,700 rcybp (Ray, Lopinot, and Hajic 1998). Below the fluted-point level more artifacts were dated about 10,900 rcyb, and below them were sparse artifacts and charcoal dated 12,950 rcybp. Also found in the pre-Clovis layers was a broken flat boulder of sandstone and an oblong chert cobble that may have been a hammerstone. These are interpreted as megamammal-bone processing tools.

The region also has mammoth or mastodont bonesites dated earlier than the Clovis era and interpreted as kills made by pre-Clovis people. Some of the sites lack lithics; examples are Burning Tree (OH) – perhaps a nonlithic cultural site dating to the early Clovis era, 11,660 and 11,450 rcybp (Fisher, Lepper, and Hooge 1994) – and several southeastern Wisconsin mammoths (Hebior, Fenske, Mud Lake, Schaefer) believed to be butchered (but see section 3.3). These sites are classified as part of the subsistence/settlement system of the so-called Chesrow complex, named after assemblages from nearby surface sites (Overstreet 1993); the lithics include variable lanceolate bifaces and other implements made of local toolstone such as quartzite cobbles. Time-diagnostic Chesrow tools have not been found associated with the mammoths. Two kinds of sites are thought to make up the Chesrow settlement system: well-drained beach ridges where only the lithics are found – mainly atop ground surfaces – and inland bogs such as Hebior and Schaefer, where mammoth bones are found with infrequent and undiagnostic lithics (Overstreet 1996; Overstreet, Joyce, Hallin, and Wasion 1993; Overstreet, Joyce, and Wasion 1995). At the Schaefer site were found a single chert flake and a biface fragment. At Hebior, two chert bifaces, a chert flake, and a dolomite "chopper" were found with mammoth bones. Dates on bones from these two sites are around 12,300 rcybp (Overstreet and Stafford 1997). Two other mammoth sites without lithics, Fenske and Mud Lake, are dated to about 13,400 rcybp, and both have yielded marks on bones interpreted as butchering traces.

The Chesrow lithic complex may be ancestral to a later Clovis pattern, or it may have nothing to do with it. Shott (n.d.) noted the many similarities of Chesrow bifaces and later Paleoindian types such as Hi-Lo. As for the mammoth sites interpreted as butchered, I return to the topic of such marked bones in chapter 3.

No fluted-point sites in the Great Lakes subregion have been reliably dated radiometrically (Lepper 1999:370). The Gainey site (MI) was dated by thermoluminescence, producing an age of 12,360 ± 1,224 (Simons, Shott, and Wright 1987) in calendar years, which is post-Clovis (see Appendix 1). The Paleo Crossing site in northeastern Ohio yielded Gainey points associated with possible pits and post molds, but these features returned radiocarbon dates clustering at two different times, approximately 12,150 and 10,980 rcybp, possibly as a result of the mixing of older and younger charcoal (Brose 1994). A subset of the available younger charcoal dates (around 10,980 rcybp) would place this site neatly into the Clovis era, but that requires unfairly ignoring the older dates. Probably the most prudent way to deal with the suite of dates (Shott n.d.) is to keep wondering why they do not cluster – do they date the Clovis-like occupation, or do they date environmental events before and after the occupation?

Dates within the range of the Clovis era have been obtained on nondiagnostic lithics in other sites, namely State Road Ripple (PA) and Enoch Fork Rockshelter (KY) (see Lepper 1999:370). Several mastodont bonesites lacking lithics and thought by some researchers to be butchered have been dated to the Clovis era or slightly later (for example Deerfield [WI], Pleasant Lake [MI], Big Bone Lick [KY], Lake Mills [WI], Marion County [OH], and Rappuhn [MI]). Some of these will be discussed further in chapter 3.

The Great Lakes subregion does have several relatively large lithic sites of possibly single occupation (such as the Parkhill and Fisher sites in Ontario), while the adjacent midcontinental subregion has numerous single-point finds, but these are not all "Clovis" although they contain fluted-point variants. The larger midcontinental fluted-point sites are quarry-related, multiple-occupation localities or are located at rich resource points such as saline springs (Lepper 1999:372, 374–5).

In the Great Lakes subregion, a sequential progression of changing Clovis-to-post-Clovis projectile-point types is thought to have accompanied changes in raw material selectivity, site distribution, and technology (Deller 1988; Deller and Ellis 1988; Ellis and Deller 1988; Storck 1991). The earliest fluted points are postulated to be Gainey, which are the most Clovis-like, followed by the Barnes type with its smaller size, longer flute, and waisted shape, and later the Crowfield type, which is wider, very thin, and with multiple fluting. The trends towards well-defined fluting and then towards thinner biface cross-section, with a resultant avoidance of deep channel flakes – often requiring more than one channel-flake removal – also characterize many western subregional typological sequences – such as the classic Clovis-to-Folsom-to-Plainview succession in the Plains.

Although no unambiguous association of *Rangifer* bones with a fluted point is known in the Great Lakes subregion, L. Jackson (1997) hypothesized that the widely scattered sites of the Gainey period (probably equivalent to the latter Clovis era) in southern Ontario were created by small human groups hunting caribou at interception points on caribou migration routes; the foragers of the younger Parkhill phase, who made Barnes fluted points 10,600–10,400 rcybp, created larger, multiple-activity sites situated along proglacial lake strandlines. The large Parkhill phase sites are interpreted as seasonal aggregations for the hunting of migrating caribou; microbands or task-specific groups had created the dispersed smaller sites during the earlier Gainey phase. But why the different phases show different settlement patterning when caribou-hunting is thought to be the main subsistence focus of both phases is not clear.

D. C. Fisher (1984a, 1984b, 1987, 1996, 1999) proposed that for more than a full millennium between 11,700 and 10,400 rcybp human foragers killed mastodonts in the Great Lakes region, sometimes caching parts of the carcasses underwater. His hypothesis that human hunting affected mastodont populations is based on several lines of evidence: some marked mastodont bones were interpreted as butchered, although lithic artifacts have not been found associated with these skeletons; the skeletons having the "butcher-marked" bones had died in the same season (around autumn), perhaps reflecting a human hunting tactic to procure meat for winter provisions; the body sizes of Great Lakes mastodonts were reduced from earlier times, a possible reaction to predation pressure by humans (acceleration of mastodont reproductive schedules compensates for hunting losses, hence smaller animals reached sexual maturity sooner); mastodonts appeared to reach sexual maturity at younger ages than they would have done if climate or vegetational stress adversely affected them; calving in-tervals in mastodonts were shorter than they would have been if climate stress affected them; and growth rates were rather high for mastodonts, as may happen in mammals subject to habitual predation losses.

However, the solid evidence for human predation on mastodonts around the Great Lakes is very slim – in fact, there is no "direct" archeological evidence, at all, according to Lepper (1999:374), who thinks that some lithics, even if only resharpening flakes, would have been left behind at mastodont "butchering" sites. I too (G. Haynes 2000a) did not find the arguments conclusive that the Great Lakes mastodonts were killed or butchered by human foragers, but these doubts should not remove the sites from the realm of debate and continued dis-cussion. It remains a possibility that pre-Clovis explorers (the Chesrow complex people) and later Clovis dispersers (perhaps the makers of Gainey fluted points) as well as post-Clovis foragers (the makers of Barnes fluted points) actually did kill or scavenge mastodonts around the Great Lakes.

The earliest fluted-point colonizers of the Great Lakes subregion entered landscapes that were freshly deglaciated, and moved from south to north as plants and animals returned to the land. Each successive phase of the fluted-point sequence may have had different subsistence and mobility patterns, although direct and unambiguous evidence about food is seriously lacking (Jackson 1997; Jackson, Ellis, Morgan, and McAndrews 2000). In the Gainey (probable later

Clovis era) phase, small and scattered sites were created especially often near lakes, and large sites have not been found, thus reflecting a non-aggregating and very mobile human population in a spruce parkland, targeting specific resources such as caribou, fish, and waterfowl. In the succeeding Parkhill phase (characterized by Barnes points), spruce was giving way to pine forests and lakes were shrinking quickly, and human foragers may have kept to the edges of these lakes to find caribou herds. Relatively large Parkhill "aggregation" sites have been found on lake strandlines, perhaps because people camped at these topographic settings seasonally to intercept migrating caribou (Jackson 1997:156–9). Finally, in the late Paleoindian Crowfield phase, the pine forests had closed in and the pro-glacial lakes were dry, effectively removing habitat for caribou and thus removing caribou itself from the human resource base.

At the Gainey site (MI), almost all the earliest diagnostic tools are made of cherts from east-central Ohio (Simons 1997). Simons interpreted the Gainey phase sites – such as Gainey (MI) and Paleo Crossing (OH) (Brose and Barrish 1992) – as places occupied by "highly mobile, seasonally migratory, groups of hunters and gatherers with a lifstyle focused, at least in part, on large game hunting" (Simons 1997:126). Perhaps macrobands during the Clovis colonizing era used ranges stretching as much as 830 km (500 miles) from southern chert sources to northern caribou migration trails in Michigan, Ontario, and other Great Lakes areas (Simons 1997). By the time of the Parkhill phase (when Barnes type fluted points were manufactured, thought to date to post-Clovis time and perhaps contemporary with Folsom in the western states), chert sources were being used nearer the residential and logistical camps (Simons 1997:117). D. G. Anderson (1990) and Simons (1997) suggest that the shift from Clovis-era long-distance north–south movement to a more east–west set of movements in the younger Parkhill phase marks the end of "southern interaction" (Anderson 1990:190–6) that might correspond to changes in subsistence – such as a change from reliance on hunting migratory caribou to hunting nonmigratory deer or other animals (Simons 1997:117–18).

Lepper followed Meltzer's lead (Meltzer 1988 hypothesized about the eastern United States in general) and proposed two distinct settlement/subsistence systems to explain the possible differences in fluted-point distributions. (1) Near the Great Lakes, the large sites may be residential (base) camps, and the smaller camps around them may attest to a generalized land-use pattern by broad-spectrum foragers in a landscape having less resource diversity and richness than farther south (Deller and Ellis 1988, 1990; Jackson 1988, 1997; Lepper 1999:378; Storck 1997). (However, I repeat the caution in these cited sources that many of the smaller fluted-point sites such as Gainey [MI] may date to an earlier time interval than the larger sites such as Parkhill and Fisher, both in Ontario, which seem to be post-Clovis [dating 10,600–10,400 rcybp].) In Lepper's view, megamammals were not often hunted. (2) In the midcontinental subregion, foraging also was generalized for a multitude of resources, but was possibly focused on white-tailed deer or elk (Lepper 1999:376, and see references); larger sites were created by multiple site revisits, indicating a low human population density in the wooded habitats. The human population seems to have maintained itself throughout the late Pleistocene/early Holocene, and gradually differentiated over space and time, producing numerous variants of fluted points and numerous small sites (and occasional larger ones).

Numerous radiocarbon dates from animal bones and organics found at Ohio's Sheriden Cave (or Pit) indicate a possible cultural association (or at the least a contemporaneity) between people and extinct fauna 11,200 to 10,600 rcybp (Tankersley 1999, 2000). The people are represented by a biface that seems to be Holcombe type (probably late or post-Clovis), flaked-stone scrapers and gravers, and two bone points. The fauna includes caribou, giant beaver, peccary, and other extinct taxa. Some bones may be butcher-marked. It may be that this is an occupation from the late Clovis era, but the cultural and noncultural inputs to the cave need to be carefully teased apart; there is no reason to believe that every animal bone inside the cave was contributed by a human forager.

In Lepper's (1999:381) view, there is no separate and isolable Clovis era in this region of the continent: "Early Paleoindian adaptive strategies appear to be essentially continuous through the early Archaic." The environmental and cultural changes from late Pleistocene through early Holocene seem uninterrupted and unspecialized, and "Clovis" in this view is therefore only an arbitrarily defined type of projectile point, not a distinctive way of life. Until Gainey phase sites and assemblages can be reliably dated, and the identifiable characteristics of Gainey phase subsistence and settlement separated from the (probably) younger phases when Barnes and Crowfield points were manufactured, a clear picture of Clovis-era foraging will remain very difficult to imagine.

Farther away from the Great Lakes, in the small subregion I call the "midcontinent" here – Iowa and Missouri – claims for pre-Clovis occupation are scattered in space and time. The bones of an adult mastodont found in the town of Miami (MO) were excavated by Carl Chapman in 1973 but never written up until the landowner T. M. Hamilton described the find in the 1990s (Hamilton 1996; Hamilton pers. comm. 1997). The associated lithic specimens were modest and perhaps questionable artifacts – a flaked pebble, two scrapers, and a "pretty little pebble" (Hamilton 1996:82) – but the bones were interpreted as obviously affected by humans. Mastodont ribs were found in a mass measuring about 1.5 × 1.2 × 0.5 m, and Hamilton believed (1997a and 1997b pers. comm. 1997) they were cut by people and stacked to align in the same direction. A second mass of smaller bones, thought to be from deer, lay under a mastodont tooth. A 60 cm long section of ivory was interpreted as cut from the rest of the tusk. Brick-sized pieces of limestone were found with a broken scapula (Hamilton 1996:85) and may have been carried to the site to break the bones. The mastodont ribs were AMS dated at around 36,000 rcybp; a thermoluminescence date of about 42,000 calendar years is in probable agreement. Hamilton imagined that foragers carried mastodont body parts up a hill to an "observation post" where the ribs were piled up for the winter. However, I suggest that other noncultural explanations can account for the bone distributions and the breakage.

Clovis points have been found in scattered surface sites located in a variety of midcontinental topographic settings. No data about the Clovis-era diet are known from Iowa, but the state did produce a cache of twenty whole and fragmentary fluted bifaces (Gainey type) that possibly date to the Clovis era (Anderson and Tiffany 1972). Morrow and Morrow (1994) surveyed Iowa fluted-point discoveries, and counted 108 Clovis or Clovis-like points and preforms distributed all across the state; the Cumberland or Barnes point type (considered to be a post-Clovis type) is very rare in the state, but Folsom does occur in the east and the west, although more commonly in the west.

Dating has been done at several midcontinental Clovis-era sites. The earliest level at the Shriver site (MO) – a lithic assemblage underlying a fluted-point occupation – was dated by thermoluminescence to 10,650 ± 1,100 calendar years old (Rowlett 1981; Rowlett and Garrison 1984), which is about the equivalent of 9,250 rcybp, too young for the fluted-point material. The site's single fluted point is not Clovis type, and may be a Sedgwick, an undated type that is considered an eastern variant of Folsom (Morse 1997), which has a date range of about 10,900 to 10,200 rcybp. Underlying the fluted-point level is an "unfamiliar congeries of chert objects characterized as unifacial flake tools" (Jennings 1983:46) dated 13,000 ± 1,500 calendar years.

No radiocarbon dates are available from the Kimmswick site in eastern Missouri (Graham, Haynes, Johnson, and Kay 1981), an interesting place where two buried and superimposed pond deposits contained Clovis lithics bedded with animal bones, stratigraphically situated under Archaic lithics. The upper pond deposit yielded two Clovis points, including one lying among mastodont foot bones, plus unifacial stone tools, a bifacial fragment, and hundreds of chert flakes, along with dermal ossicles of ground sloth and bones of shrew, rodents, deer, snake, and a canid. The lower pond deposit yielded fragments of a lanceolate point base (probably Clovis) and a fluted preform, plus chert flakes, associated with mastodont and twenty other mammalian taxa (Graham and Kay 1988). The bones of rodent, deer, and turtle were almost as abundant as mastodont. The microfauna bones may have been derived from carnivore scat (Graham and Kay 1988:233). Dermal ossicles from *Glossotherium harlani* (Harlan's ground sloth) were found in the Clovis levels, but with no other bones of the taxon, perhaps indicating that Clovis people brought sloth skins to the site. Mastodont bones mainly consisted of teeth and foot elements, and bone surfaces were too poorly preserved to show possible cutmarks.

No direct dates were possible from the site, but the stratigraphic and typological data clearly demonstrate the mastodont components date to the Clovis era. No artifacts showed any damage that would suggest redeposition, and no evidence exists of sedimentary mixing. Thus, the site unquestionably records the contemporaneity of megamammals and Clovis foragers. However it is difficult to decipher behavioral events that could account for the bone and lithic assemblage. No hearths or other undisturbed features were found that would indicate a "living floor" had been buried with minimal alteration.

Kimmswick is interesting for another reason, besides revealing a Clovis–mastodont interaction: the local paleoenvironment is interpreted as deciduous woodland with open grassy glades, a far cry from the poorly drained spruce forests often envisioned as the home of the American mastodont (for example, see Dreimanis 1967).

The central Mississippi river valley is relatively rich in fluted points (Morse and Morse 1983:41), especially between the Mississippi river and the Ozarks of Arkansas and Missouri, where mastodont bones are also found but not in primary association.

(4)   NORTHERN PRAIRIE/PLAINS

The "northern" prairies and plains of North America are actually located in Canada, but because of the stateside position of the continental glaciers so late

Fig. 2.5 The northern Prairie/Plains region, without the hard-to-define Canadian component.

in the Pleistocene, my discussion of this region mainly focuses on Montana, North Dakota, South Dakota, Wyoming, Nebraska, and Colorado (Fig. 2.5). The northernmost portions of this region were recently deglaciated in the time interval of interest here, and consisted of tundra, wetlands, and shrub habitats rather than prairies. The area of the prairie/plains part of this region is over 1,475,000 square kilometers. Nearly 800 fluted points are known from the region; but based on information in Anderson and Faught (1998a), I estimate that Folsom types greatly outnumber Clovis in the total, ranging from two to one to as much as ten to one.

Possible pre-Clovis sites in the northern Plains do exist, including some in Canada north of the glacial ice and some that would have been occupied before the Last Glacial Maximum ice sheets covered the locations. One recent candidate for a pre-Clovis site is the Grimshaw gravel pit in Alberta (Chlachula and LeBlanc 1996; Chlachula and Leslie 1998). A collection of seventeen quartzite lithics – called choppers, scrapers, and retouched flakes – was picked up in a glacial till, and the apparent nonrandomness of the flaking was interpreted as proof that humans did it. Yet the geological origin of the few pieces – glacially transported gravels that would have been knocked about under pressure – is probably a clue as to how the flakes were removed. And the old unproven claim that natural processes would never mimic human flaking on stone is worth rejecting at last (see Barnes 1939; Mason 1965; Warren 1920). Sites with nothing but crude chopper-like objects and flakes with irregular or casual "retouch" – which may have been nonculturally produced – do not solidly prove human existence in the northern Plains before about 11,000 rcybp.

Clovis type fluted point sites are not abundant in most of Canada's prairie and western provinces – for example, only "four or five" Clovis points have been found in Manitoba (Manitoba Archaeological Society 1998), because so much of the present-day province was covered by glacial ice until after 10,500 rcybp. Alberta has yielded fluted points from many surface sites, but Bryan (1968:74) noted that only three "classic" Clovis points were known up to 1968, although "two or three dozen other fluted points" could be fit into a more flexible definition of the Clovis type. T. Kehoe (1966) examined fluted point distribution in Saskatchewan, and Pohorecky and D. E. Anderson (1968) and Pettipas (1967) looked at fluted points around glacial Lake Agassiz shorelines. As Bryan (1968:74–5) pointed out, the studies show that fluted-point distribution in central Canada is limited to south of the continental ice-front, as if Clovis foragers were "roaming the region near the ice margin in search of mammoth."

Driver (1998) placed the first known human occupations of western Canada at no earlier than 10,700 rcybp, with post-glacial colonization coming up from the south. The Niska site (Saskatchewan) has one date of 10,880 ± 70 rcybp, but the artifacts are of the post-Clovis (and post-Folsom) Cody complex type, and the other radiocarbon dates range from 3,000 to 8,500 rcybp. The Vermillion Lake site (also in Saskatchewan) has a stratified component dated around 10,770 rcybp, with associated bones of snowshoe hare and an extinct subspecies of bighorn sheep. The stone artifacts are not typologically diagnostic (see Driver 1998 and references therein).

South of Canada, the possible pre-Clovis manifestations in the northern United States are scarce and debatable. Two mammoth sites lacking stone tool associations have been reported from Nebraska, namely the La Sena site, dated by radiocarbon and sedimentary position to the Last Glacial Maximum at 18,000–19,000 rcybp, and the Jensen mammoth, which is dated to about 14,000 rcybp. Both sites contained fractured and flaked mammoth limb bones, while other elements such as ribs were unbroken, leading Holen (1995, 1999; Holen and Blasing 1991) to propose that pre-Clovis people using hammerstones selectively broke bones to make tools and to extract marrow (following from earlier suggestions by Myers and Corner [1986], Myers, Voorhies, and Corner [1980], and Voorhies and Corner [1984]). If these sites are cultural and not natural, pre-Clovis foragers were present in Nebraska at the time when deep deposits of windblown silts were forming in the region, suggesting a very dry landscape with open vegetation. However, the evidence for a human presence is at best equivocal in these sites; in a later chapter I return to the topic of whether this sort of mammoth-bone breakage is authoritative evidence for human actions.

If La Sena and Jensen are authentic cultural sites, they indicate an extremely low density of extraordinarily mobile foragers long before Clovis times, when foragers were still mobile but also had become ubiquitous. Clovis points have been found throughout Nebraska, but are not as numerous as later Paleoindian point types such as Cody in the west or Dalton in the east of the state (Holen 1995).

Dent (CO) was first excavated by Jesse Figgins in 1932 (Figgins 1933), making it the first Clovis–mammoth association reported in North America (Wormington 1957). For that reason, it should have given its name to the fluted projectile points we now expect to be associated with megamammals. But the

Clovis point type was not recognized as distinct from Folsom at the time Dent
was uncovered (Holliday and Anderson 1993; Holliday 1997:25), and the type
was labeled Folsomoid or Folsom. Eventually, after Edgar Howard's excavations
that began in 1933 in Blackwater Draw near Clovis (NM), Clovis and Folsom
points were differentiated (for example, Cotter 1938), and the type that should
have been named "Dent" was given the designation "Clovis."

Dent was found in 1932 when mammoth bones began eroding out of a bank
about 160 m from the local railroad station. A Jesuit priest and students ex-
cavated the bones and discovered a fluted point, and the following year the
Denver Museum of Natural History continued the digging. The priest, Father
Bilgery, did not believe the Clovis point was the same age as the mammoth bones
(Bilgery n.d., cited in C. V. Haynes, McFaul, Brunswig, and Hopkins 1998), but
Jesse Figgins, who directed the Denver Museum excavations, did. In 1973, renewed excavations clarified the site's stratigraphy (C. V. Haynes 1974; C. V.
Haynes et al. 1998). In all, the site has yielded bones of fifteen mammoths,
mostly smaller individuals that are females or young, and three fluted points.
Radiocarbon dating of bone ranged from 11,200 ± 500 rcybp to 10,810 ± 40;
but charcoal and coke from the sediments enclosing the mammoth bones were
dated 170 ± 50 and 32,260 ± 2100 respectively, thus implying more than one
episode of redeposition had occurred at the site. The redeposition is supported
by Cassells (1983), who referred to an early observation of boulders bedded with
carbonate coatings in random orientation (suggesting they had been rolled and
reoriented from their original positions). Studies of the site's stratigraphy are
ongoing (Brunswig and Fisher 1993).

Colby (WY) contained seven mammoths that Frison (1986b) thought had been
killed over an extended period of time, possibly one at a time – judged on the
basis of differential bone weathering and the potential difficulty of killing more
than one mammoth at a time. Also at the site were found four fluted points,
with bases that are unusual in outline but technologically seem to be Clovis-like
(see Fig. 2.11 below), and thirty flakes, at least one flake tool, a hammerstone, a
split-boulder chopper, a sandstone abrader, and several possible bone tools. No
charcoal was found for dating; mammoth bones were dated to 11,200 ± 220,
10,864 ± 141, and 8,719 ± 392 rcybp. The youngest date is considered to be
incorrect. Another discovery of abundant mammoth bones less than 1 km away
from the Colby site had been made in 1907, although no further information is
available (Frison 1986a), hinting that mammoth-hunting may have been even
more frequent in the Clovis era.

In the Colby bonebed were two bone piles. One consisted of an articulated
front limb of an adult mammoth that was underneath long bones from other
individuals, all of which were covered by a young male animal's skull. Frison
(1998:14,581; Frison and Todd 1986) interpreted the pile as an unused
"cold-weather meat cache similar to those documented ethnographically in
the arctic." Another bone pile, more dispersed, was interpreted as a cache that
had been pulled apart and used. Frison (1986b:137) proposed that "planned and
deliberate trapping and killing" account for the site assemblage, a procurement
tactic repeated several times over a year or longer.

The Drake cache from a ploughed field in north-central Colorado included thirteen Clovis points, tiny fragments of ivory, and (possibly) a chert
cobble hammerstone (Stanford and Jodry 1988). Eleven of the points were

manufactured of chert from a source 560 km away in Texas. Some of the points appear to have been resharpened, but all were sharp and ready to use. Stanford and Jodry (1988) suggest the cache may have been a grave-offering rather than a utilitarian toolkit.

The Fenn cache (Frison and Bradley 1999) is a collection of fifty-six artifacts, all but one with traces of red ochre on the surface, possibly discovered in a dry cave around the Utah/Wyoming/Idaho border in 1902. Twenty-two Clovis points are in the collection, along with thirty-two bifaces, one bifacially shaped crescent, and a flake-blade. Nothing is known for sure about the provenience of these artifacts, or whether they were all recovered together.

The Anzick (MT) cache site contained seven Clovis points, several bifaces, a blade, an endscraper, utilized flakes, pieces of four or more bone rods – all of which were covered in red ochre – and fragments of one associated human child's bones (Jones and Bonnichsen 1994; Lahren and Bonnichsen 1974; Owsley and Hunt 2001; Stafford 1999a). A second child's bones were also found at the site, but dated much younger.

Frison's (1999) description of Clovis in the northwestern Plains provides ideas about mammoth-hunting tactics and lithic technology, but little can be said about ecology and social behavior. Clovis foragers killed "mammoth, bison, and pronghorn, along with an occasional horse, camel, or muskox" in environments that were changing from steppe or steppe-tundra to prairies and plains. Frison (1999:270–3) suggests that even a single hunter with Clovis-tipped spears would have had a "high probability of success" in killing a mammoth with a broadside shot into the animal's thorax. Better yet, two closely cooperating hunters would have been a "good strategy" (Frison 1999:271). Mammoth meat from Clovis kills may have been temporarily cached over winter as a safeguard against unpredictable hunting success over the harshest season.

Frison proposed that the superior Clovis lithic tools recovered from Clovis caches – such as Anzick (MT), Drake (CO), and Fenn (WY/ID/UT) – were "institutionalized parts of the Clovis cultural system" (Frison 1999:273) and may have been burial offerings, although human bones were found only at the Anzick site. If the "caches" are the remains of burials where bones have long since disappeared, Clovis groups were "relatively sophisticated" in Frison's view and had "possible status differentiation" (Frison 1999:277).

In Stanford's (1999b) summary of Clovis in the Plains and Southwest, mammoth-hunting and lithic technology also dominate the discussion, as in Frison (1999). To explain the occurrence of toolstone from distant quarries Stanford speculated that Clovis groups either exploited very large territories or were involved in trade distribution of raw materials. He also suggests that Clovis groups may have operated from base camps but temporarily occupied processing camps at sites where mammoth or bison kills had been made, possibly in the fall season.

C. V. Haynes (1966) (also see Stanford 1999b) hypothesized that drought conditions during the Clovis era in the western midcontinent and elsewhere contributed to extinctions by attracting animals to a limited number of sources for water and food. During the drought, humans and mammoths dug water-wells at sites in the southwest (see the discussion of region 5 below). Following the drought, much wetter climatic conditions led to a major increase in bison

Fig. 2.6 The Southern
Prairie/Plains and
Desert Southwest
region, without the
hard-to-define
Mexican component.

populations, and the Clovis way of life evolved into Folsom and later Paleoindian
traditions.

(5) SOUTHERN PRAIRIE/PLAINS AND DESERT SOUTHWEST

This region (Fig. 2.6) is a combination of two subregions, the Southwestern
states of New Mexico and Arizona and adjacent parts of northern Mexico, and
the southern Prairie/Plains states of Kansas, Oklahoma, and Texas plus adjoin-
ing parts of northern Mexico. Relatively little is known from northern Mexico;
prior to the late 1990s, only around twenty Clovis points had been found in
"about half a dozen locations" (Sanchez and Carpenter 2000), but a recently
studied site known as El Bajio has yielded twenty-five Clovis points and may be
"the largest known Clovis site in western North America" (Sanchez and
Carpenter 2000). Much more research needs to be carried out in and reported
from Sonora, Mexico.

My discussion here focuses only on the states of the USA. Texas is included as
a whole, but in fact much of its eastern half is covered with humid woodland as in
the eastern states. In area the part of the region I discuss covers about 1,679,000
square kilometers. Anderson and Faught (1998a) list nearly 2,000 fluted points
from the region, but only about one-third of that number may be Clovis; as in
the northern Plains, Folsom types greatly outnumber Clovis.

A solidly acceptable pre-Clovis occupation in the southern Plains and the desert Southwest, as elsewhere in the continent, is extremely difficult to find. There is no shortage of candidate sites advanced for pre-Clovis occupation, but doubts plague them all. The site called Pendejo Cave near Alamogordo, NM, is rudely named ("pendejo" is an insulting term in Spanish roughly translated as pubic hair) and unevenly interpreted. Twenty-two strata were excavated in the cave, containing modified animal bones, hair (possibly human), pits and hearth-like features, cordage, possible but very crude stone artifacts, and possible human-skin imprints on fire-hardened clay (Chrisman, MacNeish, and Cunnar 1998; Chrisman, MacNeish, Mavahwalla, and Savage 1996; MacNeish, Chrisman, and Cunnar 1998). The cave's deposits were said to have "well-defined strata" (Chrisman et al. 1996) but Stafford (1999b) reported a very mixed-up series of radiocarbon dates, indicating extensive bioturbation possibly by rodents. The site's animal bones had undergone "complex taphonomic histories," such as sedimentary abrasion, rodent-gnawing, and weathering (Johnson and Shipman 1993:73–4), and a microscopic examination of a bone sampling did not find evidence of human modifications. The bones may or may not pre-date the Clovis era, and they may or may not look similar to post-Clovis bones interpreted as tools (Chrisman, MacNeish, and Cunnar 1998; MacNeish, Chrisman, and Cunnar 1998), but they also appear to have the same breaks, surface-marks, and edge-shapes that any large collection of naturally modified bones will show (see G. Haynes 1981 for examples).

The Burnham (OK) site contained small chert flakes and bison bones dated about 30,000 years old (Wyckoff 1999). The Cooperton (OK) site (Anderson 1962, 1975) contained the bones of a still-growing male mammoth dated to 21,000–17,000 rcybp (Anderson 1975) but some question remains about the accuracy of the dating (Gilbert 1979:23). Several limb bones had been broken when still in a fresh state (Mehl 1975). Three baseball-sized rocks each weighing about 400 g and a boulder weighing about 8.5 kg were thought to be hammerstones and an anvil that had been carried to the location to break the bones, to get either marrow or fragments for tool-making. The bone breakage is not definitively human-caused (see chapter 3), and in spite of the foreign rocks the evidence is not persuasive enough that the site is cultural. Cooperton is similar to La Sena (NE) (mentioned above in the northern Plains section) in that both sites contain broken mammoth limb-bones and no flaked-stone tools, and both are dated to the Last Glacial Maximum. The two sites may be part of a pattern that is emerging from an as yet underappreciated LGM archeological record, or they may be mistakenly interpreted as cultural.

Collins (1999c) proposed that at the Wilson-Leonard rockshelter site (TX) the stratigraphic position of a small lithic assemblage found in a fluvial gravel layer indicates it is pre-Clovis, but no direct dates are yet available. Stratigraphically above this assemblage – which contains "a large biface, 3 other bifacial pieces, 3 edge-modified flakes, a uniface, and 52 flakes" (Collins 1999c:21) – is another assemblage that includes seven bifaces, a projectile point tip, thirty-one chipped stone tools, a hammerstone, and 658 flakes, all "with technological similarities to Clovis" (Collins 1999c:21). Above this possible Clovis level is another assemblage containing an unfluted projectile point, twenty-six bifaces (including ultrathin specimens), 3,000 pieces of debitage, a mano, an engraved stone, and bones of horse and bison, which could imply an affiliation with Plainview. If the stratigraphy and dating are reliably interpreted, the Wilson-Leonard site contains a long-sought stacked sequence of pre-Clovis, Clovis, and Plainview.

For the southern Plains, Holliday (1997:212–13) interpreted the paleoenvironmental evidence to show a "shift from relatively dry to more humid conditions (cool-dry grassland to cool-humid grassland) from pre-Clovis to Clovis times" with a probable increase in spring discharge and channel incision; during the Clovis period in the High Plains streams may have had the highest energy and discharge of any time of human occupation (Holliday 1997:213). After the Clovis era, stream discharge was still high but relatively reduced, with more local variability. "The environment during the Clovis period probably was the most equable of any time during the human occupation of the Southern High Plains" (Holliday 1997:177). Clovis-period valleys contained perennial streams in the southern High Plains, but an abrupt shift followed at about 10,900 rcybp with warming conditions, fluctuating water tables, and episodic droughts (Holliday 2000b).

However, Holliday (2000b) and C. V. Haynes (1991a, 1993; C. V. Haynes, Stanford, Jodry, Dickenson, Montgomery, Shelley, Rovner, and Agogino 1999) do not agree on the dating of the southern Plains drought and wet periods, especially about whether the strongest drying occurred during the Clovis or Folsom interval. Holliday (2000b:7) argued that data are sparse for a Clovis drought but clear for a Folsom drought; C. V. Haynes (for example 1993) argued the opposite – that at the Clovis site (Blackwater Draw, NM), Murray Springs (AZ), and many other sites in the American West, surface water dried up, water tables dropped, and drought conditions appeared during Clovis times. After the Clovis period, water tables once again rose. Stanford (1999b) also interpreted the evidence this way – for a serious Clovis drought. Judge's (1973) data from the Rio Grande valley (NM) also show more intensive occupation *after* Clovis times.

Stanford (1999b) hypothesized (as had C. V. Haynes 1966, 1968, 1980) that drought in the Clovis era attracted large animals to a limited number of sources for water and food, where human hunters waited to pick them off. During the drought, people dug water-wells at Blackwater Draw, NM (C. V. Haynes, Stanford, Jodry, Dickenson, Montgomery, Shelley, Rovner, and Agogino 1999) and Aubrey, TX (Ferring 1995; Humphrey and Ferring 1994), and mammoths apparently dug wells at Murray Springs, AZ (C. V. Haynes 1991a). These sites are described below.

In Holliday's view, the Clovis era may have been the time of peak occupation intensity (based on number of sites per century) in much of the southern High Plains and the "Rolling Plains" (easternmost southern Plains), although not in the Llano Estacado (Holliday 1997:218). More post-Clovis sites have been counted in the southern Plains, compared to counts of Clovis, but the occupation intensity (sites created per century of component life) is greatest for Clovis (Holliday 1997:tables 5.3 and 5.8). In the northern Plains the number of post-Clovis sites is equal to Clovis or lower in each component until later Paleoindian times.

As for Clovis-era sites, many of the buried ones are mammoth associations. Domebo in Oklahoma (Leonhardy 1966) is a mammoth site in the bottom of a gully cut through the rolling hills of the prairie/plains zone, just east of mixed prairie and the High Plains farther west. The mammoth bonebed had been twice disturbed by erosion (Leonhardy and Anderson 1966). The animal had been a fairly large but still-growing individual, thought by Mehl (1966) to be a female. Along with the bones were found two complete Clovis points and a fragment of what appears to be another point, plus three unmodified flakes. A fourth Clovis point was found washed downstream from the bonebed, as were a side scraper and a utilized flake. The three points found in the excavation, the side scraper, the worked flake, and the three unmodified flakes were made of Edwards Plateau chert from central Texas. The bone surfaces were too poorly preserved to show any butchering marks (Mehl 1966:29). There is no other clue to human group size or behavior at the site.

Leonhardy (1966:52) thought that at around 11,000 rcybp when the mammoth died a "humid woodland" covered the river valleys, while grassland covered the rest of the surrounding landscape. Winters were more moderate than today, with fewer and shorter periods of subfreezing temperature; summers were cooler than today. In this landscape moved Clovis foragers, who left behind fluted points all across Oklahoma and surrounding states. At least ninety Clovis points have been found in Oklahoma, most coming from the open prairie and plains and very few from the wooded portion of the state. No Clovis sites besides Domebo are radiometrically dated in Oklahoma (Hofman and Wyckoff 1991).

Miami (TX) is located in the north Texas panhandle, about 200 km northwest of Domebo. Miami was discovered in the early 1930s, as had been Dent (CO) and the Clovis type-site itself (Blackwater Draw, NM), described below. It was excavated by Edgar Sellards in 1937 (Sellards 1938, 1952) and re-examined in 1990 (Holliday, Haynes, Hofman, and Meltzer 1994). The bones of five mammoths, three adults and two juveniles, came out of a small depression that had filled with silt. Ploughing unearthed the first bones, which lay in playa fill above loess. Excavations recovered three Clovis points and a flake scraper; later surface collecting found a side scraper and two bifacial retouch flakes, possibly part of the original assemblage (Holliday 1997:118). Holliday and colleagues (1994) suggested four possibilities to account for the assemblage: the site may have been (1) a successful mass-kill, (2) a herd that had died after an unsuccessful attack (with Clovis points in their bodies), (3) a site where Clovis foragers scavenged mammoths found dead, or (4) a mix of several different episodes of killing or scavenging.

Blackwater Locality No. 1 (NM) (Hester 1972; Holliday 1997) is in eastern New Mexico, about 450 km west of Domebo and 260 km southwest of Miami. The site was originally known as the Clovis site, after the nearby town, but I use the more familiar designation Blackwater Locality No. 1 to avoid confusing it with Clovis-point sites elsewhere. The Clovis-era features at the site are located in or along the margins of a 300 × 500 m paleobasin formed around 13,000 rcybp. Gravel-quarrying and numerous salvage or test excavations have removed a great deal of the artifacts and bones once located in the sediments, and some of the archeological records are difficult to reconcile with others. The site has yielded eight different mammoths in separate bonebeds, two bison bonebeds (one containing seven individuals with a Clovis point, and one containing four individuals dated 10,800 rcybp), plus two campsites. These are all located near spring conduits or outlet channels. Saunders and Daeschler (1994) proposed that at least one mammoth had been scavenged after death, because the marked bones seem to suggest that stiff or frozen joints were cut by Clovis tools.

The San Pedro river valley sites in southeastern Arizona (Hemmings 1970) are justly famous for the information they afford about mammoth-hunting. The major sites are Escapule (Hemmings and Haynes 1969), Lehner (Haury, Sayles, and Wasley 1959), Murray Springs (C. V. Haynes 1976, 1980, 1981, 1982; C. V. Haynes and Hemming 1968), Naco (Haury 1953), and Leikem (Saunders 1980).

The San Pedro sites are relatively uncomplicated locales where at least one mammoth skeleton was excavated, with fluted points and other stone tools. Lehner was originally investigated by Haury and associates in the 1950s (Haury, Sayles, and Wasley 1959), and Vance Haynes reopened the site in 1974 (C. V. Haynes 1991b). Lehner had thirteen Clovis points, plus an assemblage of cutting/scraping stone tools, at least four hearths, and the bones of thirteen mammoths and various other fauna, including bird, rabbit, bear, camel, canids, snakes, a possibly redeposited mastodont, and various rodents (Saunders 1977). Haury, Sayles, and Wasley (1959) thought the mammoths had been killed "at intervals," as spaced kills. But paleontologist Jeff Saunders (1977, 1980, 1992), after determining the ages of mammoths in the site, using a scale of African-equivalent years established for modern African elephants – a technique first tried by Vance Haynes – interpreted the mammoth age-profile to mean that a herd group had been killed together. In Saunders's (1977:62) words, Clovis hunters "found it expedient, and easiest, to crop a complete family unit which huddled together in protracted defense."

Naco (AZ) yielded the partial skeleton of one large female mammoth and eight Clovis points (Haury 1953). Together with Escapule (AZ), which had two Clovis points – both with impact-flaking at the tips – and no other tools associated with a single and rather large mammoth, these two sites may have been cases of animals that had been speared in the Lehner mass kill but escaped to die alone next to water (Hemmings and Haynes 1969). Like long-lived bowhead whales who carry ancient harpoon points in their foot-thick blubber for decades (Raloff 2000), these two mammoths also may have survived their wounds for many years and died long after the Clovis hunters speared them.

Murray Springs (AZ) is a more complicated site. It has several main activity areas. One centers on a mammoth skeleton with three fluted points, three stone tools, a bone tool, and thousands of stone flakes (C. V. Haynes 1980). This mammoth kill was situated on an ancient riverbank, once a muddy expanse of mammoth footprints, which were preserved as depressions in the stratum's upper surface. Another activity area was a multi-bison kill, probably made in winter (Wilson, Todd, and Frison n.d.) in which the bones of eleven individual bison were bedded with ten Clovis points, seven stone tools, and about 2,500 thinning and resharpening flakes. The hundreds of biface thinning flakes bedded with the bones indicate that bifaces were a staple in the Clovis toolkit (Hemmings 1970). The bison skeletons were more disarticulated than the mammoths (C. V. Haynes 1976, 1980), probably because of more complete butchering. Other animals were represented by a few bones in the site – horse, camel, bear, tapir, and rabbit. A third activity area was a campsite 40–100 m distant, containing seven more fluted points, seven flake tools, six blade tools, two bifaces, and hundreds more flakes from biface thinning and tool resharpening. The three areas are closely tied together behaviorally: an impact flake from the bison kill had been removed from a damaged Clovis point found in the campsite, and the opposite also was discovered – a flake from the campsite had come from a Clovis point in the kill area. As well, mammoth bones were found in the campsite, thus linking the camp to both the mammoth and bison kills.

The San Pedro valley sites are all located within 27 km of each other on tributary streams of the San Pedro river. This little area of extreme southeastern Arizona provides us a wonderfully unique glimpse into Clovis-era foraging behavior by what could be a single family unit or macroband. E. Hemmings (1970) suggested a band size of fifty to a hundred people in the locality, judging from the amount of meat that would have been taken from the eleven bison killed and butchered at Murray Springs. C. V. Haynes (1980) estimated that the Naco mammoth may have escaped from four to eight hunters, who belonged to a local population of twenty to forty men, women, and children. These estimates are very much keeping to the ethnographic models of hunting-gathering band demography. The associated Clovis points from single-event sites such as Naco, so similar that they could have been manufactured by the same person, may be mementoes of a day when hunters tooled up and then closed with a mammoth herd, out of which two animals broke away to die alone.

Aubrey (TX) is a deeply buried Clovis site located at the boundary between Rolling Plains (which are just east of the High Plains) and the Gulf Coastal plain (Ferring 1989, 1990, 1995). This locale is situated in humid and subtropical prairie and woodland, quite unlike the dry and open setting of other Clovis sites such as those in the San Pedro valley (AZ) or Blackwater Draw (NM). The Aubrey site formed where a spring-fed pond filled with lacustrine, colluvial, and other sediments after 13,000–14,000 rcybp. Clovis-era fauna and artifacts are found on a "paleosurface" over a large area, with overlying dates on sediments placing the Clovis material's age at greater than 10,700–10,900 rcybp. Radiocarbon dates from one camp locus are 11,540 ± 110 and 11,590 ± 90 rcybp (Ferring 1995). A bison "kill" area contained a single bison's bones, one of which may have been cut and fractured by humans, along with stone resharpening flakes and a stone blade. Two "camp" areas contained over 6,000 lithic artifacts, many of which were biface-reduction debitage, along with a Clovis point, blade blanks made into scrapers, blade fragments, and a large blade core, among other items. Charcoal and burned bones were found in clusters. About 12,000 bones were recovered from pond sediments, including more than forty taxa, notably white-tailed deer, bison, rabbit, muskrat, fishes, birds, and rodents. Turtle bones were abundant, including some that had been burned. As was the case at Kimmswick (MO), ground sloth dermal ossicles were found, without other elements of the skeleton, perhaps again indicating the use of sloth skin by Clovis foragers. Most of the animal bones at the site were considered to be natural "background," not the remains of food items in the Clovis diet (Ferring 1995:277). Toolstone, as is common in many Clovis-era sites, was derived from sources long distances away that were the same as used by southern High Plains Clovis foragers. Ferring (1990, 1995) suggested the Clovis occupation was a brief encampment, possibly at a bison or mammoth kill, based on the facts that artifact clusters did not overlap, and the lithic aggregations were separate from the animal bones. Longer occupations or multiple repeat visits probably would have smeared together the remains of individual chipping features and cooking spots.

Stanford (1999b:292) refers to Lewisville, Aubrey, and Kincaid Shelter (all situated in the more humid part of Texas, not in the plains) as sites showing evidence for a "broad-based economy" practiced by Clovis foragers. The sites contain a variety of possible food remains from medium and small mammals, including mice, armadillos, raccoons, and reptiles, even amphibians and mud-dauber larvae (see chapter 5 below, and Table 5.1).

An important Clovis site in the more humid part of this region is Gault, Texas (Collins 1999d, 2001; Handbook of Texas Online 1999; T. Hester, Collins, and Headrick 1992). The site is located about 65 km from Austin, and like Aubrey is not in the southern Plains – it is situated in central Texas's Edwards Plateau, a wooded prairieland, but is examined at some length here because of the fact that cherts from the plateau were frequently used by Clovis flintknappers on the High Plains, reflecting common movement back and forth.

Gault is a multicomponent site with abundant local chert deposits. The site's Clovis levels are 40 cm thick (and up to 2 m thick in places) and may cover nearly 20 acres. The Clovis materials include fluted points and preforms, tools manufactured on both flakes and blades, possibly burins, and small bifacial adzes for working wood. Some artifacts were excavated in dense concentrations, or in "staggering numbers" as Collins (2001) phrases it on the Texas Archeological Society website. The Clovis levels also contain pit features, a possible rock pavement, and pebbles with geometric designs engraved on them. The site has yielded fifty-two specimens of engraved stones so far, but some are clearly post-Clovis in age. Bones of mammoth, horse, and bison are found in the earlier Clovis levels, but only bison continues through all Clovis levels, recording bison survival after the extinction of mammoth and horse. Burned bones of small animals also occur. Folsom and Midland points and tools are found immediately above the Clovis materials.

The Gault site was first excavated in the 1930s, and since then has been tested with care, but also looted recklessly several times (Handbook of Texas Online 1999). This site has the potential for providing critical evidence about a range of Clovis campsite activities, as well as yielding information about changes in subsistence focus throughout the Clovis era. The site also may contain unique evidence about possible Clovis-era portable art and a continuing tradition of such art during later Paleoindian and Early Archaic times (see chapter 3).

Collins (1999a:181) examined archeological evidence from south-central United States, particularly Texas, and suggested that "Clovis knappers acquired chippable stone locally when it was available, stopped at known source areas as part of subsistence rounds, explored likely geologic exposures during subsistence wandering or any other travel into unfamiliar country, and exchanged stone opportunistically as part of social encounters whether scheduled or occurring by chance." Collins also suggested that Clovis "knowledge of toolstone sources was sophisticated" and implied that Clovis groups were geographically well established in their territories (Collins 1999a:181, 182).

The Clovis blade and biface technology found throughout the continent, but especially abundant in the southern tier of central and western states, bears unmistakable similarities to western European Upper Paleolithic technology (Collins 1999a; Bradley 1997). The potential relationships between Clovis and other technocomplexes such as Solutréan and Aurignacian will be discussed further in chapter 4.

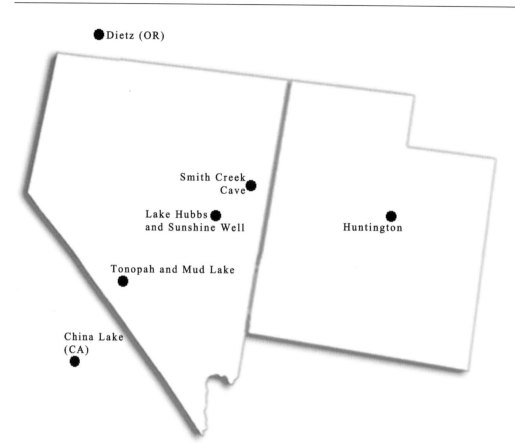

Fig. 2.7 The Great Basin and Colorado Plateau region, shown without the portions of Wyoming, Idaho, Oregon, and California that also are in the physiographically defined Great Basin.

(6) GREAT BASIN AND COLORADO PLATEAU

This region (Fig. 2.7) includes the southeastern corner of Oregon, southeastern California, nearly the entire state of Nevada, small parts of Idaho and Wyoming, the northern part of Arizona, and much of Utah. However, the relatively small parts of Oregon, Wyoming, and Idaho that are physiographically in the Great Basin are not discussed together here. All of Oregon and Idaho are discussed as part of the Northwest region, Wyoming is covered in the northern Prairie/Plains region, and Arizona is covered with the southern Prairie/Plains and desert Southwest. Also, California is discussed as a single region unto itself in section 8 below. In area, the remaining part of the region (most of Nevada and Utah) is nearly 500,000 square kilometers. At least 200 fluted points are known, most of which are Clovis or Clovis-like, rather than Folsom.

The Pleistocene archeological record is "predominantly a surface lithic record" (Beck and Jones 1997:221), and information about subsistence is not easy to come by. Often the locations that were used by Holocene foragers were the same ones used by Pleistocene people, so it is a "considerable challenge ... to try to disassemble ... lithic aggregates into collections that have some meaningful chronologic unity" (Beck and Jones 1997:221). Beck and Jones's best guess for the Great Basin, keeping in mind the limitations of the archeological materials, is that fluted-point-makers were primarily hunters of large terrestrial herbivores.

Willig (1989, 1991) suggested that initial human dispersals into the Great Basin were made by free-ranging foragers with an opportunistic diet, who tended to specialize in large mammals, as Kelly and Todd (1988) proposed; later foragers in the pluvial lake basins attached themselves to the "biotically rich littoral zones and riparian habitats of shallow lake and marsh systems and the streams that fed them" (Willig 1991:111). Willig (1991) identified some Great Basin locales where major concentrations of fluted points have been found – China Lake and Tulare Lake in California; Tonopah Lake, Mud Lake, Sunshine Well, and Lake Hubbs in Nevada; and the Dietz/Alkali Lake basin in southeastern Oregon. The California and Oregon sites are described under the next two regional summaries (California and Northwest). All the locales are in pluvial lake basins near the lowest Pleistocene strandlines, probably indicating that Clovis-era foragers sought abundant and diverse resources in these settings, such as small and large game, fish, birds, and plant foods. A few campsites were used and reused many times, producing large assemblages, while many other much smaller and less used task-specific sites are scattered over the landscape and are archeologically inconspicuous.

Bryan (1980; Bryan and Tuohy 1999 and references therein) has long advocated an early appearance for stemmed points in the Great Basin. In his view stemmed points date at least as early as Clovis or Clovis-like fluted points. Smith Creek Cave in eastern Nevada may provide the evidence to support this idea, but the argument about dating at the site is far from over. At Smith Creek Cave (Bryan 1979, 1988), radiometric dates in the oldest occupation layer range from 12,150 rcybp on nonartifactual wood to 10,420 rcybp on cordage. The artifacts include stemmed-point fragments, scrapers, and gravers. Willig and Aikens (1988), Beck and Jones (1997), Mead, Thompson, and Van Devender (1982), and Thompson (1985; Thompson and Mead 1982) do not accept that the early dates are correctly associated with the archeological materials, but Bryan (Bryan and Tuohy 1999) continues making a case that the dates actually do tell us how early the occupation began.

Basgall and Hall (1991) detected enough variation in the spatial distribution of stemmed and fluted points in the Mojave Desert to suggest that different cultural systems used the two types of points, unless stemmed and fluted points had extremely specialized and nonoverlapping uses by a single culture, which seems very unlikely. Beck and Jones (1997) pointed out that the overwhelming proportion of radiocarbon-dated stemmed-point occurrences in the American West are younger than 10,900 rcybp, which probably means that if any overlap of stemmed and fluted projectile-point traditions did occur, the stemmed points appeared later than the earliest Clovis and coexisted only for a short time.

Faught and Anderson (1996) showed that stemmed-point radiocarbon dates increase in frequency from older to younger much more gradually than do fluted-point dates. This kind of time distribution, plus the spatial distribution of stemmed points, led Faught and Anderson (1996) to propose that stemmed points spread as a radial wave into western North America from a possible point of origin in Northeast Asia. The relationship with fluted-point assemblages is still impossible to understand.

Relatively late dates (about 10,350 rcybp) on a possible mammoth-ivory point and a bone uniserial barbed point (Dansie and Jerrems 1999, 2000) from northwestern Nevada may indicate Holocene survival of mammoth in a region lacking much evidence of Clovis foraging, but many other bone and antler uni-serial barbed points (Rendall 1966; Ting 1968; Tuohy 1990) are thought to be younger, and are usually considered to be associated with Holocene fishing. Perhaps a late Clovis or post-Clovis backwash migration brought fluted points into a rather undesirable region where surface water and marshes were abundant, but herbivore forage quality was limited. Waterfowl and fish were probably the most abundant Clovis-era faunal resources. Over time these resources were concentrated in smaller areas as the drying lakes disappeared.

Another possibility is simply that the rather late dates on the ivory and bone are inaccurate and too young, which is a not uncommon problem.

The Colorado Plateau subregion is situated just east and south of the Great Basin. About twice as many fluted points have been found in the plateau as in the basin portion of Utah (Copeland and Fike 1988); Folsom-like points out-number Clovis-like specimens by about three to two. No fluted-point sites have been directly dated, and no projectile points have been found in unambiguous association with mammoth or any other megafaunal bones. The Huntington Canyon mammoth was associated with unfluted projectile points, but the asso-ciations may be fortuitous in pond sediments. The mammoth was discovered on the Wasatch Plateau at about 2,720 m elevation (Madsen 2000). A Pryor-stemmed-like point is thought to have come from the same level as the bones, but this point type post-dates the animal's death (see Table 2.4 below) which happened around 11,220 rcybp. Bones of a short-faced bear in the site were dated to around 10,850 rcybp; Madsen (2000) suggested that the bear scavenged the mammoth carcass, but the date separation does not clearly support this possibil-ity, although the dates do overlap within a two-sigma interval. A few mammoth bones were marked as if butchered, but I have examined the skeleton and in my opinion the evidence is ambiguous that humans processed this animal.

(7) CALIFORNIA

This "region" is perhaps the least logical physiographically, hydrologically, and archeologically, but a case can be made for equating California with a single region (Fig. 2.8). The state is enormous, and its physiography quite varied, but it is often treated as a separate archeological division in the continent because it is isolated by the Sierra Nevada mountains on the central east and northeast side, the extreme deserts on the southeast side, wet and rugged terrain on the north side, and the Pacific Ocean on the west. Baja California is mapped as part of this region (Fig. 2.8), but so little is known that I do not discuss it here. The area of the state is almost 404,000 square kilometers. The southeastern corner of the state is part of the Great Basin region, but is discussed apart from that region here. About 500 fluted points are known from the state, but the typology is not firmly established and not all of the points are Clovis (Anderson and Faught 1998a).

California archeology has produced "far more than its share of putative [pre-Clovis] sites – most of which are easily disqualified" (Moratto 1984:70), but some of which may be genuine examples of human behavior. Moratto (1984:39–73) has summarized them, which I depend upon here to present a brief sample. Several human bones and skeletons have come from California, none of which can be shown to pre-date Clovis (see Table 1.2).

Borax Lake

Tulare Lake

China Lake

Calico Hills

Fig. 2.8 California as a "region," without its southern extension Baja California.

Lake Manix in the Mojave Desert yielded crude artifacts interpreted as either a very old technology (Simpson 1964) – 20,000 years or more – or a much younger example of unfinished workshop debris (Glennan 1976). Another site called Calico Hills is either a very early human site (Leakey, Simpson, and Clements 1968) – over 70,000 years old – or a gravel deposit containing naturally flaked rocks (C. V. Haynes 1969a, 1973). The Yuha Pinto Wash site contained eighty objects interpreted as stone tools and utilized flakes buried in a deposit that may be over 50,000 years old (Childers and Minshall 1980). The famous Rancho La Brea tar pits yielded incised and marked bones of extinct saber-tooth cat, lion, and bison dated over 15,000 rcybp. Sites in and near La Jolla and San Diego have been advanced as containing hearths and crude flaked stone that geographer George Carter argued were signs of a human presence as old as 80,000 years (Carter 1980). None of these sites can be accepted as unambiguous examples of pre-Clovis occupations.

The China Lake basin in the northwestern Mojave Desert was studied by Emma Lou Davis for several decades, yielding thousands of surface artifacts including some described as core tools and choppers dating up to 45,000 years old (Davis and Panlaqui 1978). The basin's postulated sequence progressed from the earliest "Core Tool Traditions" through "Late Wisconsin Cultures," "Proto-Clovis Cultures," and a "Classic Clovis Phase." The assignment of dates to surface artifacts was based on the degree of weathering, the differences in material used, and the technology. Radiocarbon dates also were run on subsurface sediment and bones, although none was associated with artifacts from the hypothesized Pleistocene cultures.

If any of these pre-Clovis claims is supportable, either they provide no evidence about subsistence or settlement, or the evidence has never been properly presented (Moratto 1984:70–3). Plenty of choppers and cutting implements occur in the old collections, but no groundstone tools, indicating that regular use was not made of seeds, nuts, and other similar plant foods that require active preparation and processing. Human populations would have been very small and very scattered.

A fluted-point tradition is much more abundant in California than any culture supposedly older, but it is still inadequately known and studied. Moratto (1984:79–90) furnished a convenient summation of the better-known fluted-point sites and localities. As in the Great Basin and other parts of North America, many fluted points are in private collections, which means that the publicly accessible museum collections and the few published studies do not provide a full picture of California's Clovis-era data. For example, Tulare Lake is a relatively rich fluted-point locality, from which about thirty fluted points in one collection have been described in print (Riddell and Olsen 1969); bones of extinct fauna have also come from the locality. Borax Lake in the North Coast mountain ranges is another surface site that is uncommonly rich in fluted points – at least twenty are known – among other projectile-point types to be found there (Harrington 1948). The fluted points were originally labeled "Folsom" (Harrington 1948), but they more likely are Clovis variants (Fredrickson 1973) which are undated, although Meighan and C. V. Haynes (1970) radiocarbon-dated a buried sediment thought to be the origins of the points, and also took samples for obsidian hydration dating, with both sets of dates suggesting that the fluted points are late Pleistocene in age.

As mentioned above, China Lake in the Mojave does yield Clovis points on surface sites. The Clovis tradition, as interpreted by E. Davis (1978), was the climax of local population growth, improving hunting prowess, and evolving lithic technology. In Davis's (1978) postulated scheme, pre-Clovis cultures in the Great Basin's pluvial lake basins developed into the savanna-adapted Clovis phase by 11,500 rcybp, after which fluted-point-makers diffused to the east and entered the High Plains.

No fluted points in California have been radiometrically dated. Obsidian hydration measurements on various specimens do not contradict an estimate of 11,000–12,000 years old or more; the spatial association of fluted points with shorelines of pluvial lakes may be the result of preferential foraging along marshy lake edges at a time when the pluvial lakes were shrinking. As everywhere else, the highest-quality cryptocrystalline stone and obsidian were chosen for manufacturing fluted points. Megamammal bones have been discovered near fluted points in California sites (see Moratto 1984:90 for references), but no behavioral association can be confidently accepted.

The relationship between fluted-point-makers and people who created stemmed projectile points is very unclear in much of California, as it is in the other states in the Great Basin. There are some archeologists who insist stemmed points are as old as fluted points, and possibly older (Bryan 1991; Bryan and Tuohy 1999), but until a stratified site or a tightly dated series of stemmed and fluted points is found, the question is unsettled. Stemmed points unquestionably

Fig. 2.9 The
Northwest region.

date later than fluted points in the Plains, and it would be surprising if this
sequence did not hold for California as well.

(8) NORTHWEST

This region (Fig. 2.9) includes all of Washington state and most of Oregon and
Idaho. Because of the way records are kept (by state authorities), I discuss these
states in toto, although some parts were mapped separately on the master regions
map (Fig. 1.3). The area is about 635,000 square kilometers. D. G. Anderson
and Faught (1998a) list over 120 known fluted points from the region, most of
which are Clovis or Clovis-like except in Idaho, where Folsom points outnumber
Clovis two to one. The physiography from west to east includes the ranges and
valleys of the Pacific coast (including drowned continental shelf), plateau and
ranges inland, a small portion of the Great Basin, and the ranges on the west
side of the Rocky Mountains. A north to south transect would move from the
southern edge of the Cordilleran glaciers to the northern edge of the Great
Basin.

A pre-Clovis occupation in the Pacific Northwest has been proposed and debated for decades. Gruhn (1961) maintained that the lower level of Wilson Butte
Cave (ID) contained pre-Clovis artifacts and animal bones. Stemmed points
were found in the same stratum with bones of extinct horse, camel, and mammoth. Radiocarbon dates on a variety of materials from the basal stratum – wood
charcoal, bone, ivory – range from 16,000 to 9,000 rcybp; obsidian hydration
measurements on stemmed points range from 14,600 calendar years to about
6,000 calendar years (Bryan and Tuohy 1999:256; Gruhn 1995). This sort of

wide date range makes the precise temporal placement of each item impossible, and the claim that a stemmed-point tradition pre-dates a tradition of fluted lanceolate points in this region remains open to question.

Gustafson (1980; Gustafson, Gilbow, and Daugherty 1979) reported a possible pre-Clovis site on the Olympic Peninsula of Washington. Lying within a gravelly alluvium stratified above a glacial drift and below a stacked series of clay, peat, and Mazama ash were the bones of an old large mastodont individual, plus elements from bison and muskrat. The mastodont had one rib with an intrusive bone/antler object (called a projectile point) embedded in it, around which the rib had healed, and the skull had been completely fragmented into over 4,000 pieces. Other mastodont bones were thought to be butcher-marked, cut, and stacked by humans. The only "recognizable stone artifact" (Gustafson, Gilbow, and Daugherty 1979:163) associated with the bones was a flaked cobble spall, although several large cobbles had been broken, possibly by noncultural processes. Radiocarbon dates on organics (such as wood and seeds) in the layer enclosing the bones ranged from 10,600 ± 190 to 12,100 ± 310 rcybp (Gustafson 1980:table 1).

This mastodont may have survived a bone-tipped spear flung into one proximal end of a rib, and it may have been later butchered, but the evidence supporting it being killed by people is not firm. The bone breakage and marking, the scattering of elements, and the fragmenting of the skull are not unusual noncultural occurrences for elephant skeletons in the wild (G. Haynes 1991); and unfortunately, the "projectile" tip in the rib cannot be proven to have been a shaped artifact – it may have been an elk-antler tine that the mastodont unwisely rolled on, or even the tip of an antler that an irritated live elk somehow stuck in the mastodon.

Aside from a few sites on the margins of the Great Basin, such as Dietz (OR) discussed below, very few localities have yielded clear information about the Clovis-era occupation of the Pacific Northwest. Erlandson and Moss (1996:282) mention a "handful of fluted Clovis-like points" from the Pacific coast areas of California, Oregon, and Washington, all of which are undated. Meltzer and Dunnell (1987) suggested that a northward return migration (a "backwash") entered the Northwest some time late in the Clovis era, because many fluted points are relatively small, not of the classic Clovis morphology, and similar to Alaskan points. This idea, that smaller points with differences in fluting and finishing are younger than Clovis, is pervasive throughout the literature of other large parts of North America, such as the eastern states, Alaska and Canada, and the Great Basin, but has not been solidly proven everywhere.

Erlandson and Moss (1996:283) see evidence that the southern parts of the Pacific coastal area were occupied by the time of the Clovis era, judging from the existence of Clovis-like points in sites not far inland, such as at Borax Lake in northern California and East Wenatchee in Washington state. Possible evidence about Clovis-era subsistence was found at a Tule Lake rockshelter close to the California–Oregon border, where fish bones were uncovered in a small fire pit (Beaton 1991a) with lithic flakes and a uniface near it; wood charcoal from the pit was dated 11,450 ± 340 rcybp. Below the level of the pit were lithic flakes, bifacial pieces, and fragmented bones of fish, waterfowl, and mammals. No lithic materials were found that could be typed as Clovis, and it is possible that the lithics and the animal bones pre-date Clovis. However, rockshelter fills are often turbated by rodent burrowing, and more work should be done to support the dating.

Dated Clovis sites with buried, stratified levels are extremely rare. Two spectacular caches of Clovis materials have been found in the region – the East Wenatchee (a.k.a. Richey or Richey-Roberts) cache in the Columbia River area of central Washington (Gramly 1993; Mehringer 1989; Mehringer and Foit 1990; Mehringer and Morgan 1988), and the Simon cache in south-central Idaho (Butler 1978, 1963; Butler and Fitzwater 1965; Titmus and Woods 1991; Woods and Titmus 1995). The East Wenatchee cache was in what has been interpreted as a pit, one of two adjacent pit features; the larger feature contained fourteen fluted points, eight bifacial knives, seven fluted-point preforms, four sidescrapers, three prismatic blades (with use-dulled edges), three celts/adzes (including one fluted specimen), two thin flakes interpreted as engraving tools, two irregularly shaped flake knives, and a large, slablike agate chopping (?) tool (Gramly 1993). Several hundred very small stone flakes and bone fragments also were found in this feature. A microscopic substance interpreted as blood residue was found on most of the stone implements (Gramly 1991, 1993:7). Also found in the first feature were thirteen bone "rods" with one or both ends beveled and a possible fourteenth which had been eaten by a carnivore and its fragmented remains passed in scat. Two of the large fluted knives had red ochre on their surfaces near the basal end, and possibly other pieces had "very little" ochre on them too (Gramly 1996:19).

A fluted biface in the feature had a volcanic ash sticking to its underside, which Mehringer and Foit (1990) concluded was from the 11,250 rcybp explosion of Glacier Peak, thus dating the placement of the cache in the pits to some time after that. A second feature was found near the first, and it contained only a sidescraper and a utilized prismatic flake along with tiny agate and obsidian flakes (Gramly 1993:6). However, questions were raised about whether the features actually were pits (Gramly 1998; Mierendorf 1997), and the stratigraphic and temporal relationships of the artifacts to the dated Glacier Peak ash may be ambiguous.

The Simon site (ID) contained three fluted and three basally thinned lanceolate bifaces whose basal edges had been ground, seventeen oval bifaces, two discoidal knives, an endscraper, "an extraordinarily large flake tool" (Butler and Fitzwater 1965:38), and an unworked spall (Butler 1963). The tools were made of quartz crystal and nonlocal cherts; no obsidian was used, although younger archeological components in the Snake River plain show extensive use of this material.

Frison (1999:273), Collins (1999a:173), and others have suggested that such caches were parts of human burials, based on similarities with the Anzick (MT) cache (see the section above on the northern Plains). However, if there ever were human interments at East Wenatchee and Simon, they are no longer to be found, although the size of the East Wenatchee cache "pit" was suggestive of a grave – about 1.5 × 1.1 m. Pavesic (1985) noted that, like the Anzick burial, later Holocene burials in the northwest states also yielded red ochre and oversized tools manufactured to accompany the burial, perhaps continuing a pattern first established in the Clovis era.

The Wasden site in the eastern Snake River Plain of Idaho (Miller 1982, 1989; S. Miller and Dort 1978) is a location with three dry, cold lava tubes situated in a topographic depression; one of the tubes (a.k.a. Owl Cave) contained nearly

5 m of deposits, at the bottom of which were three broken fluted points – which appear to be Folsom – as well as channel flakes and broken bones of mammoth, bison, camel, pronghorn, dire wolf, fox, fish, reptiles, amphibians, birds, and gastropods (Miller 1989). The radiocarbon dates on mammoth bones range from over 12,850 to 10,910 rcybp. An AMS assay on charcoal from the mammoth-bone layer yielded a date of 10, 640 ± 85 rcybp (Bryan and Tuohy 1999:255, citing a 1995 pers. comm. from S. Miller), filling the expectations for Folsom. However, radiocarbon dates on bison bone from the mammoth level range from 10,470 to 9,735 rcybp, indicating that mixing of materials from different time intervals has occurred. The projectile-point morphology implies a Folsom occupation, which is post-Clovis or briefly overlaps the end of the Clovis era. What is unusual about the site is the association of mammoth bones with Folsom points, which has not been found anywhere else in North America. The mammoth bones are fragmented, possibly broken by Folsom people in preparation for the manufacture of implements out of them, such as needles, points or "foreshafts," or other types of tools found in Folsom sites (see, for example, Frison and Craig 1982). "Hundreds of fluted points have been recovered from southern Idaho," according to Titmus and Woods (1991:119), many of which are the Folsom type.

Dietz (OR) produced sixty Clovis-like fluted-point fragments in numerous clusters extending over 1,000 m along ancient shorelines of a pluvial lake basin; about half that number of stemmed points were also found in spatially separated clusters (Willig 1988, 1989). Willig (1991; Willig and Aikens 1988) proposed that "Western Clovis" people foraged around one side of a half-meter-deep lake or marsh, clearly preceding the stemmed-point occupations. Willig suggested that the reliability of water and food resources – ungulates, waterfowl, fish, snails, plants – attracted the fluted-point-makers to the marsh. No dates have come from the site, and faunal remains are unknown from the fluted-point occupation.

(9)   FARTHER NORTH

This region (Fig. 2.10) consists of unglaciated north-central Alaska and adjacent unglaciated western Canada. The area covered was extremely changeable, as glaciers retreated from mountain ranges and river valleys, and land became exposed. The area I discuss is approximately 768,000 square kilometers. D. W. Clark (1991) could count about fifty fluted points from Alaska, mostly from land surfaces or shallow deposits where vertical displacement has probably occurred, owing to natural processes such as freezing and thawing or soil flow.

The earliest identifiable archeological cultures in Alaska are not Clovis. The first arrivals were people who made blades (not microblades) and unfluted bifacial points, sometimes hunted large mammals such as wapiti and bison (as at Dry Creek [Powers and Hoffecker 1989] and Broken Mammoth [Yesner 1994, 1996]), but also ate small mammals, birds – including swans, geese, ducks, and ptarmigan – and fish (as at Broken Mammoth [Yesner 1994, 1996]). These cultures have been dated as early as 11,800 rcybp in the Tanana river valley. West (1996) hypothesized that a single earliest Beringian tradition – containing either microblades or bifaces and macroblades at different sites – were ancestral to Clovis, and that the people were speakers of Greenberg's Amerind linguistic stock. However, Hoffeker, Powers, and Goebel (1993) and Goebel (1999) found

Fig. 2.10 Farther North, showing all of Alaska except the farthest Aleutian Islands, and a part of adjacent unglaciated Canada.

important differences between a separate and somewhat older macroblade tradition (Nenana) and the younger microblade tradition (Denali, probably derived from Dyuktai in northeastern Asia). Nenana would be the probable Clovis ancestor. The Nenana assemblages contain lithics that would not be unfamiliar to Clovis flintknappers farther south, such as endscrapers and bifaces, whereas the common Denali lithics such as microblades, microcores, and burins are not considered very Clovis-like. It may be that microblades are some sort of specific adaptation to the colder conditions of the Younger Dryas in Beringia and northeast Asia (Elston and Brantingham in press; O. Mason, Bowers, and Hopkins 2001) and proliferated after the climatic shift; not all tool functions changed drastically from Nenana times – for example, instead of making endscrapers for hide-working, the Denali people used their transverse burins – but the use of much smaller cores and tools could have been a major risk-avoidance strategy in cold periods (Elston and Brantingham in press).

Based on paleontological, palynological, and archeological data from Alaska's earliest Tanana river valley sites – Broken Mammoth, Mead, and Swan Point – Yesner (1996) suggested that the landscape of interior Alaska was a mix of grassland, scrub birch, poplar, and willow, undergoing a transition from open savanna, with wetlands scattered along the rivers where human groups foraged for a broad-spectrum diet. Sites were occupied at different seasons of the year – for example, the foragers at the blufftop Broken Mammoth site killed bison, wapiti, and caribou in the fall–winter during one occupation, but ate migratory waterfowl in the spring or late summer/early fall during another occupation (dated much earlier). Mammalian bones at the Broken Mammoth site were highly fragmented, perhaps as a result of the process of making bone grease or of extracting marrow. Diverse activities took place at the sites, such as tool manufacture, animal butchering (although the sites are not killsites), hide preparation, food preparation, and so forth (Yesner 1996:267). Yesner proposed that the blufftop sites were places where multiple households or multifamily groups processed foods and hides for transport elsewhere, maintained tool-kits, and cached food and artifacts on a small scale. These sites were distributed around stable basecamps (as originally proposed by Guthrie 1983), which have probably eroded away or been deeply buried (Yesner 1994, 1996).

But these sites are not fluted-point loci. True Clovis footprints are impossible to identify in the far north. Clovis sites include Putu, Girls Hill, and Batza Téna (see discussions in Clark 1991; Hamilton and Goebel 1999). The dates on Clovis sites appear significantly younger than they are in the lower forty-eight United States (Clark 1991; Hamilton and Goebel 1999:table 2). An old radiocarbon date of 11,470 ± 500 rcyb from Putu is doubted because of evidence of sedimentary mixing (Reanier 1995), and the remaining dates range from obsidian hydration estimates of 1,800–21,600 calendar years (clustering at 8,000–10,000 calendar years) to a radiocarbon assay of 4,440 ± 90 rcybp, which must be only a minimum age limit (Hamilton and Goebel 1999:table 2). Possibly the obsidian hydration estimates and a tentative identification of mammoth blood on Alaskan fluted points (Dixon 1993; Loy and Dixon 1998) may indicate that at least some of the fluted points are late Pleistocene in age, although the recovery of blood residue has not yet been solidly proven.

Alaskan fluted points are technologically distinct from the classically defined Clovis type; they often have multiple flutes on both faces, and the bases have ears on both sides of the basal concavity. Similar fluted points from British Columbia and Alberta have been dated 9,500–10,500 rcybp (Carlson 1991; Clark 1991; Fladmark, Driver, and Alexander 1988; Gryba 1983), lending support to the hypothesis that the northern fluted points also may post-date Clovis. Multiply-fluted points are also known from the lower forty-eight states, such as in the Shoop site in Pennsylvania, as are deeply indented bases, such as from Debert (Nova Scotia) and Vail (ME). T. D. Hamilton and Goebel (1999) suggested that the multiply fluted points with deeper base indentations could be signs of a northward-spreading "barrenlands" technology adapted to caribou-hunting, which appeared during and after the deglaciation of subarctic and arctic Canada.

Goebel (1999; Goebel, Powers, and Bigelow 1991) concluded that Nenana in Alaska is technologically almost identical with Clovis assemblages from the lower forty-eight states (except for the absence of fluted bifaces), and there-fore may be the direct ancestor of Clovis technology, which ironically enough may have spread back north into Alaska about the time it was disappearing in the lower forty-eight states (Clark 1991:42–3). The ecological stimulus for movement back north is not proven, however.

Clovis-era patterning is difficult to identify in technology, subsistence, and settlement because undated assemblages may be mixed, and the fluted points may be very late variants that appeared after the Clovis dispersals down south. The fluted-point sites at the Batza Téna obsidian source were flake clusters within wide scatters found on the ground surface (Clark and Clark 1993). No information is available about diet, because the sites had no preserved or-ganic remains. However, some information about mobility can be milked from the data – for example, small and nomadic groups made tools at the tool-stone source and did not stay very long. The Batza Téna obsidian source lies 150 km south of the Brooks Range and 300 km northwest of the Tanana river valley, but obsidian taken from it was carried to distant sites across the Brooks Range and into the Tanana valley as early as 10,000–11,800 rcybp (Hamilton and

Goebel 1999), attesting to the abilities of Clovis-era foragers to make rapid discoveries of high-quality toolstone sources.

2.3   Knowledge and guesswork about the late Pleistocene

From this time forward the character of the country was changing every day.

Francis Parkman 1949 [orig. 1847]:352

The preceding section's summaries of North American finds have shown how variable the material remains are from Clovis and how difficult it is to define a single Clovis "culture." Sites from region to region differ in size and assemblage inventories, and the distributions of sites from region to region are not comparable. The fluted points in some regions are Clovis-like as often as they are not. Very few fluted-point sites have been dated, and the existing dates only imperfectly cluster around 11,000 rcybp. The regional variability may mean sites were made at different times by different ethnic groups foraging for different foods in different habitats.

Or does it mean those things? In this section, I begin trying to find an answer to this question by first summarizing the environmental conditions at 11,000 rcybp throughout the continent, and then looking for some of the key elements of nature and culture where uniformity or variability are to be expected.

Most evidence about prehistoric environments in North America is incomplete or indirect. Animal bones tell us what species lived in particular places, suggesting the vegetation and the climatic conditions of the times, and plant pollen or macrofossils provide further support for inferred climatic conditions. But often the necessary details required to understand community ecology simply are not preserved, and we must make educated guesses based on indirect data or surrogate facts. Here I simplify the late Pleistocene interpretations, deductions, and surmises in order to set the stage for interpreting Clovis-era archeological discoveries.

PLEISTOCENE CLIMATES, ENVIRONMENTS, AND SEDIMENTS

Late Pleistocene environmental changes in North America were intricate and multidirectional. Beginning in the early Pleistocene, global climates shifted to a relatively colder state, and in the northern hemisphere huge ice sheets covered large parts of North America and Eurasia, cyclically growing and contracting about every 100,000 years or so. Cycles of warming interrupted the cold periods several times. The final peak in glacial cold is called the Last Glacial Maximum (LGM). If pre-Clovis people were present in the continent, their distribution and behavior would have been seriously affected by the earlier climates and environments; therefore I begin here by briefly describing the Last Glacial Maximum, which pre-dates Clovis by thousands of years.

The LGM was the time when land-ice was at its greatest volume, dust in the atmosphere was also at a maximum, and atmospheric carbon dioxide was much reduced. This "event" is centered at about 18,000 rcybp. About 16,500 rcybp the event ended quickly – within a few hundred years – when ice volume rapidly decreased by about 10 percent (Yokoyama, Lambeck, De Deckker, Johnston, and Fifield 2000). The ice sheets in North America, vast domes of glacial ice covering nearly all of Canada, and almost 2 km thick at their peak, retreated unsteadily after that, but vegetation most likely recolonized land areas very quickly as the climate rapidly changed (see Ammann, Birks, Brooks, and 7 others 2000).

The presence of the colossal ice sheets affected atmospheric circulation, notably by forcing westerlies relatively south, which brought year-round precipitation to the Southwestern region and kept the Great Basin region much cloudier and wetter than today.

Eastern coastal regions were also affected. Mean sea levels dropped by about 120 m during the glacial maximum, doubling the size of Florida's lower peninsula and adding considerable area to the Middle Atlantic and Southeastern regions in the form of exposed continental shelf. The plunging Pacific coast continental shelf is nowhere near as extensive as the Atlantic coast shelf, and much less extra land was added to the western edge of the continent, except in the far north where a wide land connection between Alaska and Asia was created by exposure of the Beringian shelf, over 1,000 km wide.

The existence of ice covering most of Canada also had the effect of limiting biogeographic migration routes between the interior and far north of North America. Glacial geologists have been studying the landforms affected by the Cordilleran and Laurentide ice sheets, two separate ice masses in the west and east respectively, in order to understand if these masses actually coalesced, and how long they did, during glacial advances of the last 50,000 years. Some analysts say that even a brief meeting of the ice sheets would have made living conditions impossible for a long time in the corridor that eventually opened between them during deglaciation (Fladmark 1983, 1979; Mandryk 1992); others believe a complete coalescence may not have happened or have been very brief (Bobrowsky and Rutter 1990), and that at worst the land between the ice sheets was cold and perhaps difficult but not entirely uninhabitable for transient explorers. Biotic recovery following deglaciation might have been relatively rapid. This unsettled aspect of North American biogeography means that the time limits on human movements from Beringia south into the interior and temperate part of the continent cannot be incontrovertibly set. Bobrowsky and Rutter (1990) proposed that human migrations (both north and south) may have taken place any time before 15,000 rcybp or any time after 13,500 rcybp.

The trend in vegetation and climate following the LGM was a gradual rearrangement towards the patterns of the Holocene. But the rearrangements were not simply gradients of change. Punctuations of cold interrupted the warming, which then later returned; changes in precipitation amounts and its monthly distribution were not linear or neat; the ice retreat was interrupted at times by readvances in the Great Lakes region, some of which may not have been climate-caused (Wright 1991).

Additionally, to further complicate the picture, individual plants and animals reacted distinctly to changing temperatures and precipitation regimes, so that whole communities did not migrate together in a synchronized movement tracking ice retreat. Biomes did not simply stretch and drift as units; LGM biomes disaggregated, and floral and faunal elements created new associations and new biomes without analogues in the glacial interval.

Jonathan Adams compiled preliminary paleovegetation maps of North America at 1,000 radiocarbon-year intervals to model changes in biome boundaries and extents (Adams 1996; Adams and Faure 1995), which suggest conditions on a large scale at the time of Clovis and just before and after it. By 13,000 rcybp, much of the western United States was semi-desert, dry steppe, and, in the Southwest, pine woodland; in the eastern half of the United States, open spruce parkland, woods, and spruce forests covered most of the landscape, except for small areas in the Gulf of Mexico subregion and Florida where vegetation was mixed forest and oak/spruce woods.

A thousand years later, dry steppe was still present in the Rocky Mountain West, but had moved northward, and the pine woodlands of the Southwest had been replaced by steppe and open pine and juniper, while boreal forest replaced the Northwest Coast's dry steppe. Broadleafed forests covered the entire southern half of the east, while spruce parkland and woodland covered the north.

By 11,000 rcybp – the middle of the Clovis era – semi-desert in the West had increased in coverage, but dry steppe still existed in the High Plains and Rocky Mountains; the Great Lakes were almost fully uncovered by the ice, and prairie had developed in the southern High Plains. Deciduous forest covered the Southeast, with oak scrub in Florida, and a band of spruce forest stretched from the Atlantic coast to the edge of the western steppe.

At 10,000 rcybp – several hundred years after Clovis had been replaced everywhere by new technologies and adaptations – the Northeast was spruce forest, the Southeast deciduous forest, prairies covered a broad band of the midcontinent, dry steppe covered the High Plains and Rocky Mountains, and semi-deserts, woodlands, and scrub covered the Far West. Vegetational changes before and after 10,000 rcyb may have been "the most extensive and rapid in the entire record" of the late Pleistocene (Wright 1991:126, referring to Jacobsen, Webb, and Grimm 1987).

Adams's maps (Adams 1996) are preliminary simplifications and "models" that if taken literally will mask the true complexities of non-analogue communities. To call the Great Basin "semi-desert" or "mountain mosaic," or to label the Middle Atlantic region a transition from "spruce forest" to "deciduous forest" at 11,000 rcybp encourages preconceived ideas about the on-the-ground resources that were available to Clovis or pre-Clovis foragers. The Pleistocene paleoenvironments were non-analogue, and their biotic communities were different from Holocene biotic communities. Not only were plants and animals living together then that do not live together today, but many common animal taxa of the time no longer exist anymore. Forty-five different genera of mammals with body-weights over 44 kg lived in North America before 11,000 rcybp (Martin 1984; Martin and Klein 1984); but after 11,000 rcybp only twelve genera survived. Seventy-three percent of the large-mammal genera were extinguished around the time of Clovis, and the presence of these unknown animals in the past makes any attempt to label late Pleistocene biomes with familiar names an exercise in pretense. There is little about the late Pleistocene that can be seen as familiar.

When imagining pre-Clovis and Clovis adaptations, we would be unrealistic if we expect the millennium-by-millennium changes in climate, vegetation, and biota to be sustained straight-line metamorphoses from glacial to modern conditions, progressing little by little but continuously. Instead, each moment in

TABLE 2.1 Chronozones and time-stratigraphic units, scaled against radiocarbon years and calibrated calendar years before present. Younger events are at the top, older at the bottom.

CALIBRATED CALENDAR YRS BP	MIDPOINT IN RADIOCARBON YRS BP	CLIMATE/POLLEN CHRONOZONE
11,350	10,000	Holocene begins Rapid end of Younger Dryas cold
12,620	10,500	Younger Dryas cold
13,000	11,000	Rapid beginning of Younger Dryas cold Unnamed brief warm interval Intra-Allerød Cold Period ends
13,350	11,500	Intra-Allerød Cold Period begins Allerød warmth
14,065	12,000	Older Dryas cool interval ends Older Dryas cool interval begins Bølling warmth ends
15,085	12,500	Rapid beginning of Bølling warmth
15,350	13,000	
16,200	13,500	
16,950	14,000	
17,450	14,500	
17,950	15,000	
18,450	15,500	
19,150	16,000	Last Glacial Maximum ends
19,950	16,500	
20,200	17,000	
20,950	17,500	
21,450	18,000	Last Glacial Maximum

this timeline was unique, each decade different in some ways, each century a time of distinct animal and plant associations, each forager's lifetime unparalleled.

THE CHRONOSTRATIGRAPHIC DATABASE

Table 2.1 shows the hemisphere-wide climate/pollen chronozones of the late Pleistocene, as correlated with both radiocarbon years before present and calibrated calendar year scales. Even within these separate phases of the deglaciation sequence there were numerous smaller-scale oscillations from warm to cold and from wetter to drier and back again. Fiedel (1999a) provides a useful comparison of recent calibrations of radiocarbon dating, which is incorporated into this table.

With these complex trends in mind, and remembering the changing vegetation all over the continent, a new definition of Clovis is offered below.

2.4   Defining Clovis: is it a culture?

Are the differences in paleoenvironments from region to region serious enough to explain the wide variability of fluted-point assemblages? Do the regional climates and biota at around 11,000 rcybp differ enough to make a definition of a Clovis "culture" absurdly impossible? In this section of the book I first define my terms (such as "Clovis" and "culture") so that I can address the implications of variability (and similarities) in habitats and the regional archeological footprints.

CLOVIS

Is there a uniform pattern of prehistoric human behavior in North America around 11,000 rcybp that can be called by a single term such as Clovis? This is the most agitating issue of all in the debate about the peopling of the Americas. Clovis is the name of a defined projectile-point type, possibly a knife but also a spear-tip (Kay 1986, 1996) that could be either thrust manually (Frison 1986a:120–8) or propelled by a spearthrower (Hutchings 1997). A Clovis point has certain attributes such as an (intuitively) acceptable range of variation in size, shape, and flake-removal processes (see Table 2.2 parts a and b).

Aside from obvious visual similarities in shape and fluting that link projectile points as a "type," shouldn't there also be tightly defined and measurable similarities in technology and function – and stylistic features – if the Clovis *type* concept itself is to be consistently applicable? Some analysts do not think that regional variants of fluted points can be lumped together into one category called Clovis, because of differences in shape, size, use, time periods, or technological pathways in manufacturing. For example, "Gainey" fluted points from the Great Lakes region are very similar to Clovis in shapes and sizes, but analysts distinguish them as different types or "modes" (Table 2.2b) (Barrish 1995; Ellis and Deller 1997; Morrow 1996; Shott 1986; also see the discussion in Anderson and Faught 1998b). One difference between them is that Clovis points from western cache sites such as Anzick (MT) or Simon (ID) (discussed above in section 2.2 and below in section 2.5) were bifacially reduced by the removal of overshot (*outrepassé*) flakes (which span a biface from edge to edge) (Bradley 1991), a tactic not as obviously documented in midcontinental fluted points.

In the Great Lakes and midcontinent region, fluted points show changes in shape and dimensions over time – from the subparallel-sided Gainey points with a concave base (most similar overall to Clovis), to the more waisted Cumberland and Barnes points with more shallow basal concavity and longer fluting, to the Crowfield points with convex sides and sometimes no true fluting at all (see Fig. 2.12 and 2.13). In sizes and shapes, these types were defined in relation to Western Clovis points (for example, see Morrow 1996 for a comparison of Gainey and Clovis; also see Table 2.2b here), but until the variability in larger samples can be studied, the possibility remains that much of the variation is continuous and the typological divisions may not be supportable (Shott n.d.).

TABLE 2.2a A basic definition of the "Clovis" projectile-point type (partly from Wormington 1957:263, partly from Morrow 1996; partly from Hester 1972; and partly from Howard 1990; also see Tony Baker's [2000] website for interesting comments). Hester (1972:97) distinguished a Clovis type 1 from a smaller type 2; this table describes type 1 only.

SHAPE	LENGTH AND WIDTH	FLUTES	FLAKING/FINISHING	COMPARISON TO FOLSOM
Lanceolate or leaf-shaped blade with subparallel or excurvate (convex) sides and concave base; lenticular cross-section except where fluted; maximum width usually at or below midpoint. Not waisted or fishtail in shape.	Length = 25 to > 150 mm; "typical" length = 70–100 mm; Width = 25 to 50 mm	May be one-third to two-thirds length of point; usually less than half the length of face; fluting on one face may be longer than on the other; fluting may be simple (single), multiple, or composite (blended scars).	Bifacial; fine (soft-hammer) percussion flaking mainly, and flake pattern may appear irregular and "random"; possibly also minor non-uniform pressure flaking; hinge or step-fracture terminations (from fluting) may be removed by final trimming; lateral and basal edges generally smoothed by grinding.	Overlapping size ranges, but usually larger and heavier; Clovis flute is a flake with thicker bulb end and thin distal feather or hinge termination, whereas Folsom flute often is noticeably flatter without the thicker proximal (striking) end (a flake technique that Baker [2000] calls "planing" rather than "fluting").

This "sequence" of types has not been directly dated, but is supported by the different distributions of the types in unglaciated and deglaciated regions (Deller and Ellis 1988; Tankersley, Smith, and Cochran 1990).

There is also an issue of size variability (see Storck 1991:157–8 and references therein) even when shapes are closely similar; can smaller-than-average fluted points (or the "miniatures" such as found at Plenge, New Jersey, the Fisher and Parkhill sites in Ontario, Bull Brook in Massachusetts, and Debert in Nova Scotia) be considered the same type as colossal examples (such as found at East Wenatchee in Washington or in the Fenn collection found around the Wyoming/Idaho/Utah borders)? Can they all validly be lumped into a category called Clovis or Clovis-like?

Perhaps no single *type* of fluted point can be defined because there was no uniform way of making them, no uniform way to use them, and indeed nothing approaching a uniform way of life during the late Pleistocene. This point of view may be called the "no-such-thing-as-continental-Clovis" model. Proponents of this view argue that (1) although fluted points are widely distributed throughout the United States, Mexico, and central America (and are even found in South America), (2) they were invented and used at different times by geographically isolated people who (3) set about manufacturing them through different technological processes and who (4) used them while foraging for very different resources. In this way of thinking, the use of the word "Clovis" is allowed only to refer to fluted-point-makers living for a limited time interval in a small part

TABLE 2.2b The distinctions between "Clovis" and "Gainey" fluted bifaces
(from Morrow 1995, 1997; Morrow and Morrow 1999).

CLOVIS	GAINEY
Thicker average cross-section (>7.0 mm)	Relatively thin cross-section (5–7 mm)
Excurvate edges	Slightly excurvate or parallel edges
Less deep basal indentation	Pronounced basal indentation
No "guide" flutes; prepared fluting platforms isolated in center plane of biface	"Guide" flutes to create an arris for final fluting; platforms low to center plane
Fluting done in middle stages of manufacture; direct percussion and larger bulb when bifaces are larger	Late-stage fluting; indirect percussion
Flakes taken from one edge terminate at other edge	Flake scars usually meet in the center
Wider faces	Less wide faces
Ground along lower lateral and basal edges	Ground along lower lateral and basal edges; distal also may be blunt or ground
Thicker interflute measurement (~7 mm)	Thinner interflute measurement (~5 mm)

(NB: may resemble Gainey after
resharpening and reshaping)

of the United States; other fluted points and the way of life of their makers are considered too different to be lumped together.

Differences and similarities in Clovis technology in different regions have been described by – among others – Bradley (1982, 1993), Collins (1999a), Frison (1991), Morrow (1995, 1996, 1997, 2000b), Wilke, Flenniken, and Ozbun (1994), Willig (1991), and Woods and Titmus (1985). What do the differences in manufacturing mean? No one reasonably can dispute that variation exists in fluted points across the continent. Some fluted points are strikingly out of the ordinary when compared to large samples from different regions. For example, Colby point bases are unique (Fig. 2.11), and the type named Gainey is not strictly identical with Clovis (Fig. 2.12) and differs from other fluted types in the Great Lakes region (Fig. 2.13). Debert and Vail points have deeply indented bases with "ears" (Fig. 2.14). Nevertheless thousands of fluted points from every region of North America can be reasonably accommodated within the single type concept (Fig. 2.15).

Ronald Mason (1962:273) warned against "the trap of the analyst making the operational if not theoretical assumption that the makers of stone tools worked by blueprint specifications and that any deviations from a 'standard' necessarily has typological significance." The archeologists who do not see linked similarities beneath the variability in Clovis points believe that the differences prove the

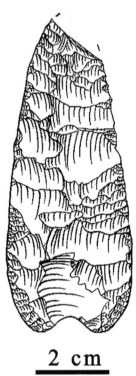

Fig. 2.11 A fluted point from the Colby site (Wyoming) (drawn by Ted Goebel).

2 cm

technology was not carried by a "single culture" and therefore either (1) the fluting was independently invented *in situ* by isolated people (an idea Mayer-Oakes introduced in South America [Mayer-Oakes 1986; Mayer-Oakes and Portnoy 2000]) or (2) otherwise the concept of specialized basal-thinning of bifaces merely spread by the diffusion of knowledge through pre-existing human populations. Bonnichsen (1991:324) cited studies he carried out that concluded the manufacturing differences in two widely separated sites' fluted points are far too great to reflect a single culture's migrations, and instead represent a kind of technological warping that follows from gradual idea-diffusion.

By emphasizing the variation in fluted-point manufacture from region to region in the United States, Bonnichsen (1991; Bonnichsen and Schneider 1999) found reason to reject the possibility that there was any single Clovis "culture." His argument was that if Clovis is a "single human culture with shared value systems . . . [then the] tool assemblages, artifact forms, and manufacturing techniques should be homogeneous and exhibit little variability from site to site and region to region" (Bonnichsen 1991:320; the phrasing is nearly identical in Bonnichsen and Schneider 1999:506). In Bonnichsen's view the fluted-point assemblages and technology are not homogeneous everywhere, and therefore no one culture can have created them.

But the basic theoretical assumption in this view of Clovis variability is that members of cultures do make artifacts from blueprint specifications. This assumption leads to an operationalized definition of the concept of "archeological culture" influenced by social anthropology's focus on ethnic self-differentiation.

Fig. 2.12 The Gainey type of fluted point; note the slightly excurvate lateral edges and indented base. The specimen on the left is from Maine (Vail site); the specimen on the right is from Illinois. (Photographed at the Anthropology Department, National Museum of Natural History, courtesy of Dennis Stanford.)

Because an archeological "culture" (consisting of artifacts, house-plans, burials, landscape use, settlement strategies) is not the same thing as an ethnic culture (language, folklore and knowledge, cosmology, etc.), the definition of "culture" must be operationalized beyond projectile-point typology to be useful. What is an archeological "culture," what do projectile point types have to do with it, and how much variability is allowable in such "cultures" before the concept breaks down?

The fundamental problem is that social anthropologists do not agree on a definition or the meaning of culture. Kroeber and Kluckhohn (1952) needed five graduate assistants, six secretaries, and two editors (Bulmer 1953:136) to amass 300 definitions and statements about the word culture, beginning with Tylor's (1871). This "all-embracing concept" has a "morass-like quality," in the view of many anthropologists (Bulmer 1953:137). American cultural anthropologists probably would like to agree about a definition but have numerous personal

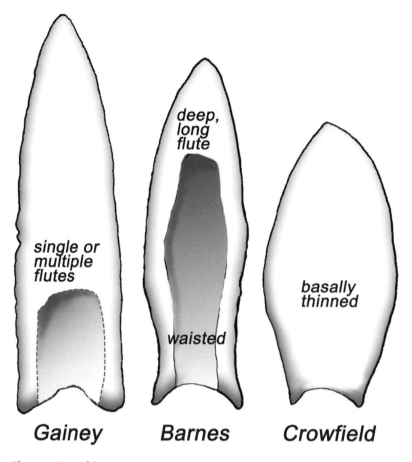

single or
multiple
flutes

deep,
long
flute

basally
thinned

waisted

Gainey   **Barnes**   **Crowfield**

Fig. 2.13 A graphic comparison of idealized Gainey, Barnes and Crowfield types. The Gainey type may have single or multiple flutes on each face and an indented base; the Barnes type has a long flute and a waist or fishtail shape to the base; and the convex-sided Crowfield type may not be truly fluted. Relative sizes may vary due to factors such as extent of resharpening or limitations of raw materials.

reservations about even the most abstract hypotheses to do with culture (Kuper 1999:227). The disagreements reflect the difficulties encountered when analyzing human thought and behavior, in both ethnology and archeology. Of major importance in the ethnological definition of culture today are several factors, including ethnic identity, language spoken, and degrees of diversity in language and behavior. Some social anthropologists think diversity and ethnic self-identity are the criteria that separate cultures, but other anthropologists accept that a great diversity is possible within populations belonging to one culture. For example, the people in Maine today do not have houses identical to those built by the people in Montana, nor do they have the same jobs; yet the people of Maine and Montana are surely *bona fide* members of an American culture, although regionally distinct in many ways. Each different region of North America, each household of people living anywhere in the United States, adheres to one set of beliefs and customs called a culture but also re-creates its personalized version of the mother culture every time it educates a new member or creates a new artifact or site. The range of variation is wide in American regional housing sizes and shapes, clothing styles, preferred furnace technology, window-frame design, the proper word-choice to use when addressing elders, the food put on the table, etc., and yet the variability is acceptable within what we call a single American culture. So how can culture

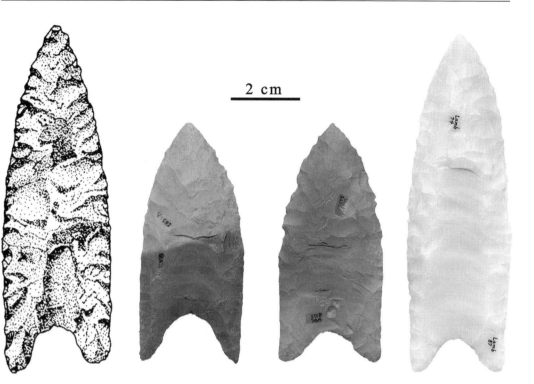

2 cm

Fig. 2.14 From the left: A Debert (Nova Scotia) fluted point (after MacDonald 1968), two Vail (Maine) fluted points, and a Lamb (New York) fluted point (the right three specimens were photographed from casts made by Pete Bostrum, Lithic Casting Lab).

be defined as an invariant set of ironclad rules and symbols expressed everywhere by the identical behavior of every member? Only a radical definition of the concept of culture would predict such strict uniformity in assemblages, artifacts, and technology, seemingly underestimating human adaptability and creativity.

Developed nations in the northern hemisphere might be misleading examples of the degree of diversity that can exist within clearly recognized cultures. In the United States, electronic and print media constantly work to homogenize American thought and behavior, as do mass advertising and structured educational systems. Examples from simpler settings – such as hunter-gatherer populations or swidden farmers – may show much less diversity and much more uniformity. "Papua New Guinea," writes Chris Gosden, "... is known for its cultural and linguistic diversity, with a seventh of the world's extant languages existing in a population of around 4 million people. However, if we were looking at Papua New Guinean diversity purely on the basis of pottery, stone tools, settlement plans, and forms of burial [which is all that archeologists hope to find], many of the fine differences in identity would be lost" (Gosden 2000:823). Thus, Papua New Guinea is an illustration of how "archaeological groupings ... for all ... prehistoric periods ... are much broader in space and time than ethnographic entities" (an idea expressed by Wotzka [1997] and reiterated by Gosden [2000:823]). An archeologist excavating sites in different New Guinea mountain valleys would see the uniformity of artifacts and village layouts and think all the sites belonged to one "culture." But an ethnologist working with living people in those same valleys would have to write separate ethnographies for each group, because the people speak different languages and assert distinct ethnic identities.

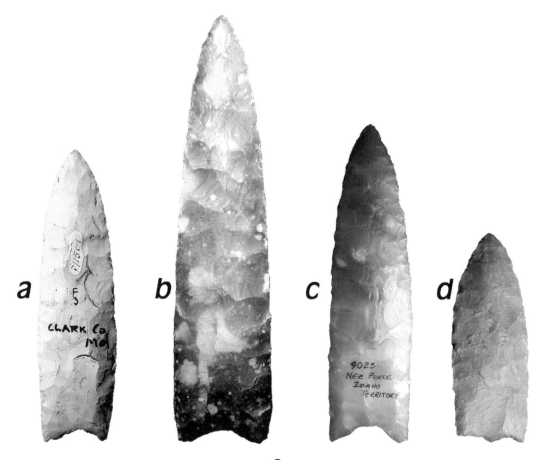

2 cm

Fig. 2.15 Fluted points usually typed as Clovis. From left to right, specimens from Missouri, Colorado, Idaho, and Virginia. The specimen on the far right is a cast of an unfinished point from the Thunderbird site (Virginia). (All specimens in the collections of the Anthropology Department, National Museum of Natural History, photographed courtesy of Dennis Stanford.)

The New Guinea example illustrates that an ethnographically recognized "culture" may be very distinct in some ways (unique language, rituals, folklore, decorative designs, and so forth) but indistinguishable in other ways (the same subsistence practices, tool manufacture and use, and settlement patterns as in other "cultures"). An *archeological* analysis of a culture, because it is limited to material remains such as lithics or camp layouts, has a view of cultural uniformity or variability very different from an ethnographic analysis. The archeologist slices time; the ethnographer slices belief systems.

Ethnographic studies also reveal that fairly clear changes do occur even within important fundamental traditions such as myths and rituals. For example, Poirier (1992) found that Australian Aboriginal people locally reinterpreted women's rituals and added elements such as new songs, without intentionally transforming the basic structure of the rituals. Poirier argued that a "dialectic" was inherent in the Aboriginal societies "between 'the forms of permanence' and those of 'openness' and creative innovations." Groups in diverse geographic and cultural areas thus could build and foster common identity at both regional and continent-wide levels, and while maintaining local differences still be mutually responsible for exchanging information and ritual knowledge (Poirier 1992). Prehistoric societies also had this same sort of dialectic. Local variations in rituals, technology, and myths surely must have been allowed to develop.

Anthropological analysis has no methodology for dealing with the relative importance and potential causes of variability within different data classes such as lithics versus language. Linguists may be able to classify different dialects when a certain degree of divergence is noted, but artifact-manufacturing "dialects" are much too tricky to distinguish. Artifact types and potential subtypes can be invented through careful analysis, but the causes of artifact variability are not automatically revealed in a typology, which is what Bonnichsen (1991) seems to suggest by assigning fluted-point diversity to idea-diffusion rather than to any other possible factor such as population spread.

Other explanations exist for variability in fluted points besides an imagined garbling during the diffusion of technological ideas. As Morrow (1995, 1996, 1997) has pointed out, many of "the characteristic biface reduction strategies" – "the reduction trajectory for fluted-point manufacture" (Morrow 1997:67) – seen in western Clovis assemblages are also found elsewhere such as in the midcontinent or eastern United States. At the same time as demonstrating continental similarities in Clovis point-manufacturing, Morrow also sensibly perceived that Clovis biface reduction strategies could be readily adapted "to cope with the ever-present uncertainties involved" in making fluted points (Morrow 1995:177). Therefore site-specific, locality-specific, and region-specific differences are to be expected among fluted-point assemblages.

Stanford (1991:2) attributed the variations in fluted-point technology to possible factors such as "idiosyncratic behavior, differences in materials, and artifact rejuvenation, as well as chronological differences." A reasonable explanation for much of the variability is the inevitable process of "drift" or the change of standards that occurs over time within fissioned groups who share the same cultural ancestry. Carlson (1991:82, 84) suggested how this drift occurred: fluting was developed to solve a hafting problem facing a founding human population, and was so efficient that the budding populations who separated from the first founders and inventors of the technology carried the knowledge with them into distant geographic regions. Over time different descendent flintknappers rethought the manufacturing process and discovered improvements or added stylish new touches through experimentation.

Morrow and Morrow (1999) provided an analysis which supports the idea that human dispersals spread fluted-point technology from its place of origin in the west-central United States. Variations in fluting were bound to develop over time and space, but the fluting technology originally dispersed by means of closely related daughter groups entering unoccupied territories – or territories where pre-existing humans were not in competition – in a fairly brief time period.

Models do exist to support the opposite notion that idea-diffusion among pre-existing human populations could have worked to keep Clovis technology noticeably similar over long distances but at the same time allowed variations to appear. Since about 1980 it has been recognized in research on diffusion that well-defined innovations that cannot be seriously changed and that appeal to distinct types of adopters actually diffuse differently than do innovations that can be locally adapted and used in different ways (Iker 1980, summarizing multiple research projects). In the latter case, innovation is not always adopted immediately, unless present and future conditions can be improved through the adoption of new technology or behavior. As well, local populations may select only part of the innovations to adopt, or change them uniquely to address local desires and needs. Even after adopting innovations, local cultures need not always continue to use them in the same way over time. These are examples of a phenomenon called "re-invention", which occurs as new technology and processes become routinized.

Innovations in the past as in the present were probably rarely adopted purely by free will alone. Instead, innovations were chosen out of a set of limits established by culture, kinship, family, personal history, and related factors. For Clovis diffusion to occur, a propagator had to be present to introduce the innovation, and some sort of network of diffusion agencies also must have existed to "teach" different cultural groups and individuals about the innovations, to deliver the innovations to the different groups, and to "service" the innovations (in other words, to act as guides for local people dealing with unforeseen problems). These social networks could have been trade contacts, mate exchange systems, or other such cultural institutions that crossed ethnic boundaries. Pre-Clovis cultures therefore must have had agencies and interactions such as mate exchange systems or specific band-spacing behaviors, in order to allow contact at individual and corporate levels. Yet no evidence can be identified in support of such pre-Clovis cultural institutions – no evidence of any sort of regular exchanges such as of toolstone material, no site distributions reflecting group territoriality or dispersal just prior to Clovis times, no hint of defined social boundaries and mechanisms of cross-boundary contact.

Equally unfortunate for proponents of the idea-diffusion model of fluted-point spread is the fact that there are no theoretically robust and practical explanations of the variability that could be expected if widely separated peoples living in different habitats in the late Pleistocene suddenly decided at almost the same time everywhere to adopt the relatively unique complex of Clovis technological traits they had never needed earlier. Ultimately diffusion has become an even more far-fetched explanation for the spread of Clovis technology and related eco-cultural features of the Clovis era.

In summary, the best alternative to idea-diffusion for explaining regional Clovis variability is a cultural founders' effect and drift. Slight differences in individual flintknapping abilities or normal variations in the ideal end-results of artifact-manufacturing were magnified after subgroups separated during dispersal into new ranges. Differences in localized toolstone attributes also affected flintknapping tactics; and local group preferences for distinctive stylistic flourishes led to further and further divergence over time and space. Yet even in different times and places the fluted points were made from the highest-quality cryptocrystalline stones, using certain identifiable biface-reduction strategies (Morrow 1995:177; 1997:67).

The people who made fluted points this way over much of North America also shared other significant cultural traits: (1) they did not establish year-round camps; (2) they did not create large accumulations of living-site debris such as seen in Old World Upper Paleolithic/Epipaleolithic sites of the same time period; (3) they did not create rock art or in most cases leave artwork in camps (although negligible amounts of possible art have been found in some sites, and one site in Texas [see above and chapter 3 of this book] has yielded possible Clovis-age engraved pebbles); (4) they maintained high mobility; (5) they did not create artifacts or features needed for a reliance on plant foods or fish or smaller mammals; and (6) they may have actively killed or scavenged mammoths and mastodonts more often than any other large mammal. These characteristics may be as much influenced by the climates and biota of the times as by ethnic relatedness.

Whether or not the makers of Clovis fluted points actually self-identified as members of one "culture" is an unanswerable question, even if they behaved similarly over a wide area. If different groups in different geographic locales were closely involved with each other, and identified with each other, they may have spoken a uniform language (see LePage 1968) as a result of mutually accommodating their speech behavior (Nettle 1998) to reduce risk and create access to resources. Contemporary foragers do maintain close economic and social contact with neighboring groups, and their social bonds may "form a dense web of relationships . . . often reinforced by biological and cultural kinship . . . which may form the basis for common ritual activities and celebrations, common . . . hunting, gifts, and food sharing, as well as trade" (Nettle 1998:359, citing Milroy 1980).

Uniformity in material culture is a characteristic not only of Clovis. Uniformity also appears across broad regions and a wide expanse of land during other peopling events or, "repeopling" events, such as the Magdalénian colonization of interior Europe out of a Franco-Cantabrian refugium, following deglaciation (Jochim, Herhahn, and Starr 1999). In this latter case, as Jochim and co-authors argue, the uniformity was a reflection of "active strategies of interaction in an uncertain social and ecological world." Certain strategic processes were used to "emphasize commonalities and facilitate interaction" (Jochim, Herhahn, and Starr 1999:139–40). Magdalénian groups were discontinuously and thinly dispersed on the ground, having leapfrogged over large areas; to maintain social contact and uniformity in culture, groups expended great effort to visit each other and exchange items, such as portable art with its recognizable elements of style, or raw materials such as shells or flint, or information and mates.

Great time and effort surely would have been needed to maintain cultural uniformity in the Clovis era, because so few people lived in the entire continent. D. MacDonald (1997, 1999) compared data from contemporary hunter-gatherers, and found that at very low population densities, foraging groups expanded social networks and increased mating distances. To overcome regional separations and yet maintain social contact, Clovis groups may have been exogamous and "traveled extreme distances [up to 2,000 km] to find eligible mates" (MacDonald 1997:120), perhaps acquiring exotic toolstone on these trips.

The Clovis time interval is clearly a unique time in North American prehistory – never again is the archeological record from so many different parts of the continent so similar. The similarities of later times are minimal. During later times there are some apparently near-synchronous trends in projectile-point shapes, such as changes in basal notching and stem proportions, but the rest of the continent's archeological record is tremendously different region to region – in site sizes, associated artifacts and proportions of different tools, site densities, site distributions, selection of raw material quality, mobility ranges, and so forth, characteristics that had been similar everywhere in the Clovis time interval.

Is there a universally acceptable way to define and measure variation within the Clovis time interval, so that we can speak of one culture existing at the time? And if there really was a pan-continental "culture" during the time when fluted points were manufactured, what should it be called? We can try avoiding the word culture, because of unreconciled differences between the familiar ethnographic focus on *diversity* and the routine archeological focus on *uniformity* when defining a "culture." Using Clovis as a designation for a culture may contribute to a potential veiling of diversity – interassemblage diversity, interregional diversity – whose significance we simply do not understand and cannot yet measure. My preference in this book – a compromise intended to make the discussion less cluttered – is to use the term "Clovis era" as often as "Clovis culture" when I mean the general characteristics of fluted-point assemblages dated to an interval centered on 11,000 rcybp. Clovis is an archeological horizon within a bounded time period.

In my usage, the Clovis era is the time when the following artifact/assemblage characteristics appeared, although not all will be found in each site or assemblage (see Stanford 1991):

> the presence of bifacial, fluted projectile points;
> frequent presence of bifaces used for a variety of functions and also serving as point preforms;
> occasional presence of blades and blade-cores;
> regular presence of cutting and scraping tools made on flakes or blades;
> presence of multiple-use tools, such as scrapers with graver spurs;
> virtually all tools made of high-quality toolstone, sometimes derived from sources hundreds of kilometers distant from the sites where the tools are found;
> infrequent presence of bone and ivory implements that are "finished," that is fully shaped, sometimes polished and/or decorated;
> even rarer presence of bone and ivory fragments from *unfinished* implement-manufacturing events;
> occasional presence of relatively small or limited-use features such as hearths;
> the remains of plant foods and small animals very rare overall or in any one site;
> site associations either with water sources exclusively, or with water sources near toolstone quarries;
> radiometric dates roughly around 11,000 rcybp;
> if sites are stratified, never any stemmed or notched projectile points *below* fluted points, and Folsom is never below Clovis type points;
> if animal bones are preserved, mammoth the most likely taxon present, followed by mastodont or bison.

Occasionally sites have been found that lack several attributes. In fact, some sites lack most of the attributes. For example, the Pleasant Lake mastodont in

Michigan (Fisher 1984a, 1984b, 1996; Shipman, Fisher, and Rose 1984) contained no stone tools at all, and was dated 10,395 rcybp (see Table 2.3). Maybe it is a Clovis-related site, maybe not. The radiocarbon date is perhaps too young to be Clovis, but it is only a limiting date on the mastodont, because it was run on wood that had filled the tusk pulp cavities after death. Statistically speaking, the chances are greater that the find, if it was created by human behavior and is not a noncultural site, is indeed a Clovis association, because only two other archeological finds are known in all of North America with associated non-Clovis projectile points possibly bedded in primary context with mammoth/mastodont skeletons – Santa Isabel Iztapan in Mexico and Huntington Canyon in Utah (a third site, Owl Cave in Idaho, contains only fragmentary mammoth bones rather than a skeleton) (see Table 2.4). In contrast, at least sixteen proboscidean sites are known to have Clovis-point associations.

The list of attributes I provide for defining something that is inchoate and wispy called Clovis may seem like a rather loose set of vague characteristics, especially when compared to the very specific criteria that distinguish archeological "cultures" and horizons – such as the precise measurements and proportions of different implement classes in typologically separate forms of the Old World Paleolithic (for example, Bordes 1961; Débénath and Dibble 1994). In my application of the Clovis-era criteria, 1 percent or 10 percent or 75 percent of a single-component tool assemblage may be endscrapers, but as long as a Clovis-like fluted point is in the inventory and/or a date around 11,000 rcybp is attached, the assemblage is in the archeological class Clovis.

The practical term Clovis era is the name of a "chronozone" when the loose set of Clovis behaviors were evident over a wide geographic area. Each region in North America shows variability in artifacts and sites, and the similarities that do exist are lumped into a new category of contemporaneity and cultural uniformity.

THE TIMING OF THE CLOVIS ERA

Because of the nature of radiocarbon dating, which is merely a statistical probability of an age bracketed between standard deviations, high precision is no more than a relative virtue whenever one tries to determine the period when Clovis culture actually existed. A site's radiocarbon date of, say, 11,000 ± 100 rcybp must be interpreted to mean that the site has a 66 percent chance of being truly dated between the standard deviations, or in other words between 11,100 and 10,900 years old. The site has a 95 percent chance of being actually dated within two standard deviations, or between 11,200 and 10,800 years old. So when I say that a Clovis site dates between 11,500 and 10,500 rcybp, I may as well say that it has a fairly good chance of dating within a much wider time interval. What is the time interval I call the Clovis era? In this book, I set the midpoint of the interval at about 11,000 rcybp, and accept radiocarbon dates up to 500 years before or after that date as being within a Clovis era; however, some flexibility must be accepted in dealing with the radiometric record.

Fiedel (1999a, 2000a) has pointed out that radiometric dating of materials from the time interval of about 12,500 to 10,000 rcybp (calibrated around 15,000 to 11,300 calendar years) – which was before, during, and after the Clovis era as defined here – is extremely complicated because of plateaus

TABLE 2.3 Mammoth and mastodont sites with definite or possible Clovis association.

SITE (REFERENCE)	TAXON AND MINIMUM NUMBER OF INDIVIDUALS PRESENT	CULTURAL ASSOCIATION AND RADIOCARBON DATE(S) (AVERAGED/UNCALIBRATED)
Blackwater Locality No. 1, NM (1)	mammoth, MNI = 8	Clovis lithics; 11,630–11,040
Burning Tree, OH (2)	mastodont, MNI = 1	No lithics; possibly butcher-marked bones; 11,660; 11,450 (gut contents?)
Coats-Hines, TN (3)	mastodont, MNI = 1	Untypable lithics (flakes, scrapers, biface, gravers); disturbed sediments, wide date range (6,530–27,050)
Colby, WY (4)	mammoth, MNI = 7	Clovis lithics; 11,220; 10,864
Dent, CO (5)	mammoth, MNI = 15	Clovis lithics; 11,200; 10,670–10,980
Domebo, OK (6)	mammoth, MNI = 1	Clovis lithics; ~11,000
Dutton, CO (7)	mammoth, MNI = 1	Clovis lithics; <11,710
Escapule, AZ (8)	mammoth, MNI = 1	Clovis lithics; no date
Heisler, MI (9)	mastodont, MNI = 1	No lithics, possibly butcher-marked bones; 11,770 ± 110
Hiscock, NY (10)	mastodont, MNI = 9	Clovis points; 9,150 ± 80 to 11,390 ± 80
Kimmswick, MO (11)	mastodont, MNI = 2	Clovis lithics; no date
Lange-Ferguson, ND (12)	mammoth, MNI = 2	Clovis lithics; no direct date
Lehner, AZ (13)	mammoth, MNI = 13	Clovis lithics; 10,900
Leikum, AZ (14)	mammoth, MNI = 2	Clovis lithics; no date
Lubbock Lake, TX (15)	mammoth, MNI = 2(?)	Clovis lithics; 11,100
Miami, TX (16)	mammoth, MNI = 5	Clovis lithics; no date
Murray Springs, AZ (17)	mammoth, MNI = 2	Clovis lithics; 10,900
Naco, AZ (18)	mammoth, MNI = 1	Clovis lithics; no date
Navarette, AZ (19)	mammoth, MNI = 1	Two Clovis points, no date
Pleasant Lake, MI (20)	mastodont, MNI = 1	No lithics, possibly butcher-marked bones; 10, 395 ± 100

TABLE 2.3 (cont.)

SITE (REFERENCE)	TAXON AND MINIMUM NUMBER OF INDIVIDUALS PRESENT	CULTURAL ASSOCIATION AND RADIOCARBON DATE(S) (AVERAGED/UNCALIBRATED)
Rawlins, WY (the U.P. mammoth) (21)	mammoth, MNI = 1	Untyped lithics; 11,280
Sloth Hole, Aucilla river, FL (22)	mastodont, MNI = 1+	Fluted-point variants, lithics, bone tools, 33 ivory points; no direct dates

References
1 Hester 1972; Holliday 1997
2 Fisher, Lepper, and Hooge 1994
3 Breitburg, Broster, Reesman, and Strearns 1996
4 Frison and Todd 1986
5 C. V. Haynes 1993; Stafford 1988; Stafford, Hare, Currie, Jull, and Donahue 1991; Wormington 1957
6 Leonhardy 1966
7 Stanford 1979
8 E. Hemmings and C. V. Haynes 1969
9 Fisher 1996
10 Laub 1994
11 Graham, Haynes, Johnson, and Kay 1981
12 Hannus 1985, 1989, 1990
13 Haury, Sayles, and Wasley 1959; C. V. Haynes 1993
14 Saunders n.d.
15 Johnson 1987
16 Sellards 1952; C. V. Haynes 1964
17 C. V. Haynes and Hemmings 1968; C. V. Haynes 1964
18 Haury 1953; C. V. Haynes 1964
19 Saunders n.d.
20 Fisher 1996
21 C. Irwin, Irwin, and Agogino 1962; H. Irwin 1970
22 Hemmings 1999; Webb and Dunbar 1999

and dips in radiocarbon, caused by atmospheric inconsistencies. Hughen, Southon, Lehman, and Overpeck (2000) reported that the largest change in atmospheric carbon simultaneously occurred with the abrupt Younger Dryas climatic cooling. The implication is that a radiocarbon date within the 15,000–10,000 radiocarbon-year range may not clearly indicate an isolable "age" but rather a range of possible ages. For example, a radiocarbon date of 10,300 (rcybp) could be produced by assays on different organic objects whose actual ages are 12,400 calendar years and 11,700 calendar years.

Radiocarbon dates earlier than my arbitrary Clovis cut-offs have been produced at a very few Clovis sites – such as Aubrey (TX) (Ferring 1995) with dates of around 11,550–11,600, and Big Eddy (MO) (Lopinot, Ray, and Connor 2000, 1998; Fiedel 2000a:52, citing a personal communication from N. Lopinot 1998) with a date of 11,900 ± 80 – but these dates are often outliers from slightly younger dates in the same strata or components, hence they are possibly not accurate.

TABLE 2.4 Mammoth sites with associated artifacts that are typologically not Clovis. Note: Other sites have been found with associated lithics that cannot be typed.

SITE (REFERENCE)	TAXON PRESENT AND DATE	ARTIFACT(S) PRESENT
Huntington Canyon, UT (1)	One mammoth, 11,220 ± 110 (AA-4936)	One "Pryor stemmed" point thought to have come from the mammoth level (also Scottsbluff points on ground surface)
Santa Isabel Iztapan, Mexico (2)	One mammoth, no date	One "Scottsbluff" point, plus two flake scrapers, one flake knife, one blade scraper or spokeshave, one retouched blade

References
1 Madsen 2000
2 Aveleyra A. 1955; Aveleyra A. and Maldonado-K. 1953

(1)   PRE-CLOVIS

In some ways, the concept of "pre-Clovis" is a key element in trying to define the Clovis era. In this book, I use the term pre-Clovis to refer mainly to finds (1) that do not contain any Clovis artifacts *and* (2) that are directly dated older than 11,500 radiocarbon years old *and* (3) are either stratified under Clovis or are enclosed in strata that geologically were deposited before the Clovis era.

Currently, the archeological record from scattered and rare pre-Clovis sites contains numerous diverse technologies, but simple bifaces and a core-and-flake technology dating back to 17,000 rcybp (or earlier) have been suggested as precursors to Clovis. Such materials were found in the Topper site (SC), Meadowcroft Rockshelter (PA), Wilson-Leonard Rockshelter (TX), and Cactus Hill (VA), which were described above.

What is the potential significance of a pre-Clovis stage existing in North America? Pre-Clovis materials claimed for the continent (see examples in Krieger 1964; MacNeish 1976; Payen 1982; Stanford 1983) are usually very different from Clovis-era materials in all respects. The sites are extremely sparse, the assemblages tend to be small, perhaps indicating small and very mobile foraging groups having an unfocused subsistence and making few or no recognisable classes of artifacts (such as typable projectile points). These differences may be the result of two distinct "colonizing strategies" – the earlier transient explorers (pre-Clovis) used generalized tools and carried out the same tasks in each small site, whereas later estate settlers (Clovis) used specialized tools and varied their activities at sites (Beaton 1991b:table 8–1).

The possibility that pre-Clovis populations existed in North America means that Clovis could be an Orphan Culture, whose archeological ancestry was an unknown culture indigenous to the continent and belonging to one of the pre-existing low-density populations, but which has been lost or ignored in much research. These ancestors had different lithic preferences, did no biface fluting, and lived in small groups who stayed in nearly unrecognizable campsites.

A second possibility is that Clovis was an Alien Culture which rapidly invaded a continent with low human population density, successfully outcompeted the scattered indigenous cultures, and left behind highly visible sites – which the pre-existing populations did not create very often – while eventually giving rise to descendent cultures. The continuity of descendent cultures can be seen in the eastern continent's Paleoindian to Early Archaic techno-settlement similarities from late Pleistocene to early Holocene, such as at Thunderbird (VA) (Gardner 1974).

A third possibility is that Clovis was a Fugitive Culture with untraceable roots, very well adapted to exploratory dispersals, that for a time coexisted with other developing cultures and possibly even exchanged mates, ideas, and genes with the others, then later became absorbed into the evolving American deme (suggested by those who speak of "co-traditions" – implying separate adaptations to many different habitats at the same time – discussed further in section 6.2).

The archeologists who argue for a widespread and poorly explored existence of pre-Clovis in the continent propose that such sites are rare because they are deeply buried in deposits conventionally ignored when surveying for late Pleistocene sites. Another hypothesis is that pre-Clovis sites did exist at one time but were flushed out of valley bottoms during erosional periods that preceded the Clovis-era aggradational phase. In both cases, more geoarcheological surveying is called for to locate the older strata that may contain remnant or protected pre-Clovis assemblages. Some such work is ongoing (for example, Nials 1999), but the chances are exceptionally poor that we will be able to predict exactly where buried Clovis sites are to be found, because human population density was so low and camp locations would have been very scattered and sporadic. As far as I know, only one stratified or buried Clovis site has ever been discovered by near-blind prediction – all the others were found after exposure of tools or bones following erosion. The one case is Murray Springs (AZ), discovered by Vance Haynes and Peter Mehringer who compared its topography to eroded locales or sites where Clovis lithics and mammoth bones had already been found.

Pre-Clovis sites continue to hide from us until they are ready to appear. Nials (1999), Goodyear (1999a), and others have made efforts to locate or predict the locations of buried pre-Clovis sediments in order to model more efficient sampling procedures. Archeological excavations at both Topper (SC) and Cactus Hill (VA) found possibly pre-Clovis lithics underlying Clovis levels, so perhaps future research will begin uncovering more and more information about the potential ancestors of Clovis in North America.

(2)   RADIOCARBON DATES AND ARCHEOLOGICAL AGES

Radiocarbon dating is based on the statistical probability that a specified amount of radioactive carbon still remains in an organic material after its death. The procedure is based on scientific principles and known rates of decay of radioactive carbon; but not all the variables in the measured process have remained consistent over time, such as the amount of radioactive carbon in the atmosphere that organisms take up into their tissues through photosynthesis or feeding. Because of differences in ^{14}C from year to year, the estimated measurement called a radiocarbon year does not always equal a calendar year in length, and some sort of calibration must be done to attach meaningful time values to radiocarbon year values.

Several different methods have been developed to do this. One method is the radiocarbon dating of separate tree-rings, which are records of wood growth from year to year in many tree species. Ideally, each progressively older tree-ring should radiocarbon-date to progressively older "rc" years (radiocarbon years) before present ("bp"), which is a point in time set at 1950 AD, before above-ground testing of nuclear bombs permanently altered the natural ratios of stable to radioactive carbon in the earth's atmosphere. But the relationship is not simple and linear. Fortunately, a long series of radiocarbon-dated tree-rings has been produced, showing the corrections necessary to appreciate the calendar (or "solar" or "sidereal") year equivalencies of radiocarbon dates. Other calibration methods are the radiocarbon dating of annual growth increments in varved sediments or coral rings, and the counting of ice layers in Greenland and Antarctica. Fiedel (1999a) has discussed calibration of radiocarbon dates from around the Clovis era.

To avoid cluttering the text with two sets of calibrated dates in every instance, I have placed a table of calibrations in an appendix correlating late Pleistocene radiocarbon and calendar year dates. It can be seen that Clovis-era radiocarbon dates tend to be on the order of 2,000 years too young when compared to actual calendar year ages. But because the archeological literature has referred to radiocarbon dates for over fifty years, for me to use only calibrated calendar year dates in this book would be confusing. Therefore, I continue to use the dates as published, citing them as "rcybp" or radiocarbon years before present (1950 AD).

(3)   FORAGING, SUBSISTENCE, AND SPECIALIZATION DURING THE CLOVIS ERA

These terms have specific meanings and connotations in this book. "Foraging" refers to the search for food and the obtaining of it. In cultural studies, the term also may mean the search for information, mates, toolstone and other raw materials, status improvement, or other goal, but here I refer only to food. "Subsistence" refers to the means of supporting life, specifically the obtaining of food and other necessities. Here I mean food more than any other necessity. Subsistence refers to a set of co-varying aspects of foraging behavior – including diet breadth, technology, mobility, and demography. "Specialization" refers to behavior that indicates a preference for a relatively narrow range of subsistence activities. All these terms will be discussed at greater length in chapters 5 and 6.

2.5   The course of regional developments: the megamammal connection

With the regional summaries and my idiosyncratic definition of Clovis in hand, now I will try to compare trends and to come up with an idea of the progression of Clovis-era settlement in the continent. Ultimately I intend to argue that a very special strategy of human foraging existed during the Clovis era, one in which megamammals were opportunistically exploited.

First, it is necessary to establish the source of the first American foragers, so there is some idea about the distances moved and the nature of the migrants' original economy and settlement system (this discussion is based mainly on Goebel 1999). As mentioned in chapter 1, some archeologists are taking seriously the possibility that the earliest Americans floated across the Atlantic ocean from a homeland in Spain over 17,000 rcybp; other archeologists believe Pacific ocean trips were possible from the Pleistocene coasts of southern Asia. In spite of these suggestions, "virtually all scientists involved consider . . . [Siberia and Northeast Asia] to be the homeland of the first Americans" (Goebel 1999:208).

Archaic *Homo sapiens* may have colonized the mountain zones of southern Siberia between 200,000 and 100,000 years ago; and modern humans appeared in the same region 45,000–35,000 years ago (see maps in Orlova, Kuzmin, and Zolnikov 2000). Either archaic or modern *H. sapiens* occupied at least one arctic locale by around 35,000 rcybp, but far to the west of Beringia (Pavlov, Svendsen, and Indrelid 2001). Not until 25,000 radiocarbon years ago were modern humans able to penetrate into the extreme conditions of subarctic Siberia, not yet reaching the far northeast of Asia (Dikov 1996; Goebel 1999; Goebel and Slobodin 1999; Orlova, Kuzmin, and Zolnikov 2000; Slobodin 1999).

Between 35,000 and 30,000 rcybc, human groups repeatedly reused basecamps, made tools from local raw materials, and hunted diverse prey. Between 30,000 and 20,000 rcybp, human groups lived in large basecamps in the harsh, open "mammoth-steppe" habitats of the north, surrounded by task-specific and resource-extraction smaller camps. Toolstone often came from far away. Higher mobility characterized the foraging groups, and technology was light and portable.

Toolkits, possibly carefully tended and "curated," consisted of microblades and cores and bifaces in different subregions. Single taxa of mammals dominated faunal assemblages at separate sites. Many sites were repeatedly re-occupied, but few appear to have been long-term basecamps. Extremely mobile foragers regularly returned to rich locales, possibly to procure resources such as migrating waterfowl.

Human populations "disappeared from most of Siberia at the height of the last glacial" 19,000–18,000 rcybp (Goebel 1999:222; Goebel and Slobodin 1999). The earliest known archeological sites in western Beringia (in Asia) are no more than 14,000 years old. Goebel (1999:222) suggested that the eastern part of Beringia was populated by mammoth-steppe foragers either *before* the Last Glacial Maximum (25,000–20,000 rcybp), or long after it (14,000–12,000 rcybp), because no archeological traces are known from the intervening millennia in Northeast Asia and Siberia and hence no antecedent cultures were present to give rise to Alaskan populations. Goebel thought the earlier interval very unlikely for the initial migrations – no sites are known in either eastern or western Beringia with those ages, and the ecological conditions were awfully severe for humans, with treeless periglacial zones lying between the continents. More importantly, glaciated mountain ranges in northeast Asia (Yakutia) probably blocked human access to Beringia. The barrier kept out any groups that might have been able to survive Beringian conditions.

This has been an extremely abbreviated discussion of northeast Asian prehistory, but that is because Clovis "origins" do not lie directly in Asia – Clovis is an American culture, even though the people who developed their traditions

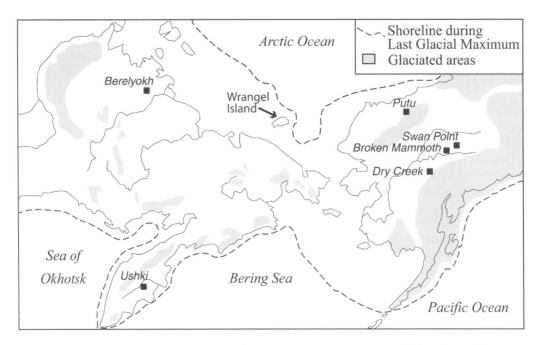

Fig. 2.16 Northeast Asia and North America during the Late Glacial, showing Wrangel Island and the sites of Berelyokh, Ushki, and Broken Mammoth (from a map drawn by Ted Goebel).

into Clovis did come from Asia originally. One reported "fluted point" from Asia (King and Slobodin 1996) is not technologically the same as American fluted points, and it may have come from an early Holocene context.

Frederick Hadleigh West (1996:546) proposed that the "peopling of America was . . . an environmental accident" caused by the deterioration of western and central Beringian habitats, which forced small groups of human foragers to move east from Asia into Alaska. By the time American Beringia was populated by these first migrants, woolly mammoths (*Mammuthus primigenius*) and other large animals already may have been extinct in most of the north, although a population of mammoths did survive until about 4,000 radiocarbon years ago on Wrangel Island (Fig. 2.16) in the arctic (Arslanov, Cook, Gulliksen, Harkness, Kankainen, Scott, Vartanyan, and Zaitseva 1998; Vartanyan, Garutt, and Sher 1993). Hence, a Clovis subsistence base oriented mainly towards mammoths would not have developed in American Beringia, although other large mammals were hunted, along with waterfowl and smaller game (Guthrie 1983; Yesner 1996). I return to this topic in chapter 6.

Is it possible that a pre-Clovis subsistence base focused on mammoths could have developed in Beringia? The extreme scarcity of archeological sites in Asia's far northeast probably reflects the lack of archeological prospecting as much as anything else, but it is usually interpreted to mean that foraging humans were not present in the north before 14,000 rcybp, which is the earliest occupation-time at the Ushki site in Chukotka (Goebel 1999). Recent data seem to indicate that this early date from the lowest level of the Ushki sites may be in error, and in fact the earliest occupation may be around 11,000 rcybp (Goebel pers. comm. 2001). The only other late Pleistocene Asian site so far north and east is Berelyokh (Fig. 2.16), an archeological locus 200–300 m from a mass of mammoth bones that pre-date the human occupation by about 1,500 radiocarbon years (Mochanov 1977; Vereshchagin 1977). Berelyokh is reminiscent of Broken Mammoth in Alaska

(Fig. 2.16), where subfossil mammoth ivory also may have been scavenged by humans who never set eyes on a live mammoth.

Thus, the evidence is at best very scarce and at worst nonexistent for mammoth-hunting in the Asian part of Beringia (G. Haynes 1989), but because the region is remote and has not been systematically surveyed, a possibility still remains, however negligible, that mammoth-hunters lived there or passed through briefly near the end of the Pleistocene.

Although Clovis subsistence and settlement patterning have not been identified in the far north, fluted points do occur in Alaska. These points are usually viewed as a return migration of foragers entering Alaska from the south, a later part of the continent-wide dispersal of fluted-point-makers from southern centers in unglaciated regions. West (1996) and others (Goebel 1999; Hamilton and Goebel 1999; Hoffeker, Powers, and Goebel 1993) saw a clear relationship between classic Clovis and earlier Beringian traditions. "Viewed from the northern perspective," West wrote (1996:553), "[classic] Clovis [in the lower forty-eight states] has a distinctly Upper Paleolithic appearance, more specifically a *Beringian* Upper Paleolithic appearance" [the italics are in the original] (see West 1996:fig. 12-2 for a visual comparison of tool classes in Clovis, American Beringia, and western Europe). Goebel (1999) has made a strong case for the earliest defined Beringian tradition – Nenana – being technologically and culturally ancestral to Clovis in the south.

By about 11,000 rcybp, Clovis-point-making groups were present over most of unglaciated North America. Population numbers were apparently low in all regions, since artifact numbers are relatively low compared to later times. Anderson, Faught, and Gillam (1998) counted over 12,000 fluted-point finds reported so far from the continent, of which nearly 10,000 were Clovis, Clovis-like, or similar in shape and size (Anderson and Faught 2000). Not all of the points would have been manufactured by contemporaneous people, of course, and not all points have been recovered. Disagreement is strong among archeologists that these thousands of fluted points can be fit into workably compact typologies; some authorities insist the morphological variability within the sample of 10,000 points is so huge that reductive typing is impossible. Others such as Gardner (1983:57; also Gardner and Verrey 1979) note that some of the "tremendous variety of styles" is an illusion resulting from projectile-point modifications from use, resharpening, and manufacturing using different raw materials; only basecamp maintenance stations and hunting camps reasonably close to quarries will provide projectile points of original-manufacture sizes and shapes. Thus, not all the projectile points in Anderson and colleagues' fluted-point surveys can be considered representative.

Anderson, Faught, and Gillam (1998) estimated that probably no more than 30,000 fluted points will ever be reported. The numbers are rough and the typology is unsettled, but perhaps the counts do suggest where we might begin trying to make a rough estimate of human population numbers and densities, especially when considered against the "hypothetical colonization scenario" in Anderson and Gillam (2000:55). If the first of the fluted points were manufactured within 500 years of the appearance of the very earliest dispersers, and similar point types were manufactured over the next 500–1,000 years (with stylistic variations, of course), a population of nearly 1 million people – over 30,000 separate groups of twenty-five people each – may have been responsible for making all the points that have been found or are waiting to be found in the continent.

I venture a wild guess – inspired by Anderson and Gillam (2000) – that at one moment on the Clovis timeline, specifically at 11,000 rcybp, the Clovis population of North America stood at not much more than 25,000 people, distributed unevenly over the continent in about 1,000 separate groups (microbands of twenty-five people). This number is about one-half the estimate offered by Fiedel (2000a:78), who suggested that 100 territories of about 100,000 km² each were occupied by a combined total of 50,000 people at 11,000 rcybp. Fiedel also suggested that social organization and human distribution in the time period just before this "late, stabilized" situation might have been very different (Fiedel 2000a:78). As with several other topics mentioned in this section, I will return to these themes in chapter 6.

Others have attempted to make estimates of *regional* or *local* human populations and territorial ranges – for example, Feidel (2000a:78), citing McAvoy (1992), suggested that 100 people may have used a range of about 20,000 km² around the Williamson site (VA); Fiedel also noted Anderson's (1995) estimate that at about 11,000 rcybp, fifteen macrobands (100–150 people) east of the Mississippi river may have foraged in territories of 20,000–80,000 km². Plenty of other examples exist of estimates of territory sizes.

D. G. Anderson (1990, 1996) proposed that the earliest Paleoindian population centers were "staging centers" (Fig. 2.17) where people aggregated after dispersing into the continent (through the ice-free corridor) by following major river valleys into the center of the continent. The best-defined routes into the Eastern Woodlands followed the Ohio, Cumberland, and Tennessee rivers. Clovis foragers either walked the terraces or floated the rivers in watercraft. Animals were abundant in the valleys, and some of the best lithic sources in the region could be found there, accounting for their appeal. Some of the initial dispersers "slowed their movement, settling in" the staging centers (in different subregions) over the course of years or generations (Anderson 1996:36), and in so doing allowed an increase in population growth rate. Mating and information networks were developed, and individuals or groups could bud off and disperse into new ranges.

Dincauze (1993a, 1993b) proposed a similar pattern of what she termed "marshalling" sites where the first groups settled and which they then used as bases from which to disperse in the Northeast, accounting for very large sites such as Bull Brook (MA). At these large sites, group ties could be reinforced, information and resources could be exchanged, and foraging trips could be organized on a community scale (Curran 1999). Yet some sites at this time were small, because Clovis foragers adjusted group size and mobility to fit resource availability (Dincauze and Curran 1983). Clovis pioneers could afford to select only the best environments to settle in, and only the best toolstone to utilize; seasonally, they could move north to take advantage of resources, then return to the aggregate residential sites.

Especially noteworthy is the fact the greatest densities of fluted points (minus the distinctive and differently dated Folsom, Cumberland, Suwanee, and Simpson types) occur not in the American Plains – often considered the heartland of Clovis – but in the eastern United States (Anderson 1990; Anderson and Faught 2000; Anderson, Faught and Gillam 1998). "If Clovis did originate . . . [in

Fig. 2.17 The main "staging areas" during the fluted-point period, as proposed by David G. Anderson (1990, 1996).

the Plains], the people producing this technology didn't stay long enough to leave much of an archaeological record behind" (Anderson, Faught, and Gillam 1998; also see Frison 1999). According to Anderson and colleagues, the highest densities of points in the eastern states occur in (listed in descending order of magnitude) the Tennessee river valley, parts of the Ohio and Cumberland river drainages, eastern Massachusetts (mainly at Bull Brook), and parts of Florida, New Jersey, North Carolina, Ohio, Pennsylvania, South Carolina, and Virginia. The densest clusters are in central river valleys, in the karstic terrain of north-central Florida, and along former shorelines of the Great Lakes. Can these be the centers of origination for ever-dispersing and expanding Clovis populations and Clovis technology?

Anderson and colleagues point out that relatively few fluted points are known from the southeastern coastal plains, as also noted by Dincauze (1993a), as well as in lower peninsular Florida and the lower Mississippi river valley. Few clusters have been found in the Appalachian mountains, too. These were the least populated parts of the Clovis ranges, occupied by scattered and few people who were highly mobile and fugitive. Indeed, these areas could be considered barriers to rapid Clovis dispersal, especially if it is assumed that human populations spread their range through wave-like diffusion of people in all directions. The existence of such large Clovis-poor patches in the continental landscape indicates that Clovis dispersal was not at all a true diffusion of groups, but instead was much more like a directed "telegraph" model of invasions (Hengeveld 1989; Holmes 1993) in which Clovis people moved in preferred directions and passed through certain areas without settling in them.

Dincauze (1993a, 1993b) also thought that the differences between fluted-point site distribution in the southern and northern states are significant. Large and small sites are known in the north; the larger sites may have been locales where clusters of different families aggregated at one time for group hunting (Fitting 1977; G. F. MacDonald 1982; Storck 1983:35), or alternatively they were places that smaller groups revisited several times. Clustered artifact loci often do not overlap, artifact fragments have been refit between different loci within the sites (Gramly 1982; Grimes *et al.* 1984), and the exotic toolstone found at some large sites is similar throughout the sites, suggesting that different groups did indeed camp together at the same time.

The central riverine subregion does not have such large multifamily residential sites. At or near cryptocrystalline quarry locales can be found sites that contain mixed residential/flintknapping-workshop debris, probably "accretions" from small groups periodically returning to them (Dincauze 1993a:284). Many single fluted-point finds made of local stone are common, perhaps reflecting higher mobility or smaller group size than in the north.

Clovis sites in the north and in the south of the eastern United States yield very similar (if not identical) tool inventories, but assemblage complexity and diversity vary significantly by distance to stone sources in each subregion (Goodyear 1979; Meltzer 1988; Dincauze 1993a:286).

Dincauze (1993a:288, 1993b) estimated an eastern forest Clovis population that was very "thin" on the landscape, capable of dispersing or migrating up to 200 km a generation, and making substyles of fluted and unfluted points that changed in morphology about every 250 years. Gramly (1982) proposed that some northeastern Clovis groups spent most of the year at large aggregation camps; single-family units ventured away from such camps towards the northern reaches of their ranges to hunt and gather, stopping at lithic sources on their foraging travels. The larger sites are those such as Debert (Nova Scotia) or perhaps Bull Brook (MA); the smaller sites are those relatively few known with low artifact counts in the New England states.

In the western states, a few rich sites show up as high-density localities, such as the East Wenatchee a.k.a. Richey-Roberts cache site (WA) and Borax Lake (CA) surface site. Other relatively large clusters of points appear along former strandlines of pluvial lakes in the Great Basin. Apparently some of these sites were places on the landscape where repeated visits were made, or larger groups camped for longer periods of time.

D. G. Anderson (1990, 1996; Anderson and Faught 2000; Anderson, Faught and Gillam 1998; Anderson and Gillam 2000) has observed that while fluted-point-makers were very unevenly distributed in North America they apparently often used fixed ranges, having dispersed through a leapfrog strategy, jumping over less productive or less appealing landscapes to find regions where they can be said to have settled. It is extremely unlikely that any pre-Clovis populations occupied most or all of these settled ranges before the appearance of fluted-point-makers, since no remains underlying them have been found in virtually all Clovis sites, with the possible exceptions of Cactus Hill (VA), Big Eddy (MO), and Topper (SC).

It is deceptively easy to try modeling continental social behaviors for the Clovis era. As numerous researchers have pointed out, environmental conditions in the many different regions occupied by Clovis foragers "were far from uniform, and likely the operative social units and their political interactions with other social units were equally variable" (Collins 1999a:180). Hence, pan-continental models will inevitably gloss over differences in densities, subsistence, technology, or settlements that may prove important in future research.

The transition from Clovis to post-Clovis landscape-use is not dramatic in most regions but it does seem clear from the archeological record. By the time of the transition from Paleoindian to Archaic strategies in the east, quarry-centered settlement systems show at least two possible patterns. In one pattern, quarries were centers near which basecamps were seasonally occupied, then groups broke up into smaller subgroups which traveled to satellite maintenance stations. In the other pattern, all the group members from basecamps near quarries largely moved together to killsites, where they stayed longer periods of time than in satellite camps (Carr 1975, 1986; Gardner 1974, 1979).

In post-Clovis times a trend can be identified of occupational debris appearing in the once emptier areas of the eastern United States, with some significant continuity in much of the technology (such as preference for high-quality lithic toolstone, careful flintknapping, similar range of tools). More people in more groups were scheduling site revisits or foraging trips to resource patches more often than during the Clovis era, and were apparently choosing to extract resources from habitats and landscapes that Clovis foragers had not utilized. For example, Dalton use of rockshelters is noticeably frequent when compared to the earlier fluted-point era (Walthall 1998).

But in some subregions the post-Clovis packing is harder to see. Human populations did not clearly begin to pack themselves into new ranges during and after the Clovis era in the Great Lakes, but site sizes and numbers do increase after the Gainey phase (possibly Clovis era as I define it), indicating that more groups were present and were carefully scheduling movements into different resource patches.

Meanwhile, in the High Plains, the number of sites from each different post-Clovis component also shows no clear trend of packing. In the southern Plains, the numbers of sites created per century go down and drop most noticeably around 10,000 rcybp, while in the northern Plains the numbers of sites created per century drop sharply immediately following Clovis to reach a low point also around 10,000 rcybp (Holliday 1997:tables 5.3, 5.7, 5.8). The post-Clovis environment in the east was apparently far more productive than in the Plains, or encouraged far more people to restrict their foraging ranges year-round.

In the Great Basin and California, fluted-point centers or concentrations also have been found (Willig 1991), and a post-Clovis "packing" of the emptier in-between locales can be discerned. Post-Clovis stemmed points (see Beck and Jones 1997 for discussion of dating) are much more frequently found than fluted points, occurring in open-air sites, along ancient lakeshores, within rockshelters, in upland locales, etc. The earlier Clovis-like fluted-point concentrations are all open-air sites in a very few lake basins (Willig 1991:table 1). However, the morphology of many fluted points (Willig 1991:figs. 4–7) could indicate they were made rather late in the fluted-point era, perhaps as late as Folsom times (10,900–10,200 rcybp), and they are perhaps contemporaneous with Alaskan fluted points and the points of the so-called "late Paleoindian" phase that follows Clovis in the eastern United States (see Gardner 1974; Gardner and Verrey 1979).

Clovis foragers in the east seem to have made what can be called *serial movements* (series of exploratory or dispersing walkabouts, perhaps up to 200 km) overlain by *cyclic movements* (periodic return visits to known quarries or refugia patches); this pattern appears in the quarry-based settlement patterns of the eastern United States. Serial settlement systems are found where lithic resources are relatively plentiful, not widely separated, and secondary sources also can be found. There are few to no true quarries in these conditions, although toolstone-related basecamps are possible. Tools are minimally curated, and are replenished often. Resharpening of tools is not a staged process – tools are discarded before going through multiple stages of resharpening or refurbishing. Biface reduction may be done in stages, but not elaborately.

In cyclic settlement systems, sites are created by groups that center their movements around heavily reused quarry sources. Biface reduction is done in clear stages in this sort of system. Projectile points are sharpened until exhausted, then replaced. Curation of tools is careful, and the highest-quality toolstone is used.

Serial settlement systems may be no more or less mobile than cyclical systems. A need for higher mobility in foragers does act to reduce the frequency of return visits to quarry locales, but the tactic of caching toolstone far from the quarry can reduce the costs of travel, and allow cyclical systems to persevere even when mobility must be extremely great. In the western United States there must have been a need for higher Clovis mobility, acting to reduce cyclic movements such as periodic revisitation of quarry localities, and hence the highest-quality toolstone was carried long distances or selectively cached in widely separated loci.

Why were Clovis caches created in the different regions? Clovis-era caches are still uncommon, but the past three decades have seen a spirited rise in the number known from the continent. Western caches outnumber eastern ones by a considerable margin (ten in the west versus two in the east, see Table 2.5). The scarcity in certain regions may result from Clovis peoples making full use of their original caches, removing them and leaving no evidence of their existence, or by post-Clovis salvaging by other people. Or perhaps foragers in certain regions saw less need for caching raw materials than foragers in other regions.

TABLE 2.5 Clovis-era lithic cache sites.

NAME (REFERENCE)	CONTENTS
Anzick, MT (1)	8 fluted bifaces, 85 biface fragments, 11 bone rods, cranial fragments of 2 humans (of different geological ages)
Busse, KS (2)	[no Clovis preforms or points] 1 large cobble, 1 edge-abrader cobble, 13 large bifaces, 25 large blades and fragments (some used as scrapers), 2 flake gravers, 48 flakes and fragments (including some used as tools); some pieces refit to each other; red ochre streaks on several pieces
Crook County, WY (3)	2 bone cylinder/rods, 9 bifaces (including 7 Clovis preforms, 1 fluted knife, and 1 reworked and near-exhausted Clovis point) covered with red ochre
Drake, CO (4)	13 Clovis points, fragments of ivory
East Wenatchee, WA (5)	14 Clovis points, 8 biface knives, 7 fluted-point preforms, 4 sidescrapers, 3 blades, 3 celts, 2 flake engraving tools, 2 flake knives, 1 large "blank," 13 (possibly 14) bi-beveled bone rods; all lithics were "well-used"
Fenn, WY/ID/UT (6)	54 bifaces (including 22 Clovis points), 1 flake-blade, 1 bifacial crescent
Kevin Davis, TX (7)	[inferred to be Clovis] 14 blades
Lamb, NY (8)	10 fluted bifaces (Gainey/Clovis), 8 unfluted bifaces
Rummels-Maske, IA (9)	20 complete and fragmentary fluted points (Clovis/Gainey)
Sailor-Helton, KS (10)	[inferred to be Clovis] 10 cores, 151 blades and flakes, 5 unifacial tools (made on blades and flakes from 4 of the cores)
Simon, ID (11)	3 fluted bifaces, 3 lanceolate unfluted bifaces, 17 oval bifaces, 2 discoidal knives, 1 endscraper, 1 large flake tool, 1 unworked spall
Udora, Ontario (12)	[inferred to be Gainey, based on nearby surface finds] 24 unretouched flakes, 27 retouched flakes, 21 worked flakes, 3 unifaces, 2 scrapers

References
1 Jones and Bonnichsen 1994; Lahren and Bonnichsen 1974
2 Hofman 1995   3 Tankersley 1998
4 Stanford and Jodry 1988   5 Gramly 1993
6 Frison and Bradley 1999   7 Collins 1999   8 Gramly 1999
9 Anderson and Tiffany 1972   10 Mallouf 1994
11 Butler 1963; Butler and Fitzwater 1965; Woods and Titmus 1985
12 Storck 1990; Storck and Tomenchuk 1990

Caches are thought to reduce costs when foragers preferentially use the highest-quality toolstone, which is usually unevenly distributed in most regions. By caching, the foragers move the toolstone nearer their activities but do not need to carry it constantly. Perhaps the foragers fortunate enough to have subsistence rounds situated nearer toolstone sources did not cache tools and raw materials, while foragers unsure of toolstone sources and intending to move far away from familiar toolstone sources chose to cache. I return to the topic of caching several times in the rest of the book.

3

Clovis archeological culture

3.1   Introduction

In this chapter I try to find a context for understanding Clovis. I primarily attempt to model Clovis-era subsistence in order to understand Clovis "culture", especially Clovis technology. In chapter 4, I will provide a discussion of global patterns in the late Pleistocene prehistory of the northern hemisphere. I do not mean to argue that Clovis is directly descended from any one tradition found thousands of miles away in Europe or Asia. Rather I hope to find the universals or commonalities that Clovis shared with other later Paleolithic adaptations, and in this way explore the origins or pragmatics of certain behaviors, as well as the possibility that new and efficient ideas about technology and social organization either diffused rapidly or were carried by dispersing foragers across large parts of the northern hemisphere during the late Pleistocene.

One unique feature of the Clovis era is the existence of large mammals which disappeared for ever within no more than several hundred years of the first Clovis appearance. I begin my description of Clovis-era technology by discussing the uniqueness of the North American landscapes entered by dispersing hunter-gatherers 12,000–11,000 rcybp.

CLOVIS-ERA MEGAFAUNA, MEGAMAMMALS, AND MEGAMAMMAL LANDSCAPE

Megafauna is usually defined as referring to animals with body mass greater than 44 kg (Martin 1967; Martin and Klein 1984). This is about the size of a small human adult. A different term, "megamammal," is here defined as a mammal with body mass "in excess of one megagram, i.e. ten to the power six grams, 1000 kg" (Owen-Smith 1988:1, who thus defines a megaherbivore). All megamammals in North America at the end of the Pleistocene were herbivores. I hope to avoid confusing readers with the use of these two terms; but keep in mind that one term (megafauna) includes animals as small as a wolf or a petite human being, while the other (megamammal) includes only mammoth and mastodont. These gigantic animals were distinct from all the other "megafauna" of the late Pleistocene in almost every aspect of ecology (Owen-Smith 1988:1).

A "megamammal landscape" is an environment where megamammals have lived and affected other large and small animals, plants, the local geomorphology, and other features of the neighborhood ecology. Readers with a background in the humanities and social sciences may consider "landscapes" primarily to be mental constructs which can be studied by interviewing people and recording beliefs about places and the history of their use of places. Readers with a background in earth sciences or ecology may consider landscapes to be distinct terrains and habitats where the objects of study are plants, animals, geology, and physical geography. In this book I use the word "landscape" in the latter way to refer to ecosystems in physical space.

A megamammal landscape has networks of trails and fixed resource points used by megamammals (and other animals), vegetation patches affected by feeding and trampling, water holes enlarged and deepened by wallowing and trampling, and a variety of other effects such as an abundance of dung beetles feeding on droppings, presence of animal taxa that feed on coppiced trees or open vegetation shaped by megamammal-feeding, and so forth. Megamammals profoundly affect community ecology in their ranges, and their signature impacts turn environments into unique settings (see Owen-Smith 1988 and references therein).

I introduce the term "megamammal landscape" here because I think Clovis-era human foragers were expert in reading megamammal-landscape signs to determine community health and ecological changes locally. In fact, the features of North America's megamammal landscapes were critical to the foraging success and rapid dispersal of Clovis people.

Other terms that may be unfamiliar, such as patch, diet breadth, marginal value theorem, migration, dispersal, and colonization, will be defined when introduced in appropriate sections below.

3.2   Clovis-era technology

STONE TECHNOLOGY

A "typical" Clovis toolkit may exist only in the minds of archeologists. No one site has contained all the tool classes recorded across the continent. Clovis flaked-stone tool classes and technology from different sites are well described by several authors, including Bradley (1982), Callahan (1979), Collins (1999a), Morrow (1996), Wilke, Flenniken, and Ozbun (1991), and Woods and Titmus (1985). Stanford (1991:2, 1999b) has described and illustrated a selection of Clovis artifacts from different sites, and suggested that an "inferred Clovis lithic tool kit" would contain: (1) bifacial, fluted projectile points, (2) large bifaces used as tools and also as point preforms, (3) blades and blade cores, (4) cutting and scraping tools made on blades and flakes, (5) gravers, and (6) a variety of endscrapers. These forms occur together in many sites, but certainly not in all the known Clovis findspots. A few Clovis-era sites have yielded burins or possible burins, and other forms not identified as frequently as in Old World assemblages. Multiple-use tools such as spurred endscrapers, denticulates, spokeshaves, and many other functional categories have been recognized in Clovis sites. Unmodified flakes and blades were sometimes utilized, as well. Debitage can consist of simple flakes, flake-blades, true blades, biface-thinning flakes, and very specialized biface-thinning flakes such as controlled plunging or overshot (outrepassé [Tixier 1974]) flakes.

Other common tools in Clovis sites also may exist, but some – such as pièces esquillés (scaled pieces, often labeled wedges or bipolar cores) (Shott 1999) – seem to be abundant in eastern sites but not in western ones, and may date to relatively late in the Clovis era (or may be post-Clovis). Unfortunately, unless each and every Clovis assemblage is solidly dated, we may not be able to distinguish changes in artifact classes and types over time, and our definition of a typical toolkit will remain fuzzy.

THE OLD WORLD BASIS OF CLOVIS LITHIC TECHNOLOGY

Bradley (1993) and Stanford and Bradley (2000) summarized what they consider to be the foundations of Clovis lithic technology, which has its heart in bifaces, blades, and core-and-flake production. Clovis technology is similar to the Old World Upper Paleolithic stone industries of the Solutréan tradition. Both Clovis and Solutréan are characterized by the presence of concave-based projectile points; by biface-thinning through the removal of large flat soft-hammer-percussion flakes that traveled more than halfway across each face, sometimes all the way across to remove part or all of the opposite edge (*outrepassé* flaking); by bifaces without a central lengthwise ridge; by special biface-flaking platforms that were isolated, ground smooth on the proximal part of a guiding arris, and further isolated by the careful removal of small flakes on both sides of the platform; by similar biface sizes and shapes (unfluted); by the presence of engraved limestone tablets (such as found at the Gault site, Texas, where most are post-Clovis in age); by similar ranges of bone tools; and by the caching of very large bifaces (Stanford and Bradley 2000).

According to Bradley, the Solutréan was primarily a blade technology but bifaces did become more frequent towards the latter part of its time range (19,500–17,500 rcybp). Hence the similarities to Clovis seem to be greater when the two technologies approach each other in time; yet the fact remains that Solutréan disappeared in Europe thousands of years before Clovis first appeared in America.

The Solutréan was distributed near the coasts in northern Spain and along waterways in SW France and Spain, which might imply an ability to use watercraft, although direct evidence is lacking. The focus was clearly on riparian habitats rich in flora and fauna. Boat-making left no identifiable remains in either the Solutréan or Clovis, so the possible direct spread of Solutréan people across the Atlantic and their subsequent dispersal in North America by watercraft are unsupported hypotheses. Straus (2000) discussed more facts and interpretations about Solutréan and its differences from Clovis. For example, Solutréan assemblages may contain bipointed and shouldered bifaces, which do not appear in Clovis. Cave paintings are associated with the Solutréan in Europe, but are not known from the Clovis era in North America. Another fact that militates against seafaring Solutréaños is the absence of Solutréan-age Upper Paleolithic industries even as near to Spain as the Balearic Islands, 100–200 km offshore, or any other Mediterranean island (Malta, Sardinia, Corsica, Cyprus, Crete), destinations requiring much less challenging trips than a cold voyage across the north Atlantic.

Although a Clovis toolkit from region to region and site to site may contain different assortments of classes and different proportions of implements, there still are underlying features that some analysts think clearly tie together the technologies. Callahan (1979), Morrow (1995, 1996), and others have defined the basic biface-reduction sequences and strategies that link Clovis technology across sites and regions (see Table 2.2). Clovis points are basally thinned or "fluted," having had channel flakes removed from the base towards the tip, but the flutes do not approach the broad and long scars of Folsom-point fluting. Ahler and Geib (2000) have elegantly made a connection between Folsom fluting and the human ability to control projectile-point penetration, repair efficiency, and stable hafting, which were features critical to extremely mobile Folsom-era foragers on the track of a single prey taxon, bison. But Clovis points are not as specialized as Folsom, perhaps suggesting that Clovis foragers had fewer worries about access to raw materials, or alternatively that Clovis people were still learning how to enhance mobility through flintknapping virtuosity.

INFERRED USES OF FLAKED-STONE IMPLEMENTS

Some Clovis-era stone tools are not exclusively diagnostic of the times. Thumbnail scrapers can be found in late Holocene assemblages, as well as in Clovis-era assemblages. Bifacial knives are common in many different time periods. The functions these tool classes had were not Clovis-specific.

Some Clovis-era tool classes are assumed to have limited functions, based on their morphology, such as spurred endscrapers, whose sharp spurs are usually thought to be gravers or piercing tips (Morris and Blakeslee 1987; Rogers 1986). The spurs on many specimens may have been deliberately engineered graving elements, but they also may have been merely the unplanned side-effects of scraper-resharpening (see Shott 1993) or fortuitous and unutilized elements of a special scraper edge (Shott 1995, n.d.). Tomenchuk and Storck (1997) make a case that widespread spurred pieces from Paleoindian assemblages (as well as from Eurasian Upper Paleolithic sites) were actually "single- and double-scribe compass-gravers and coring gravers" whose functions were to engrave single or concentric circles on organic materials, cut thin disks, and bore holes.

Besides the shapes of stone tools, other features have been examined for clues to tool function. Usually analysts select edges to study, seeking polish, striations, and scratches, which are then compared to similar modifications on replicated tools used experimentally to cut, scrape, and chop hard and soft materials such as animal skins or wood (Keeley 1980; Semenov 1976).

For example, flake tools from the Udora (Ontario) site were examined for traces of possible use-wear. The site contained a possible Gainey phase cache of informal tools (Storck 1990; Storck and Tomenchuk 1990). The analytical results supported suggestions that the cache was a store of tools used seasonally to split roots, possibly of jack pine or black spruce, in order to make line or cordage.

M. Kay (1996) examined microwear traces on replicated tools – fluted points and a uniface – which had been used in butchering African elephants, and he compared them with fluted points recovered from the Colby (WY) mammoth site. Based on the surface marks and alterations, Kay found that two Colby points had been used only once as spearpoints, and the other two had been used several times as projectiles and also as butchering knives.

Tomenchuk (1997) examined over 2,000 pieces of lithic debitage, utilized flakes, and fluted points from the Fisher site (Ontario), which is a manifestation of the Parkhill complex (Barnes type projectile points) thought to date to just after the Clovis-Gainey phase. Tomenchuk found evidence that the lithic materials had been used to work wood (specifically unseasoned jack pine and black spruce and partially seasoned white birch), bone, and antler; as well, Tomenchuk proposed that some tools had been used to butcher fish. He also suggested that several tools had been used to butcher immature caribou, perhaps to skin them, and that bone beads or disks were manufactured at the site.

Shott (1993) identified what he considered to be macroscopic use-wear traces on endscrapers from the Leavitt site (MI), another Parkhill phase (post-Gainey/Clovis) site; he concluded that this class of Paleoindian tool had a wide range of cutting and scraping uses.

Other studies at both the macroscopic and microscopic levels have been carried out on fluted-point assemblages, contributing to our understanding of site tasks and tool functions, but the fact is that most Clovis-era tools have not been closely examined.

TOOLSTONE SOURCES, MOBILITY, AND TECHNOLOGICAL ORGANIZATION

Clovis-era sites are generally small and scattered, except for the infrequent large "aggregation" sites such as Bull Brook (MA) where a relatively large group of several families camped together a few times (or alternatively, single families camped repeatedly over and over again, giving the impression of a large group). The general assumption about Clovis-era toolstone acquisition is that small mobile groups traveled directly to the sources and did not trade for it (see Meltzer 1989b).

Clovis-era artifact assemblages differ because different activities may have taken place at each site; they also differ because of preservational biases, sampling mistakes, and any of a number of other reasons. Tools were probably carried out of some camps to use elsewhere, and many sites do not fairly sample the range of implements that had been used in them (see Shott 1986). The same campsites may have been used for different purposes at different times, thus mixing toolkits (see Binford 1982:12–16).

Numerous studies of Clovis-era toolstone have shown that some raw materials in Clovis tool assemblages often came from far distant sources – up to 1,800 km away (for example, Gramly 1988). To make their tools from the preferred materials, Clovis-era foragers had either to go directly to toolstone sources or find neighbors in intervening ranges to engage in trade for the raw material. If foragers did travel to sources, they may have done it purposively, which Binford (1979:259) considered unusual, or they "embedded" the travel in other foraging trips through the landscape. Either strategy might leave different telltale sequences of tool-making, reworking, and discard on the trail of the mobile foragers.

Most regions in North America have Clovis-era sites where toolstone sources are distant. Not all toolstone sources have been reliably identified, so the attempt to measure distance that Clovis foragers moved between toolstone sources can be tricky – potentially yielding distances that are either too high or too low. Even some well-studied toolstone sources contain so much variability that raw materials in some sites may be unrecognized. Therefore trying to identify Clovis-era forager range-sizes based on distances between toolstone sources may greatly overestimate or underestimate the true distances traveled. As well, tools may have been scavenged by later people and moved far away from old sites, further contributing to an overestimate of range sizes.

Curran and Grimes (1989) examined toolstone in several large assemblages from the Northeast, and determined that if fluted-point foragers used direct acquisition, they had a range almost as large as all of New England (Shott n.d.), which is much greater than the ranges of recent ethnographic foragers. Other studies have come up with range sizes based on distances to sources. For example, Hester and Grady (1977) attempted to estimate ranges ("catchment areas") utilized from individual campsites in the *llano estacado* of the Southwest; Custer and Stewart (1990) modeled range sizes for Middle Atlantic Paleoindians; and Storck and Tomenchuk (1990) estimated a possible "residential core area" between Lakes Huron and Ontario in Canada. These studies and others that depend on distance-to-source measurements assume that sites in the studies are contemporaneous, which is usually impossible to demonstrate, and that toolstone acquisition was 100 percent by direct travel, which is also impossible to prove. Estimates of straight-line distances walked by Clovis foragers have varied from as little as 75 km in one direction in central Virginia (Gardner 1974) up to 1,800 km (Gramly 1988). An average figure from studies in the Northeast is 250 km (Custer and Stewart 1990), which is similar to the distances walked by recent subarctic foragers. When distances to all potential toolstone sources are used to draw "range" boundaries, the sizes exceed the average yearly range of modern foragers such as Alaska's Nunamiut people, who are often considered similar to northeastern Paleoindians in terms of subsistence and social organization (MacDonald 1968; Ritchie and Funk 1973; Storck and Tomenchuk 1990; see also Binford 1983).

Besides affecting range size, Clovis-era toolstone acquisition closely shaped settlement patterning and task scheduling. Gardner's (1974, 1983) settlement model for the Shenandoah Valley sites (VA) described a "cyclical or direct procurement pattern," in which Clovis-era foraging groups cycled their movements from quarry to quarry – bedrock outcrops or cobble deposits – with the scheduling of their quarry visits dependent on toolkit needs such as replenishment. Toolkits in quarry-related sites include worn-out implements made of nonlocal material, as well as many more implements made of local material. This patterning is called cyclic.

A second and different pattern emerged where the toolstone sources were relatively plentiful and not widely separated. In this case, toolstone procurement was embedded in other activities (Binford 1979), and toolkits include implements made of a variety of materials, with minimal tool curation and minimal resharpening of tools (unless some of the lithic materials used were of relatively low quality) (Custer, Cavallo, and Stewart 1983:271–3). This second pattern is called serial.

OTHER USES OF STONE

Going beyond flaked-stone lithic technology, we can hardly see any other uses of stone. Only rarely is another kind of stone artifact uncovered in a Clovis assemblage. For example, Laub (1995) reported a small (7.5 × 9.5 × 6 mm) bead of sandstone from the Hiscock (NY) site, and a stone bead was found at Charlie Lake Cave (British Columbia), associated with bone dates of around 10,500 rcybp (Driver 1988; Driver, Handly, Fladmark, Nelson, Sullivan, and Preston 1996; Fladmark, Driver, and Alexander 1988), which Driver and associates see as far too young to have had anything to do with the original peopling process. Ritchie (1953, 1957:plates 15 and 17; also see Gramly 1992:40) reported eleven small trianguloid pendant-like pieces of steatite, each with a perforation at one narrower end, and some with a lengthwise groove. These pieces came from the Reagan fluted-point site (VT), and have been found nowhere else. They are not directly dated and not necessarily associated with the fluted-point occupation, which is likely post-Clovis in age (see Deller and Ellis 1992:128, and fig. 88).

Cobbles and rocks used as hammerstones, abraders, or pounders have been identified in Clovis-era sites; hammerstones are especially abundant in quarry-related sites. But only one stone grinder – a mano or handstone – has ever been found in a Clovis assemblage (see Table 5.4 below); metates or milling stones have never been found in dated Clovis assemblages. Apparently people in the Clovis era did almost no grinding but had no end to cutting and scraping tasks.

Adhesive technology

The technology of adhesives was probably critical in Clovis times, but we know little about it. One obsidian Clovis point from the Fenn cache (described in section 2.2) had traces of amber in scratches on the channel-flake scars of both sides (Frison and Bradley 1999:19). Tankersley (1994b) examined an Oregon fluted point and found microscopic traces of an organic, resinous material on one channel-flake scar. The artifact had been surface-collected at the Hoyt site in central Oregon, not far from the well-known Dietz site. Tankersley called the material amber, and speculated that fossil resins such as amber were used as an adhesive ("mastic") for binding stone points to the beveled ivory or bone rods that have been interpreted as foreshafts (described below) in Clovis assemblages. Amber or similar fossil resin also has been found in eastern European Upper Paleolithic sites (Adovasio and Soffer 1992; Pidoplichko 1976; Soffer 1985), and at the Lindenmeier Folsom site in Colorado (Wilmsen and Roberts 1984), suggesting a globally widespread usage of the material's adhesive properties. Tankersley further speculated that fossil resin beads and pendants – occasionally found in Upper Paleolithic sites and interpreted as artwork or adornment – could have served as both decorative items and quick tool-repair kits when melted, making them especially useful in open environments where pitch-bearing trees were scarce (see also Soffer 1985:438). C. W. Beck (1996), a materials analyst, did not accept Tankersley's use of the word "amber," but this quibble cannot invalidate Tankersley's (1994b, 1996) proposal that fossil resins were potentially useful and the knowledge of their usefulness was present across the northern hemisphere during the late Pleistocene. Clovis-era industries undoubtedly made use of such materials in hafting and attaching components of their multi-part tools.

Residue analyses of the surfaces of stone artifacts (described in a later chapter; see Table 5.2) occasionally turn up evidence interpreted as traces of blood, either animal or human, and the implication is the blood resulted from tool-use on animals; an alternative explanation is that blood was used as an adhesive on hafted tools (Gramly 1991). Storck and Tomenchuk (1990) found microscopic traces of a foreign (unidentified) substance that might have been a hafting cement on three flake tools from the Udora (Ontario) site. The substance had quartz particles embedded in it, possibly to make it gritty and increase friction.

Wood technology

Holman (1986) reported a wooden object 23 cm long with a tapered point and four striated sides in the Dansville (MI) site, which also contained a mastodont skull. The mastodont, a sexually mature female, died in a bog in the early spring and is not thought to have been killed by humans. Whether the wooden object is a spear point or staff used to lever bones is thus unclear, but the object does seem to be similar to another late Pleistocene wooden object recovered in Florida. The Florida specimen is also tapered, with four striated sides, and was found lying between the collapsed upper and lower shells of an extinct giant land tortoise (*Geochelone* sp.) in the underwater site Little Salt Spring. The Florida specimen was interpreted as either a killing spear, still in place after the tortoise was cooked, or a stick used to help in the cooking. The Florida stick was dated to 12,030 rcybp (Clausen, Cohen, Emiliani, Holman, and Stipp 1979), which gives the impression that a pre-Clovis population could have preyed on animals whose escape speeds were slow. However, Purdy (1991) wondered if this "spear" is actually an artifact.

A more careful comparison must be made between these possible wooden spears and poles broken by noncultural processes such as gnawing beavers (*Castor canadensis*). Beaver-gnawed sticks can be deceptively spear-like when slightly weathered. Wittry (1965:18–19) noted how sticks that looked like spears in another Michigan mastodont site (Rappuhn) were "unquestionably made by beavers," although he interpreted a layer of thicker poles just under the "spears" as a platform built by people. Beavers do create mats and shelters of large sticks, shredded wood and fresh vegetation (Gore and Baker 1989; Jenkins and Busher 1979; Warren 1927), and the Rappuhn site poles may be an ancient beaver construction. If ambiguous discoveries like the possible spears are ever going to become clear additions to the Clovis-era inventory, a better understanding is needed of noncultural processes that could create pseudo-artifacts in sites without stone tools.

Sharpened spears have a surprisingly deep history in the Old World's mid-Pleistocene archeological record, and so the existence of wooden spears, digging sticks, and staffs is to be expected in the Upper Paleolithic or the New World's Clovis era. Pieces of wooden spears were found at Kalambo Falls, Zambia (Clark 1974, 2001), estimated to be 90,000–200,000 years old, and at Schoningen, Germany (Thieme 1997), dated to around 400,000 years ago. At Schoningen, three sharpened spruce spears, a bipointed stick, and two grooved wooden objects (probably handles) were found with thousands of horse bones; the javelin-like spears were killing implements carefully made by a pre-modern form of *Homo*.

The potential ineffectiveness of sharpened wooden spears against the thick and hairy skin of large mammals may have made their use as killing weapons relatively rare by Upper Paleolithic times when bigger prey animals were sought, but even so the technology and know-how would have remained in place to manufacture a portable, tough, and flexible wooden cylinder capable of delivering a stone-tipped projectile such as a Clovis point.

Other uses of wood probably would have included simple architectural constructions, such as supports or roof and wall elements in shelters and dwellings. The floor of a possible shelter that may have been built of wood was excavated at the Thunderbird site (VA), but the only material traces of the construction were post molds in the sediments and the distribution of artifacts within the space outlined by the post molds (Gardner 1974).

Unfortunately, organic preservation is notoriously poor over much of North America, especially in the east, and no indisputable wooden artifacts are known from any region. Yet the existence of wooden implements in Clovis technology is probable. In other places in the world where unusual conditions have allowed organic materials to be preserved, such as at waterlogged or underwater localities, even very old cultural traditions that at every other contemporary site lack traces of wooden remains may contain preserved pieces of wood, such as found at the 20,000-year-old Ohalo II site in Israel (Krause 2001; Nadel and Werker 1999).

If preservation were better from Clovis sites, we probably would find wooden spearshafts, wooden handles for knives and other tools, wooden bowls, perhaps spoons, decorated items, clubs, and so forth. As things stand, we can do no better than speculate about Clovis wood technology until the sites with ideal preservation are discovered.

Textiles, basketry, cordage

Soffer, Adovasio, Illingworth, Amirkhanov, Praslov, and Street (2000) argue that fiber technology was well developed by the Last Glacial Maximum in a large part of Europe, stretching from France across to Ukraine. Upper Paleolithic weavers could make "plaited basketry and twined and plain woven cloth which approach levels of technical sophistication heretofore associated exclusively with the Neolithic and later time periods" (Soffer, Adovasio, and Hyland 2000:531). Soffer and colleagues propose that Upper Paleolithic people in different geographic regions made a variety of items from fiber-based textiles – woven caps, hairnets or netted snoods, clothing with straps or bands, belts, string skirts, and bracelets and necklaces. Fibers were also used to make baskets, nets, ropes, and bags (Soffer et al. 2000). Such a widespread and useful technology is postulated to have existed for thousands of years, and thus was probably rather advanced in later traditions such as Clovis.

The "invisible Palaeolithic majority – the women, the children, and the elderly" (Soffer et al. 2000:819) would have used many of the fiber-based perishables, and fiber industries thus may provide information about gendered and age-specific activities. For example, communal net-hunting may have been practiced by the groups which could make certain kinds of textiles such as knotted nets (Adovasio, Soffer, Hyland, Klíma, and Svoboda 1998). Another possible implication of the technology is status differentiation: the finer textiles woven by women may have been "valuables [that] functioned in prestige economies" (Soffer et al. 2000:819).

Analogous evidence about similar possibilities in North America is not known from the Clovis era. However, a late Paleoindian hunting net has been found dating to about 8,900 rcybp (Frison, Andrews, Adovasio, Carlisle, and Edgar 1986), and relatively "advanced" textiles (diamond-plaited construction) are associated with the 9,400-radiocarbon-year-old Spirit Cave skeleton from western Nevada (Dansie 1997; Dansie in Wheeler 1997; Tuohy and Dansie 1997). These finds imply that earlier cultures such as Clovis also may have been competent textile-manufacturers.

Clovis technology probably included ropes and cordage, bags, belts, roll-up matting, wraps, and a host of clothing, containers, binding aids, and so forth. It will be nice to find some of these things one day. Their presence may help us better appreciate gendered Clovis-era subsistence, personal appearance, and activities other than "men in furs knapping stone tools to kill megafauna" (Soffer et al. 2000:819).

Bone, antler, and ivory

The European Upper Paleolithic is justifiably famous for the variety and abundance of bone, antler, and ivory artifacts. These range from the elegant simplicity of such items as sagaies (the pointed rods without barbs – the name sagaie has the same roots as the familiar "assegai" of Bantu Africa), the arrestingly shaped implements once called bâtons de commandements, delicately fashioned bone needles, decorative discs and beads, painted bones, carved and polished bone objects, and the splendid carved and decorated figurines such as the German ivory lion man, the little mammoths of central Europe, and the so-called "venus" figurines (a fine span of examples is illustrated in Leroi-Gourhan 1967 and Wehrberger 1994).

Many of the the organic artifacts in Upper Paleolithic assemblages probably functioned as tools as well as decoration or art. Yet the very richness of the artwork and decoration must have had an underlying symbolic weightiness, as suggested by images as extraordinary as animal heads on human bodies. The hunting scenes, the "therioanthropes," the fabulous creatures (Bahn 1998; Bahn and Vertut 1997; Bosinski 1994; Hahn 1994; Hahn, Müller-Beck, and Taute 1985; Leroi-Gourhan 1967; Wehrberger 1994) leave us wondering at the imagery of the Upper Paleolithic. In contrast, the designs on pre-Clovis and Clovis-era organic artifacts are uncomplicated and almost uninvolving to the viewer. A few implements are incised with angled lines, or in one Clovis-era case sinuous lines (see below). The plain Clovis artifacts may also have a symbolic weight to them, one that is indecipherable to us, but nearly all appear to be objects created to have nothing more than unadorned functionality.

Abundant amounts of worked and semi-worked bone, antler, and ivory can be found in European sites. Many assemblages contain scrap and debris from the working of organic material, as well as rough, half-finished, or rejected specimens. These kinds of workshop debris may be under-reported, perhaps tossed out of excavated inventories, because their potential for revealing information about prehistoric behavior is not fully appreciated. But a visual examination of collections will show that such materials are not especially rare in the Old World.

The Russian archeologist Semenov contributed useful guides to the inferred uses of stone and bone tools, and the possible techniques and practices used by prehistoric people to shape bone, antler, and ivory (Semenov 1976 [the original in Russian appeared in 1957]), which have had a lasting impact on archeological interpretations of Upper Paleolithic organic technology.

Several North American collections of pre-Clovis and Clovis age contain marked, broken, or minimally modified organic objects, sometimes interpreted as artifacts or the end-effect traces of human butchering. These are the nearest examples to European workshop debris.

The inventory of Clovis-era bone, antler, and ivory implements is surprisingly modest continent-wide. The decay of organic materials in Clovis sites was a factor in removing such items, but their scarcity relative to Old World inventories may be due to other circumstances such as higher mobility and shorter occupational times in North America.

In the rest of this section I describe the artifactually modified bone, antler, and ivory items found in Clovis-era sites, other than possible artwork, which is summarized in section 3.4 to follow. Clovis-era organic artifacts are so rare that they deserve detailed presentation.

Leroi-Gourhan (1967) categorized portable Upper Paleolithic bone, ivory, and antler objects into "decorated weapons, tools, and ornaments" and "objects of religious significance," but Clovis specimens are too scarce and simple to divide into such categories. The categories I use here are terms of inferred function already attached to the Clovis objects. Following the functional categories (numbered 1 through 7), the simplest organic artifacts – unmodified bone fragments – are described and discussed at some length because not all of them may be the results of deliberate human actions.

(1)   Foreshafts, osseous rods, *sagaies*, harpoons

Table 3.1 lists the known examples of cylindrical bone/antler/ivory implements. These objects are the most common organic artifacts in Clovis-era assemblages (and assemblages that are uncertainly dated), but they are so variable in shape and size as to defy a single descriptive term or functional category. Some rods are beveled at both ends; some are beveled at only one end while the other end is pointed. Some are very long and thin; others are relatively short and stout (see measurements in Lyman, O'Brien, and Hayes 1998:table 1).

Lyman, O'Brien, and Hayes (1998) examined the mechanical possibilities of the cylindrical shape, the scarfed or beveled end with roughened surface, and the measurements of girth and length, and suggested that the bi-beveled examples were used as levers to tighten the sinew binding around the haft-ends of lithic tools such as fluted knives or saws (Fig. 3.1). Other possible uses that have been suggested in the literature include *foreshaft* (a piece mounted between the fluted point and the main spear shaft) (Fig. 3.2) (Lahren and Bonnichsen 1974), *spear tip* if one end is pointed and the other is beveled (Cotter 1954; Jenks and Simpson 1941), *pressure-flaker handle* (Wilke, Flenniken, and Ozbun 1991), *pry-bar or lever* used to separate bones during butchering (Saunders and Daeschler 1994), and *sled shoes* (Gramly 1993). At least one proboscidean-ivory specimen from Florida has a hooked barb on one side (and other barbs may have been present before the specimen broke); one bone specimen from Wizards Beach on Pyramid Lake, Nevada, directly dated 10,340 ± 50 rcybp, has an extremely sharp tip and a full series of sharp (and possibly worn and resharpened) barbs on one side, indicating its intended use as a projectile point. The barbed specimens may have been fish-spear heads, but barbed points are also commonly used on terrestrial mammals in Africa, and Upper Paleolithic barbed points were used on caribou and other Late Glacial land animals. The Pyramid Lake specimen is one of a dozen examples known from the lake and usually assumed to be fishing gear (Tuohy 1990), but it was found near a possible proboscidean-ivory point having one beveled end and a very sharp tip, directly dated 10,360 ± 50 rcypb, perhaps indicating the relatively late survival of mammoths in the western Great Basin (Dansie and Jerrems 1999, 2000); the dates and the identification of the ivory may need re-evaluation.

TABLE 3.1 Clovis sites or Clovis-era sites where bone or ivory rods have been found.

SITE (REFERENCE)	NUMBER AND TYPE OF RODS	ASSOCIATED ARTIFACTS
Anzick, MT (1)	11 bone (2 complete, 4 beveled ends, 5 midsections)	8 fluted points, 85 biface fragments
Aucilla River, FL (2)	33 ivory	possibly associated fluted points and lithics
Blackwater Locality No. 1, NM (3)	4 bone (1 complete, 3 others fragmentary)	fluted points, other lithics, faunal remains
Broken Mammoth, AK (4)	1 ivory	(possibly older than associated lithics, scavenged from long-dead skeleton)
Drake, CO (5)	possible ivory rod	13 fluted points
East Wenatchee (Richey-Roberts), WA (6)	13 bone (a possible 14th found as fragments in carnivore scat), 2 with decorations	14 fluted points, 15 bifaces
Goose Lake, CA (7)	6 bone	
Klamath Lake, OR (8)	2 bone	
Saskatchewan, Canada (9)	1 bone	
Sheaman, WY (10)	1 ivory	1 fluted point, Clovis lithics
Sheridan Pit (or Cave), OH (11)	1 bone	non-fluted stone projectile point, lithics; stratum date of 11,060 ± 60, bone date of 10,920 ± 50
Wizards Beach, Pyramid Lake, NV (12)	1 ivory point, plus 11 bone or antler uniserial barbed points	ivory point directly dated 10,360 ± 50 (UCR-3796), one bone point directly dated 10,340 ± 50 (UCR-3795)

References

1 Jones and Bonnichsen 1994; Lahren and Bonnichsen 1974
2 Hemmings 1999; Webb and Dunbar 1999
3 Hester 1972
4 Yesner 1994
5 Stanford and Jodry 1988
6 Gramly 1992, 1993
7 Riddell 1973
8 Cressman 1942, 1956
9 Wilmeth 1968
10 Frison 1982
11 Redmond and Tankersley 1999; Tankersley 1997, 1999
12 Dansie and Jerrems 1999, 2000; Rendall 1966

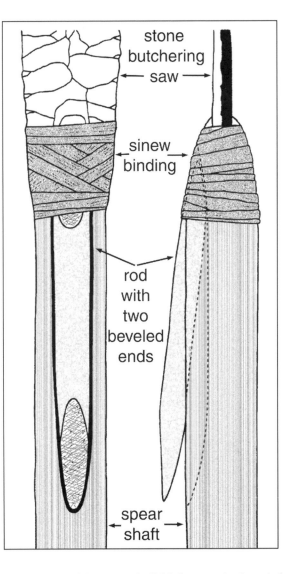

Fig. 3.1 Hypothesized use of Clovis-era bone rods as levers to tighten bindings on hafted butchering tools (after Lyman, O'Brien, and Hayes 1998).

The Old World Upper Paleolithic bone/antler/ivory industries are known for projectile weaponry, beginning with Aurignacian types and changing shape over time (Knecht 1993; Peyrony 1933). The earliest are split-based points with distinctive haft-widths and lengths (Peterkin 1993:57), and later types include simple-based points, including "lozenge-shaped" and "spindle-shaped," which do not have beveled bases. The earliest organic points with beveling on one end appeared in Gravettian assemblages (see Pike-Tay and Bricker 1993 and references, and Knecht 1993 and references). Other types of organic point include "whittled-base," double-beveled-base, forked-base, and bi-pointed (Delporte, Hahn, Mons, Pinçon, and de Sonneville-Bordes 1988). Each of the different forms was hafted differently. Another form of point, the mammoth-rib point, is known from Gravettian levels in southern Germany (Knecht 1993:43, plate 3.1).

By the time of the Magdalénian in western Europe, *sagaies* were numerically very common in archeological assemblages (see Peterkin 1993). Size ranges seem to be remarkably consistent among the types with different bases. Later,

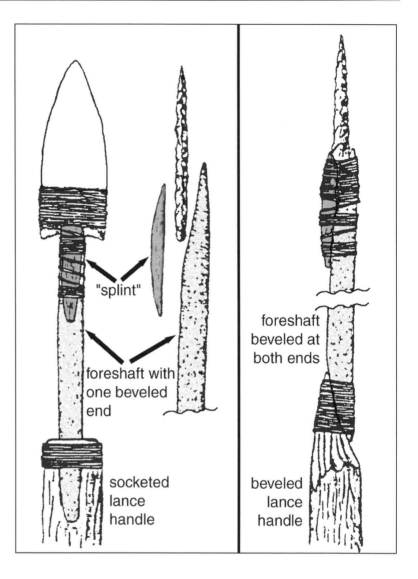

Fig. 3.2 Hypothesized use of Clovis-era bone rods as spear foreshafts (after Lahren and Bonnichsen 1974).

"splint"

foreshaft with one beveled end

foreshaft beveled at both ends

socketed lance handle

beveled lance handle

during the final Magdalénian, barbed organic points appeared and are usually labeled "harpoons," some having basal perforations. Harpoons are either uniserially or biserially barbed.

The Clovis-era specimens from North America would certainly seem familiar to Old World analysts, but the Clovis-era examples do not include split-based or lozenge-shaped bases. If some of the Wizards Beach Pyramid Lake specimens (see Table 3.1) are indeed made from proboscidean bone and ivory, including the barbed specimen that Dansie and Jerrems (1999, 2000) think is made from a mammoth rib, then the range of shapes and sizes of Clovis-era organic points is conspicuously similar to the ranges in the Old World.

(2)   Shaft straightener or shaft wrench

Only a single specimen of a worked bone with a hole bored through one widened end is known from all of North America. The undecorated specimen (Fig. 3.3)

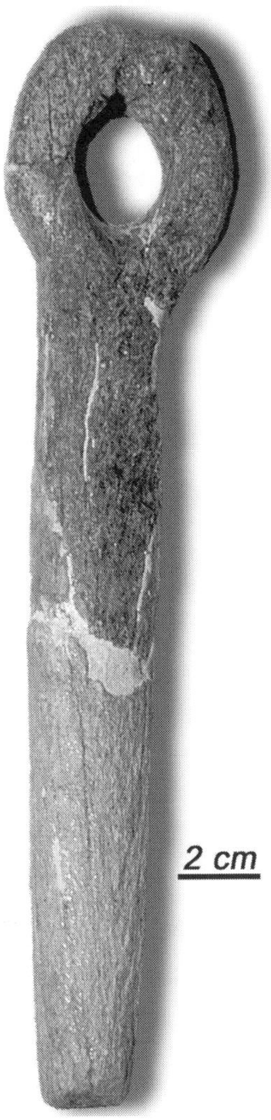

Fig. 3.3 The Murray Springs (Arizona) shaft wrench; length of the specimen is 259 mm (photographed on exhibit at the Arizona State Museum).

was discovered in two parts beneath a "black mat" sediment blanketing a mammoth skeleton and Clovis implements in a channel deposit dated 10,900 ± 50 rcybp (average of eight dates), at the Murray Springs (AZ) Clovis site (C. V. Haynes 1980; C. V. Haynes and Hemmings 1968). It is often described as a shaft wrench or straightener, and its similarity is noted to Old World Upper Paleolithic tools once called *bâtons de commandement* – a term which evokes "an aged . . . general directing . . . an assault on a mammoth" (Leroi-Gourhan 1967:59) – but now more often descriptively termed *bâtons perforés* or *bâtons perçés*, pierced staffs. The term in German is *Lochstab* (baton). The uses of these perforated items – often made of antler in the Old World and also decorated with incised designs – are not clearly known, but their applicability to straightening spear shafts or *sagaies* is as good a guess as any. Next to awls, says Leroi-Gourhan (1967:59), pierced staffs are the most common bone implement in every time period of the Upper Paleolithic. Many in the Old World were decorated with geometric or curvilinear designs, or carved animals (most often horses), but the single Clovis-era piece from Arizona is plain.

The Murray Springs Clovis-era specimen does not show polish or rounding of the interior hole, which has pronounced beveling at the top and bottom. C. V. Haynes and Hemmings (1968) suggest these characteristics mean the implement was not used as a rope twister or thong stropper but was used to straighten wood or bone spear-shafts. The Murray Springs specimen is very similar in size and shape to ethnographically recorded Klamath Indian arrow-shaft straighteners (made of wood) in the Barrett collection of the University of California, Berkeley's Phoebe Hearst Museum (accession 303, specimen numbers 12352, 12713, and 12628) (Barrett 1911), which were collected in 1907. The Murray Springs specimen has a much larger hole in the working end, as befits a spear straightener – 25 to 30 mm wide – when compared to the Klamath specimens whose holes are the smaller widths of arrow-shafts – 10 to 19 mm.

(3)   Possible harpoon-head socket

Stanford (1996) (also Dillehay 2000:xix; Dixon 1999:251–3) illustrated a bone implement interpreted as a socket that could have held a fluted point at one end and at the other end slipped over a spear shaft, where flaring basal tangs might have toggled once it had been propelled inside an animal's flesh, functioning much as do Eskimo harpoons with sockets connecting bone foreshafts to wooden main shafts. However, the prehistoric piece was collected from an Indiana peat bog, and while its distal socket is a good fit for a Clovis fluted point and its tapering proximal socket is a good fit for a typical Clovis-era bone rod, the AMS date on the specimen (7,990 ± 120 rcybp) shows it cannot be a Clovis tool, even if the date is seriously affected by contamination (Stanford 1996:46). Yet Stanford believes the hafting technology seen in this socket may have been used much earlier by Clovis foragers. Lyman, O'Brien, and Hayes (1998:893) politely suggest the specimen may have been modified by natural processes such as ungulate-chewing (Gordon 1976) and may not be an artifact at all.

(4)   Ivory burnisher/billet

Saunders, Agogino, Boldurian, and C. V. Haynes (1991) reported on a mammoth-ivory artifact from the Clovis level of Blackwater Locality No. 1 (NM). The object had been broken when uncovered and then was stabilized with dental plaster. It was photographed (Fig. 3.4), but while the artifact was being cast-replicated, the casting technician died, and the implement is now lost. The object appears to have pitted, polished, and striated surface zones, and is similar in size and shape to ten mammoth-ivory objects interpreted as flintknapping billets from the European Upper Paleolithic site Předmosti (Czech Republic) (Saunders et al. 1991:fig. 2). The Blackwater Locality No. 1 object may have had multiple uses – for example, as a burnisher in preparing animal hides, and as a flintknapping billet (Saunders et al. 1991:362).

Another kindred object was described and illustrated by Norton, Broster, and Breitburg (1998:fig. 1) from the Trull site (TN), and interpreted as a mastodont-ivory billet. As with the Blackwater Locality specimen, one end of this piece was rounded as if from pounding against very hard surfaces, which is similar to the wear that develops on soft hammers such as antler billets used in flintknapping.

Fig. 3.4 Clovis-era mammoth-ivory burnisher/billet from Blackwater Locality No. 1 (New Mexico) (image scanned and edited from a photographic mosaic in Saunders, Agogino, Boldurian, and C. V. Haynes 1991, used here with permission).

(5) Bone bead

J. Hester (1972: 116, fig. 103d) reported an elongated bone bead from Blackwater Draw (NM), recovered from the Clovis level. The cylindrical piece was drilled towards the center from each end, but one of the drilling attempts apparently emerged prematurely through the side of the piece.

A single, poorly made bead does not imply Clovis-era self-adornment on a grand scale. The bead may have had a utilitarian role, such as a moving part in an as-yet-unimagined artifact.

(6) Segmented tusk/semifabricate

Saunders, C. V. Haynes, Stanford, and Agogino (1990) reported a segment of proboscidean tusk from Blackwater Locality No. 1 (NM) which they deemed a "semifabricate" or unfinished piece (Fig. 3.5). The piece has graving or whittling

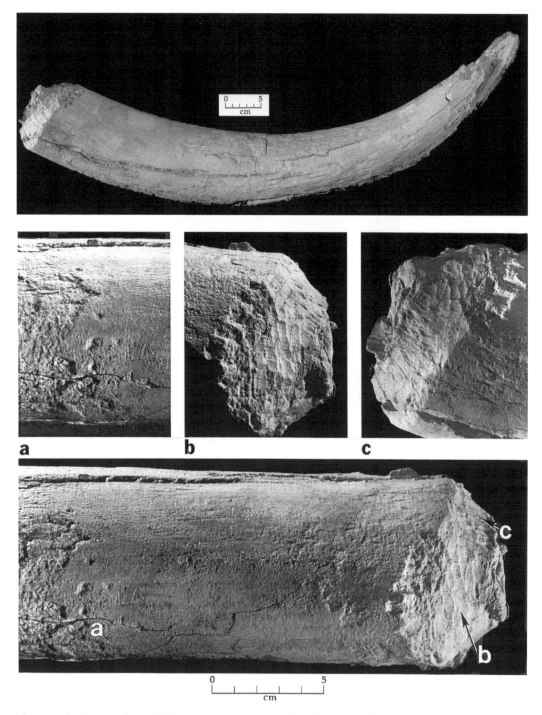

Fig. 3.5 Clovis-era tusk semifabricate from Blackwater Locality No. 1 (New Mexico). Features include (a) guidemarks for sectioning the tusk, (b) guide channel, and (c) notch-like groove (photograph at top by Marlin Roos, Illinois State Museum; photographs at bottom by K. B. Farnsworth and L. Hansen, Center for American Archaeology, Kampsville, Illinois; these images appeared in Saunders, C. V. Haynes, Stanford, and Agogino 1990, used here with permission).

Fig. 3.6 Tooth marks made by modern beaver on oak log; the tooth grooves run left and right on the image, truncated by drying cracks in the wood (photographed by G. Haynes, specimen collected by Stephen Jenkins).

marks on one end where a Clovis craftsperson is thought to have cut through the segment to separate it from the rest of the tusk. Saunders and colleagues interpret the marks as made by the repeated drawing of a unifacial knife ("in a drawknife fashion" [Saunders *et al.* 1990:fig. 4 caption]) at right angles to the tusk's long axis. The marks are similar to modifications that the Russian analyst Semenov (1976:148–51) interpreted as traces of ivory-working in Eurasian Upper Paleolithic assemblages.

The Clovis tusk's graved grooves are noticeably similar to the tooth grooves that modern beavers (*Castor canadensis*) produce on gnawed hardwood (Fig. 3.6). Also, the section lengths marked off on the Clovis-era tusk segment are similar to the lengths of tree segments that beavers preferentially separate by gnawing though the wood. Even the angle of the ends of hardwood gnawed by beavers are similar to the angle on the graved end of the Clovis tusk (Fig. 3.7). However, the lengths of the individual whittling marks are so different on the Clovis-era tusk segment (Table 3.2) that its interpretation as a humanly worked fragment is sound and plausible.

(7) Minimally modified bone tools

Possible bone tools have been described from the Hiscock (NY) site (Laub 2000; Laub, Tomenchuk, and Storck 1996; Tomenchuk and Laub 1995). These items remain questionable because they came out of a deposit that also contains gravelly sediments and occasionally reworked/redeposited bones. The manufacture-and-use sequence envisioned for the specimens seems singular and odd to me.

Fig. 3.7 Beaver-gnawed modern oak logs (photographed by G. Haynes, specimens collected by Stephen Jenkins).

TABLE 3.2 Measurements from Blackwater Locality No. 1 semifabricate (sectioned tusk) compared with measurements from beaver-gnawed wood. *Sources:* Saunders, C. V. Haynes, Stanford, and Agogino (1990:114), and G. Haynes (unpublished field notes).

	WIDTH	LENGTH
Beaver toothmarks (n = 20)	3.0–8.0 mm mean = 5.0 mm	28.0–95.0 mm mean = 56.8 mm
Marks on tusk (n = 17)	5.2–9.0 mm mean = 6.5 mm	2.9–9.0 mm mean = 5.3 mm

Nevertheless, the authors reporting these two objects have made a case for the minimal shaping of a mastodont-rib fragment they believe was used as a skin scraper and a mastodont-vertebra fragment they believe was used as a handle for a scraping tool. The rib piece was directly dated 10,990 ± 100 rcybp and the vertebra was directly dated 10,810 ± 50 rcybp. The existence of these possible tools, both so little modified as to be easily overlooked in Clovis-era assemblages, should inspire a deeper search for related evidence of human use of proboscidean carcasses and bones. Hemmings (1999) reported an ivory-working station at Sloth Hole, Florida, and if the interpretation is correct the criteria can be established to discover other such work stations.

J. Hester (1972:110) states that "artifacts of bone are an important and var-ied portion of the [Blackwater Draw Clovis] artifact asemblage," with the bone tools having "almost as many uses as the stone implements . . . [including] flak-ing, scraping, cutting, piercing, ornamentation, digging, and the killing of game" (Hester 1972:118). Most of the twenty-five implements described and illustrated appear to be only fragments of mammalian bones with rounded edges (for example, Hester 1972:figs. 101a–e, 102a–j, 103a, 104b–d) or marks on parts of surfaces (Hester 1972:fig. 104a). These sorts of modifications can-not automatically be interpreted as artifactually created, and indeed may have resulted from sediment abrasion or trampling.

I doubt that the bone assemblage illustrated by Hester (1972) does contain real tools, but perhaps the original breakage was done by people to extract marrow or to prepare bone slivers for making needles and other such implements.

(8) Broken proboscidean limb elements

Blackwater Locality No. 1 (NM) yielded many nonproboscidean-bone fragments and two mammoth-bone fragments thought to be artifacts, possibly fleshers or digging implements (Hester 1972:fig. 117a, 117d). The mammoth bones were ribs, not limb-elements. Only one Clovis-era site contains both Clovis lithics and broken megamammal limb-bones – Lange-Ferguson (SD). Several other Clovis-era sites that contained broken limb-bones completely lacked Clovis lithics. I discuss Tocuila (central Mexico) and Duewall-Newberry (TX) as examples of these, together with Lange-Ferguson (SD), in section 3.3 below.

Another site, Owl Cave (Wasden) in Idaho contained fragments and flakes of mammoth cortical bone associated with three partial fluted points and the bones of bison, pronghorn, and other fauna (Miller 1982, 1989; Miller and Dort 1978). The deposit containing this assemblage had been deformed from sedimentary loading and ice wedging, and was capped by rockfall. The layer was radiocarbon dated from 12,850 to 9,735 rcybp and artifacts were dated by obsidian hydration from 12,600 to 11,200 calendar years old (which calibrates to about 10,500 rcybp to 10,000 rcybp). The projectile points appear to be Folsom, whose association with bison bone is as expected, but whose association with mammoth is unique. The assemblage may be a sedimentary medley of Folsom and pre-Folsom materials, or an example of late-surviving mammoths utilized by Folsom people, or a case of Folsom scavenging of Clovis-era mammoth bones. I return to the site's interesting mammoth-bone breakage later in this book.

Discussion

Old World Upper Paleolithic assemblages often contain abundant quantities of bone, antler, and ivory fragments from large mammals (for example, see Klíma 1994 who describes the material from Pavlov I in Moravia). Many fragments had not been further modified after the initial simple breakage from impaction, but many others were chopped, hammered, sawn, scratched, or deliberately incised. Old World sites may be full of such workshop debris – the rejected bits, the segments of bone, antler, and tusk left over from manufacture of implements, the incomplete objects (semifabricates), the finished but worn out implements (for examples, see Gvozdover 1995:figs. 9, 10, 60, 61, 64, and 65). Upper Paleolithic workshop assemblages are also frequently associated with abundant lithic tools and debitage, finished organic tools, and artwork (Fig. 3.8).

Antler is the ideal material for many tools, because when fresh it can be broken by bending with less force than bone, thus making it easier to work, but when dry is much tougher at absorbing shocks and sudden impacts (Currey 1979; MacGregor 1985). Yet dated Clovis-era artifacts made of antler are completely unknown. The fact that bone and ivory were used in manufacturing certain tools expected to withstand impacts or great force – such as points and foreshafts or the one known shaft wrench – may indicate that Clovis-era foragers did not have access to antler in many regions, since antler would have stood up better to heavy use.

Antler, bone, and ivory soaked in water for a day or two is much easier to carve, incise, and whittle than dry specimens (MacGregor 1985:63–6). The fact that almost no examples of elaborately incised or carved osseous material are known from the Clovis era, unlike the hundreds of specimens from Old World sites, may indicate that Clovis foragers did not choose to spend the time – forty-eight hours or more – waiting for hard tissue to be softened in water or any other liquid, such as urine. One of the rare examples of Clovis-era artwork on osseous material is an incised rib from Blackwater Locality No. 1 (NM) (Saunders and Daeschler 1994), but this rib was carved without the fine control and lightness of touch so evident in Old World carvings (see Fig. 3.26 below). It was probably not soaked before carving, and the work was quickly done by the carver, once again perhaps suggesting much less time spent in crafting nonfunctional items in North America than in the Old World. I have more to say about Clovis-era artwork below in section 3.4.

There is plenty of evidence that a bone-tool industry was an important part of Europe's Upper Paleolithic technology (Semenov 1976:144–95). If Clovis people in North America were also regularly manufacturing useful objects out of bones, antlers, and tusks – such as the Murray Springs shaft straightener or

Fig. 3.8 At the top, a worked piece of mammoth ivory from an early Upper Paleolithic level of the Vogelherd site, Germany, showing impact points and numerous incisions. At the bottom, four carved mammoth-ivory figurines from the site's early Upper Paleolithic levels: (a) horse, length 48 mm; (b) panther, length 68 mm; (c) cave lion, length 64 mm; (d) woolly mammoth, length 50 mm. (Figurines photographed by Hilda Jensen, specimens from the Institut für Ur- und Frühgeschichte, Tübingen, Germany, which has permitted their use here and which retains all rights for further reproduction; the top specimen, also from the Institut, photographed by G. Haynes.)

TABLE 3.3 A sample of fossil proboscidean sites that contain broken bones interpreted as culturally modified. The sites are arranged chronologically, starting from the earliest at the top.

SITE (REFERENCES)	TAXON	DATE (ESTIMATE OR ^{14}C)	PROPOSED EVIDENCE
Old Crow, Yukon (1)	mammoth	290,000–13,000	Flaked bones
Grundel, MO (2)	mastodont	25,100 (large sigma errors)	Broken bones
Cooperton, OK (3)	mammoth	20,400–17,575	Broken bones, transported boulders
Inglewood, MD (4)	mammoth	20,070	Broken bones
La Sena, NE (5)	mammoth	18,000	Flaked bones
Selby and Dutton, CO (6)	mammoth	16,000–12,000	Flaked bones; Clovis point; 7 lithic flakes
Boaz, WV (7)	mammoth	13,510	Broken bones
Fenske, WI (8)	mammoth	13,470	Butcher marks
Mud Lake, WI (9)	mammoth	13,440	Butcher marks
Lamb Spring, CO (10)	mammoth	13,000–11,000	Flaked bones
Pleasant Lake, MI (11)	mastodont	12,845; 10,395	Butcher marks; cut and burned bones; bone tools
Owl Cave, ID (12)	mammoth	12,800–10,920	Flaked bones
Monte Verde, Chile (13)	mastodont	12,500	Flaked bones; bone tools; burned bones
Duewall-Newberry, TX (14)	mammoth	12,000–10,000	Flaked bones
Tocuila, Mexico (15)	mammoth	11,200	Flaked bones
Lange-Ferguson, SD (16)	mammoth	11,140	Flaked bones
Hiscock, NY (17)	mastodont	11,390–9,150	4 percent of broken bones are tools?

References
1 Bonnichsen 1979; Irving, Jopling, and Beebe 1986; Irving, Jopling, and Kritsch-Armstrong 1989; Morlan 1979, 1980, 1986
2 Mehl 1967
3 Anderson 1975
4 G. Haynes 1991
5 Holen 1995, 1999; Holen and Blasing 1991
6 Stanford 1979
7 Palmer and Stoltman 1976
8 Overstreet and Stafford 1997
9 Overstreet, Joyce, Hallin, and Wasion 1993; Overstreet and Stafford 1997
10 Mandryk 1998, 1999; Stanford, Bonnichsen, and Morlan 1981; Rancier, Haynes, and Stanford 1982
11 D. C. Fisher 1996, 1987, 1984a, 1984b
12 Miller 1989; Miller and Dort 1978
13 Dillehay 1997
14 Steele and Carlson 1989
15 Arroyo-C., Gonzalez, Morett A., Polaco, and Sherwood 1999; Morett A., Arroyo-C., and Polaca 1998; Siebe, Schaaf, and Urrutia-Fucugauchi 1999
16 Hannus 1990
17 Laub 1990, 1995, 2000; Laub and Haynes 1998; Laub, Tomenchuk, and Storck 1996; Tomenchuk and Laub 1995

the cylindrical rods found in sites from Washington state to Florida (see Table 3.1) – where is the site-to-site workshop debris that should have been left over from the process? Why aren't there far more broken mammoth and mastodont bones, chopped and sectioned tusks, worked cervid antler, or partially finished implements in the larger Clovis sites?

I offer a three-part answer: First, as mentioned above, the larger Clovis residential sites are generally located in eastern North America where organic preservation has been very poor, except in a few localities such as the underwater sites in Florida; therefore the workshop debris may have long ago decayed away. Second, the sites that do contain some organic materials – such as the mammoth killsites in the western United States – were possibly very short-term occupations where little if any bone-working would have been done. And third, there actually *are* a few possible sites where some deliberate bone-breaking may have been done, such as Lange-Ferguson (SD) and Tocuila (Mexico).

In the next section I turn attention to these Clovis-age sites, after first clarifying my theoretical and paradigmatic views of archeological interpretation. Then I go on to consider the pre-Clovis sites containing broken megamammal bones that have been interpreted as evidence of a bone-flaking industry (Table 3.3).

3.3   Clovis-era megamammal bone-breakage

Three Clovis-era sites contain broken limb-bones with the rest of the mammoth skeletons – Lange-Ferguson (SD), Tocuila (Mexico), and Duewall-Newberry (TX). Only one of these three sites – Lange-Ferguson – also contained lithic artifacts, which included Clovis points. Another site with a broken-bone assemblage that may or may not be from the Clovis era is Owl Cave in Idaho, but the mammoth-level lithics are much more Folsom-like than Clovis, and the dating also suggests a post-Clovis age for the earliest human occupation of the site (see chapter 2).

Before I interpret these sites, and then others from pre-Clovis contexts, I provide my views here on the process of interpreting ambiguous archeological specimens.

REPLICATION IN SCIENCE

The word "replication" has three different definitions in archeology. The most common use of the word is the experimental process of making copies of artifacts, features, or other prehistoric items, in order to understand the manufacturing process or the object's possible uses. A second definition is the discovery of sites, artifacts, or assemblages that are similar to other finds. Many archeologists prefer to know that there is more than one example of an object or special site before accepting the reality of the first find.

In this book, I use a third definition of the word – it is *the necessary agreement among different researchers studying the* **same** *site, assemblage, or artifact.* If a site, assemblage, or artifact is interpreted completely differently by different prehistorians, then the disagreeing archeologists have not replicated the data's possible meaning. If different observers do not agree on the interpretation of a pre-Clovis site's stone inventory or modified mammal bones, they certainly will not be able to agree on the possible human behaviors those sorts of items could indicate.

As a specific example, one pit in the Calico site in southern California has yielded over 800 examples of stone "tools" and flakes (Budinger 1999, 2000; Leakey, Simpson, and Clements 1968; Patterson 1999; Simpson, Patterson, and Singer 1986), while the entire site is said to have over 11,000 artifacts in it. The interpretation that these items are tools – scrapers, denticulates, gravers, burins, choppers, etc. – is based on the specimen sizes and shapes, and the presence of certain features such as bulbs of percussion. Yet the startlingly early date on the enclosing sediments – over 150,000 years – plus the occurrence of these items in an alluvial fan containing massive amounts of gravels, and the local nature of the chalcedony which makes up most of the "tools," lead some archeologists to disagree that the specimens are artifacts and to judge them nonculturally produced during the buildup of the fan (C. V. Haynes 1973). Minshall (1989) claimed that the "best" pieces in Calico's lithic assemblage were once "finally accepted as manmade" when shown to professional archeologists at the 1985 annual meeting of the Society for American Archaeology in Denver. Yet Calico is not a site in the mainstream of American archeological belief, and only a minority of professionals accept the assemblage as legitimate artifacts.

Perhaps selective sampling (suggested by Dixon 1999, but disputed by Patterson 1999) has given the impression the Calico site yields numerous unambiguous tools, when in fact it may contain a much wider range and variability of modified specimens that when seen together do not look so much like an artifact assemblage.

What is missing from the Calico case is a frame of reference that all archeologists share. The specific ranges of platform angles, flake scar patterns, and other features on flaked-stone objects that unequivocally define humanly made artifacts are not based on lawlike generalizations. Nature too creates these features from time to time. So the recording of angles and scars on broken cobbles does not directly translate into interpretations of human behavior. Different observers of the identical data will not produce reports and interpretations that are superimposable.

Some disagreement over the finer points of archeological meaning is probably inevitable, especially because much of archeological evidence is by nature relatively ambiguous; artifact uses in prehistory are not observable and neither is foraging or camping behavior in the past. We can only reconstruct in our minds how people lived, a visualization that may seem to be no better than psychic divining if supporting arguments are neglected.

Archeologists are conditioned to argue with each other – we train for combat. We mistrust unusual experimental results, we scoff at revelation, sacred texts, and arguments from authority; we insist on cross-examining all the evidence (see Yun 1995 and Sokal and Bricmont 1999 for case studies of how actors in scientific debates can disagree on even the basics such as epistemology and methodology). Competing theories exist in almost every aspect of archeology, and the theories may be equally (but equivocally) convincing because they do not have powerful tests. Competition is therefore normal in archeological interpretation. But a disagreement in archeology over whether excavated materials actually qualify to be called evidence is not normal, and indicates that either archeological methods in use are defective or the methods are simply not appropriate to the case at hand. With many archeological examples – such as Calico, perhaps – a cold and objective look at the site and the materials will not necessarily end the debate, because the evidence will always remain ambiguous in the extreme and no universal methods exist to reduce the ambiguity.

An archeological site's excavation is an experiment of sorts, but one in which the years of excavation, cataloguing, interpreting, and publishing cannot be reproduced. If the interpretations are sound, a fresh set of eyes and thoughts – not from a true believer (Simon 1999:129) but from an ethical yet skeptical colleague – should be able to review the data representing the site (Simon 1999:114–16) and come up with a replica of the interpretations.

The critical importance of replication in archeology should be apparent. Without the necessity for replication, clever archeologists could interpret almost anything in stratigraphic context as an artifact having certain specified (but unproven) behavioral implications. Fortunately we do not automatically take each other's word that archeological interpretations are always proven and correct – instead we demand to examine the evidence and appraise the reasoning, and as scientists we are duty-bound to disagree and challenge deficient cases. Educated guesses or unwarranted suspicions must be questioned and those that do not hold up to scrutiny are to be jettisoned. A pronouncement about artifacts or assemblages – even the pronouncements coming from experts – are not the same as scientific *proofs*. If an archeological interpretation is questioned, and the best response to the questioning is: "After doing archaeology for more than 30 years now, I believe that I have managed to learn what is a human artifact" [a verbatim response I once received to a query about a questionable artifact], the time is right to prepare for a fierce – but honorable – scientific battle. The existence (and meaning) of actual artifacts is dependent not on the depth of any archeologist's experience, but upon objective criteria that everyone should be able to evaluate. This is the meaning of "replication."

BROKEN BONES

The Tocuila site, located in Texcoco Municipality, Mexico, contains mostly disarticulated bones of at least seven columbian mammoths, plus a few bones of horse, bison, camel, and rabbits, buried in a mud flow dated between 12,616 rcybp and 10,220 rcybp (Arroyo-C., Gonzalez, Morett A., Polaca, and Sherwood 1999; Morett A., Arroyo-Cabrales, and Polaco 1998; Siebe, Schaaf, and Urrutia-Fucugauchi 1999). No stone tools are associated with the bones, but several mammoth-bone fragments may have been percussion-flaked. Siebe *et al.* (1999) propose that a 14,000-year-old volcanic fallout deposit was captured by water and redeposited or buried the mammoth skeletons around 11,000 rcybp, after the animals were already dead.

A bone fragment that looks like a core with flake scars came from the site. A bone flake can be refitted to the core (Figs. 3.9 and 3.10), leading investigators to wonder if humans of the Clovis era quarried well-preserved limb-bones for toolmaking. No unmistakable cutmarks have been identified on the bones, nor are there any related hearths or any other unambiguous cultural features present in the site.

A second ambiguous site with broken mammoth limb-bones is Duewall-Newberry, located on the Brazos river in southeastern Texas, between Waco and

Fig. 3.9 A mammoth-bone flake with a series of flake-scars – a "core" – from the Tocuila site, Mexico (photographed by G. Haynes at the Instituto Nacional de Antropología e Historia, Mexico City).

Houston (Carlson and Steele 1992; Steele and Carlson 1989). A partial skeleton of an adult mammoth was found at the edge of the riverbank, with the bones resting atop sandy muds and muddy sands of a natural levee that had been buried under clayey silt alluvium. The sedimentary position of the bones led to an age-estimate of 12,000–10,000 (radiocarbon) years, thus placing the site in the Clovis era. No stone tools or debitage were discovered, but the possible presence of humans was suggested by the fact that both humeri and a femur had been fractured, and possible impact points could be seen on them. Steele and Carlson did not think mammoth-trampling broke these bones, since other, less robust elements had survived unbroken. The site's fine-grained sediments indicate a low-energy environment of final deposition, and hence there are no

Fig. 3.10 The Tocuila core with a flake refitted on it (photographed by G. Haynes at the Instituto Nacional de Antropologia e Historia, Mexico City).

obvious indicators of noncultural processes capable of breaking such thick-walled bones. D. G. Steele and Carlson (1989; Carlson and Steele 1992) thought humans piled bones around and below the skull, then deliberately broke the long bones with hard hammers (which were not found at the site), possibly to get at the bone marrow or to produce thick bone fragments to use in tool-making. Quite possibly a naturally defleshed carcass was scavenged by Clovis foragers for the bones or for grease.

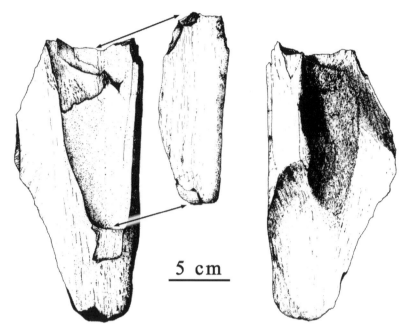

Fig. 3.11 Bone core and refitting flake from the Lange-Ferguson (South Dakota) Clovis site (after a drawing in Hannus 1989).

5 cm

The only known Clovis-era site with Clovis type fluted points together with broken mammoth limb-bones is Lange-Ferguson (SD) (Hannus 1985, 1989, 1990), where remains from an adult and a juvenile mammoth were found 15 m away from three fluted points, all in buried and stratigraphically corresponding contexts. Several mammoth limb-bone elements had been broken and flaked at the site. A scapula fragment was interpreted as a cleaver; four other bone fragments were said to be cores or flakes. One flake could be refit to a core (Fig. 3.11).

The breakage and flaking of the mammoth bones from these three sites appear to have been done when the bones were fresh, and the interpretations of the specimens deem them either tools that were created by people planning to use them in the butchering process, or preforms and preparatory stages in the reduction process of bone fabricates. The specimens described as flaked often show features that appear to be percussion bulbs, hackle lines, and ripple marks, as well as striking platforms and feather terminations (Hannus 1989:figs. 7–20; Miller 1989:figs. 3, 5, 7, 8, and 13; Stanford, Bonnichsen, and Morlan 1981), which are the same features of conchoidal fracturing that flaked-stone specimens possess (see Cotterell and Kamminga 1990). The argument made about the evidence is that because the bone specimens possess the same characteristics seen on humanly flaked stone, they too must have been flaked by human beings when the bones were fresh.

However, I can make another argument about the evidence. Weathered bones do not flake in the same way as do fresh bones, and the flaked fossil bones were indeed in an unweathered state when modified. But what can be questioned is the time when the flaking was done. Quaternary mammalian bones may be preserved extremely well in certain sediments, sometimes for thousands of years, and when struck, bent, or flaked, they may behave as if "fresh" even millennia after the death of the animal. Whenever heavy equipment – such as bulldozers, dragline engines and buckets, tractors, and so forth – pass over sediments, especially wet sediments or peaty deposits enclosing bones, the bones and the sediments are deformed, sometimes severely. In addition, bone surfaces can be gouged, cut, incised, and rubbed by the moving parts of the equipment, sedimentary particles, or other clasts in the enclosing matrix, even while below ground, and the marked bone surfaces very quickly take up coloring or staining from minerals in groundwater and sediments, thus appearing to be ancient marks.

Figure 6.11 in G. Haynes (1991) shows the extreme distortion of subsurface sediments at a late Pleistocene mammoth site in Maryland; the site's stratified and partly waterlogged deposits had been deformed and split apart by heavy construction and landscaping equipment driving over and scraping the ground surface. Mammoth bones – dated to around 20,000 rcybp – in the disturbed part of the site were fragmented as if they were still green and fresh, while bones of the rest of the skeleton 5 m away where the heavy equipment did not pass were found unmodified.

Buried fossil bones in anaerobic sediments can be affected by modern processes in such a way that they appear as if they had been already modified when first deposited. Subsurface probing, repeated surface scraping by heavy equipment, and repeated sediment block movements can bend, deform, and fracture bones embedded in sediments. Bones and tusks when bent too far by these and other kinds of distortions will break apart in chunks, flakes, and spalls, some of which will appear to be percussion-flaked, because they possess features such as one thick end (appearing to be a striking platform) and one thin end (a feather termination), hackle lines on ventral surfaces, ripple marks, and ring-cracking or depression fracturing where solid pressure was applied, either directly, such as when parts of the equipment contacted the bone surfaces, or indirectly, such as when the force of the equipment was applied through intermediate bodies such as other bones, pebbles, fragments of bones, or other clasts in the sediment.

The end-effects of solid-tissue bending failure – deceptively appearing to be the result of percussion-flaking – are much more widely present in fossil assemblages than generally believed, I think. I have written about this process (G. Haynes 1983, 1986, 1988a, 1988b, 1991) and pointed out its inevitable confusion with percussion-flaking, but references in the literature to this work are vanishingly scarce. I resignedly believe that archeological analysts are notoriously unfamiliar with and unheedful of the processes in nature which modify animal bones, and as a result many analyses are little better than drive-by reviews of data. Even worse, some modified-bone analyses are echo-chamber appraisals, where consultants state in their interpretations exactly what they perceive is expected. For these reasons, I spend some time here on the taphonomic issues of bone-breaking, flaking, and cutmarking.

Figures 3.12 and 3.13 show collections of fragments of modern elephant tusks that were broken by bending failure while still in place in live animals; these specimens were all broken by elephants pushing, shoving, and fighting with their tusks. Many of these fragments look like flakes and cores themselves, because they have hackle lines, ripple marks, bulbs of "percussion," and other features thought to be exclusively diagnostic of percussion fracturing. But the specimens in the figures are not percussion-flaked. Well-preserved fossil tusks and bones also would show these same features when subjected to bending failure.

Fig. 3.12 Breakage of modern African elephant tusks, done by the animals fighting over access to water; the mechanical pencil is 13.5 cm long (photographed by G. Haynes in Zimbabwe).

There are some mechanical differences between ivory and bone tissue that may affect how these materials respond to bending stresses. Wet elephant ivory has a lower "bending strength" or toughness than wet bone when subjected to laboratory table testing (Currey 1979; MacGregor 1985), meaning that as a material ivory can absorb less energy than bone before breaking; ivory also is less stiff than bone – that is, it deforms sooner than bone under the same stress. But these differences are not huge, and it is important to remember that laboratory measurements comparing ivory and bone toughness and stiffness were made on tissue-slivers machined to long and thin wafer-like sizes. Complete ivory tusks are solid and usually much thicker than the bone-walls on limb elements, and the fact that they can be broken in nature means that bones too could be broken by natural processes. The features created when ivory breaks by bending are not unique. Bone that is not dry or weathered will break in similar ways when subjected to stress from bending, and will also show hackle lines, ripples, and bulbs.

In addition to the natural processes that can flake bone, there are processes that spirally fracture whole elements. Figures 3.14–3.18 show specimens collected in Zimbabwe during studies of noncultural bone-modifying processes. The specimens were spirally fractured by elephant trampling or traumatic breaks during life. The fracturing of such specimens is of the sort that might be

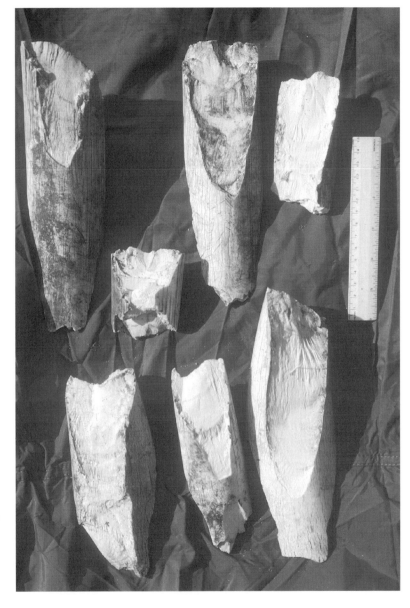

Fig. 3.13 Modern African elephant tusk breakage. Note the features identical to percussion-flaking features, such as hackle lines, negative bulbs, seemingly "prepared" platforms, and ripples; the scale bar is 15 cm long (photographed by G. Haynes in Zimbabwe).

mistakenly interpreted as the result of human actions. Yet this type of modification and the end-effects of bending failure *occur frequently in nature*.

My arguments about the evidence are not claimed here to be conclusive proof that humans never broke any of the fossil mammoth and mastodont specimens. These arguments are worth addressing by analysts who disagree with me. My alternate propositions may be impugned during a new round of argumentation, but if they are accepted, they succeed in producing a reasonable doubt that fossil bones which appear to have been percussion-flaked were not broken by cultural processes.

Fig. 3.14 Spirally fractured elephant femur in Zimbabwe, produced nonculturally; the scale bar is 15 cm long (photographed by G. Haynes in Zimbabwe).

In the next section I advance my argument that bending failure of bones has frequently been misinterpreted as percussion-flaking.

PRE-CLOVIS BONE-FLAKING "TECHNOLOGY"

Pre-Clovis-age broken mammoth bones and tusks from Old Crow, Yukon (Bonnichsen 1979; Irving and Harington 1973; Irving, Jopling, and Beebe 1986; Irving, Jopling, and Kritsch-Armstrong 1989; Morlan 1986, 1980, 1979;

Fig. 3.15 Spirally fractured elephant humerus in Zimbabwe, produced nonculturally (photographed by G. Haynes in Zimbabwe).

Stanford, Bonnichsen, and Morlan 1981) were interpreted as percussion-flaked tools manufactured by pre-Last Glacial Maximum foragers, whose flintknapping knowledge and technology had been conveniently transferred to bone as a raw material because of a scarcity of toolstone or an unfamiliarity with lithic sources in the north. To these archeologists, bone-flaking was a "paralithic technology." Pleistocene-age flaked bones had also appeared in the Old World such as at the Lower Paleolithic sites Torralba and Ambrona, Spain, and several other sites in Italy, and in early Pleistocene levels in Olduvai Gorge loci (Tanzania) (see G. Haynes 1991:236–9 for references). To lend further

Fig. 3.16 Spirally fractured elephant femur in Zimbabwe, produced nonculturally (photographed by G. Haynes in Zimbabwe).

plausibility to the hypothesis that bone can be flaked by people in the same way as stone, Biberson and Aguirre (1965) flaked and trimmed modern elephant bones using percussion-flaking, Bonnichsen (1979) carried out experiments with fresh animal bones, and Stanford, Morlan, and Bonnichsen (1981) experimentally butchered a euthanized zoo elephant named Ginsberg (who, it was widely believed, had once been a star in the John Wayne movie *Hatari*). Notably, Stanford and colleagues produced a valuable and clear record of their experiments, greatly improving the state of knowledge about bone-flaking.

I quote extensively from Stanford and colleagues (1981) on the way to making my counterargument about the fossil bones not being artifacts. Stanford and colleagues described the process of preparing bone for percussion-flaking, and the properties of flaked pieces.

The first step in producing percussion-flaked bone is to fragment a fresh thick-walled element such as a limb-bone. Stanford and colleagues felt that only a hard impactor such as a boulder weighing no less than 9–10 kg must be used to break apart elephant leg-bones; less massive impactors do not produce the fracturing or cracking needed to separate potential bone cores. Even a heavy enough impactor must have a relatively small point of impact that is to be carefully directed onto optimal zones on elephant limb-bones, where fractures can propagate, or otherwise cancellous bone or especially sturdy bone-walls will prevent the successful fragmenting of the element. The impactor must be flung with ample force against the right places on different bones, or else it will bounce off and merely create networks of shallow cracks and faults. Often, the successful fragmentation of elephant bone leaves ring-cracks and intersecting fracture fronts at the point of impact (Fig. 3.19).

Once the element has been fragmented, an appropriate segment of dense bone is then selected for further reduction and the removal of sharp-edged flakes. But before usable flakes can be removed with any degree of control, the selected fragment must be shaped into a workable core. Suitably created bone flakes (Fig. 3.20) are useful cutting implements, but as with flintknapping the working of bone requires technological know-how and care in preparing the raw material.

"Green bone is highly elastic and flexes when impacted" and "green bone fracture patterns are quite variable" (Stanford *et al.* 1981:439). Hence, bone flakes could be wide and short, long and narrow, or scale-like in form. The ideal

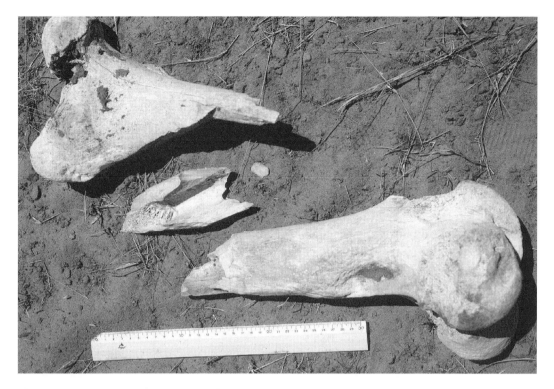

Fig. 3.17 Spirally fractured giraffe femur in Zimbabwe, nonculturally produced; the scale bar is 30 cm long (photographed by G. Haynes in Zimbabwe).

flake would be long enough either to grasp in the hand or to attach to a handle, and one long edge ideally would be sharp along its entire length. The distal terminations on useful bone flakes may be feather, hinge, or step. Tip-shapes on flakes may be pointed or blunt.

"Green bone fracture surfaces are usually quite smooth, and they often form acute and obtuse angles not only with the long axis of the bone, but also with its outer surface" (Stanford *et al.* 1981:439). An acute angle is important between the striking platform and the dorsal face of the core, because it prevents an impactor from slipping off the top of the core at the moment of impact. Small flakes of bone can be removed to prepare the striking platform (Fig. 3.21), producing a negative hinge scar "on the core platform as the fracture front is deflected by the longitudinally oriented collagen fibers" (Stanford *et al.* 1981:439). Platform preparation need not always be done by the percussion removal of scalar flakes along the dorsal surface of the core. "In another platform preparation technique, the platform surface is smashed with the impactor until a suitable acute-angle platform is created" (Stanford *et al.* 1981:439) (Fig 3.22).

To summarize and explain: a bone core readied for flake removal will have an especially prepared striking platform usually with adjacent scalar flake scars on the dorsal surface of the bone fragment's proximal end, and also may show evidence of grinding or crushing of the striking platform. The platform will form an acute angle with the dorsal surface of a bone element used as a core. To maximize flake lengths, the bone core must be prepared with its striking platform set up at a right angle to the bone element's longest collagen fibers, because flake lengths are determined by the fiber orientation; otherwise, flakes directed across the grain of bone fibers will be choppy and short.

Fig. 3.18 Spirally fractured elephant femur showing features similar to percussive ring-cracking; this specimen was broken and modified by elephant-trampling (photographed by G. Haynes in Zimbabwe).

Thus a percussion-flaked bone core (1) will have a crushed/ground/smashed platform end, and/or (2) will show scalar flaking along the dorsal edge of the striking platform, and (3) will have its flake scars oriented along the bone's long axis (or whichever direction the element's longest collagen fibers were oriented). These identifiable features characterize the replicated bone cores and flakes in the Ginsberg experiments (which I examined during the experiments in 1978 and later in the collections of the Smithsonian Institution, courtesy of Dennis Stanford in December 2000). An additional feature present on many bone fragments from the Ginsberg replicative experiment was variable scratching on the outer surfaces of fractured bones, created by the scraping away of periosteal tissue so that fragmented bone pieces would separate, and also so that cortical-bone striking platforms could be directly impacted without the enclosing soft tissue deflecting or absorbing the blow. Both flakes and cores showed this scratching on parts of dorsal surfaces, as did many fragments that had not been

Fig. 3.19 Ring-cracks on cortical bone of a modern African elephant (Ginsberg) experimentally fragmented by a hammerstone and reported by Stanford et al. (1981) (photographed by G. Haynes, from collections of the Anthropology Department, National Museum of Natural History, courtesy of Dennis Stanford).

percussion-flaked after the initial breakage of the elements. It seems reasonable to expect the presence of identical features on fossil specimens interpreted as percussion-flaked.

Stanford and colleagues (1981:439) describe bone flakes as "simple to produce" and "effective butchering tools" but they discovered that such flakes are not successful at cutting through elephant skin, and are not "particularly effective for cutting through thick myelin sheaths that surround muscle" (Stanford et al. 1981:439). Bone flakes worked best on frozen elephant meat during the Ginsberg experiment, since warm meat adhered to bone-tool edges and made them ineffective for cutting. Bone tools were difficult or impossible to resharpen when dulled.

I have not closely examined every fossil megamammal-bone fragment interpreted as percussion-flaked; but the examples I have seen – in person or in photographs – do not display the very specific features that Stanford and colleagues (1981) produced in their replicative experiments. Sometimes authors refer to one or another of these features on flaked proboscidean bones, such as Hannus (1989:fig. 11) and Morlan (1980:plates 4.11 and 4.12) who call attention to "prepared" striking platforms on Clovis and pre-Clovis specimens, but they do not provide itemized descriptions or fine-scale illustrations of the micro-features needed to demonstrate that a platform was indeed deliberately prepared.

One example of flaked mammoth bone comes from the Clovis-era (but lithics-free) Tocuila site (Mexico), mentioned above, which yielded the bone "core" and refittable bone flake in Figure 3.10. When I examined the specimens I found they

Fig. 3.20 Bone flake from the Ginsberg experiments, showing scraping marks on bone surface and flake removal from the proximal end (photographed by G. Haynes, from collections of the Anthropology Department, National Museum of Natural History, courtesy of Dennis Stanford).

did not have the grinding, crushing, or scalar-flaking on the "platform" end of the core – or on the proximal end of the refittable flake – where striking platforms would have been prepared (Fig. 3.23). Bone cores and flakes from Old Crow (Yukon) that I examined in the University of Toronto's collections do not unambiguously or consistently show the features of periosteal removal by scraping or the multiple modifications resulting from actual platform preparation. The illustrations of broken bones from the pre-Clovis La Sena (NE) site (Holen 1995, 1999) do not show evidence of actual platform preparation, or other unambiguous evidence for percussion-flaking described from the Ginsberg experiment. The photographs published of the Owl Cave (ID) mammoth-bone flakes (Miller 1989) do not show scraping marks or platform preparation by smashing or small-flake removal.

The authors of reports about other putatively percussion-flaked megamammal bones have not described or highlighted these sorts of features, which may mean the features do not exist or have been overlooked.

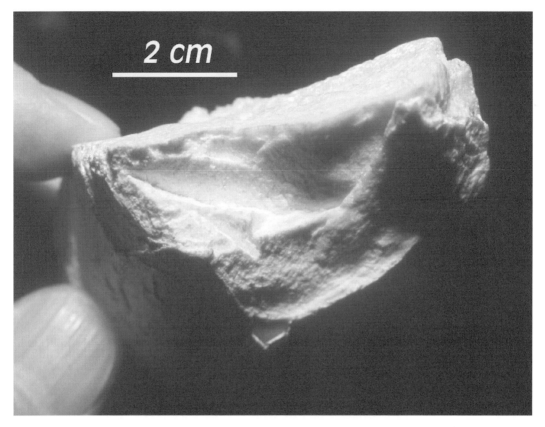

Fig. 3.21 Proximal end (striking platform) of an experimental Ginsberg bone flake, oriented with the dorsal surface towards the bottom of the figure, and showing platform preparation by removal of scalar flakes (photographed by G. Haynes, from collections of the Anthropology Department, National Museum of Natural History, courtesy of Dennis Stanford).

If these fossil specimens were not percussion-flaked – that is to say, if they were not broken originally by human beings wielding heavy impactors, and not deliberately broken up into cores and flakes by technologically savvy bone-knappers trying to prepare striking platforms in certain necessary ways – then *they are not artifacts*. They are "naturefacts" or pieces that look deceptively like artifacts but in fact were produced in nature. They broke most likely by bending failure, either from postdepositional trampling, from loading when buried in sediments that preserved the bones well for millennia, or from deformational forces exerted by another natural agent such as river ice. The forces of compression, tension, and shear produced while bending or point-loading created the specific features – the bulbs and ripple marks and flake morphology – that have been mistaken for evidence of percussion-flaking by human beings.

BONE MARKING ("CUTS," "BUTCHER-MARKS," ETC.)

Surface marking is another category of bone modification that is frequently misinterpreted. Scratches, gashes, nicks, furrows, and incisions are often uncritically called butcher-marks and cutmarks on fossil bone surfaces. Most archeologists believe that there is an ample literature showing how to diagnose the agencies responsible for surface marks; I think there is not. Even if there were better and more comprehensive guides, the fact remains that different agents of bone marking do produce identical end-effects, a condition called "equifinality."

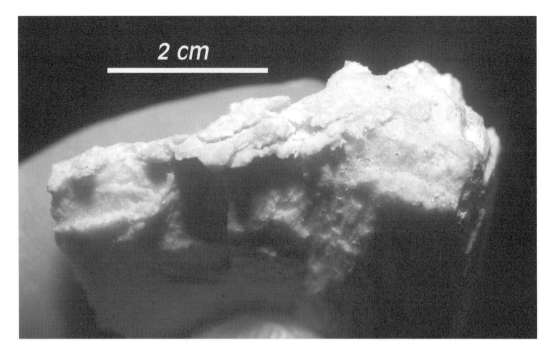

2 cm

Fig. 3.22 Proximal end (striking platform) of an experimental Ginsberg bone flake, oriented the same way as in Figure 3.21, showing an alternate method of platform preparation by percussive crushing; this sort of crushing also may be accomplished through grinding (photographed by G. Haynes, from collections of the Anthropology Department, National Museum of Natural History, courtesy of Dennis Stanford).

In G. Haynes (2000a:267–8) I roughly estimated that even if a very small proportion of Pleistocene megamammal bones were preserved with noncultural modifications identical to cultural modifications such as spiral fracturing and cutmarking, there would still be many such specimens awaiting discovery (and misinterpretation) – anywhere from 16 to 16,000 sites dating 18,000 to 10,000 rcybp in North America.

Replicative studies of elephant-butchering are helpful guides to understanding some butcher-marking on bones. But butchered elephant carcasses will show greatly variable cutmarks and chopping damage. The degree of surface marking depends on the butchers' haste in dismembering or filleting the carcass, the types of tools used in the butchering, and the anatomical knowledge possessed by the butchers. Butchers who use heavy axes to remove meat and to separate bone elements may not flinch from cutting or chopping hard against bone surfaces, thus marking the surfaces deeply and clearly. Steel knives can be re-edged quickly if butchers carry sharpening steels, so if knife edges scrape against hard bone surfaces and lose some of their sharpness, little time is lost in restoring the sharpness or continuing the carcass-processing. Heavy axes do their work adequately even when less than razor sharp, so chopping against bone does not necessarily slow down the butchering process.

Another difference in the degree of bone marking results from a variation in background experience when butchering proboscidean carcasses. Butchers who are not accustomed to processing huge carcasses or who are not fully experienced with the details of skeletal shapes and connections will misjudge where to slice and they will press hard against bone surfaces sometimes, whereas more experienced butchers know how and when to twist or angle their cutting tools and which directions to move the tool in order to avoid damaging tool edges. Hence, inexperienced butchers mark bones much more than do experienced butchers who are concerned with preserving their tool edges.

Fig. 3.23 Proximal end of the Tocuila (Mexico) Clovis-era bone core, oriented with the dorsal surface towards the top of the figure, showing no identifiable evidence of platform preparation by crushing or small-flake removal (photographed by G. Haynes at the Instituto Nacional de Antropología e Historia, Mexico City).

Examples of butcher-marking I would expect to be produced by experienced and efficient butchers who avoid unnecessarily dulling their tools are shown in Figs. 3.24 and 3.25; these examples are direct results of my observation-participation in the butchering of African elephant carcasses in Zimbabwe during the mid-1980s (see G. Haynes 1991:177–91). I was a member of a Zimbabwe government team of hunters, scientists, and laborers which killed and fully butchered over 9,000 elephants in Hwange National Park. As a member of the team, I closely observed the stalking, killing, and the field butchering of over 500 elephants. I also participated directly in the butchering of forty carcasses, and returned to cullsites to look at bones several times after the sites were abandoned. I took many bones away from butchering sites to be cleaned and examined for marks.

Additionally, I observed or participated in the butchering of a series of individual elephants shot as problem animals or to provide meat rations for laborers in Hwange National Park between 1983 and 1999.

The differences between the types of sites – mass kills that were butchered by experts versus single-animal kills butchered by inexperienced people (who were impressively expert at butchering goats and cattle, but not at butchering elephants) – are simple: the expert butchers never left a mark on post-cranial bones that they completely stripped of meat or disarticulated, while the inexpert butchers left occasional chopmarks and cuts on leg bones and other elements.

However, it is conceivable that if the expert butchers ever had cut distractedly against bone when removing masses of meat, their potential cutmarks would have been located on limb elements in very patterned orientations and places. The mapping of such cuts needs to be done while elephant carcasses are still allowed to be butchered in Africa.

Fig. 3.24 A modern elephant femur in Zimbabwe, after removal of muscle meat. The distal end is at the bottom of the figure and the anterior aspect is oriented towards the right. The arrows show the locations and directions of filleting and disarticulation cuts. None of these cuts left marks on the bone surface.

There are no reliable guides to understanding cutmarking of proboscidean bones during butchering. Jones and Vincent (1986:fig. 19.1) illustrated marks on a modern elephant scapula but the text confusingly refers to the marks only when discussing accidental cutmarks made by excavators and "naturally occurring nutrient channels" on bone surfaces (Jones and Vincent 1986:185). E. Johnson (1987:150–2, and fig. 10.2) discusses "actions" taken during mammoth-butchering and bone-processing in the late Pleistocene levels of Lubbock Lake (TX), based on marked and broken bones from the site, but the actions are *ad hoc* accommodations rather than demonstrably useful steps necessary for carcass processing. Many hypothesized actions that would have produced the marks on mammoth bones illustrated from Lubbock Lake are for the most part unnecessary or impractical during meat-removal or carcass-sectioning. Processes other than butchering may better explain the marks. The

Fig. 3.25 Another modern elephant femur, proximal end to the left, showing locations and directions of cuts used to remove muscle meat. None of these cuts left marks on the bone surface.

marks on the fossil specimens could be the result of noncultural processes, such as trample-caused scratching, localized rounding, and fracturing.

Bone-surface marks in locations other than these I illustrate in Figs. 3.24 and 3.25 could conceivably result from butchering, but the actions needed to produce them would not be efficient or even very useful sometimes. Because noncultural trample-marks appear sharply incised and may be oriented preferentially along bone surfaces, as are real butchering marks, the safest interpretations of possible cutmarks will be those that are cautious and guarded. If doubt exists about marks, the interpretation of them as butchering marks really does require a more careful evaluation of their features and their placement.

The oldest possible butcher-marked specimen I know is one rib from the partial skeleton of an adult mammoth (*Mammuthus* cf. *imperator*) found in the Anza-Borrego Desert State Park in extreme southern California. Uranium-thorium dates indicate the bones are older than 300,000 years old; a paleomagnetic date on sediments below the bones shows they are younger than 720,000 years old (Graham 1988; G. J. Miller pers. Comm. 1988; Miller, Remelka, Parks, Stout, and Waters 1991; Minshall 1988). Although Minshall (1988:3) states that four bones from the skeleton had cutmarks on them, Miller and colleagues (1991:5, 27–9; G. J. Miller pers. comm. 1988) mention only a single specimen showing variably shaped marks that appear similar to the kinds of bone-surface damage in noncultural assemblages such as I have collected in North America and Africa. The marks, which were on the skyward surface of the Anza-Borrego rib as it lay in the ground, are said to be the result of chopping against the rib by a *Homo erectus* group which scavenged a recently dead or dying mammoth (Miller and colleagues 1991:33).

A number of Clovis-era and younger mastodont sites in the Great Lakes region have been interpreted as kills made by humans (Fisher 1996, 1999). These sites possess several characteristics in common, including (1) inferred death of individual animals in the fall or winter (as judged on the basis of ivory growth increments), (2) presence of burning, bone-breakage, rounded edges of fragments, and marks on some bones thought to be prying damage and cutmarks (for example, Shipman, Fisher, and Rose 1984), and (3) spatial arrangement of bones in more than one case thought to be the result of underwater caching of body parts and meat held underwater by mastodont gut lengths weighted with rocks.

One example is the Pleasant Lake mastodont in Michigan (Fisher 1984a, 1984b, 1987, 1996, 1999). Wood fragments found within the tusk pulp cavities were radiocarbon-dated to 10,395 ± 100, and wood from just below the bones was dated 12,845 ± 165; Fisher suggested the skeleton's age is closer to the younger assay, too young for Clovis but possibly still within the fluted-point period (which is essentially undated yet in the Great Lakes region). Pleasant Lake contained a partial skeleton of a single mastodont that was apparently healthy before it died in the autumn. The skeleton was in a compact cluster, and most bones were present. Because of the presence of marked and broken bones, the mastodont (and others like it from other sites) is interpreted as killed and butchered by human hunters (Fisher 1996, 1999). In contrast, other mastodont sites such as Johnson and Taylor (both in Michigan), which consisted of isolated skulls from individuals that were growing relatively slowly before death in the winter, are interpreted as scavenged noncultural deaths.

The Heisler (MI) site (Fisher 1987; Hall 2000) has another partial skeleton of a 17-year-old male mastodont thought by D. C. Fisher to have been killed by people, although no lithic artifacts were found with the partly clustered and partly dispersed bones, some of which were gouged and cut. Fisher proposed that parts of its carcass were disassembled but the meat was not removed, then the segments were stored underwater in an open pond to refrigerate and protect the meat from four-legged scavengers. Two small spruce trees were found with their tips down in almost vertical position, like stakes driven into the pond bottom, and pockets of coarse sediments were shaped like proboscidean gut segments that may have been filled with sand and cobbles to anchor the meat cache. Pollen and bacteria were recovered that reasonably could occur in a mastodont's gut.

Fisher experimentally stored a piece of a modern horse carcass underwater, and retrieved it later to eat, lending plausibility to what seems to be a fanciful scenario about mastodont-meat storage. Fisher also tried to add more plausibility by citing an ethnographic report (J. G. Taylor 1969) of caribou-hunters with "similar styles of caching" (Fisher 1987:315), but in truth, as Shott (n.d.) has noted, the ethnographic caches were not underwater and in fact were not all true "caches" – some were dumps which were raided by hungry people, and some were stores used to feed dogs. The underwater caching scenario is questionable.

Fisher identified several mastodont sites in Michigan with the pattern he considered indicative of kill/butchering sites, and other sites with a

noncultural-death pattern (Fisher 1984a, 1984b, 1987, 1996). Not every example
with marked and broken bones was discovered by a dragline or by dredging
operations, but the possibility that recent activities could be responsible for
marking and breaking bones should not be overlooked, because the ponds and
bogs recently drained in the twentieth century also may have been subjected to
attempted draining or probing decades – or a century – earlier, before the bones
finally did come to light. The illustrations (Fisher 1984a:fig. 4c, g) of "cutmarks"
on Pleasant Lake specimens show marks that could be produced by agents other
than stone tools, and the staining in some marks also seems to be a lighter color
than the rest of the bone surface, perhaps indicating recency of the marking. No
amount of microscopic examination of marks will tell us if the cuts are ancient
or recent ones, because marks made by many different cultural and noncultural
agents are indistinguishable.

But let me be of two minds about these sites. The published interpretations of
Pleasant Lake, Heisler, and other mastodont sites in Michigan may be evidence
about Paleoindian subsistence. Because bones are my specialty I am not yet
willing to be convinced that the sites are firm examples of human foraging
behavior. My background has shaped – some might say warped – this cautious
point of view. In the end, however, I acknowledge that these sites should not be
ignored when discussing late Pleistocene foraging.

3.4   Clovis-era artwork, decorative work, "symbolic" objects

Clovis "artwork" of any kind is unusual. The bone and ivory rods (see section 3.2
above) are sometimes marked with geometric designs or zig-zag lines that could
be decorations, ownership marks, or some other kind of symbolic message. Two
relatively thick and wide bi-beveled bone rods from the East Wenatchee Clovis
cache site (WA) are marked with "ramiform" incisions (zipper-like) along their
long axes, also perhaps decorative elements or marks with symbolic import.

Saunders and Daeschler (1994:fig. 9) discovered one possibly decorated
mammoth-bone rib segment in the Blackwater Locality No. 1 (NM) Clovis assemblage; rodent-gnawmarks truncate wavy-line incisions that look bilaterally
symmetrical on this specimen (Fig. 3.26). One hypothesis to account for the
marks is that they may be a distracted excavator's doodlings with a dental pick
or trowel edge, unaware that a bone fragment was emerging from the ground,
after which a rodent briefly gnawed the piece, perhaps overnight before it was
removed from the ground. But Saunders and Daeschler (1994:21) are on to
something much more intriguing when they speak of a "floral or flame motif
[of sinuous and diagonal engravings] that may have been associated with an
applied substance, perhaps hand-transferred body oils" on the fragment, helping to explain why rodents gnawed the piece so much after it was carved by a
Clovis-era hand.

Laub (1995) reported a single small sandstone bead from the Hiscock (NY)
Clovis site. It is not finely made, and by itself speaks very little about adornment.
Small perforated steatite "pendants" from the post-Clovis-age Reagan fluted-
point site (VT) are as suggestive as the lone bead of a prehistoric urge for personal
adornment, but it is still nearly impossible to picture individual Clovis foragers
bedecked with ornaments.

Fig. 3.26 Mammoth rib fragment from Blackwater Locality No. 1 (New Mexico), showing possible artwork truncated by rodent gnawing (photographed by G. Haynes, from collections of the Philadelphia Academy of Sciences, courtesy of Ted Daeschler).

Ritchie and Funk (1973:plate 15; also see Gramly 1992:fig. 53) illustrate a single fist-sized cobble with a ladder-like pattern scratched into it, recovered from the West Athens Hill (NY) Clovis site. Its age and provenience are not clearly known.

Over the last seventy years, the multicomponent Gault site in east-central Texas (Collins 1999d, 2001; Collins, Hester, and Headrick 1992; Collins, Hester, Olmstead, and Headrick 1992; Handbook of Texas Online 1999; Hester, Collins, and Headrick 1992) has yielded several dozen limestone pebbles engraved with gridlike geometric designs, plus one possible animal figure and one plant-like image. As many as fifty-two engraved stones (Fig. 3.27) have come from the site. The limestone is local, as is most of the high-quality chert used for flintknapping at the site. At least twenty-one engraved pebbles from recent excavations near a spring could possibly be from the Clovis era, but other specimens are associated with later components. The evidence may indicate the act of engraving portable pieces of stone originated in the Clovis era and continued through the later Paleoindian and Early Archaic periods, too. Most of the site was destroyed by relic collectors, but it was – and still is – a huge site (perhaps more than 20 acres in extent) with a large inventory of stone artifacts and animal bones. Ongoing excavations may reveal the way the engraved pebbles were created and used. The Clovis levels contain fluted points and a wide variety of other tools, so it may be possible to understand examples of Clovis portable art in the context of camp-life and daily subsistence activities.

Two other sites contained engraved stones, but in Folsom-age deposits – Wilson-Leonard Rockshelter (TX) and Blackwater Draw (NM) (Collins, Hester, and Headrick 1992; Collins, Hester, Olmstead, and Headrick 1991). These and the post-Clovis examples from Gault may indicate that the Clovis-to-Folsom transition was a technological shift but not an ethnic replacement in the region. The descendants of Clovis foragers became Folsom foragers over time, but continued the tradition of carving limestone pebbles and cobbles. Perhaps they also spoke the same (but evolving) language.

The symbolic import of engraved and portable artwork is very difficult to understand clearly, and it is possible to overinterpret and assign far deeper meaning than these pieces may deserve. The fact that the designs were incised

CM

Fig. 3.27 Both sides of two engraved limestone pebble/slabs from the Gault site (Texas) (photographed from casts made by Pete Bostrum, Lithic Casting Lab).

into stone instead of animal bone perhaps indicates a desire that the engraved objects have greater permanency, which in turn may reflect unusually strong human feelings of attachment to the site and landscape. The Gault site is located in a superbly rich locality, with freshwater springs and abundant toolstone, and must have been considered an outstanding place to camp, make and repair stone tools, and forage for plant and animal foods. As well, the possibility of uninterrupted manufacture of the engraved stones from Clovis through later components does seem to suggest social and symbolic continuity over at least 1,000 years in this region.

Mol, Agenbroad, and Mead (1993) propose that pecked figures from rockfaces on the Colorado Plateau in southern Utah are proboscideans, and hence these petroglyphs would date to the Clovis era. One photographed figure (Mol, Agenbroad, and Mead 1993:16) – the so-called Moab mastodon (Anonymous [*Scientific Monthly*] 1935) – could pass for a proboscidean, with an upraised trunk, but it is a very rough likeness and undated. The toes are depicted as separated, unlike the pillar-like feet of proboscideans, and nothing suggesting tusks can be discerned. These petroglyphs, if they actually do represent mammoths, are sketchy and very much unlike the Old World representations of mammoths in Upper Paleolithic sites.

The rough petroglyph is visually comparable to the two "elephant pipes" found in Iowa in the nineteenth century and the big "Elephant Mound" in Wisconsin (Putnam 1886). The clay smoking pipes and the effigy mound certainly look like elephants (or mastodonts), more than any other animal (except possibly non-native anteater), and their prehistoric authenticity seems assured, but disbelievers could point to the lack of tusks in all three effigies. Also, the pipes and the mound clearly date to a late Holocene time period; mastodont bones do not date this young. (Occasionally later Holocene artifacts have been found with mastodont elements, such as the "salt-pan" pottery holding mastodont bones in a Mississippian site in the state of Missouri, interpreted as the remains of either a native ceremony or salt-extraction from the permeated fossil bones [Adams

1941, 1949]). The animals depicted in the Iowa pipes and the Colorado Plateau petroglyphs remain a mystery, unless an imperfect folk-memory of a vanished long-nosed animal survived in midcontinental Native Americans thousands of years after mastodont extinction.

There are no known cave paintings, portable artwork, carved figurines, or petroglyphs that *clearly and unambiguously* portray Clovis-era images. A bison skull at the Cooper (OK) site had a red zig-zag painted on it, but the site contained post-Clovis (specifically, Folsom) artifacts (Bement 1999). Non-representational items are also extremely rare at Clovis sites. Jewelry or items of apparent adornment such as beads are scarce in any Clovis or later Paleoindian assemblages, but a few examples are known, mostly from post-Clovis contexts. In short, what we know of Clovis decoration and design is exceptionally limited. This contrasts markedly with the rich and varied design-world of the Eurasian Upper Paleolithic, where cave paintings are abundantly known, portable artwork such as carved figurines is plentiful, and fancifully and creatively decorated bone/antler/ivory tools abound in all parts of the Old World's northern hemisphere.

Red ochre in the Clovis era is a potentially symbolic material whose use is evident at several sites, especially the biface caches such as Anzick (MT) and Simon (ID) (see chapter 2 above). Anzick contained the bones of two young children, but only one was dated to the Clovis era; this 1–2-year-old's bone fragments were covered in red ochre, as were the lithics, thus closely linking the artifacts and the one set of bones (Owsley and Hunt 2001; Stafford 1999a). Red ochre restores the blush of life to dead faces, and it also may be coloring used in design work on painted clothing or human skin. The symbolism is apparent, and there may have been functional applications of ochre as well, such as colored clays used to bind and attach objects.

The evidence for possible ritual behavior in post-Clovis Paleoindian times is known but scarce. For example, two raven skeletons were probably left deliberately by people at the Charlie Lake Cave site in British Columbia, associated with mammal-bone dates of 10,500 to 9,500 rcybp (Driver 1999). The Caradoc site in southwestern Ontario, dated to almost the same interval, contained the pieces of at least seventy-one broken lithic artifacts lying within a possible structure where they had been "sacrificed" or ritually broken (Deller and Ellis 2001). Both these possible examples are too young to be Clovis, but their existence may imply that earlier cultures such as Clovis also performed sacred rituals or ceremonies from time to time.

4 The Old and New World patterns compared

4.1 Dispersals and diffusions: Old World Upper Paleolithic and New World Clovis

In this section, I briefly describe Upper Paleolithic patterns existing between about 30,000 and 10,000 rcybp in northern Eurasia. Somewhere in the long span of time and list of cultural achievements is the "ancestry" of Clovis adaptations and behavior. The Upper Paleolithic began 40,000–50,000 years ago in Europe, 50,000 years after the first appearance of anatomically modern *Homo sapiens sapiens* in Africa. Throughout the long sequence of Upper Paleolithic technological change, many tool classes remained in use, and some changes in morphology possibly were as much style-related as function-related.

The specific sequences of events region-by-region in Europe are not simple and linear. Culture-historical sequences differ from place to place and time to time. Certain landscapes were abandoned and recolonized more than once; other landscapes such as those around the Mediterranean were almost continuously occupied by Upper Paleolithic people.

The Aurignacian is the first recognizably distinct Upper Paleolithic culture, possibly originating in central Asia (Kozłowski and Otte 2000). The culture is characterized by flake and blade tools with controlled retouch around tool edges, and by limaces, burins, numerous classes of scrapers such as carinated and nosed, and bone points. Aurignacian has traditionally been interpreted as the culture of Cro-Magnon *Homo sapiens sapiens*, possibly overlapping for a time with Mousterian industries before the final disappearance of Neanderthal hominins. During the Aurignacian, blades were apparently made by the hammer-and-punch technique, a major innovation. Tool classes and types changed over time during the millennia that Aurignacian traditions lasted – for example, bone points in the early part of the sequence were conical with split base, while in the later part they tended to have a beveled base (Knecht 1993). The beveling or scarfing was usually deeply scratched in sets of parallel incisions similar to the effects of a wood rasp, in order to increase the friction between the bone point and a connecting spear-shaft or handle. This method has been in use for thousands of years around the world, and is an effective way to put together multi-part tools.

Aurignacian-like industries dominated the archeological record from after 40,000 to 27,000 rcybp in western and southern parts of Europe. The oldest known cave art in western Europe – found at Grotte Chauvet, France (Clotte 1995), and Fumane Cave, Italy (Balter 2000), dating 36,500–32,000 rcybp – was produced by people of the Aurignacian traditions.

During the Last Glacial Maximum, the range of people using Aurignacian technologies and industries shrank back to refugia in the Iberian peninsula and parts of southern Europe. The Aurignacian traditions gave rise in western Europe to the Upper Paleolithic industries called Gravettian and Upper Périgordian between 30,000 and 27,000 rcybp. Gravettian industries of western and central Europe are known especially for abundant burins, endscrapers, backed blade tools such as Gravette points, and carved bone or ivory figurines, among other things.

Archeologists in Europe debate whether the appearance and spread of Gravettian was a human migratory movement or merely the diffusion of ideas and technological changes among pre-existing populations, much as Clovis archeologists still argue over the spread of fluting. In some parts of Europe, such as the middle Danube river subregion, Gravettian culture is said to have originated as early as 30,000 rcybp (Kozłowski 1986, 1990; Otte 1981; Svoboda 1994), pre-dating hypothesized migrations from the Middle East that brought certain genetic markers to Europe's human population (Semino, Passarino, Oefner, Lin, and 13 others 2000). The genetic markers may or may not validly reflect the appearance and movements of archeological cultures such as Gravettian or Aurignacian (see Gibbons 2000). The postulated timing of the proposed population movements is uncertain, and new genetic studies and interpretations undoubtedly will emerge in the future.

The last of the Gravettian coincided with the development of the Solutréan in western Europe. Although regionally differentiated after 20,000 rcybp, the other Upper Paleolithic industries of Europe were nevertheless broadly similar to Gravettian variants in several ways. For example, later Solutréan assemblages in France and Spain began to include shouldered points, which were hallmarks of the Kostenki variant of Gravettian in central and eastern Europe.

HUMAN FORAGING SYSTEMS BEFORE, DURING, AND AFTER THE LGM

The roots of Clovis – like the roots of all other Upper Paleolithic adaptations in the northern hemisphere – go back to Aurignacian industries, but the clearest similarities appear in Eurasia just at and after the Last Glacial Maximum. The Last Glacial Maximum (LGM) in Eurasia dates between 19,500 and 16,100 rcybp (Mix, Bard, and Schneider 2001). The coldest midpoint is usually taken to be 18,000 rcybp. Maps of paleovegetation and biomes that existed during this time interval show a "'glacial' world that differs radically from that of today" (Prentice, Jolly, and BIOME 6000 participants 2000:509), with compressed and fragmented forest zones and "a kind of steppe" where today's forests are located. Tundra greatly expanded, and there was a "long common frontier or intergradation zone" between tundra and steppe, perhaps possessing characteristics of both biomes. Beringia was "unambiguously tundra," but the huge region of central Asia and southern and south-eastern Europe "was clearly steppe" (Edwards, Anderson, Brubaker, and 16 others 2000; Prentice, Jolly, and BIOME 6000 participants 2000:510; Tarasov, Volkova, Webb, Guiot, and 9 others 2000). Therefore, the Upper Paleolithic inhabitants of Europe must have been adapted mainly to steppe conditions around the Last Glacial Maximum, and I would expect their material culture, settlement, subsistence, and social behavior to show specific adjustments to such habitats.

I start my discussion of the later Upper Paleolithic adaptations with the Gravettian and "similar if distinct" (Mussi and Roebroeks 1996:698) variants in Europe. The earliest Gravettian is known from central Europe, and dates to 30,000 rcybp at Willendorf II in Austria (Svoboda 1994:table 1) and Dolní Věstonice I and II in the Czech Republic (Klíma 1963, 1995). The artifact assemblages contain numerous burins – unlike Clovis assemblages later appearing in North America – as well as endscrapers (an ubiquitous Paleolithic implement). The environment was steppe-like with temperate climate at this time (Svoboda 1994). An abundant bone industry marks the following phase 27,000–24,000 rcybp; localized art styles had become recognizably distinct by then. The most striking artwork is seen in the small female figures carved from ivory, bone, stone, and clay. They are often nicknamed "Venus" figurines because of their exaggerated female anatomical features (Leroi-Gourhan 1967:90; Soffer 1989; Soffer and Conkey 1997). Sites containing figurines are distributed from France to Ukraine.

Important sites with information about technology and subsistence during this phase are located in the Czech Republic; these include Dolní Věstonice (Absolon 1945a, 1945b; Klíma 1963, 1995), which contained the bones of at least 150 mammoths, plus signs of shelters made of mammoth bones, wood, rocks, and dirt, plus hearths and thick ashy deposits, more than 2,300 fragments of clay figurines, and a large inventory of lithic and organic artifacts; Pavlov I (Svoboda 1994), with evidence of semi-subterranean dwellings, the use of mammoth bones in dwelling structures, thick ash lenses, over 1,000 fired clay objects, abundant bones of animals hunted for food and fur, decorated bones and antler and ivory objects, and possible boiling pits; and Předmosti (Absolon and Klíma 1977), which is said to have contained the bones of over 1,000 mammoths.

The final phase of Gravettian lasted from 24,000 to 20,000 rcybp and saw the spread of shouldered points; important sites are Moravany in Slovakia (Kozłowski 1998) and Kraków-Spadzista Street in Poland (Escutenair, Kozłowski, Sitlivy, and Sobczyk 1999; Kozłowski, Kubiak, Sachse-Kozłowska, Van Vliet, and Zakrzewska 1974).

The 10,000-year-long span of Gravettian and Gravettian-like industries (also called Pavlovian and Kostenkian in different subregions) left a rich archeological record – both large and small sites, some with enormous mammoth-bone dwellings, and splendid artwork such as the beautiful little pieces of carved ivory and bone, some representing dynamic animal figures (see Fig. 3.8) and some depicting humans, notably the diverse figures of women and a striking statuette of a lion-headed man (Wehrberger 1994).

But the environmental and social conditions of this time are not as well known as they should be. It used to be assumed that this was a period of deteriorating climates as the Last Glacial Maximum approached, and that "the rich and varied artistic production . . . and the appearance of large settlements (Dolní Věstonice, Kostienki [sic – a spelling variant of Kostenki]) . . . [were] ultimately triggered by the need to cope with climatic stress" (Mussi and Roebroeks 1996:697). Yet recent studies now indicate that while the climate was relatively cold and landscapes were open or steppelike (where today there are forests), no arresting or rapid ecological changes were occurring. Climates had begun cooling and drying much earlier, and in parts of Europe such as Spain the climate from 30,000 to 20,000 rcybp was actually warmer than it had been earlier. Ecological change was "miminal" in the north (Mussi and Roebroeks 1996:698). The Last Glacial Maximum therefore seems to have abruptly begun around 22,000 rcybp, and was not the culmination of a long, slow icing up.

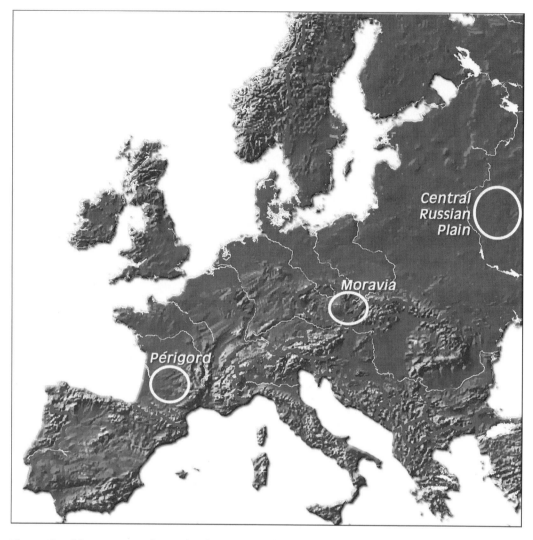

Fig. 4.1 Possible centers of human population and cultural developments in Europe during and just after the Last Glacial Maximum.

The productive steppes of Europe were not uniformly occupied by human groups – large sections of the Iberian peninsula, Italy, Greece, and the north-western region were nearly empty of the human presence. In western Europe, sites were distributed in "nodes of concentration" separated by large, empty or near-empty zones (Bocquet-Appel and Demars 2000). The French Périgordian region, Moravia in the Czech Republic, and the central Russian Plain were the evident centers of human activity (Fig. 4.1). Site densities overall throughout Europe seem to be relatively low during this period (Roebroeks, Conard, and van Kofschoten 1992).

Yet people maintained contact over even the empty areas, judging by the distribution of exotic items such as Mediterranean shells found in German archeological sites. Local toolstone – often of very good quality – was not always exclusively preferred for tool-manufacture, and some sites in Moravia, the central Russian Plain, Germany, and France contained items made of materials transported 100 to 300 km from their sources. People dispersing or exploring out of permanent refugia may have made long-distance movements across the emptier zones and repopulated them from time to time. Bocquet-Appel and Demars (2000) suggest the human population of western Europe – stretching from southern France to northern Germany and the British Isles – stood at just 4,000 people during Aurignacian times, rose to 7,700 by the end of the Gravettian, and rose further to 8,900 people by the end of the Last Glacial Maximum, when populations were concentrated in the refugial centers.

The similarity of contemporary industries (Gravettian, Pavlovian, Kostenkian) masks differences that may be expressions of localized style or alternatively may be functional-ecological. The participants in a 1995 workshop on the Paleolithic occupation of Europe called the lithic record from 30,000 to 20,000 rcybp a "big mosaic" (Mussi and Roebroeks 1996:698). In some regions of the continent, certain characteristics of Gravettian seemed to be continuous from the earlier Aurignacian tradition (for example, pendant manufacturing), while other characteristics were distinct (such as choice of raw materials used). "The really new thing from this period" (Mussi and Roebroeks 1996:699) are the huge settlement sites such as Dolní Věstonice and Pavlov, with their tremendous inventories of lithics, bone, ivory, and antler objects, grinding stones, fired-clay figurines, and central hearth features within separate dwellings. The dwellings may not have been occupied all at the same time, and the site sizes may indicate multiple use by smaller groups rather than a single or limited number of large-group occupations.

Soffer and Praslov (1993) discussed the possible similarities and differences between the European Gravettian-like cultures and Clovis in North America. Gravettian people occupied regions where earlier people had lived for millennia, and coexisted with different cultural entities (or "co-traditions"?) in some parts of their range; Clovis people did not invade occupied ranges – they colonized an empty continent, or one where pre-Clovis groups were scattered so sparsely as to be nearly invisible in the archeological record. Both Gravettian and Clovis spread over huge geographic regions, but the arguments still rage about whether the spread was human migration or exchange of ideas among pre-existing populations. Both Gravettian and Clovis people hunted large animals such as mammoths, but researchers disagree over the relative importance of the larger mammals in the diet. The Gravettian faunal record through the continent of Europe seems dominated by reindeer and fur-bearing carnivores (fox, wolf), but mammoth has a commanding presence on faunal lists from numerous larger sites in Moravia, Poland, and the central Russian Plain (see Table 5.7 below); Clovis faunal lists are most often dominated by mammoth, with bison and a few other taxa rarely represented. Clovis colonizers eventually gave rise directly and lineally to regionally distinctive complexes and industries in early Holocene North America; but the Gravettian-like cultural entities of Europe seem to have "dissipated in a time and space transgressive fashion" (Soffer and Praslov 1993:11). Gravettian sites sometimes contain elaborate "facilities," and items of personal adornment are relatively abundant; Clovis sites have yielded no recognizable artwork (although see Saunders and Daeschler 1994 and section 3.2 above on bone technology), but Soffer and Praslov (1993:12) speak of "elaboration" within Clovis culture in the painstaking lithic technology and a few possible burials.

Fig. 4.2 A large biface from the Fenn cache (Wyoming/Utah/Idaho border region) (Frison and Bradley 1999), showing near-parallel *outrepassé* flaking (photographed from a cast made by Pete Bostrum, Lithic Casting Lab).

2 cm

While Gravettian-like cultures were fading away or disappearing, a new complex of industries was surfacing in France, Spain, and Portugal, the Solutréan of 21,000 to 16,500 rcybp (Straus 2000 cites the original sources for these dates and other information about the Solutréan). This tradition was an adaptation to Last Glacial Maximum conditions in a southwestern European refugium whose northern limit was the Loire river valley of France, well south of Paris. The Solutréan era "was a time of inventiveness and ingenuity under environmental and resource stress" (Straus 2000:223). Solutréan art is diverse and more plentiful than often realized; cave art is found in Spain and France, and portable art items such as engraved stone slabs and perforated animal teeth and shells are distributed throughout Spain and Portugal (see Straus 2000:223 for references).

There are limited similarities between Solutréan and Clovis technology. Clovis preforms were thinned by the percussion removal of flakes with isolated and

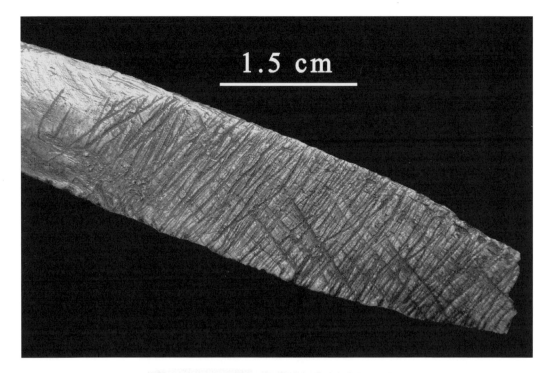

Fig. 4.3 The beveled end of a bone point from Sheriden Cave (Ohio) showing the incised marks commonly found on such ends (photographed from a cast made by Pete Bostrum, Lithic Casting Lab).

well-prepared striking platforms; these flakes often extended most or all the way across a face, and some plunged or overshot to remove the opposite edge (Fig. 4.2). Dennis Stanford and Bruce Bradley (Stanford 1999a) considered overshot-flaking far more often associated with the Solutréan than with any other Upper Paleolithic technology, although Straus (2000:221) disagreed and considered overshot flakes "common whenever facially working techniques were used, as they were in many times and places in the prehistory of the world."

Biface shapes and sizes are also considered by Stanford and Bradley to be very similar among Solutréan, Clovis, and pre-Clovis specimens, the latter represented by bifaces from Meadowcroft Rockshelter (PA) and Cactus Hill (VA) (see Fig. 2.2). But Solutréan bifaces are never fluted, unifacial points are not uncommon, bifacial points come in a wider variety of shapes and sizes, and shouldered and stemmed points may be found together in Solutréan assemblages. This sort of variety and diversity is not seen in Clovis assemblages. Blades and bladelets dominate some Solutréan inventories; blades are not rare but certainly not common in most Clovis sites. Burins are common in Solutréan sites, but rare in Clovis assemblages.

Another similarity Stanford and Bradley have noted between Solutréan and Clovis is in the shapes and design of bone points or foreshafts. Scarfed or beveled ends on pointed bone and ivory pieces, often incised and roughened (Fig. 4.3), are found in both Solutréan and Clovis inventories. However, these particulars of form and design occur throughout all the European Upper Paleolithic and later traditions, and continue into the late Holocene almost around the world. Another Solutréan–Clovis similarity is the use of red ochre, but once again as Straus (2000:222) pointed out red ochre has been used worldwide by modern human foragers long before and after Clovis.

Around 16,500 rcybp in western, southern, and central Europe, a new set of industries appeared and began spreading through regions recovering from the Last Glacial Maximum. This new tradition is called Magdalénian, and wherever found commonly includes such tools as microlithic implements – such as backed bladelets and geometric forms (triangles, semi-lunates, etc.) – as well as numerous burins and bone or antler points, especially barbed points sometimes called harpoons.

The Magdalénian recolonization of Europe was once considered to be a population explosion that moved as a front expanding out of French and Spanish glacial refugia, coinciding with the Bølling warming phase of about 13,000–12,000 rcybp (de Sonneville-Bordes 1974). More recent work views the Magdalénian expansion as beginning earlier, during the Oldest Dryas phase when climates were still markedly continental but pioneer vegetation had appeared in the northern reaches of Europe. Now the human recolonization process is believed to have proceeded more slowly, in stages of exploratory foraging, abandonment, and return over the course of several centuries. Still, the Magdalénian must be seen as a "lasting re-settlement" following after the Last Glacial Maximum (Vencl 1999:290, referring to the Czech Republic), whose developing adjustments and false starts were parts of an inevitable process of landscape filling.

In the far peripheries of western and northern Europe – Britain, the Netherlands, northern Germany, Belgium, Scandinavia – the Magdalénian settlement (called Creswellian in Great Britain and Hamburgian on the continent) was possibly in two stages (Housley, Gamble, Street, and Pettitt 1997). The first stage in Britain may have been no more than an extension of the annual rounds of a few groups of southern hunter-gatherers, and may have lasted only about 500 years – a "short-lived pulse of activity" (Barton 1999:83) consisting of infrequent seasonal visits to new ranges in the north, perhaps to find high-quality flint sources or to hunt (Rensink 1999:98). The timing and sociocultural details of this widespread and brief pulse of dispersal are ambiguous, because the dates fall in a radiocarbon plateau that deceptively widens what could be a narrower span of time (Barton 1999; Burdukiewicz 1999). Scattered, small sites spread over a wide geographic area and the scarcity of coincidental radiometric dates characterize much of the periphery during the earliest Magdalénian phase. High-quality flint seems to have been moved long distances, as it had been in the earlier Gravettian phase, also implying temporary visits from far away. Few if any sites seem to be occupied year-round in this initial phase. No artwork dating to this phase can be found in many regions. Large lithic assemblages are uncommon to nonexistent, dwellings with prepared hearths are rare, and all signs point to very mobile and transient foraging groups. In many ways the phase is similar to the Clovis era in North America.

Pioneer Magdalénian hunter-gatherers may have travelled up river valleys and along ocean coasts to move north, sometimes sticking to the now-submerged continental shelf. The first visits may have been summer treks from distant home ranges to gather toolstone; later visits may have been group relocations into the new ranges (see Straus and Otte 1995). An alternate interpretation is that first visits were seasonal hunting expeditions after reindeer; later and longer visits took place after other resources had become rich enough to support year-round foraging (Bratlund 1996; Housley, Gamble, Steet, and Pettitt 1997).

In central and eastern Europe, Gravettian traditions diverged into Mag-dalénian in the west and into Epigravettian in the east; both traditions appear to have expanded northward after post-glacial warming began (Kobusiewicz and Kozłowski 1999a, 1999b). The first settlements were not as small, scattered, or ephemeral as those in the north, and they date earlier (up to 16,000 rcybp). Intermittent return to cold and drier conditions interrupted human occupational histories in many regions, and glaciated landscapes such as northern Poland had to wait until the early Bølling for their first colonists, so the sequence of ex-ploration, colonization, abandonment, and recolonization differs from place to place in northern Europe. Between 16,000 and 10,000 rcybp, some regions and individual sites were repeatedly abandoned and reoccupied by groups carrying different technologies and distinctive tool styles (Kabaciński, Bratlund, Kubiak, Makowiecki, Schild, and Tobolski 1999; Kobusiewicz 1999); yet evidence also exists that some regions were never fully abandoned during the cold periods such as the Younger Dryas (Dolukhanov 1997; Larsson 1999; Otte 1999).

COLONIZATION, ABANDONMENT, AND RECOLONIZATION IN THE UPPER PALEOLITHIC

A fairly extensive literature continues to grow about the Upper Paleolithic set-tlement, abandonment, and resettlement of northern Europe during the Last Glacial Maximum and afterwards (see Kobusiewicz and Kozłowski 1999a, for example). Some patterns emerging from the studies may be worthwhile seeking in the evidence about the peopling of the Americas.

Jochim, Herhahn, and Starr (1999) examined the causes and context of Magdalénian expansion into southern Germany, and some of their talking points are relevant to the Clovis case. Following Clark (1994) and Anthony (1997, 1990), Jochim and co-authors (1999) suggested some biotic factors may have "pushed" foragers to disperse away from old ranges – such as limited range size, perhaps contributing to "crowding," as well as declining faunal diversity – and they also suggested factors that "pulled" foragers into new ranges – such as improve-ments in climate and habitats outside the refugia. Support for the idea that the refugia were no longer adequate can be found in paleoenviromental data – for example, reindeer body size was reduced, reflecting poorer forage – and also in archeological data (see Jochim, Herhahn, and Starr 1999 for original citation references). Technological innovations, such as the spearthrower in-troduced during the Solutréan and the bow-and-arrow introduced during the Magdalénian, and changes in settlement patterning, may indicate "considerable dynamic adjustments to varying environmental and demographic conditions" (Jochim, Herhahn, and Starr 1999:133). The almost explosive flourishing of cave art during the Solutréan and early Magdalénian "may reflect increasing territo-riality and ritual mediation as responses to the social problems of demographic circumscription" in Late Glacial refugia (Jochim, Herhahn, and Starr 1999:133).

A possible factor influencing the almost irrepressible impulse of Magdalénian dispersal may have been the distances that foraging groups had to travel. Widely separated forager groups must maintain social contact to find mates and stay so-cially attached, and this may involve extremely long-distance and costly outings. During the period of post-glacial dispersal, open networks of mating (Wobst 1974) and exchange would have been effective not only for keeping peripheral groups in touch with sources and centers of culture, but also for encouraging exploration beyond the periphery.

Jochim and colleagues (1999:134) describe the Magdalénian spread as a "streamlike, leapfrog pattern of movement" by very dispersed groups which occupied specific, preferred habitats but left certain parts of ranges empty. As will be discussed in chapter 6, this description fits well for Clovis dispersal, which can be called linear, streamlike, telegraph, or leapfrog – all of which mean that dispersing groups did not move in a wavelike diffusion front across the landscape, but traveled intelligently to find specific goals such as toolstone sources, water, megamammal refugia, or other objectives.

Clovis dispersal was a process probably very similar to the spread of Magdalénian. Certain Clovis sites were merely one-time visits by nonresident foragers out on an annual round to hunt megamammals or explore for toolstone in one season; other sites were multiple-visit loci used by regionally resident populations beginning to settle into new ranges. I return to these topics in chapter 6.

4.2   The American Upper Paleolithic

Clovis is the American Upper Paleolithic, but its artifact diversity and richness are modest and newborn when compared to the fullness of Europe's late Pleistocene record. Many traits are similar between the technologies of the late Pleistocene Old and New World, such as the shapes of bone tools, the stone-working strategies, and an apparent reliance on large animals for subsistence. But there are important differences between Clovis and the European culture complexes. The European archeological record spans tens of thousands of years, in a geographic area currently one-and-a-quarter times the size of the forty-eight United States but which would have been much reduced by ice-cover during the late Pleistocene. The Clovis era, in contrast, lasted less than 1,000 years – possibly only a few hundred years. Timespan alone could account for the greater richness and quantities of artifact classes in Europe; but the intensity of site-use also differed. European sites may have been occupied by larger groups and visited much more often than most Clovis sites, with the possible exception of the largest fluted-point sites such as Shoop (PA) and Bull Brook (MA) (possibly also El Bajía, Mexico), each having 20-acre sizes and nonoverlapping loci that suggest synchronized use by multiple family groups.

Clovis sites do not contain the discernible workshop debris from bone- and ivory-working that can be found in large European sites. Clovis sites (with the possible exception of Gault, Texas) do not contain artwork and decorative work that European sites are famous for. Perhaps if Clovis had lasted for a longer time, and site inventories had increased steadily, the assemblages might have included a broader range of tools, artwork, scrap, and other sorts of things that are rare or missing. An alternative reason for the lack of artwork in Clovis is that there was no need for such visual displays of information or social identity.

Clovis lithics are similar to Upper Paleolithic assemblages, with a wide assortment of tool classes, including typical Upper Paleolithic forms such as end-scrapers. However, Clovis is much more a biface-oriented technology than a blade-oriented one, as are many Upper Paleolithic complexes, although this may be only a minor distinction not profoundly important to the original Pleistocene flintknappers who were competent enough working in both modes. Upper Paleolithic flintknappers produced both blade tools and bifacial implements in Europe, and Clovis knappers seem to have been equally adept.

It is worth remembering that the Later Stone Age in Africa, which is technologically parallel to the European Upper Paleolithic and similarly dated, also seems very closely kindred to Clovis. The existence of so many corresponding traits in both hemispheres should bring home the lesson that Clovis is not unilineally derived from a later Paleolithic tradition on any one continent or another – but it is one member of a global family of contemporaries sharing abilities, experiences, and historical traditions.

Figures in the landscape: foraging in the Clovis era

> The more important objections [to the theory] relate to questions on
> which we are confessedly ignorant; nor do we know how ignorant we are.
>
> Darwin 1872

5.1   Introduction

The purpose of this chapter is to discuss three aspects of human behavior
during the Clovis era, namely (1) the environmental and social conditions of
foraging, (2) the foraging strategies available to Clovis people, and (3) the foraging outcomes – specifically megamammal extinction, range exploration, and
population dispersal.

CLOVIS EVIDENCE: NOISE, SIGNAL, AND STOCHASTIC RESONANCE

Before presenting my arguments about Clovis foraging behavior, I introduce
some thoughts about the nature of Clovis-period evidence. I acknowledge that
this evidence – about paleoenvironments, megamammal biology, Clovis subsistence, etc. – at best is incomplete. In fact, the evidence is of a kind that may
be confusing. It is helpful in actualistic field studies to think about bonesite evidence in terms of the concepts "signal" and "noise." The "signal" is the specific
set of material remains that allows us correctly to reconstruct human or animal
behavior. "Noise" is the result of a process or event that alters material remains
or produces its own set of remains that is wrongly interpreted. At a primary level,
the Clovis signal of main interest would therefore be the actual patterning of
landscape use by Clovis foragers, the tool assemblages that reflect technology
and subsistence, and the remains of foods eaten by Clovis people. This primary
signal would allow us to reconstruct a Clovis way of life, so to speak, the Clovis
"culture" itself. Noise at the primary level, or interference with the signal, may
take the form of a complete loss of patterning in sites and assemblages, giving
the appearance of random site placement, random selection of food resources,
and random technological variance. This, a frequent variety of noise, prevents
us from making any generalizing statements about Clovis.

At a secondary level, the Clovis signal may be somewhat "noisy," but still retain
meaning. For example, projectile points left where they had been used, used up,
or imperfectly manufactured, and tool assemblages even if palimpsests may reflect definable tasks and functions, even if they do not tell us clearly about overall
foraging strategies. The remains of food resources tell us something about what
we must presume to be important foods eaten or processed at the sites where
they are found. Reoccupied sites may reflect visits by the same or similar groups,

telling us something about landscape use but not everything. Noise also exists at the secondary level, such as when noncultural patterning obfuscates cultural patterning: erosion may remove stratigraphic contexts; changes in landscapes may remove clues about geomorphic conditions that once existed; changes in food distribution or food resource behavior may make it impossible to reconstruct Clovis hunting tactics. A particularly bad kind of noise is the kind that loses information: for example, subtractive taphonomic processes may completely eliminate all evidence about diet. Constant cultural readaptation may be a form of noise in a way, if each reoccupation of a single site is functionally unrelated to earlier ones. Perhaps the worst noise is the addition of unrelated materials to assemblages left behind by Clovis foragers – such as when streamflow washes bones into sites, or scavenging carnivores carry unrelated bones to camps and killsites.

Stochastic resonance is what happens when noise actually upgrades an otherwise ambiguous signal, or one that cannot be clearly interpreted (see Bulsara and Gammaitoni 1996). The resonance produces evidence that allows a correct reconstruction of past events. A more concrete example may help make these concepts clearer. Imagine a Clovis band with a hunting "rate" of one animal killed per each 5 km of trails within a range. The actual hunting is done by either encounter contact, stalking, or chase, but the overall rate is generally fixed by deliberate decisions made by the foragers. The rate may be increased if desired, wherever the prey base is not being utilized fully. The rate also may be decreased, if desired.

Within the Clovis band's immediate range that is criss-crossed by 75 km of animal paths, migration trails, and other landscape linkages such as natural passes, river valleys, and so forth (these numbers are entirely hypothetical, although not beyond the range of possibilities), there would be a maximum of fifteen carcass sites produced where kills and processing occurred, if the foragers follow the trails sequentially (Fig. 5.1). Note that this is simply a spatial measurement without a temporal dimension – the fifteen kills may be produced in a season, a year, or any other unit of time. However if the Clovis people were hungry or otherwise motivated to hunt more intensively, they may have decided to raise their rate from one kill per 5 km traveled to two per 5 km traveled (Fig. 5.2). With gregarious game this could have been done by killing two animals together or killing twice as often over time. Or, if the food was not patchy, the foragers may have decided to reduce their rate to one per 10 km traveled. The "signal" in this case would be the number of carcasses per kilometer traveled.

Now imagine some noise. The carcasses decay away to leave no remains. The trails disappear, as do the natural features that defined the range boundaries. Other animals also die along the trails, from noncultural causes. Out of the thirty actual killsites left behind by the foragers, only three are preserved, while ten more unrelated skeletons are preserved from the natural deaths along the trails and at water points. Stochastic resonance is occurring in this situation: a very weakened signal about Clovis foraging has now been strengthened by the addition of the natural deaths, and the appearance of Clovis predation on mammoths has been restored to a recognizable pattern.

Let me invent another Clovis scenario, in which a band of foragers kills two mammoths in a two-week period. The foragers eat as much as possible and then leave behind two Clovis points and bone fragments from the mammoth

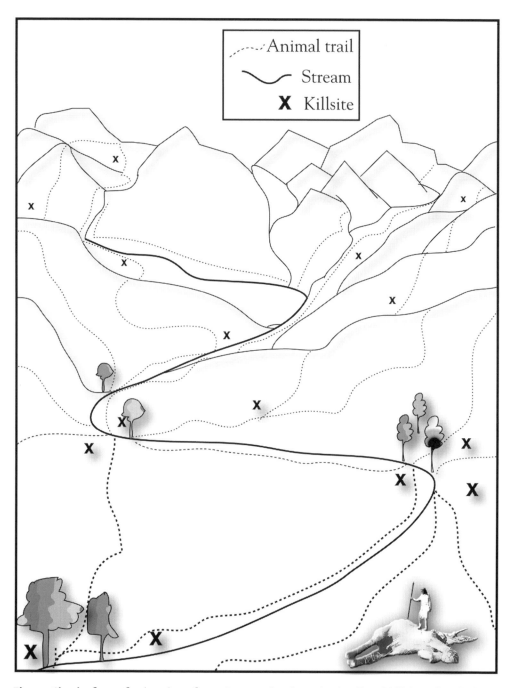

Fig. 5.1 Sketch of part of an imaginary forager's range showing animal trails and killsites when the kill rate is about one kill per 5 km of trail (measured over any appropriate unit of time). There are ~15 kills per 75 km of trails. The small hunter standing on the dead proboscidean is after a photograph by Stuart Marks (1971), used with his permission.

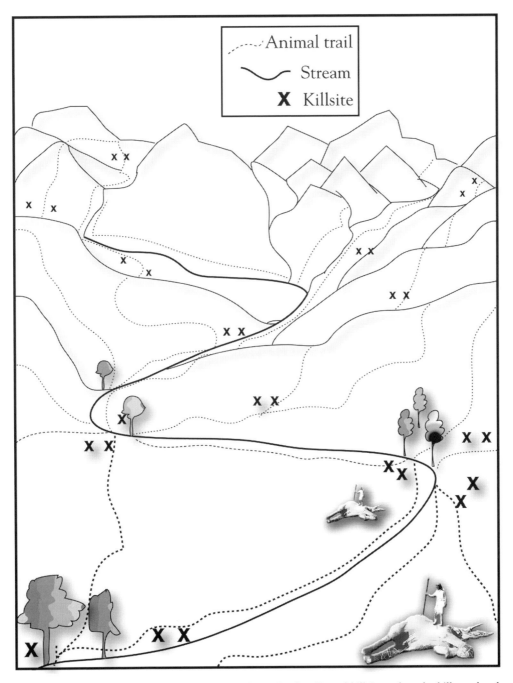

Fig. 5.2 Sketch of the same forager's range showing animal trails and killsites when the kill rate has been increased to about two kills per 5 km of trail. Now there are ∼30 kills per 75 km of trails.

skeleton. Ten years later nine mammoths starve to death in the same place; and a year after that, another Clovis band comes to the same place and over the course of three days kills three mammoths, using three Clovis points. Two months afterwards stream deposits bury about 80 percent of the three speared mammoths and 60 percent of the starved mammoths. The rest of the bones are washed away or weather into unidentifiable splinters. The bones from ten years earlier (the two speared animals) by now have been completely destroyed or removed.

What is the signal here? The bones should ideally tell us that small Clovis bands reoccupied a site and killed mammoths there more than once, butchered the carcasses quickly and wastefully, did not store food, and seldom returned. They also broke up limb bones to manufacture foreshafts and other bone tools. The noise in this case is created by the subtracting of bones, which has removed information about the numbers of mammoths killed. However, the presence of the unrelated noncultural deaths makes the Clovis kill seem to be larger than it actually was. The process of erosion, weathering, trampling, and fluvial subtraction of bone elements may remove other evidence about the kills and the handling of the carcasses; perhaps some bone elements were fragmented by trampling, giving the appearance that Clovis people broke up far more long bones than they actually did. But with the stochastic resonance of this situation, the resulting archeological remains (80 percent of the speared and 60 percent of the starved mammoths) can be interpreted as created by mammoth-hunters who were mobile and who made multi-animal kills. There has been a resonance here between the noncultural and the cultural evidence that allows at least some important events to be reconstructed, which may not be possible otherwise.

Another scenario may illustrate how noise actually overwhelms signal and fools us. Say twenty-five mammoths starved to death at one site; one month later sediments rapidly bury the remains. Three years afterwards, at the end of an erosional period when the articulated mammoth bones are beginning to be naturally uncovered, Clovis people visit the site to eat salad greens, build fires, and roast lizards. Another episode of rapid sedimentation buries the artifacts and features, bedding them in the same sediments the mammoth bones are in, and enclosing everything together in a narrow vertical spread. The resonance in this case produces a site that appears to have been created as a Clovis camp beside poorly used mammoth kills. The true signal – generalist nomadic foragers who ate plants and small creatures – is well hidden.

The lessons I have to offer are derived from studies of natural deathsites in the midst of archeological landscapes (see Conybeare and Haynes 1984; G. Haynes 1980, 1981, 1982, 1983, 1984, 1985, 1986, 1987, 1988a, 1988b, 1989, 1991, 2000a). In other words, these Clovis scenarios are not simply daydreams or groundless cautionary tales. They are based on actual observations of the ways in which bones and artifacts and site features that result from human behavior on three continents are affected by noncultural processes in temperate and tropical regions. One point these stories make is that the signal-to-noise ratio in bonesites need not be perfectly clear, and that archeological interpretations based on apparent spatial associations may be more than a little naïve in the absence of real-world experiences with site-formation processes. Even in the absence of actualistic experiences, perhaps we should think more critically and skeptically all the time, and constantly evaluate signals, noise, and potential resonance that could have shaped archeological sites dating from Clovis times.

There are no commandments to guide such a skeptical analysis. I cannot provide rules for factoring out each site's signal or noise; the actualistic studies described in the literature offer some guides, but they will never answer all the possible questions arising from the study of fossil megamammal sites. What I hope to accomplish here is to point out that Late Pleistocene mammoths were undoubtedly living and dying because of different stresses such as starvation or drought, at the same time as competent big-game hunting people were present in their ranges. Clovis behavioral signals will be overlain by (or themselves will overlay) noise from paleoenvironmental processes affecting the mammoths and the sites, and every site's stochastic events may or may not resonate with either the signal or the noise to create variance in the local evidence. In other words variance is to be expected from site to site, especially in regards to animal bones, and need not exclusively result from simple sequences of foraging events. Clovis hunting behavior in different parts of the United States will probably never be seen as identical or especially similar, and the reasons for the variance may be either cultural or taphonomic.

5.2 Archeological evidence about hunting and gathering in megamammal landscapes

> The buffalo are strange animals; sometimes they are so stupid and infatuated that a man may walk up to them in full sight on the open prairie, and even shoot several of their number before the rest will think it necessary to retreat. At another moment they will be so shy and wary that in order to approach them the utmost skill, experience, and judgment are necessary.
>
> Francis Parkman 1949 [orig. 1847]:309

> These smaller whales [cows and calves] . . . evinced a wondrous fearlessness and confidence, or else a still becharmed panic which it was impossible not to marvel at. Like household dogs they came snuffling around us . . . till it almost seemed some spell had suddenly domesticated them.
>
> Herman Melville 1948 [orig. 1851]:384

CLOVIS FORAGING, DIET, AND ECOLOGICAL "FOOTPRINTS"

Mammoth skeletons co-occur with Clovis tools in several sites in the western United States (see section 2.2), implying that Clovis people ate proboscidean meat. However, many archeologists do not acknowledge that prehistoric people would hunt megamammals for a living. Archeological finds related to diet – such as bones preserved from eaten animals, or identifiable parts preserved from gathered plant foods – should be able to tell us important characteristics of the Clovis way of life. Unfortunately, Clovis sites usually consist of lithic assemblages and little else. Thousands of fluted points have been picked up in the United States (Anderson and Faught 1998b, 2000; Anderson and Gillam 2000), but associations with food remains are exceptionally rare. Nonetheless, archeological interpretations of Clovis diet can be made, based upon the few sites that contain possible foods, as well as upon pollen analyses of sedimentary matrix, paleoenvironmental reconstructions, and comparisons with nearby or similar sites containing evidence about diet.

Caribou were thought to be the main prey of Clovis hunters at the Vail site in Maine (Gramly 1982), yet this is a theory based not upon direct association with caribou bones, but upon guesswork about the site's location on a potential caribou migration route. Steadman, Stafford, and Funk (1997) found the direct evidence very slim that Clovis foragers hunted caribou in the Great Lakes and eastern states (individual sites – namely Dutchess Quarry Cave [NY], Bull Brook [MA], Whipple [NH], Udora [Ontario], and Holcombe [MI] – are reported in Gramly and Funk 1990; Morlan 1991; Spiess, Curran, and Grimes 1985; Spiess and Storck 1990; and Storck 1988, 1990).

Some western Clovis sites contained the bones of large to medium species other than proboscideans, such as *Equus* (horse), *Camelops* (American camel), *Antilocapra* (pronghorn), and *Bison* (bison), or other species such as bear (*Ursus americanus*), tapir (*Tapirus* spp.), and jackrabbit (*Lepus* spp.). In many sites, the species other than mammoth were represented by far fewer bone elements. In addition to the larger mammals, the Clovis sites also contained remains of much smaller animals, such as *Ondatra* (muskrat), *Vulpes* (fox), and a variety of rodents. The small mammals often are considered to be only background bone accumulations at sites where people ate the other, larger animal species. The partial skeletons of larger mammals associated with Clovis lithics are usually thought of as consumed, hence probably hunted by Clovis foragers. Table 5.1 lists the possible faunal food remains from eighteen sites. Some of these remains could be noncultural bones, but their proximity to Clovis tools or features may be evidence that they were part of Clovis diets.

Other archeological evidence can be found to support a model of Clovis big-mammal-hunting (Table 5.2). One line of evidence is organic residue analyses, although these are tricky procedures whose results may or may not be supportable; in some cases species identification remains unproven because lab tests do not reliably discriminate the blood of different taxa, and in other cases postdepositional contamination may give false results (see Eisele, Fowler, Haynes, and Lewis 1995; Fiedel 1996; Hyland, Tersak, Adovasio, and Siegel 1990; Kimura, Brandt, Hardy, and Hauswirth 2001; Loy 1983).

Blood residue analyses of Alaskan fluted points produced possible evidence of mammoths (Dixon 1993; Loy and Dixon 1998), and analyses on the East Wenatchee Clovis cache from Washington state turned up possible evidence for bison, cervid, lagomorph, and human (Gramly 1993). Humans presumably were not on the Clovis menu, and the blood may have been from a flintknapping accident, but the bison, cervid, and lagomorph blood could have come from butchered prey animals. Other studies (Table 5.2) have found possible traces of cervid, bovid, and horse on fluted points.

Remains of foods possibly eaten by Clovis people have been recovered in single site contexts, such as hawthorn plum, grape, hackberry, and blackberry seeds from Shawnee Minisink (PA) (Dent and Kauffman 1985) (Table 5.3). Shawnee Minisink is somewhat noteworthy because the Paleoindian assemblage contained one fluted point and consisted mainly of endscrapers and debitage (McNett 1985) made mostly of local chert, contemporary with a fire-floor area. Perhaps the site functioned differently from other Clovis sites that contain

TABLE 5.1 Sites with possible associations of Clovis artifact(s) and bones of animals other than mammoth or mastodont. (Notes: Some of these sites also contain megamammal bones; "Clovis lithics" refers to assemblages containing both Clovis fluted points and other stone implements.)

SITE (REFERENCE)	CULTURAL ASSOCIATION	TAXA
Aubrey, TX (1)	Clovis lithics	Deer, bison, rabbit, muskrat, fishes, birds, turtles, rodents, ground sloth
Blackwater Locality No. 1, NM (2)	Clovis lithics	Bison, horse, camel, box turtle, carnivores, rodents, plus teeth only of antilocaprid, extinct paleolama, flatheaded peccary
Bull Brook, MA (3)	Clovis lithics	Caribou, beaver
Colby, WY (4)	Clovis lithics	Pronghorn, camel, hare, ass, bison
Escapule, AZ (5)	Clovis points	Horse
Hiscock, NY (6)	Clovis points	Caribou, stag-moose, California condor, pied-billed grebe, small unidentified mammal
Holcombe, MI (7)	Clovis lithics	Caribou
Kimmswick, MO (8)	Clovis lithics	Micromammals (mainly rodents)
Kincaid Shelter, TX (9)	Clovis lithics	Alligator, slider and box turtle, armadillo, badger, raccoon, mice
Lehner, AZ (10)	Clovis lithics	At least 11 taxa, incl. micromammals, and horse (teeth), American camel, bison
Lewisville, TX (11)	1 Clovis point, hearth features	Small mammals, amphibians, reptiles (and reptile eggs), mud-dauber larvae, hackberry seeds – in hearth features
Murray Springs, AZ (12)	Clovis lithics	Numerous taxa, incl. micromammals, and horse (teeth), American camel, bison
Naco, AZ (13)	Clovis points	Bison

TABLE 5.1 *(cont.)*

SITE (REFERENCE)	CULTURAL ASSOCIATION	TAXA
Sandy Ridge, Ontario (14)	[Inferred Gainey/Clovis] lithics (no points)	Calcined cervid bone in possible hearth feature (but AMS date too young)
Shawnee Minisink, PA (15)	1 Clovis point, many scrapers, debitage	Calcined bones of unidentified fish, micromammals, and reptiles
Sheridan Pit (or Cave), OH (16)	Possibly late Clovis or post-Clovis (Holcombe-like point), bone point, lithics	Snapping turtle, caribou, flatheaded peccary, giant beaver, plus microfauna (noncultural?)
Udora, Ontario (17)	Gainey/Clovis lithics, calcined bones (possibly hearth sweepings)	Cervid (including caribou), hare/rabbit, arctic fox
Whipple, NH (18)	Clovis lithics	Caribou

References

1 Ferring 1995
2 Lundelius 1972
3 Spiess, Curran, and Grimes 1985
4 Frison and Todd 1986
5 Saunders n.d.
6 Laub 1994; Steadman 1988
7 Fitting, DeVisscher, and Wahla 1966
8 Graham, Haynes, Johnson, and Kay 1981
9 Collins, Evans, Campbell, Winans, and Mear 1989
10 Saunders n.d.
11 Stanford, Jodry, and Banks 1995, cited in Stanford 1999b
12 C. V. Haynes 1980
13 Haury 1953
14 Jackson 1997
15 Dent and Kauffman 1985
16 Tankersley 1997, 1999; Tankersley and Munson 1999; Redmond and Tankersley 1999
17 Spiess and Storck 1990; Storck 1990
18 Spiess, Curran, and Grimes 1985

more fluted points and knives. It may have been a collecting locality, rather than a knapping workshop, basecamp, or animal killsite. Its evidence possibly reflects elements of Clovis foraging behavior other than the hunting and killing of animals.

Taphonomic processes may account for some site-specific differences in dietary evidence, and distinct localized paleoenvironmental conditions may account for others. The fact that more and more sites seem to yield more and more variation in food remains (or, more often, *no* food remains) has led some archeologists to interpret Clovis subsistence strategy as opportunistic and very unspecialized, including the hunting of smaller game, opportunistic scavenging of larger game, and probably snaring, netting, trapping, and plenty of gathering of plant foods, bird eggs, insects, and whatever else generalists would be capable of harvesting from the wild.

TABLE 5.2 The results of blood residue studies on Clovis tools.

SITE (REFERENCE)	TAXA IDENTIFIED
East Wenatchee (Richey-Roberts), WA (Clovis cache) (1)	Human, bison, bovine, deer, rabbit
Shoop, PA (1 endscraper in Clovis site) (2)	Cervid
Alaskan fluted points (3)	Mammoth
Wally's Beach, Alberta (Clovis points) (4)	Bovid, horse
Martins Creek, OH [Note: not a proven Clovis site; site contains mastodont and deer bones associated with flakes and scrapers] (5)	Elephant and deer
Western Iowa (Northern Loess Hills) Clovis/Gainey point (6)	Cervid

References
1 Gramly 1991, 1993
2 Hyland, Tersak, Adovasio, and Siegel 1990. One endscraper out of forty-five tested had cervid residue
3 Dixon 1993; Loy and Dixon 1998
4 Kooyman, Newman, Cluney, Lobb, Tolman, McNeill, and Hills 2001; Kooyman, Tolman, Hills, and McNeil 2000
5 Brush, Newman, and Smith 1994; Brush and Smith 1994; Brush and Yerkes 1996
6 Molyneaux 2000

TABLE 5.3 Clovis sites that contained plant macrofossils or pollen evidence suggesting plant-food items in the diet.

SITE (REFERENCE)	ASSOCIATION AND DATES	FLORA IDENTIFIED AND PLANT-PART
Shawnee Minisink, PA (1)	1 Clovis point, other lithics, hearth/fire floor, ~10,900 rcybp	76+ botanical specimens, including examples of *Chenopodium*, *Rabus* (blackberry), carbonized *Crataegus* (hawthorne plum) seeds, *Physalis*, *Acalypha*-like, *Vitis* (wild grape) seeds, *Celtis* (hackberry)
One site in Israel River valley, NH (2)	Excavated feature	1 charred water lily seed

References
1 Dent 1985, 1999
2 McWeeney 1999, 2001

No forager refuses unforbidden food, if food is available, of course, but I doubt that Clovis foraging was actually so unfocused or wholly dependent on small food packages. For one thing, some late Pleistocene paleoenvironments may not have provided enough of such table fare; for another, a strategy

TABLE 5.4 Clovis sites with milling stones, roasting pits, or other tools/facilities indicating routine use of nuts, seeds, or other plant foods.

SITE (REFERENCE)	ARTIFACT/FACILITY PRESENT	COMMENTS
Blackwater Locality No. 1, NM (1)	One grinding stone ("small mano")	Used for pounding and reciprocal grinding; not known if used for seed preparation or flintknapping
Debert, Nova Scotia (2)	Possible processing implements: "pulping planes, cleavers"	Suggested use: processing vegetable products for food or fuel
Michaud, ME (3)	Possible processing implements: cobbles	Possibly used for grinding, pounding, plant processing

References
1 Hester 1972:107, 108, 109
2 MacDonald 1968:111, table 15
3 Dincauze 1993a; Spiess and Wilson 1987

of targeting *bigger* game probably would have been optimal at the end of the Pleistocene. I discuss this later at more length.

The archeological evidence about food items other than mammoths is notably scarce, and the stone tools recovered in unquestionable Clovis contexts have been almost exclusively cutting, piercing, and scraping implements rather than plant-processing tools or facilities (Table 5.4), so there is no data-based model of diet, technology, and generalist foraging that can replace the megamammal-hunting model. I suggest the empirical and theoretical evidence be interpreted to mean that extensive and intensive megamammal-hunting in North America was an end-of-the-Pleistocene activity. I also suggest the evidence can be interpreted to mean that megamammals were killed by Pleistocene foragers more often than scavenged after death (see G. Haynes 1991 and 1999 for evaluations of the evidence about human scavenging versus killing of mammoths).

Yesner (1995) pondered the types of archeological evidence that might help distinguish whale and mammoth scavenging from hunting. He suggested sex- and age-profiles in death assemblages would reflect hunting techniques or op- portunism, and carcass-utilization would differ when carnivores – including humans – feed from a scavenged carcass versus a freshly killed one (G. Haynes 1991). But a careful examination of these attributes in bone assemblages may not be enough authoritatively to distinguish hunting from scavenging in all cases, owing to "equifinality," which is the frequent tendency of very different post-mortem agencies to create very similar end-effects in bone assemblages.

Yesner (1995:158–60) suggested two criteria that might help make the dis- tinction between scavengers and killers: with true hunters, butchery sites are located near settlements (because the animals were deliberately sought and killed in these locations), and dedicated hunting gear is present in artifact in- ventories. Yet even these criteria can be ambivalent, as Yesner noted. Settlements may be moved to carcass locations, whether the carcasses were actually killed by people or not; and technological gear may be multipurpose and not exclusively used for hunting or killing.

TABLE 5.5 Comparison of cultural and noncultural elephant-bone accumulations (from G. Haynes 1988a, 1988b, 1999).

	SERIAL DEATHS ONLY			MASS DEATHS ONLY	
VARIABLE EXAMINED	CULTURAL ORIGIN	NONCULTURAL ORIGIN	VARIABLE EXAMINED	CULTURAL ORIGIN	NONCULTURAL ORIGIN
Carnivore use	often light	varies	Carnivore use	light to moderate	light to moderate
Weathering	mixed	mixed	Weathering	mostly similar	mostly similar
Bone representation	selective	nonselective	Bone representation	nonselective	nonselective
Age profile	varies	selective	Age profile	nonselective	selective

Yesner (1995:159) believed that artistic depictions of hunting "are perhaps the *best* criterion for distinguishing hunting from scavenging" [italics in the original], but they are extremely rare in archeological assemblages created by whaling cultures, and do not exist at all in North America's Clovis assemblages.

The specific evidence that I think supports Clovis foragers as megamammal-killers rather than post-mortem scavengers has been put forward elsewhere (G. Haynes 1999). I cannot argue that the evidence is fully conclusive, but the arguments are based on testable hypotheses derived from actual empirical data. Studies of African elephant bonesites in the wild have uncovered important differences between modern bone accumulations that resulted from noncultural death events and bone accumulations resulting from humans killing the animals. Table 5.5 lists very brief descriptions of the characteristics of each kind of bonesite.

A comparison of fossil and modern sites and a supporting review of the descriptive literature led me (G. Haynes 1999) to propose that the largest Clovis-age mammoth sites (such as Lehner and Dent) were short-term kills, and the large mammoth-bonesites in Europe such as Mezin and Mezhirich in Ukraine and Kraków-Spadzista Street in Poland were made from the bones of serial or short-term kills. Note a critical observation from the actualistic studies: *artifacts in bonesites do not necessarily indicate that the bones resulted from humanly made kills.*

Another line of evidence besides the subtle differences in bone assemblages can be found to support the thesis that fluted points were used to kill proboscideans rather than merely cut them open after finding their dead bodies. M. Kay (1996:330) examined two fluted points from the Colby mammoth site in Wyoming and found microwear traces "indicative of use exclusively as projectile points." The microscopic unidirectional impact striae, abrasive microparticles still adhering to surfaces, and the razor-sharp edges attested to one-time use of the two fluted points as projectiles launched into the body of an animal. Two other fluted points from the site showed a more complex functional history, including multiple uses as projectiles and later use as heavy-duty butchering tools (Kay 1996:332).

The archeological record from around 11,000 rcybp in North America is *not ambiguous in indicating that megamammal-hunting was practiced.* An exceptionally high number of mammoth and mastodont killsites in North America is a signal about Clovis foraging that should astonish us with its implications.

MAMMOTH-HUNTERS OR MAMMOTH-SCROUNGERS?

Before discussing the implications of Clovis and megamammal associations in the United States, I discuss further what sorts of evidence are expected at a genuine megamammal killsite, so that the meaning I attach to terms such as killsite, noncultural site, and megamammal-hunting may be made clear, and my reasons for assigning these meanings can be evaluated by other prehistorians. I follow the same lines of reasoning and use the same terminology employed by G. Haynes and Stanford (1984) in their re-examination of possible human hunting of Pleistocene *Camelops* in North America.

The ideal set of standards of acceptability for evidence about human hunting and killing behavior is probably rarely reached, and the actual standards are loosened often to accommodate sites and assemblages that ideally should remain equivocal. G. Haynes and Stanford (1984:217–22) distinguished three levels of evidence about the ways that prehistoric humans interacted with Pleistocene mammals. The first level is the vaguest, and is called *Contemporaneity*. This is a word used in a geologist's sense, meaning the life forms whose remains or residues are preserved at sites were alive in about the same time period, or in the case of bones were deposited at around the same time as co-occurring artifacts were left behind. The word does not mean there is evidence that humans hunted, killed, or butchered the animal, or that there is evidence the animal's bones were used in any way by prehistoric people. Contemporaneity explicitly means that the possibility of sediment mixing has been eliminated, and that artifacts and bones are chronostratigraphically the same age. But no behavioral association is to be implied.

The second level is called *Association*, which means that although prehistoric people may have somehow interacted with an animal's skeleton or single bones, they cannot be shown to have killed or butchered the animal. People may have moved bones into piles, carved them into tools, burned them in fires, or broken them to make useful items. But bones are objects that can be found and utilized by people regardless of whether the people actually killed the animals. When a site's evidence shows some Association, it has moved well beyond Contemporaneity.

The third level, and the one of most interest here, is called *Utilization*, referring to evidence indicating that humans actually killed and butchered animals. Unmistakable artifacts must be clearly associated with bones in one and the same natural stratum; some bones (ideally) would bear cutmarks made in logical positions on bone elements to remove skin and meat or to disarticulate body parts; no contradictions exist in radiometric data or physical studies of the site. To avoid ambiguity, no anomalies should be acceptable, such as the presence of carnivore gnaw-damage seemingly intermixed on bone surfaces with suggested cutmarks, or sedimentary abrasion marks and edge-rounding on specimens that also are thought to show tool-use modifications.

"These definitions are conservative, and . . . [if analysts apply them stringently, they] run the risk of ignoring true archeological specimens" (G. Haynes and Stanford 1984) that cannot manage to meet these requirements; yet I also would argue vigorously that it is an acceptable trade-off in a social science such as archeology to overlook potential data if it means that by so doing we can be sure we are not inventing fictive data.

So what exactly would constitute an indisputable killsite of a mammoth? What sort of site would fit into the level called Utilization, as defined above? An answer is that there seems to be an archeological *template*, or a preconceived image of large-mammal killsites that I think archeologists share – the ideal picture is of one or more animal skeletons, bedded with projectile points (for example, the Danish aurochs figured in Aaris-Sørinsen and Brinch Petersen 1986), perhaps partly sectioned and scattered but retaining some semblance of an actual carcass from an animal that fell down on the spot. A modest number of sharp-edged tools may be bedded with the skeletal parts, and some may show use-wear. Relatively few to no bones may be cutmarked, few to none burnt, and few to none broken by hammerstones. These latter kinds of modifications are thought to occur more often in secondary processing locales or campsites, rather than at actual killsites.

Compare the "killsite" maps and photographs in Hester (1972), Aaris-Sørensen and Brinch Petersen (1986), and MacCalman (1967), for example. Archeological interpretations have converged on a set of characteristics that are to be expected at true killsites. I have seen dozens of modern killsites of African elephants in Zimbabwe, and these skeletal sites also appear much like the ancient sites interpreted as kills. Hence, I argue that the conventional archeological wisdom about what can be interpreted as a killsite is logical and supportable.

Are there any of these kinds of killsites present in North America? A survey of the literature shows that megamammal-bone associations with human behavioral traces can be found in North America, and many of them in fact appear to be true killsites. In spite of the difficulties and risks often envisaged by archeologists imagining the killing of mammoths and mastodonts in the past, prehistoric people did indeed kill these creatures, to judge by the evidence, and furthermore it is not fair to claim the megamammal kills are rare (Meltzer 1993a). The data clearly show how breathtakingly abundant the associations are. Megamammal sites that were likely kills, scavenged carcasses, or other kinds of human–mammoth spatial associations number at least twenty-two in North America (see Table 5.6).

The United States contains more megamammal killsites than there are elephant killsites in all of Africa – a land mass that is much larger than the United States. Not only is Africa much larger, but its hominin presence extends back at least 100 times the chronostratigraphic span of the human presence in North America. Yet there are fewer than a dozen probable killsites, spanning a time range from Plio-Pleistocene to mid-Holocene (see G. Haynes 1991:table 6.1). North America, of course, has far more archeologists on the ground than does Africa, and also has suffered relatively more intense recent landscape modifications, which makes the discovery of sites easier. But nonetheless, the archeological record of mega-mammal killsites from Africa seems unexpectedly very poor by comparison.

The North American artifact-bearing (or likeliest to be cultural) sites are striking also because they cluster in an extremely tight time range – they date to the latest Pleistocene, and most in fact date to within a few centuries of each other or less (see Table 1.1). This makes their abundance all the more extraordinary. The large mammoth-bone sites in northern Eurasia also cluster in time, for the most part, although their dates spread over a wider range than in North America. Table 5.7 lists several sites containing many mammoths, their approximate ages, and the numbers of mammoths represented by bones.

TABLE 5.6 Mammoth and mastodont sites with definite or possible Clovis association. (Note: This is Table 2.3 repeated for convenience.)

SITE (REFERENCE)	TAXON AND MINIMUM NUMBER OF INDIVIDUALS PRESENT	CULTURAL ASSOCIATION AND RADIOCARBON DATE (AVERAGED/UNCALIBRATED)
Blackwater Locality No. 1, NM (1)	mammoth, MNI = 8	Clovis lithics; 11,630–11,040
Burning Tree, OH (2)	mastodont, MNI = 1	No lithics; possibly butcher-marked bones; 11,660; 11,450 (gut contents?)
Coats-Hines, TN (3)	mastodont, MNI = 1	Untypable lithics (flakes, scrapers, biface, gravers); disturbed sediments, wide date range (6,530–27,050)
Colby, WY (4)	mammoth, MNI = 7	Clovis lithics; 11,220; 10,864
Dent, CO (5)	mammoth, MNI = 15	Clovis lithics; 11,200; 10,670–10,980
Domebo, OK (6)	mammoth, MNI = 1	Clovis lithics; ~11,000
Dutton, CO (7)	mammoth, MNI = 1	Clovis lithics; < 11,710
Escapule, AZ (8)	mammoth, MNI = 1	Clovis lithics; no date
Heisler, MI (9)	mastodont, MNI = 1	No lithics, possibly butcher-marked bones; 11,770 ± 110
Hiscock, NY (10)	mastodont, MNI = 9	Clovis points; 9,150 ± 80 to 11,390 ± 80
Kimmswick, MO (11)	mastodont, MNI = 2	Clovis lithics; no date
Lange-Ferguson, ND (12)	mammoth, MNI = 2	Clovis lithics; no direct date
Lehner, AZ (13)	mammoth, MNI = 13	Clovis lithics; 10,900
Leikum, AZ (14)	mammoth, MNI = 2	Clovis lithics; no date
Lubbock Lake, TX (15)	mammoth, MNI = 2(?)	Clovis lithics; 11,100
Miami, TX (16)	mammoth, MNI = 5	Clovis lithics; no date
Murray Springs, AZ (17)	mammoth, MNI = 2	Clovis lithics; 10,900
Naco, AZ (18)	mammoth, MNI = 1	Clovis lithics; no date
Navarette, AZ (19)	mammoth, MNI = 1	Two Clovis points, no date
Pleasant Lake, MI (20)	mastodont, MNI = 1	No lithics, possibly butcher-marked bones; 10,395 ± 100

TABLE 5.6 (cont.)

SITE (REFERENCE)	TAXON AND MINIMUM NUMBER OF INDIVIDUALS PRESENT	CULTURAL ASSOCIATION AND RADIOCARBON DATE (AVERAGED/UNCALIBRATED)
Rawlins, WY (the U.P. mammoth) (21)	mammoth, MNI = 1	Untyped lithics; 11,280
Sloth Hole, Aucilla river, FL (22)	mastodont, MNI = 1+	Fluted-point variants, lithics, bone tools, 33 ivory points; no direct dates

References

1 Hester 1972; Holliday 1997
2 Fisher, Lepper, and Hooge 1994
3 Breitburg, Broster, Reesman, and Strearns 1996
4 Frison and Todd 1986
5 C. V. Haynes 1993; Stafford 1988; Stafford, Hare, Currie, Jull, and Donahue 1991; Wormington 1957
6 Leonhardy 1966
7 Stanford 1979
8 Hemmings and Haynes 1969
9 Fisher 1996
10 Laub 1994
11 Graham, Haynes, Johnson, and Kay 1981
12 Hannus 1985, 1989, 1990
13 Haury, Sayles, and Wasley 1959; C. V. Haynes 1993
14 Saunders n.d.
15 Johnson 1987
16 Sellards 1952; C. V. Haynes 1964
17 C. V. Haynes and Hemmings 1968; C. V. Haynes 1964
18 Haury 1953; C. V. Haynes 1964
19 Saunders n.d.
20 Fisher 1996
21 C. Irwin, Irwin, and Agogino 1962; H. Irwin 1970
22 Hemmings 1999; Webb and Dunbar 1999

TABLE 5.7 A sample of European Upper Paleolithic sites containing large numbers of mammoths, arranged alphabetically. (Sources: Absolon and Klíma 1977; G. Haynes 1991; Soffer 1985; Svoboda 1994; P. Wojtal pers. comm. 2001)

SITE	RADIOCARBON DATES	MINIMUM NUMBER OF MAMMOTHS REPRESENTED BY BONES
Dolní Věstonice, Czech Republic	27,000–24,000	150
Kraków-Spadzista Street, Poland	23,000–21,000	80
Mezhirich, Ukraine	19,000–14,000	149
Mezin, Ukraine	29,000–21,000	116
Předmostí, Czech Republic	~26,000	estimated > 1,000
Yeliseyevichi (also spelled Eliseevichi), Russia	33,000–13,000	60
Yudinova, Russia	15,660–13,650	56

I next address the questions about distinguishing American campsites and killsites, and offer some thoughts about their distribution in the continent.

WHERE ARE THE PLACES THAT CLOVIS-ERA FORAGERS CAMPED OR MADE KILLS IN THE DIFFERENT REGIONS?

Sites that can be solidly interpreted as "camps" – as opposed to killsites, butchering or processing sites, caches, or quarry-related knapping sites – are extremely variable. Under a loose set of interpretive standards, small surface sites with a few artifacts may qualify to be called camps; setting the standards higher will mean that only buried fire-floors surrounded by lithics and bone debris may qualify to be called camps. The ideal Clovis-era campsite would retain evidence of work and sleeping arrangements, consisting of debitage or discarded lithics and organics, plus hearths or fire features with some remains of food and fuel in them.

Any site with an assemblage that comes close to this ideal undoubtedly already has been interpreted as a camp. Debitage piles indicate a nonmobile episode of flintknapping, and if debitage occurs with possible food remains, especially burned bones or plant bits, the site will be considered a "camp," since that designation may refer to anything from a temporary halt to an overnight stop to a multi-night settlement.

Clovis sites that are deposits of separate and nonoverlapping materials may have been created by people camping together but maintaining subgroup separation, such as detached family units; alternatively such deposits may have been created by one group staying in almost the same place several times. I return to this topic later.

Campsite locations may be understandable once they are discovered, but they are very difficult to predict without some outward clue such as artifacts exposed by erosion. The ideal campsite locations of today were not the ideal locations of 11,000 rcybp. Some Clovis-era campsite locations at first glance are not difficult to understand – for example, the Hell'n Moriah Clovis site in Utah (Davis, Hurst, and Westfall 1993), a surface site that yielded 146 lithic artifacts made of (1) four different kinds of chalcedony derived from local nodules, (2) an obsidian found 70 km away, (3) a quartzite found 6 km away, (4) two kinds of local chert, and (5) a clear quartz from 34 km away. Seven broken and unbroken Clovis points, three biface fragments, one sidescraper, one hammerstone, and many biface thinning flakes in the debitage, when taken together, indicate the site was a short-term stop where a mobile foraging group replaced or repaired tools after collecting raw materials possibly while out searching for food.

The Murray Springs (AZ) campsite, in contrast, yielded about 3,000 pieces of debitage, near a multi-bison kill/butchering locus and a mammoth kill. An impact flake from the bison locus refits to a Clovis point from the camp; and an impact flake from the campsite refits to a killsite point. The refits show the camp is intimately related to the killsite. One may wonder if the other Clovis-era megamammal killsites also had associated campsites nearby that were not discovered or that did not survive erosion and the ravages of time.

As with campsites, killsites also defy prediction. Although we may be able to predict where water sources were once located, and where bone preservation may be ideal, and where hunters could have taken advantage of topographic features to launch attacks on megafauna – such as in steep-sided arroyos where the animals' escape would be difficult – we have not been able to pinpoint where the sites actually were created, simply because Clovis hunting was spread so thinly on a huge, nearly empty landcsape. The best we can do is to explain the locations once they have been found through erosion.

I suggest that the ideal places for megamammal-hunting in the American West were upland meadows or stream valleys where streamflow was sluggish, such as near springs emerging from deep aquifers, and mineral accumulation rates were relatively high – attracting megafauna, especially if certain minerals were available in the sediments or groundwater. I return to this topic in much more detail below.

CAN DIFFERENCES IN MEGAFAUNA BEHAVIOR ACCOUNT FOR DIFFERENCES IN CLOVIS ASSOCIATIONS WITH MAMMOTHS OR MASTODONTS FROM REGION TO REGION?

There is ample evidence from North American fossil proboscidean finds that *Mammut* and *Mammuthus* usually segregated in terms of habitat and diet. Thus certain parts of North America must have had much different numbers of mammoths and mastodonts. Dreimanis (1967) proposed that Ontario mastodonts preferred spruce forests or woodlands, especially those with poor drainage. These same habitats yield a much poorer record of mammoths. In Shoshani's (1990) census of *Mammut* finds reported from all of North America, the distribution of the total number of 1,473 individuals clearly shows most sites to be in the eastern United States, with noticeable clustering in the Great Lakes region and Florida. While mammoths also were found in these same subregions, the evidence about the mastodonts shows that the genus *Mammut* without doubt preferred the eastern USA, where wooded habitats were more extensive and thicker than in other parts of the continent. Saunders (1996) described the distribution of *Mammut* as effectively continent-wide, but unmistakably the most dense in the Great Lakes area of the eastern USA. Late Pleistocene mastodonts have been found in New Mexico, Utah, Washington, even Alaska, but at very low fossil frequencies. The implication is that specific kinds of wooded habitats made up the mastodont's preferred range. Johnson and Kost (1988) reported that most mastodonts found in Kansas were from the eastern half of the state, where woods were denser. McAndrews and Jackson (1988) described far more mastodont finds than mammoths in southern Ontario, a mostly wooded part of the province.

The evidence is very strong that mastodonts predominated in woodlands and forests; mammoths, on the other hand, probably survived well in some wooded habitats but preferred the more open grassland or steppe-like regions of North America. Judging from tooth morphology – specifically the enamel configurations – *Mammut* was well adapted to browsing diets, and *Mammuthus* was efficiently adapted to a grazing diet. Based on studies of isotopic bone chemistry,

D. C. Fisher (1996) concluded that *Mammut* had a mixed browsing and grazing diet, but with at least seasonally apparent preferences for browse. Agenbroad (1984) and associates (Agenbroad and Mead 1987; Mead, Agenbroad, Davis, and Martin 1986) analyzed *Mammuthus* habitats and the evidence about diets, such as the study by Davis, Agenbroad, Martin, and Mead (1984), and determined that grasses were the preferred food of mammoths, although browsing also was done.

These and other studies (for example, Drumm 1963; King and Saunders 1984) show that *Mammut* and *Mammuthus* were segregated in terms of preferred habitats and diets, although overlapping ranges were probable in certain regions and at certain times during the late Pleistocene.

Other characteristics of the two proboscidean taxa may have been distinct, as well. Many finds of *Mammut* and *Mammuthus* have been made of single individuals whose bones were discovered in waterlain sediments. It would be useful to determine whether there are relatively more finds of single *Mammut* skeletons than of *Mammuthus*. It also would be useful to determine if the age profiles are different between "typical" mass sites of mastodont and mammoth. The depositional environments also may differ in mammoth and mastodont sites.

If some differences do exist in the proportions of single animals found dead for each genus, compared to the total population of dead animals, what reasons could be found to explain them? Are there ecological and behavioral distinctions between *Mammut* and *Mammuthus* that would have led to different proportions of ages and sexes in mass sites, or different kinds of sites where the deaths occurred? This query leads to a second question whose answer will address the query too.

WHY ARE THERE FEWER KILLSITES OF MASTODONTS IN THE EAST THAN THERE ARE OF MAMMOTHS IN THE WEST?

I think the archeological record will contain as many mastodont kills as there are mammoth kills, but the data from the different regions currently do not support this belief. To help explain the differences in site distribution and visibility, I first address possible behavioral differences between mammoths and mastodonts.

I believe that the social groupings of both *Mammuthus* and *Mammut* were similar. The basic social group was probably mother and young, and individual mothers preferred to associate with other adult females and young in bonded groupings called mixed herds. Sexually mature males did not stay in mixed herds, but instead lived on their own or in fluid-membership male bond groupings (Douglas-Hamilton 1972; McKay 1973; Moss 1982; Sukumar 1989). Sexually active females and males sought each other out for mating, but there was probably little seasonal synchrony of mating activity. The mixed herds and the males in groups or alone were generally segregated throughout the year.

Both taxa would have been water-dependent, although at certain times of the year the available forage would have provided abundant moisture content along with nutrition, allowing longer intervals of time between trips to water. Seasonal feeding preferences and habits would have changed to optimize diets, as is seen with modern Asian and African elephants. During the seasons when moisture was least available in forage and in water sources, members of each taxon would have centered their nomadic feeding movements around water sources. These seasons would have been the times of the year when proboscideans were most vulnerable to human hunting, because feeding and socializing movements were much limited, precise tracking of targeted individuals could be easily done by foraging humans, and the animals themselves would have been continually losing condition and vigor.

I recognize that some differences between mammoth and mastodont sites may be explained by behavioral or ecological distinctions between *Mammuthus* and *Mammut*, but I think the greater explanatory power for the differences of interest to paleoecologists and archeologists is in habitat and environment. The behavioral responses of mammoths and mastodonts to habitat characteristics and climatic change were probably identical, and when bonesites do differ be-tween the genera, the differences may be due more often to water distribution than to taxon-specific behavioral distinctions.

The proportion of single-mastodont bonesites may seem to be large, when compared to mammoths (see Table 5.8), and this difference has led to specula-tion that mastodonts were perhaps solitary animals, or lived in smaller groups than mammoths or the recent elephants. I suggest that the preponderance of single-mastodont sites may be accounted for by the distribution of water sources in the ranges preferred by *Mammut*. Both mammoths and mastodonts were water-dependent, but paleoenvironmental studies show the genera did not uni-formly inhabit ranges with identical water source distributions. In mastodont ranges, water sources were closer together and perhaps less often strictly ephemeral or seasonal than in mammoth ranges, since in general the pre-cipitation totals would have been greater during the year than in mammoth ranges. One predicted result of the denser water distribution (including point sources and ribbon, linear, or streamway sources) is that in mastodont ranges – in general and more often than not – one should relatively often find bones of single individuals. The deaths may have resulted either from normal mor-tality over the range, or from serious and sustained drought. Mammoths, on the other hand, including any of the several species within the genus *Mammuthus*, preferably inhabited grasslands, open woodlands, and steppes, which are habitats that did not have the same dense distribution of water sources. Water-related skeletal sites should frequently contain several mammoth in-dividuals.

The main difference in bonesites is the scarcity of fluted-point associations with mastodonts, when compared to mammoths. Some researchers believe that a relatively large number of mastodont sites do contain evidence of butchering by humans, although stone tools are lacking in the assemblages. These sites are dated to a time interval consistent with the fluted-point cultures in the United States. One possible explanation for the difference in fluted-point associations between *Mammut* and *Mammuthus* may have to do with the distance between water sources in woodland versus grassland or wooded steppe, and with the nomadic movements of mastodonts in their more closed and better-watered habitats versus the movements of mammoths in their drier and more open habitats. If fluted-point-makers were targeting proboscideans to hunt in the Late Glacial interval, the relatively greater distances separating mammoth water sources from feeding patches probably led to widely scattered mammoth killsites in large ranges, although multiple-kill locales should be clustered at the largest and longest-lasting water sources. In mastodont ranges, the kills were more

TABLE 5.8 Comparative sample of North American mammoth and mastodont sites (arranged alphabetically). (Sources: Hay 1923; G. Haynes In press; Osborn 1936, 1942.)

SITE	TAXON	MNI	AGE/SEX	PLACE OF DEATH	DATE ESTIMATE, RANGE, OR MIDPOINT	POSSIBLE ARCHEOLOGICAL EVIDENCE
Alma, MI	mastodont	1	adult female			
Angus, NE	mammoth	1		stream	12,000–10,000?	Fluted point? (maybe not contemp.)
Aurora, IL	mastodont	3		postglacial lake		
Babine Lake, BC	mammoth	1	adult male(?)	pond	34,000	
Bakertown Marsh, MI	mastodont	6		marsh		
Barnhart, MO	mastodont	17	mixed	streamside/slackwater	12,000–10,000	
Big Bone Lick, KY	mastodont	10+	mixed	salt springs/pond	10,600	
Blackwater Draw, NW	mammoth	8+	adults	lake	11,630–11,040	Fluted points and lithics
Boaz, WI	mastodont	1	adult male	bog/marsh	12,000–10,000	Fluted point?
Boaz, WV	mammoth	1			13,510	Broken bones
Boney Spring, MO	mastodont	31	mixed	springfed pond	16,540–13,550	
Burning Tree, OH	mastodont	1	adult male	small lake	11,660; 11,450 (gut contents?)	Butcher-marks; cached bones?
Case High School, WI	mammoth	1		bog/marsh?	13,000–10,000	Butcher-marks
Coats-Hines, TN	mastodont	1		small stream		

Site	Taxon	Count	Age/Sex	Context	Date	Remarks
Colby, WY	mammoth	7	mixed (incl. fetal)	small stream	11,200	Fluted points and lithics
Cole, MI	mastodont	1	adult male(?)			
Cooperton, OK	mammoth	1	young adult male	stream/pond	20,400–17,575	Broken bones; transported boulders
Crappie Hole, NE	mammoth	1+		stream/lake?		Broken bones
Dansville, MI	mastodont	1	young adult female	marsh		Wooden spear
Deerfield, WI	mastodont	3			11,140–9,065	Butcher marks
DeLong, NV	mammoth	3+		stream/lake	16,000–10,000	Fluted, stemmed, square-based points
Dent, CO	mammoth	15	mixed	streamside/ford?	11,200; 10,980–10,670	Clovis points; butcher-marks; season-of-death
Denver, IN	mastodont	1	adult male	bog		
Domebo, OK	mammoth	1	young adult female	slackwater stream/pond?	11,490–10,810	Fluted points and lithics
Dry Gulch, NM	mammoth	1		springfed pond		Transported boulders
Duewall-Newberry, TX	mammoth	1	young adult male	streamside	12,000–10,000	Flaked bones
Elkhart, MI	mastodont	1	young adult male			
Escapule, AZ	mammoth	1	adult male	small stream	12,000–10,000	Fluted points and lithics
Farview, MI	mastodont	1	young adult male			
Fenske, WI	mammoth	1		bog/marsh?	13,470	Butcher marks

TABLE 5.8 (cont.)

SITE	TAXON	MNI	AGE/SEX	PLACE OF DEATH	DATE ESTIMATE, RANGE, OR MIDPOINT	POSSIBLE ARCHEOLOGICAL EVIDENCE
Fulton, IN	mastodont	4	females	stream/floodplain		
Grandville, MI	mastodont	1	adult male			
Grundel, MO	mastodont	1		loess	25,100 (large sigma errors)	Broken bones
Hackettstown, NJ	mastodont	5	4 adults, 1 calf	small "basin"		
Hajny, OK	mammoth	2	adult males	floodplain spring	34,000–21,500 (also 165,000–140,000)	
Haley, IN	mammoth	1			13,850	Broken bones
Hallsville, OH	mastodont	1		kettlehole lake	13,695–12,685	Transported boulders
Hazen, AR	mammoth	1				
Hebior, WI	mammoth	1		pond	12,480; 12,250	Untyped lithics; butcher-marks
Heisler, MI	mastodont	1	adolescent male	pond	11,770	Butcher marks; season-of-death
Hiscock, NY	mastodont	9+	mixed	springfed lake	10,945–9,150	Fluted points, lithics; bead; 4 percent of bones are tools?
Hot Springs, SD	mammoth	50+	males, mixed ages	sinkhole pond	26,000	Flaked bones
Huntington Canyon, UT	mammoth	1	adult male		11,500–9,500	Lithics; cutmarks(?)

Site	Taxon	No.	Age/Sex	Setting	Date	Evidence
Inglewood, MD	mammoth	1	adolescent male	stream/marsh	20,070	Broken bones
Ivory Pond, MS	mastodont	1		bog	11,440; 11,630	Cutmarks; toothmarks
Johnson, MI	mastodont	1	adult male	point bar in stream		
Kimmswick, MO	mastodont	2	mixed	springs/pond/stream	12,000–10,000	Fluted points and lithics
Koehn-Schneider, KS	mammoth	2		slow stream	11,050; 11,170 (overlying sediment)	Butcher-marks; bone distribution
Kuhl, MI	mastodont	1	middle-aged male	pond margin		
La Sena, NE	mammoth	1		loess?	18,000	Flaked bones
Lake Mills, WI	mammoth	1		bog/marsh	9,065	Butcher-marks
Lake Willard, OH	mastodont	1			9,250	
Lamb Spring, CO	mammoth	30+	mixed	spring pond/stream	13,000–11,000	Flaked bones
Lange-Ferguson, SD	mammoth	2	adult and subadult	pond/marsh	11,140	Flaked bones
Latvis/Simpson, FL	mastodont	1		sinkhole in river channel		
Lehner, AZ	mammoth	13	mixed	streamside/pond	11,470–10,620	Fluted points and lithics
Leikum, AZ	mammoth	2		stream	12,000–10,000	Fluted points assoc. with 1
Lindsay, MT	mammoth	1		loess	11,925; 10,980; 10,700; 9,490	Cutmarks; transported rocks; stacking

TABLE 5.8 (cont.)

SITE	TAXON	MNI	AGE/SEX	PLACE OF DEATH	DATE ESTIMATE, RANGE, OR MIDPOINT	POSSIBLE ARCHEOLOGICAL EVIDENCE
Lubbock Lake, TX	mammoth	2	adult and 2 subadults	point bar in stream	11,100	Butcher-marks
Manis, WA	mastodont	2?	old adult male and subadult	stream/pond	12,000; 11,850	Bone point (?) embedded in rib
Marion County, OH	mammoth	1	young adult	lake	10,340	Broken bones
McLean, TX	mammoth	1				Fluted point?
Miami, MO	mastodont	1		loess	35,900; 35,773; 41,700 (TL)	Piled ribs; boiled bone scraps? cut tusks?
Miami, TX	mammoth	5	mixed	pond in loess	12,000–10,000	Fluted points and lithics; cutmarks?
Milwaukee, WI	mastodont	1		bog		
Monte Verde, Chile	mastodont	7	mixed	streamside	12,500	Flaked bones; bone tools; burned bones
Moon, PA	mammoth	1		springfed kettlehole lake	12,210	Netstones; butcher-marks; bone distrib.
Mud Lake, WI	mammoth	1		bog/marsh?	13,440	Butcher-marks
Murray Springs, AZ	mammoth	2	adult females(?)	streamside/pond	11,190–10,710	Fluted points and lithics
Naco, AZ	mammoth	1	adult		12,000–10,000	Fluted points and lithics
New Hudson, MI	mastodont	1	female(?)	point bar in stream		

Site	Taxon	MNI	Age/sex	Environment	Date	Evidence
Noble County, IN	mastodont	3	2 adults, 1 calf			
Oak Creek, NE	mammoth	1				Broken bones
Oakes, WI	mammoth	1		bog/marsh	13,000–10,000	Butcher-marks
Old Crow, Yukon	mammoth	5+	mixed	lake/stream	290,000–13,000	Flaked bones
Orleton Farms, OH	mastodont	1	adult	bog/marsh?		
Owl Cave, ID	mammoth	1+		cave	12,800–10,920	Flaked bones
Owosso, MI	mastodont	1	adult female			
Parker, MI	mastodont	1	adult male			
Petronila Creek, TX	mammoth	1+		sandbar beside slow stream	18,180 (bone); 16,880 (overlying clay)	Cutmarks; flaked mammoth teeth
Pleasant Lake, MI	mastodont	1	middle-aged male	bog/lake	12,845; 10,395	Butcher-marks; cut & burned bones; bone tools
Powers, MI	mastodont	1	adult female			
Quagaman, MI	mastodont	1	adult male			
Rancho La Brea, CA	mammoth	5+	mixed	slow stream/ephemeral ponds	20,000–10,000	
Rappuhn, MI	mastodont	1		bog/pond	9,250	Pole platform? Burnt and cut bones
Rawlins (U.P.), WY	mammoth	1	adult male		11,280	Untyped lithics

TABLE 5.8 (cont.)

SITE	TAXON	MNI	AGE/SEX	PLACE OF DEATH	DATE ESTIMATE, RANGE, OR MIDPOINT	POSSIBLE ARCHEOLOGICAL EVIDENCE
Russell Farm I, MI	mastodont	1	adult male			
Russell Farm II, MI	mastodont	1	female			
Sakstrup, MI	mastodont	1	middle-aged female			
Saltillo, PA	mastodont	1				
Saltville, VA	mastodont	1+		salt spring/stream	13,990	Flaked bones; transported lithics rocks;
Saskatoon, Sask.	mammoth	2	adult and subadult	meltwater stream	35,000+	Broken bones; cutmarks; lithics
Schaeffer, WI	mammoth	1		lakeshore	12,480–10,960	Untyped lithics; butcher-marks; piled bones
Sedalia Swamp, MO	mastodont	8+	"all ages"	spring		
Selby and Dutton, CO	mammoth	2+		pond/loess	16,000–12,000	Flaked bones; 7 tiny lithic flakes
Sheathelm, MI	mastodont	1	young adult female			
Shelton, MI	mastodont	1	adolescent female		12,320; 10,970	
Sloth Hole, FL	mastodont	1		sinkhole in river channel		Ivory "foreshaft"; cut/chopped bone
Springdale, OH	mastodont	1				

Site	Taxon	N	Sex/age	Context	Date	Notes
Stanton County, KS	mastodont	1				
Stolle, NM	mammoth	1				Broken bones
Taylor, MI	mastodont	1	male	pond margin		
Thames river, Ontario	mastodont	1		pond/stream?	12,000–10,000?	Fluted point(?)
Tocuila, Mex.	mammoth	5+		atop volcanic ash, in mudflow	11,188 (5 dates)	Flaked bones
Tolo Lake, ID	mammoth	8+		lakeside		
Trull, TN	mastodont	1		springfed small stream		Tusk billet
Valley of Mexico, Mex.	mammoth	2	adult male (?)	lake	16,000; 11,003; 9,670	El Jobo points
Van Sickle, MI	mastodont	1	adult male	bog margin		
Waco, TX	mammoth	22	mixed	stream	28,000	Age profile
Wakulla Spring, FL	mastodont	3+		karst sinkhole/spring		
Warren, NY	mastodont	1	adult male			
Wattles, MI	mastodont	1	young male			
Whitewillow, IL	mastodont	6		artesian spring/bog		
Winameg, OH	mastodont	1		pond		

closely spaced and selective, since mastodont populations were spread more evenly or distributed more accessibly throughout the woodland habitats.

I restate my propositions: (1) Mammoth and mastodont bonesites do differ in some features. (2) The differences are most apparent in proportions of sites containing single individuals, and proportions of sites showing unambiguous cultural affiliation. Mastodonts appear to have died alone more frequently than did mammoths. Mammoths appear to have been hunted or scavenged by prehistoric people more often than were mastodonts in North America. (3) The possible differences in the proportions of mammoth and mastodont Minimum Number of Individuals (MNI) may be due to differences in the Pleistocene distribution of water (in streams, as point sources such as springs, or in ephemeral ponded sites).

I have not discussed in depth the possible differences in megamammal social behavior or ecology that could explain the taxon-specific proportions of MNI. Instead I have offered what I consider to be a plausible but still hypothetical reason behind some bonesite differences. In the next sections, I return to the behavioral and ecological characteristics of mammoths and mastodonts, and I provide what I hope will be a potentially more satisfying answer to questions about hunting.

5.3   Why hunt megamammals? Why not hunt megamammals?

> The lower animals . . . live in a world without time . . . This is what has made it so simple to shoot down whole herds of buffalo or elephants. The animals don't know that death is happening and continue grazing placidly while others drop alongside them.
>
> Ernest Becker 1973:26–7

INTRODUCTION

Scientific philosophers who do not desire to hunt elephants today, especially if they have no choice except to be armed only with stone-tipped spears, also do not want to imagine Clovis foragers hunting megamammals. The reasons usually advanced for not hunting megamammals are no more decisive than the sentiments that can be advanced in favor of a belief in active megamammal-hunting. Megamammal-hunting, especially mass killing, if it ever existed, surely had to be a cooperative or communal effort, a distinction made by Driver (1995) – "cooperative" refers to hunters (usually all male) acting together, whereas "communal" refers to the involvement of all members of a group or community acting together. The social costs and benefits of organized hunting for huge prey are not self-evident. Driver (1995:26–7, 35) explored the possible ecological conditions under which social hunting may occur, such as low prey diversity, seasonal scarcity of prey, low reliability of alternative food sources, or aggregated prey. In rich environments social hunting would not be common, owing to the high social costs of marshaling labor and the institutionalizing of control. In late Pleistocene North America, prey diversity was relatively high compared to the Holocene in most places, but possibly the isolation and scattered distribution of megafaunal refuges would have created the conditions that made Clovis social hunting a frequent occurrence.

TABLE 5.9 Possible reasons to hunt megamammals.

WHY HUNT MEGAMAMMALS?

1. Nutritional advantages: mammoths and mastodonts are the largest possible fresh-meat source; mammoth meat is storable for future use.

2. Symbolic advantages: even at the expense of biological fitness, Clovis social groups may have acquired some psychocultural sense of well-being or improved social positioning by killing megamammals (see, for example, de Garine 1996 for ethnographic cases of this sort of trade-off).

3. Status-gain advantages: a Clovis individual would have gained some prestige associated with procuring the biggest and most difficult prey species (Jones 1990; also see papers in Wiessner and Schieffenhövell 1996).

4. Social advantages: social solidarity would have been fostered through the cooperative hunting and processing required in megamammal-procurement.

TABLE 5.10 Possible reasons not to hunt megamammals.

WHY NOT HUNT MEGAMAMMALS?

1. Social disadvantages: mammoths and mastodonts were so large that meat would have been wasted, creating social tensions; redistribution would be awkward or impossible, or the social institutions would be too expensive for the organization of the hunt, the kill, and the post-mortem operations such as processing and storage (see Driver 1995).

2. Danger and technological challenges: mammoths and mastodonts were too difficult to kill and process; the skin was too thick, the Clovis weapons were too ineffective (see Frison 1986a or Meltzer and Smith 1986).

3. Search-time costs: mammoths and mastodonts were too rare, hence rarely hunted (Webster and Webster 1984).

4. Advantages in scavenging rather than killing: megamammals did not have to be hunted – they were dying out anyway, and frequently could be found already dead (see G. Haynes 1991).

5. Social taboo: mammoths and mastodonts may have been a proscribed species; modern people often relate mentally to elephants in almost totemic ways, and find them too humanlike to consider hunting (see Kalland 1993; Peterson 1993).

Aside from the obvious benefit of providing protein, fat, and other nutrients, the hunting of mammoths and mastodonts may have had other benefits and costs. In Tables 5.9 and 5.10, I list ideas advanced to explain why the biggest animals would have been hunted, and other ideas advanced to argue against the hunting of megamammals.

Some of these suggested issues can be addressed in future studies. For example, it should be within reach to determine if mammoths and mastodonts were impossible to kill with thrown spears (or arrows propelled from bows of different pulls). In spite of at least four known recent instances when stone-tipped weaponry was thrown, thrust, or jabbed into dead elephants, the definitive study of weapon effectiveness has not yet appeared in the literature (see Frison and

Todd 1986:115–34; Huckell 1979; Laub 1992; Rippeteau 1979; Stanford 1987; Stanford, Bonnichsen, and Morlan 1981). It should also be possible to study the energetics of partitioning and redistribution of megamammal body parts and meat, the nutritional advantages of megamammal meat, the symbolic advantages of proboscidean-hunting, and the social solidarity that big-game procurement may provide to cultural groups (for example, see Marks 1971). Some of the other suggested issues may already be resolved or not worthy of future debate.

The question about whether human foragers ever would wish to hunt megamammals can be answered with opinions, empirical evidence, or theories. Each archeologist has an individual answer. I have phrased the question in a specific way so that I can begin addressing it as rigorously as I can in this book. My version of the question – why would Clovis-point-makers actually kill megamammals and why would they behave as if they preferred this prey category? – can be addressed using actual information and a conscientious application of biological and anthropological theory.

PLEISTOCENE FORAGING CONDITIONS

Right now we may not be able to understand Clovis foraging behavior if we rely only on the published literature to shape our thoughts. The literature is polarized and adversarial. In this section I try to describe the stage upon which Clovis foragers first strode 11,500 rcybp, so that I can model how Clovis-era foraging was adaptive under unique ecological conditions.

HABITATS, PRODUCTIVITY, MOSAICS, "EQUABLE" CLIMATES, NON-ANALOGUE COMMUNITIES

Megafaunal taxa during the Pleistocene seem to have partitioned resources and had specialized (or "stereotyped") diets. For example, Florida mastodonts were primarily browsers, while mammoths were grazers, based on interpretations of geochemistry, isotopic ecology, and tooth morphology (Koch 1998; Koch, Hoppe, and Webb 1998), a conclusion which probably applies to the taxa in all regions (although note that Gobetz and Bozarth 2001 found conflicting evidence in their study of opal phytoliths on the teeth of a very small mastodont sample). Climate change at the end of the Pleistocene would have affected all varieties of vegetational distributions, so it is unclear why animals with different stereotyped diets would have been uniformly affected by the same vegetational changes. Some animals would have felt the stresses of disappearing forage, but others would have been favored by the changes.

Evidence about the nature of Pleistocene vegetational mosaics comes from isotopic studies of bone chemistry (for example, Hoppe, Koch, and Carlson 1995; Hoppe, Koch, Carlson, and Webb 1999; Koch et al. 1998), and may provide essential clues about how forage resources were actually partitioned by megafauna destined to become extinct. Pleistocene biomes were large patches of different vegetational types (such as woody plants, steppic species, or grasses). Koch and associates argued that Pleistocene animals with stereotyped browsing diet (mastodont especially) fed in closed-canopy woodlands and not in low-density trees widely scattered in steppes and grasslands (Koch et al. 1998), as often envisioned in artistic reconstructions. Evidence also exists that animal movements in the Pleistocene can be tracked by trace element analysis of fossil bones (Hoppe *et al.* 1995; Hoppe *et al.* 1999). Some large taxa such as mastodonts and mammoths had nonoverlapping, fixed ranges, up to 100–200 km in diameter, similar to the ranges used by modern African elephants in southern Africa. These data lead to the interpretation that patches in parts of the continental United States were 100–200 km in their maximum dimension – a far cry from the sparsely scattered trees dotting open grassland/shrubland or lining rivers, as Pleistocene mosaics are usually visualized. The large patches of trees or woodland abutted other vegetational types to form Pleistocene mosaic biomes.

After the Last Glacial Maximum, many of the once associated plant and animal species radically and individually rearranged their geographic distributions in response to changing climatic factors. Some species retreated south, some retreated north, and some changed their elevational distributions. Thus ended the existence of the Pleistocene mosaics of mixed species that do not live together now. There is evidence that in many parts of North America the cells making up these non-analogue biomes did not simply coalesce into bigger and bigger zones as diversity disappeared; instead the patches were reduced in numbers first, and the diverse mixtures of plants and animals became fewer and fewer, as well as more and more separated from each other, as a result of the establishment of broad zones of uniform vegetational types, where biotic diversity was much reduced. This reasoning is based on studies such as King and Saunders (1984) and on open possibilities about the meaning of the evidence. The last mosaics of highly diverse cells (woodland species abutting steppic associates living nearby shrubby taxa, for example) may have survived in unknown numbers and densities by the last few millennia of the Pleistocene. We do not have the data or expertise to predict whether there were hundreds of these last diverse islands of biota, or dozens, or thousands. We do not know whether there were remnant mosaics spread throughout the interior of the continent, or if they were limited to only a few latitudes or longitudes. I suggest that these islands of high productivity and diversity were refugia for species that could not easily retreat into different latitudes.

If climate changes caused extreme shrinkage of patches or the wide separation of abutting cells, the diversity and productivity of Pleistocene refugia (the ecotones where several cells came together) would have been dramatically reduced. Each different type of cell (woodland, grassland, etc.) may have become isolated, greatly reduced, or eliminated. Fewer rich ecotones would have survived over time. The ranges of grazing and browsing animals would have become widely separated from each other in most places, although a few refugia may have continued to provide a wide variety of forage suitable for animals with stereotyped diets.

Even if the idea of mosaics (or refugia) that effectively isolated big-game populations cannot be robustly supported or proven, other climatic/paleo-environmental trends would have served to cluster and isolate taxa such as the largest terrestrial mammals at the end of the Pleistocene. The 10,900 rcybp drought in the Southwest and Plains states would have forced mammoths and other large mammals to congregate at a much reduced number of sources of water and forage (see C.V. Haynes 1984, 1993, 1996, among others). Research in the Great Lakes states provides further evidence that terminal Pleistocene refugium patches existed there too, providing either better food, more of the essential dietary minerals, or some other requirement in quantities or quality higher than in the surrounding country. For example, the Hiscock site in north-western New York state (see Laub 1994; Laub, Dufort, and Christensen 1994; Laub, Miller, and Steadman 1988) contains evidence of lowered water table at the time mastodonts were dying off there (between about 11,390 and 10,300 rcybp) – for example, wells were apparently dug by mastodonts seeking clean water, and tusk-tips were broken off during fights over access to the wells. (Note that small trees earlier reported in the Pleistocene levels and interpreted as growing where water tables had dropped have recently been dated to the late Holocene, and cannot be used as support for the drying up of the site.)

I suggest here a few stresses and selective disadvantages to be expected in a megamammal population during the difficult time of the terminal Pleistocene – a time of rapid climatic reversals, increased seasonality and extremes of seasonal climate patterns, and a severe reduction of preferred habitats. These disadvantages have been seen in recent field studies of large mammals in fragmented and crowded ranges (for example, see Rachlow 1997). Examples are (1) increased incidence of oftentimes violent agonistic encounters, resulting in widespread poor health; (2) heightened feeding competition leading to mortality of young animals first, followed by older females; and (3) extremely differential reproductive success within a population, as some males become territorial and others form coalitions, resulting in a reproduction rate that is in fact much lower than numbers of animals alone would predict.

OTHER FACTORS AFFECTING MEGAMAMMAL DISTRIBUTION DURING THE LATE PLEISTOCENE

Megamammals were not randomly distributed in late Pleistocene ranges. Mammal distribution is affected by habitat features – such as the availability of water sources or forage patches – and by population size. Proboscidean density is generally higher around water sources, especially point sources in ranges where water is limited. Modern elephants sometimes reach densities of one animal per square kilometer or higher. Elephants in some African ranges may have a standing crop over seven times greater than white-tailed deer in same-size ranges of North America (Laws, Parker, and Johnstone 1975; Petrides and Swank 1966) so their density may greatly exceed that of other, much smaller herbivores (Owen-Smith 1988, 1999:66). Certain parts of megamammal ranges were much more densely occupied than others.

Harris (1985) analyzed the distribution of vertebrate fossils from the late Pleistocene, and his data show that neither longitude nor latitude correlates with the specific taxa found in the fossil record throughout the American West – the only geographic variable that significantly correlates with taxa is elevation. In other words, the same or similar faunal associates were found throughout most of the American West, from Canada to Mexico, varying only by elevation. Typical big-game animals were mammoth, horse, bison, and camel; typical medium-game animals were deer, elk, antelope, and wild sheep. High-altitude (equator equivalent of 5,000–7,000 + ft asl) fossil sites in California, Arizona, or Colorado were dominated by sheep; medium-altitude sites (equator equivalent of 2,000–5,000 ft asl) were dominated by deer or smaller animals;

low-altitude sites (equator equivalent of 0–2000 ft asl) were dominated by bison; yet overall, the faunal inventories are quite similar over the entire region.

The key observation is that elevation mattered more than latitude or longitude in large-mammal distribution during the late Pleistocene. The largest game animals had no widespread barriers to their western distribution. Of course there would have been latitudinal gradient differences in vegetation, woody cover, temperature and seasonality, surface water, and other environmental factors across the vast expanse of the western United States, and local differences in these factors would have affected megamammal densities.

One important factor has been poorly studied until recently – the availability of micronutrients in the environment. Perhaps the most critical micronutrient for large mammals is the element iodine, which also seems to be the least studied (Milewski 2000; Milewski and Diamond 2000, n.d.). Biologist A. V. Milewski has recently proposed a theory of the pivotal role that the micronutrients iodine, cobalt, and selenium play in megamammal distribution and nutrition. Of the three, iodine is the most critical catalyst of metabolism in large herbivores, allowing rapid use of energy and regulating the function and production of other metabolic catalysts such as enzymes and hormones. Iodine has crucial effects at small amounts, and is essential for brain development and function (Milewski and Diamond 2000).

Iodine is necessary in animal and human diets, because a deficiency leads to a variety of conditions and diseases such as neonatal death (Ramakrishnan, Manjrekar, Rivera, Gonzales-Cossio, and Martorell 1999), severe cretinism with mental retardation, debilitating weakness, memory impairment, and enlargement of the thyroid (a condition called "goiter") which may cause serious breathing difficulties (Baldini, Vita, Mauri, Amodei, Carrisi, Bravin, and Cantalamessa 1997; Geelhoed 1999). Iodine must be obtained regularly to offset metabolic losses, but obtaining a balanced supply within very narrow tolerances (too little is as dangerous as too much) is precarious for humans and other animals (Milewski and Diamond 2000; Shiraishi, Muramatsu, Los, Korzun, Tsigankov, and Zamostyan 1998). Vegetarian diets put people at risk of iodine deficiency, if supplements are not taken (Davidsson 1999; Remer, Neubert, and Manz 1999). Very large herbivores require more iodine than they can practically ingest from palatable plants in most ranges; yet obtaining iodine where it is commonly found in thermal springs can be seriously toxic when fluorine and radioactive iodine are also ingested, even at concentrations that are normal for the other micronutrients.

Fortunately, iodine is input regularly into the terrestrial and biotic environment. The source of iodine in terrestrial ecosystems is the sea. Marine algae concentrate iodine from sea water. Iodine continually volatilizes from algae at the sea surface and is blown to land by wind. Iodine is depleted by the gravitational flow of water, leaching out of soils and into aquifers, so it does not accumulate on the earth's surface, although it can bind with organic matter and to a lesser extent with clay particles or dust. Plants are an unreliable source of iodine, because it is not required for their survival and their tissues store negligible quantities. Many plants produce secondary compounds that induce iodine deficiency in herbivores, as is well known from domestic livestock. This seriously affects offspring, because the goiter-causing breakdown product of the toxin passes unimpeded across the placental and mammary barriers. The most practical sources of iodine in megamammal diets are thus certain kinds of iodine-rich sediments such as mineralized earth or potable ground water issuing up through spring vents from deep aquifers that have accumulated iodine. Springs are variable in iodine content, owing to the quality and position of aquifers.

Iodine deficiency leads to a sluggish ability to utilize energy. Young animals suffer impaired brain development; adult animals suffer reduced fecundity. Megamammal populations – even those with adequate protein, energy, water, and vitamins in the diet – may still be seriously deficient in micronutrients, and the animals will show chronic ill-effects such as lack of body hair and poor skin condition, stunted growth, lower reproductive rate, aborted or weak offspring, depressed brain function, and smaller brain size. Even a subclinical deficiency of iodine which does not produce noticeable symptoms in adults is likely to depress reproductive rates.

The most important effects on mammoth and mastodont fecundity in iodine-poor regions would have been a sharp increase in the age of first reproduction, plus a high proportion of offspring not living to maturity (see Milewski 2000). Thus, mammoths and mastodonts may have been both less "intelligent" than modern elephants and also less fecund. The most noticeable effect on intelligence would have been a lack of appropriate anti-predator behavior by megamammals. Both these effects would have made megamammals much more vulnerable to hunting by Clovis foragers. A. V. Milewski's megacatalyst theory proposes that the iodine supply was sufficient for megamammals in the Pleistocene when human predators were absent, but late in the Pleistocene vulnerability was heightened owing to the biological ill-effects of iodine deficiency and the appearance of humans preying on and outcompeting megamammals for access to whatever scattered iodine-rich springs and licks could be found.

Iodine is not continuously distributed in North America. Because a primary source is rain water (Truesdale and Jones 1996), those areas of the continent with low rainfall and at great distances from the sea have less iodine replenishment. In those areas where the natural iodine is low, the most commonly consumed foods and water do not provide a minimum necessary intake, resulting in a high incidence of diseases (for examples of human case studies, see Geelhoed 1999; Hou, Chai, Qian, Liu, Zhang, and Wang 1997; Longvah and Deosthale 1998; for example of effects on animals, see National Research Council 1968a, 1968b). If secondary sources such as mineralized groundwater or mineral licks – or food supplements, in the case of modern human communities – cannot be found, then surviving without adequate iodine would be a critical challenge for humans and wild animals. Survival would be especially precarious in regions where iodine sources are reduced by factors of geography or climate – for example, in once-glaciated areas where the long-term iodine bank was bankrupted by flushing and removal of soils. North America possesses several goiter belts such as the Pacific Northwest (where high rainfall flushes iodine promptly back to the sea), the Great Lakes region (heavily glaciated), Indiana, Illinois, Ohio, Pennsylvania, the Dakotas, Nebraska, Utah, Nevada, Colorado, Idaho, and Montana (National Research Council 1968b:6–7). Great variation in iodine within a single region can exist even in adjacent groundwater and springs (Milewski 2000).

Modern-day elephants sometimes behave in what appear to be extreme ways attempting to ingest earth sediments, such as at mineral licks and termitaria. In Africa and Asia, elephants have been known to spend considerable time during dry seasons excavating seepage pits in river beds instead of drinking streaming surface water. These sorts of behaviors suggest that elephants seek something more than just water and tasty minerals for their diet; perhaps they seek iodine to supplement what they ingest from plants (Milewski 2000).

The use of mineral licks by wild animals (Cowan and Brink 1949; Weir 1969, 1972) and the ingestion of earth (geophagy) is well known, but guesswork at the motivation for such behavior has led to conclusions about sodium cravings, potassium deficiencies, or other possibilities. However, in habitats where palatable plants provide adequate sodium and other elements, the heavy use of mineral licks or the digging of wells even when surface water is available could be an expression of another need by mammals, specifically for micronutrients such as iodine.

How would the dependence on iodine potentially affect megamammal populations during the Clovis era? To answer this question scientifically, and to go beyond the theoretical nature of the "megacatalyst" model briefly presented above (Milewski and Diamond 2000), we need to know the realistic amounts of iodine available in mammoth or mastodont forage, mineral licks, and groundwater in the different regions of North America. Unfortunately, few measurements have been made of iodine concentrations in wildland ranges or regional aquifers. Humans worldwide who depend on plant foods and surface waters, and who do not have access to bovine milk and seafood – good sources of iodine – suffer iodine-deficiency symptoms in up to 30 percent of the population (Hetzel and Dunn 1989; World Health Organization 1996). Herbivores living in the same ranges where humans are prone to deficiency symptoms also suffer from iodine deficiency (National Research Council 1968a, 1968b). Hence, a comparison of iodine concentrations in each different region of the continent is a potential proxy measure of megamammal fecundity and intelligence during the Clovis era, if these measurements can be found. Table 5.11 (data taken from Milewski 2000) shows the quantities of plant matter, sediments and rocks, and water that a modern elephant would have to ingest each day to supply its daily iodine requirement. Note that many potential iodine sources do not provide a realistically useful amount.

Mammoths, mastodonts, and most other large mammals of the late Pleistocene were water-dependent; water would have been the primary factor in the daily lives of big-game animals, searched out and craved more intensely and more often than anything else. Second to water was the necessity for food; and third was the need for micronutrients. If food, minerals, or micronutrients such as iodine were depleted in local ranges, megamammals nonetheless would have preferred to stay near water sources to avoid long-distance searching for what was missing from the diet. Pleistocene megamammals – like modern elephants today – if need be preferentially lived without micronutrients first, then food second, and lastly water. Elephants cannot survive more than a few days without water, unless forage is especially moist; but elephants can fast for much longer, although they will fill their stomachs with indigestible fibers or soils to take the place of plant food. Elephants under these conditions starve to death eventually, of course, but the process takes many weeks if water can be found.

TABLE 5.11 Potential sources of iodine for a modern elephant (average body mass 3,000 kg, requiring 10 mg/day iodine) (taken from Milewski and Diamond 2000). Every day an average elephant eats about 30 kg of forage and drinks about 30 liters of water.

SUBSTANCE	IODINE (MG/KG)	MAXIMUM QUANTITY REQUIRED/DAY	COMMENT
Dry organic matter			
Cultivated herbaceous leaves	0.3	33 kg	Lethally risky
Goitrogenic wild leaves	0.2	>60 kg	Requires supplement
Seaweed	500	20 g	Ample
Marine organic sediment	50	120 g	Inaccessible
Rocks and soil			
Volcanic rock	0.1	100 kg	Impossible
Shale	0.1	100 kg	Impossible
Sandstone	0.1	100 kg	Impossible
Mineralized earth	8	1.25 kg	Possible
Dust on plants	5	2 kg	Unlikely amount
Waters			
Thermal spring	0.5	20 liters	Risky for fluorosis
River in moist areas	0.003	3,300 liters	Impossible
Melted snow	0.001	10,000 liters	Impossible
Groundwater in dry areas	0.1	60 liters	Possible

Adult elephants do not die from deficiencies of iodine or other micronutrients, unless it is extreme and chronic.

A possible difference between modern elephants and Pleistocene megamammals is in water needs. Modern elephants are strikingly inefficient with water, and they urinate prodigiously, perhaps because they drink much more moisture than actually needed in an effort to ingest minerals dissolved in the water. In ranges with adequate iodine and other micronutrients, herbivores have reduced water requirements (Milewski in prep.). Quite possibly, mammoths and mastodonts might not have needed to drink as much or as often as do modern elephants, because ice-age ranges were drier than in the Holocene, and iodine (and other minerals) were not flushed so readily. If Pleistocene habitats did provide more micronutrients, megamammals could have ingested them without the need to drink as much as do modern elephants; thus, ice-age megamammals would have avoided large energy losses from drinking so much cold water.

In summary, the main factors governing megamammal distribution during the late Pleistocene are the availability and distribution of water, nutritious forage, and micronutrients. Cover and protection from predators would have been much less important. Higher densities of megamammals were found where all the factors were optimal or rich.

The largest and densest populations of megamammals predictably would have been in geographic regions whose habitats met the following criteria: (1) the primary (plant) productivity averaged at least what modern elephants require, which is around 250 grams of dry matter per square meter (250 g DM/m^2), of which 10–15 percent must be crude protein (approximately the requirements for modern elephants, averaged over a year); (2) either numerous springfed water sources were present to provide potable water, adequate iodine, and other micronutrients such as cobalt and selenium, or bedrock and sediments containing iodine were available along with abundant surface water.

It should be possible to predict where optimal habitats were located as well as where productivity was too low to support megamammals, if information such as late Pleistocene pollen diagrams and paleohydrology are obtainable. Many modern habitats clearly cannot support megamammals today.

The ideal spot to find mammoths or mastodonts in the Pleistocene probably would have been in or near permanently wet grass and sedge meadows on gentle slopes, with the water flow fed by springs (especially mineral springs, as long as their waters were not too high in fluorine, which is toxic) and situated in uplands with sluggish drainage, underlain or surrounded by volcanic sediments or fine-grained sedimentary bedrock.

The Valley of Mexico had an abundance of this sort of ideal setting, and indeed mammoth sites are exceptionally common there (Arroyo-C., Polaco, and Aguilar-A. 1999; Arroyo-C., Polaco, Johnson, and Guzman 1999; Gonzalez, Arroyo-C., Turner, Pettit, and Sherwood 1999). One of the better-known jokes in central Mexico is that Mexico has three stratigraphic levels – the modern one on top with Spanish-language litter and recent buildings, under which are the ubiquitous pre-Hispanic materials you can find nearly everywhere, both resting atop the mammoth layer (Oscar Polaco, pers. comm., 15 Nov. 2000).

The Great Lakes region seems to be another such optimal region for finding megamammal bones. In Michigan, numerous localities with surface saline water are known, as are numerous proboscidean sites, and it has been proposed that the mastodonts and mammoths were perhaps attracted to the saline waters for the sodium. Possibly other micronutrients were acquired as well. Soils and plants in the Great Lakes region are very low in iodine, but the abundant saline springs and stagnant post-glacial ponds probably provided adequate minerals and micronutrients.

The idea that Pleistocene proboscideans were attracted to salt licks can be found in archeological interpretations of sites from the Old World, too. Derevianko, Zenin, Leshchinskiy, and Mashchenko (2000:53) hypothesized that one site in western Siberia, Shestakovo, was created 25,600 to 18,040 radiocarbon years ago by humans seeking mammoths attracted to a "local geochemical landscape, i.e. solonetz soil" rich in potassium and magnesium. Leschinsky [a spelling variant of Leshchinskiy] (1999) proposed that Upper Paleolithic humans in northern Eurasia balanced the search for suitable toolstone against the search for large mammals. The largest archeological sites are found where toolstone sources are located near mammoth migration routes in landscapes rich in calcium, magnesium, and sodium. Soffer (1993:40) suggested that some central European (Moravian) mammoth-bone archeological sites were located where they are because of the local mineral-rich sediments.

Abraczinskas (1992) tested this kind of speculation with a spatial analysis of Michigan mastodont sites, but she discovered that the megamammal bonesites are poorly correlated with the saline waters, although about one-third of the fossil megamammal finds were situated within 33 km of a salt site. Both fresh and saline water sources were probably relatively abundant in late Pleistocene Michigan, partially accounting for the unclustered distribution of megamammal finds; but it would be interesting to learn what this region provided in the way of iodine and other micronutrients. A critical attractant in the Michigan fossil sites, and in many mammoth-rich sites in the Old World, may have been micronutrients in the water, such as iodine, rather than exclusively sodium, potassium, or other minerals, although large mammals were probably using the presence of salts and other minerals as an indicator of iodine in soils and waters.

Nevada is in an iodine-poor region. Surface water was abundant during the late Pleistocene, in the form of huge pluvial lakes (Grayson 1993), and the vegetational communities of the times probably provided adequate dry matter and crude protein for herbivores in many places (G. Haynes 2000b), yet mammoth fossils are infrequently found in the state. In the Pleistocene, plant productivity was considerably higher, especially around pluvial lakes, so forage should have sufficed for mammoths. One partial explanation for the relative scarcity of mammoths is that deep exposures of bone-bearing Pleistocene strata are uncommon, since the region is inwardly draining and sediments do not deeply erode over large areas; another explanation is that the known scarcity of essential micronutrients kept mammoth populations low and widely scattered.

Keeping in mind the factors limiting megamammal distribution and population health, I now turn to evidence that Clovis foragers took advantage of megamammal ecology and behavior, specifically the knowledge of megamammal distribution and behavior under different environmental stresses.

DID CLOVIS PEOPLE HUNT MAMMOTHS AND, POSSIBLY AS OFTEN, MASTODONTS?

Ethnographic records show that recent people did not make a living hunting the biggest game animals such as elephants. I repeat what I think is a necessary caution about relying exclusively on ethnographic knowledge to predict everything we do not yet know about the prehistoric past (Binford 1967; Hodder 1982; Kelley and Hanen 1988; Levine 1997; Salmon 1982; Wobst 1978; Wylie 1985). Ethnographic observations are useful as inspirations and consciousness-expanders, but they cannot be binding guides. Many modern foraging groups live in habitats quite different from those inhabited by the foragers of the Pleistocene. Holocene ranges are not as biotically diverse, for example, as they were in much of Pleistocene North America. Clovis foragers had very different choices to make than Holocene foragers (a point well made by Kelly and Todd 1988). Pleistocene foragers would not have had pastoralist or farming neighbors, or colonizing invaders, as did (and still do) the known foragers ethnographically described in the literature. The archeological record contains information about a more colorful and richer range of forager behavior in the past than we can observe in the ethnographic present.

It has been argued (see Dincauze 1993a; Levine 1997; Meltzer 1988, 1996; Meltzer and Smith 1986, among others) that Clovis people did not "specialize" in big game, and in fact no hunter-gatherers ever do show such specialization. To evaluate this type of argument, the word "specialist" first must be defined. Dincauze and Curran (1983:8, cited in Levine 1997:238) defined the Paleoindian specialty as being no more than a flexibility in procurement strategies. Other authors seem to have other meanings in mind for the word "specialty." It is defined in different ways by scientists using different methods in their fields. For example, biologists define specialization as the anatomical and behavioral features that function in an unvarying way to obtain specific resources. The flexibility or versatility of the features is limited; the features can be used in only one way. If this definition is the one used by archeologists who reject big-game specialization by Clovis or any other foraging group, I would have to point out that clearly this is a straw-man argument, hardly worth taking seriously. No human forager "specializes" this way. Flaked-stone tools are rarely restricted to single purposes (as seen in multiple-use results from use-wear analyses, or predicted in models of technological strategies [Morrow 1996; Odell 1996; Shott 1986, 1993]) in both the Pleistocene and the Holocene. It cannot be imagined how Pleistocene tools could have been obligately limited to use on only one species of animal, or on only animal rather than plant tissue.

This sort of unvarying tool use is not what a fair rejection of Clovis "specialization" can be based on; but what else can the critics' case be founded on? The inability to see Clovis as a big-game specialization follows from a typical ethnographic definition of specialization as a focusing of technology, social organization, and settlement patterns into a narrow range of activities in order to survive. The narrowness of the range is in need of clarification, obviously, if subsistence specialization is to be understood one way or another. The Clovis literature does not do enough to clarify this. For example, one discussion of specialization (Johnson 1991) categorizes hunter-gatherers as specialized if they emphasize "collecting" (in the sense defined by Binford 1980), while others are called "generalists" if they forage (also in the sense defined by Binford 1980). Foragers, in this scheme, are people who move their camps sequentially to food patches, and collectors are people who maintain home basecamps while task-specific groups harvest food and return it to the camp where it can be stored, redistributed, or consumed. Yet either one of these defined types – collectors or foragers – could in fact be specialists under certain conditions. The word specialist cannot be synonymous with "collector" in archeological interpretations.

"Specialization" should not be understood as another way of saying "ranking" of food items. Specialization refers to a behavior that, while it may be based partly on food-ranking, is also shaped by several other variables and perceptions. Even "specialists" would take higher-ranked foods than the ones they specialize in whenever they are encountered, and would not preferentially take low-ranked foods first. To be rational and subject to selection, specialization would have to be no more than a reducing of the number of items chosen for a forager's diet. Later I discuss the modeling that pertains to diet-breadth and prey selection. Here I wish only to suggest that some participants in the debate about the impossibility of Clovis foragers specializing in megamammal-hunting may be defining "specialization" in an irrational way – by assigning megamammals to a ranking that is lower than they deserved in the late Pleistocene.

If megamammals were indeed very hard to find, hunt, and kill, or to process and digest, then they may have been relatively little sought and hunted rarely if ever, unless no other prey existed. Yet when one judges megamammal-hunting by analogy to the hunting of modern elephants, the conclusion is inescapable that Paleoindians never would have irrationally ranked megamammals at the low end of the scale. Modern elephants leave unmistakable marks on their habitats. Some of these marks are subtle, but most are quite obvious and full of information. Modern proboscideans make complex mental maps of water points, mineral sources, forage patches, fruit trees, travel routes, and socializing

Fig. 5.3 Modern
elephant trail in sand,
showing well-flattened
surface, dung boluses,
and a water source at
the end of the trail
segment
(photographed by
G. Haynes in
Zimbabwe).

sites, creating travel routes between these important places that can be easily
followed by human foragers and other animal taxa. Proboscidean trails are well
used, clearly identifiable (Fig. 5.3), and easy to follow. They tend to be flat-
bottomed (because elephants have flat feet and weigh so much), measure about
45 cm wide or more, and are consistently placed year to year. Human foragers
would have recognized and made use of these trails to track animals moving
from water source to forage to cover to mineral licks and back again. Trails
made or used by other animal taxa also provide information useful for foragers;
for example, the size and shape of habitually used bison trails are recognizably
distinct from the dimensions and morphology of habitually used horse trails
(G. Haynes unpublished field notes 1979–87), thus indicating the prey taxa to
be found along such trails.

Another source of foraging clues is proboscidean dung. Modern elephant
dung is large and visible to anyone in elephant country; its freshness and the time
elapsed since its deposition are apparent to knowledgeable hunters. The diet of

Fig. 5.4 Poorly chewed and undigested plant parts (including a long strip of bark to the left, and parts of identifiable leaves in the center) dissected out of modern African elephant dung at a die-off locality (photographed by G. Haynes in Zimbabwe).

megamammals is readable in the droppings. Elephant biologists carefully record dung composition and decomposition in order to reconstruct diets, animal numbers passing per unit of time, and animal health (Barnes and Jensen 1987). Dung provides a wealth of information about an elephant's age, its traveling speed, and its diet. Poorly masticated plant fibers such as bark (Fig. 5.4) or other items indicate badly worn and inefficient teeth, perhaps reflecting great life-age in proboscideans, or unselective feeding by very hungry individuals.

Masses of clay or sand in dung may be left by hungry animals trying to fill their stomachs where forage is scarce, or alternatively by animals that have drunk out of pits and wells dug to reach subsurface water. Such indications are produced by stressed animals in droughty habitats.

Elephants can travel great distances in a day, owing to their long legs, so gut transport signs such as unchewed fibers or sandy dung may be up to 30 km or more from the place where these substances were first ingested. Seeds in dung may be passed unchewed or only partly chewed (see Dudley 1999, 2000; Janzen and Martin 1982), and a human forager can make a mental map of an elephant's feeding ranges from such information.

Great quantities of dung are found in proboscidean ranges, thus making them very high-profile animals to human foragers. Elephants are bulk feeders and inefficient processors, and only around 50 percent of intake is digested (Benedict 1936). Adult elephants ingest around 150 kg of forage every day, feeding at all times of the day, and hence dung is well scattered over their daily range (Laws, Parker, and Johnstone 1975; Sikes 1971). Food consists of an eclectic mix of grass leaves and stems, woody twigs, bark, and tree leaves. Visual traces of elephant feeding are often commonly found, such as broken and debarked trees, excavated roots, and pulled-up bunches of grass partly eaten. Every day an enormous fibrous dung volume and mass (over 100 kg per adult) is dropped by elephants. The dung is deposited not only in feeding patches but also along the trails, at water sources, and around and within mineral licks. The dung is passed as boluses which, because elephants are such tall creatures whose anuses are up to 2 m or more above ground, tend to fragment as the height and travel speed increase. Elephants travel at different speeds, ranging from a brisk walk (which approaches the speed of a human run) to a leisurely amble (which is similar to a slow human jog). The dung passed by elephants at variable locomotion speeds breaks apart differently upon impact with the ground, providing a clue to the speed of moving animals. A clever tracker can examine dung boluses to estimate (1) how large the animal was (based on bolus size), (2) how long ago the dung was passed (based on the degree of freshness of the boluses) and how fast the animal was traveling (based on the dung's fragmentation) – hence, how far ahead the animal may be, and (3) the animal's relative health, appetite, and feeding preferences. All these clues would improve the efficiency of foraging, thus reducing the cost in time and energy needed to hunt elephants. Human foragers in prehistory surely examined elephant dung – as do modern biologists who study elephant populations – to determine individual animal sizes, age and sex, locomotion speed, direction of travel, and feeding patterns (Barnes and Jensen 1987).

Elephant habits such as migration to daily water sources are clear from an examination of trails. Experienced big-game hunters can read the environmental notes left behind by elephants, or by mammoths and mastodons. Therefore, it is no surprise that megamammals were hunted relatively heavily (as argued above, and elsewhere [G. Haynes 2002]). In fact, megamammals must have been ranked very high by Clovis foragers for reasons that include (1) their large body size and high-value energy returns (which is a strong predictor of food ranking); (2) their late Pleistocene crowding into refugium patches where they could be found easily (discussed below); and (3) the cycles of late Pleistocene stresses they suffered at both the population and the individual level (also discussed below).

So if mammoths and mastodonts would have been so important to late Pleistocene foragers, were the foragers "specialists" in hunting proboscideans? What is needed is a workable definition of specialization in Clovis studies. Following from Pianka (1994:268–93), I offer a definition and discussion of the archeological implications of specialization. Pianka points out that the word "niche" is the fundamental term and concept needed to study the ecology of natural ecosystems. Niche is defined as "the sum total of the adaptations of an organismic unit," or the various ways an organismic unit (individual, population, or species) conforms to its environment (Pianka 1994:269). Niche therefore refers to the ways an organismic unit uses and interacts with its environment. Patterns of resource use are usually thought to be "niches." Niche breadth (= width = size) can be described only comparatively, or that is by comparisons between given organismic units. Relatively narrowed tolerances for relevant environmental variables make a niche "specialized" – such as habitat requirements or food needs. Generalized organisms have flexible habitat requirements, exploit more food types, occupy more habitats, and build up larger populations. However, generalists cannot be viewed in the human context as being invariably superior or more fit than specialists. Generalists are, in a way, jacks-of-all-trades but masters of none; while they are flexible and opportunistic, they are also less efficient exploiters of habitats and food resources than specialists.

When and why would foragers reduce niche breadth and become specialists? In food-rich environments, foragers may choose to bypass suboptimal prey in favor of searching for the optimal taxa, thus narrowing niche-width. It is possible that the late Pleistocene ecotonal refugia were food-rich patches. Also, an optimal forager may choose to utilize only those food patches which have the higher expectations of yield, especially if there is resource competition. Such patches may have been late Pleistocene refugia, and the competition may have been perceived as fellow carnivores and scavengers such as Pleistocene lion or short-faced bear. As resource availability increases, niche width tends to decrease, creating specialization – and once again, I suggest that late Pleistocene insular refugia were enriched in food resources compared to the preceding full Glacial and succeeding early Holocene patches. In short, "rich food supplies . . . lead to selective foraging and narrow food niche breadths" (Pianka 1994:283). And when the degree of difference between patches in an environment increases (such as occurred at the end of the Pleistocene), the advantages of being specialized also increase.

"Organisms that spend disproportionate amounts of time in different patches [that is, out of proportion to the actual sizes or densities of the patches] are said to use their environment in a *coarse-grained* manner" (Pianka 1994:285, after Levins 1968). Fine-grained use of the environment occurs when patches are visited for amounts of time proportionate to their existence in the environment. If patch sizes are relatively small, organisms tend to utilize their environments in a fine-grained manner; large patch sizes may lead to a coarser-grained use of the environment. Late Pleistocene patches were probably relatively small, and packed together complexly, unlike the more homogeneous and zonal arrangement of Holocene patches. But late Pleistocene foraging people selected only particular prey types, thus utilizing a perhaps relatively fine-grained environment in a coarse-grained way, which is not impossible. This kind of foraging is considered a form of specialization.

What would motivate foragers to select food prey out of proportion to what is found in the environment's patches? To address this question, I refer to optimal foraging theory, also sometimes called optimization theory.

OPTIMIZATION THEORY AND MEGAMAMMAL-HUNTING

Good theory should help explain not only what foragers such as Clovis could *not* do, but also what they actually did do. One model of Clovis foraging behavior is based on theories in behavioral ecology and population biology, subfields of the biological sciences using the analytical approaches known as evolutionary ecology, optimization theory, and related perspectives on the behavior of foraging organisms.

At one time it was thought that foraging animals chose their food types from the environment in proportion to the availability (abundance and density) of those types (Allee, Emerson, Park, Park, and Schmidt 1949:517; also see Lee 1968, who suggested that hunter-gatherer diets directly reflect the availability of animal and plant foods). Now it is clear this is not at all true (for example, Foley 1982), and that in fact selection shapes food choices. Foraging Theory ideally predicts that foraging animals behave rationally but also make decisions based on optimality models, which describe the relationships among variables such as feeding costs and the energy benefits gained per unit of time spent locating, capturing, and handling food. In short, because selection acts on feeding behaviors, foraging by animals is not simply a series of fixed behaviors or automatic harvest-responses to resources, nor does foraging behavior depend mainly on the order and proportions of food types encountered in the environment. Foraging is much more than an attempt to get the most food at the least cost.

Research in Foraging Theory has examined the types of observed deviations from modeled predictions (for example, Alvard 1995 on why game conservation is not always perceived as optimal foragings, or C. Kay 1994 on aboriginal resource-exploitation in North America). Foraging theorists use models and mathematical formulas to understand unique as well as universal decisions and selective processes, and not merely to make programmed predictions about foraging behavior. The models take into consideration a set of probable tradeoffs between getting the best food for the time and energy required. When there is an observed congruence of foraging behavior and the predictions of rational modeling, it can be said that the theory has explanatory value. Where there are incongruences, it can be said that the model needs to take other perceived costs and benefits into consideration, or more closely examine the assumptions and goals of foraging behavior.

Here I discuss three important components of the body of theory about cost-benefit tradeoffs, namely diet breadth, marginal value, and foraging time spent in patches, and I suggest how these conceptualized relationships or theorems accommodate different predictions about Clovis foraging (including the possibility of "overkill" and the so-called "blitzkrieg" model). I have simplified these concepts to make them undemanding and more understandable to nonexperts (see Kelly 1995 and references therein for more technical definitions and discussions).

Diet-breadth modeling is a technique used to understand forager ranking of food items and the possible reasons why some foods and not others are included in a forager's diet. The "breadth" of a diet refers to the relative inclusiveness of items that are ranked from high to low; narrow diet breadths are restricted to high-ranked items such as easy pickings with high return rates (easily killed animals, for example); wider diets also include high-ranked items but depend on foods with lower rank (such as seed grains, which are time-consuming and difficult to harvest, process, and store). The way in which diet breadth is modeled involves an examination of the costs (measured in units of time and energy) of acquiring a food item relative to other food items. Many diets are chosen because of the long-term average costs and benefits associated with foods in forager ranges. However, diet modeling for human foragers also must take into consideration cultural proscriptions and beliefs about foods, which may alter rankings.

A popular approach to interpreting diet choices in the recent literature is called "Prey Selection" modeling, referring to predictions of diet based on measurements of costs and benefits associated with different prey taxa encountered by foragers at different times and places.

"Specialization" is a deliberate narrowing of diet breadth by foragers who arrange their behavior to make certain food items easier or less costly to procure. Specialization may be long-term or it may be temporary, as an adjustment to changes in availability or vulnerability of certain food items.

To illustrate the insights that diet-breadth modeling can provide about prey "specialization," I here set up an example from an imaginary Pleistocene region.

IMAGINING MAMMOTH-HUNTING

To make a reality-based model of mammoth-hunting, I will first set values for an imaginary local mammoth density (which depends on food sources), body size, spatial distribution (which is mainly affected by water distribution), and a number of other variables that are not precisely known from prehistoric localities. As a starting point, I set density and distribution to the same levels observed in modern African elephant populations. In general, *Loxodonta* densities are artificially affected by human management policies, such as the protection afforded from hunting in game reserves and national parks, or the susceptibility to hunting experienced by elephants outside such protected areas. I take these into consideration when setting my mammoth values.

Elephant densities of about one animal per square kilometer are considered rather high nowadays. Here I begin modeling by setting mammoth *density* 12,000–11,000 rcybp in an imaginary American stream valley at one animal per 2 to 3 square kilometers. Modern elephant *distribution* is not random, since it is directly shaped by water distribution (for example, see Williamson 1975). I set a higher mammoth density around streamways. These numbers are fairly realistic.

To further simplify, I consider my imaginary study area to be a rectangle 40 × 64 km in size. Within the rectangle are fairly productive patches of vegetation, such as wet meadows, riparian woodlands, and grassy glades. If a human forager on foot in this area can walk about 16 km a day without hardship, she or he would never be more than 1.5 day's walk from the central streamway, which I call the White river. If 1,000 mammoths live in this area, and are nonrandomly distributed according to water needs, forage preferences, and traditional routes to and from feeding and watering points, the single human forager may not expect to encounter mammoth herds every day, but probably would be able to track and find animals within three days of walking.

TABLE 5.12 Resource returns compared.

RESOURCE	MAXIMUM SEARCH TIME (HOURS)	MAXIMUM HANDLING TIME (HOURS)	ENERGY KCAL/UNIT (AVERAGE ADULT)	POST-ENCOUNTER RETURN RATE (KCAL/HR)	UNITS ENCOUNTERED IN THE TIME ONE MAMMOTH IS ENCOUNTERED
Mammoth	72	6	2,600,000	30,000	1
Bison	72	3	430,000	5,512	0–1
Deer	24	2	42,000	1,615	0–3
Fish (netted)	8	24 (smoke-drying time)	~1500?	~2000	0–50+

Mammoth *search cost* is defined as the time in hours that must be spent searching for an average weight of useful meat (see Kelly 1995:79–85). If one or more mammoths can be found in three days (72 hours) within the valley, and the average mammoth-unit weight is 4,000 kg, the search cost under these idealized conditions is therefore 72 hours divided by 4,000 kg, or 0.018 hr/kg. This is an extremely low cost. Search costs can change, owing to changes in resource densities. A three-day search could be reduced to two hours or increased to three weeks under different conditions. Search costs can be minimized when foragers acquire more accurate information about food locations (Kelly 1995:80).

Handling cost is defined as the time needed to procure and process the mammoth after locating it, divided by the energy yield. An imaginary forager might set this post-encounter expense of time maximally at six hours – two hours needed to kill the mammoth and four more hours needed to remove skin, meat, and perhaps some bones. One kilogram of lean meat (70 percent water, 25 percent protein, 5 percent fat) contains about 1,300 Kcal energy; an "average" mammoth weighing 4,000 kg might yield 2,000 kg of usable energy, or about 2,600,000 Kcal. The maximum handling cost thus would equal six hours divided by the total energy yield less the energy burned by a human forager in killing and butchering the mammoth. Like search cost, the handling cost for a mammoth in such a region would be very small. Handling cost may change with improved technology, lowering it even more.

The return rates of foraging may change as the usable technology's manufacturing costs change, pursuit styles change, degrees of butchering change (such as, for example, adding bone-breakage to retrieve marrow when body-fat levels on carcasses are relatively low), and preparation for storage is discarded or added to the handling process.

In the imaginary modeling region, mammoth search time may be five minutes to seventy-two hours; handling time is consciously limited by my imaginary foragers to three hours (allowing the butchers to take about one-third the available meat). In this model, the return from a butchered mammoth would be about 700 kg of meat, or 910,000 Kcal per unit, plus organs and fat. Skin, bones, cartilage, tendons, connective tissue, and most viscera are not utilized, and plenty of meat is also left behind, including the bits difficult to remove quickly.

Table 5.12 compares this model's post-encounter return rates from mammoth, bison, deer, and netted fish in the imaginary region. The population of bison is set at 500 in the region; there are 250 deer; and the freshwater fish number about 5,000 in the 64 km stretch of the fictional White river. The search times are based on estimates of time needed for tracking, and vary from season to season.

These numbers are partly arbitrary and partly reality-based. For example, I have not mentioned the "danger" cost of searching for mammoths or trying to kill them. In this model, and based on real-life observations, I propose that less than the total available amount of energy (Kcal) would be harvested from each mammalian carcass, because of wastage and inedibility, but the model does allow the maximum amount of energy to be harvested from each fish. The return from each prey item is calculated by finding the total of Kcal actually recovered from one butchered unit and dividing by the combined search and handling times, minus the expenditure of Kcal burned by the hunter/butcher. The return from a foraging plan that includes all possible items in the diet is calculated by first adding all the totals of energy harvested from each unit, then dividing by the combined search and handling times (note that the highest-cost scenario is assumed – that is, search times for all items are additive). Adding bison, deer, and fish to mammoth in the diet reduces the net return from 30,000 Kcal per hour for mammoth alone, to 14,600 Kcal per hour. In this model, thus, adding any other prey item to mammoth to the diet is not necessarily optimal; the foragers should stick to mammoth alone. The other prey items would be optimally ignored when encountered, even if encountered far more often than mammoth. However, if search cost ever goes sharply up for mammoth and/or bison, then deer and fish are much more likely to be added to the diet.

The question then arises: how rare must mammoth become to force the diet breadth to be widened? I return to this topic below, after discussing the concept of "patch choice" modeling.

"Patch choice" modeling refers to the measurement of costs and benefits associated with forager decisions to travel to certain specific patches in the environment where food may be sought; patch choices also take into account decisions about how much time is to be spent in each patch, and how much time is to be spent traveling to another patch. The forager evaluates the total amount of time and energy needed to travel to a patch where food may await the forager, versus the energy return expected from staying in the patch.

In modeling, patches are defined as spatial areas that contain at least one food resource (although human foragers may define viable patches as sources not only of food but also of water and a range of other resources such as toolstone). A "patch" is not the same thing as a habitat or an environment. Patches are usually of three types (Fig. 5.5). Most terrestrial patches provide diminishing returns over time, or abruptly cease returning energy if prey are all killed. The word "patchy" refers to an inconsistent or irregular distribution of resources in an environment. Very patchy resources are clumped in space, rarely available, appear only for a short time, and have a small unit size. Non-patchy resources are uniformly dispersed, available often, appear for a long time, and have a large unit size. Mobile resources are patchy; migratory resources are patchy. Mammoths confined to refugia are not a patchy resource.

The graph in Figure 5.6 depicts the way food items may be ranked for inclusion in a forager's diet. The highest ranking (1, 2, 3, ...) of a resource results from a low handling time-per-calorie value (which takes into consideration an

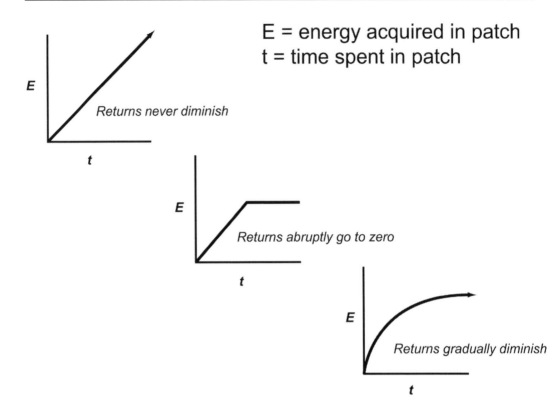

E = energy acquired in patch
t = time spent in patch

Fig. 5.5 Potential energy returns graphed against time spent foraging in three different kinds of patches. Most terrestrial patches may provide returns as in the graph in the bottom right, diminishing over time. However, some patches in the late Pleistocene may have provided returns as in the other two graphs.

animal's body mass, its ability to return usable food, and the difficulties of killing, butchering, and processing meat) and a low search time-per-calorie value. Very large animals usually require more search time than the smaller ones (being less common), and while they may be ranked highly they may not necessarily rank the highest. The ranking of one item may vary if search and handling times change – in other words, if an animal taxon becomes easier to track or find and kill, as a result of environmental variables (such as drought that forces some species to crowd into refuges, or the human invention of new and more effective technology).

Figure 5.7 shows how foraging theory tries to predict the time a forager spends in a patch. A forager who must walk from a distant point to reach the patch in mind would want to spend more time foraging in that patch (time = T_y) than one who travels a shorter time (spending T_x in the patch), if the patch can return enough energy to make the stay acceptable. The forager makes up for the lengthy travel time by staying longer in the patch, until the return rate drops off below the rate the other distant patches provide on average.

The Marginal Value Theorem as originally articulated by Charnov (1976) and carefully re-evaluated by others afterwards (see Martin 1983 for examples) states that foragers are aware of the energy yield per time in each feeding patch, and they are therefore aware of the optimal time to quit the patch – which is when the capture rate in the patch is equal to the average energy per time obtainable over the entire environment (including travel-time, and other variables). In other words, Marginal Value Theorem attempts to predict the time a forager spends in a patch, based upon the time elapsed between the last successful capture and her/his departure from the patch. In richer environments, where patches may

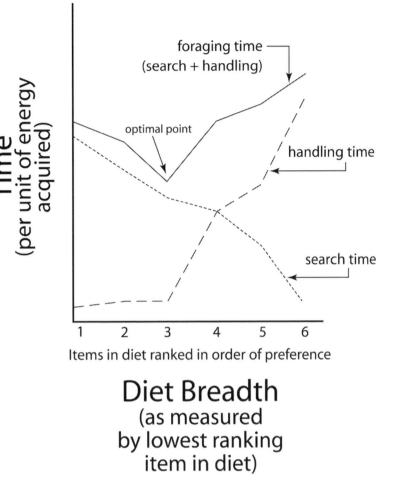

Fig. 5.6 Search time and handling time when added together provide foragers with a possible measurement of the major costs of foraging for different food items. The highest-ranked items may have longer search time but much shorter handling costs, while lower-ranked items require much greater handling. Thus, "diet breadth" is a gauge of the range of lower-ranked food items included in the diet. (Redrawn from Bettinger 1991, after MacArthur and Pianka 1966.)

be more productive, the "giving-up" time may be shorter, but decisions about patch abandonment time may based on perceptions of prey distribution.

In trying to understand the length of time Clovis sites were occupied, rarely do archeologists refer to another ecologically critical aspect of foraging behavior, namely the mental modes used by rational foragers who try to estimate the quality of resources available in habitats or food patches (see Giraldeau 1997:42–68 for background in theory and research). In conjunction with a better understanding of models describing or predicting prey choice and patch residency, a greater familiarity with models used to estimate quality may help us develop a sensitive and scientific theory of Clovis behavior. Here I simply wish to make reference to Bayesian models. Potentially these models help illustrate the reasoning used by Clovis foragers, which may have been behind Clovis site use and behavior. Bayesian models are decision-making "rules" that update mental pictures of resource value. The models operate by continually acquiring information from experiences during foraging searches, and this current information is processed to condition foragers' *a priori* expectations and views about resource distribution (I am explicitly referring here only to one aspect of information use, as discussed in Giraldeau 1997:45–8).

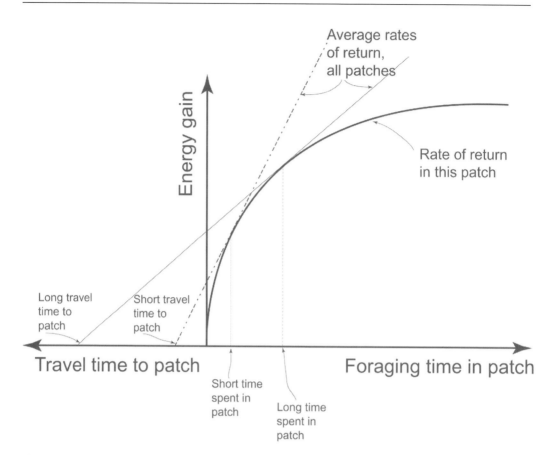

Fig. 5.7 One possible reason foragers decide to spend more or less time in a patch is the cost of travel time involved in getting to patches. This graph illustrates the way an optimizing decision may be made – by evaluating returns from all food patches, and then relatively measuring the costs of leaving each patch to travel to others instead of staying in the patch. (Redrawn from Charnov 1976 and following Bettinger 1991.)

The amount and quality of information available to a forager make a tremendous amount of difference in a forager's patch choice decisions. Especially important are decisions about the quality of the patch as reflected by the distribution and density of food items such as prey taxa. Figure 5.8, after Giraldeau (1997) and Iwasa, Higashi, and Yamamura (1981), shows predictions about a forager's decisions in three different situations within an environment – when prey are "underdispersed," "overdispersed," and "random." In these cases, foragers think about the distribution of prey in these three abstract ways: "underdispersed" means the prey are not uniformly dispersed in the range and are absent or rare in some patches; "overdispersed" means that prey individuals are everywhere distributed through the range and are expected to be found in every patch; "random" means the prey are randomly or independently dispersed, without predictability in their locations. Foragers predict their success very differently when they think of prey and patch quality in these terms. When a forager who expects prey to be underdispersed in the environment encounters a prey individual in a certain patch, that forager then may think the likelihood is increased that the patch contains still more prey. The "updated estimate of the number of prey remaining in the patch increases following each encounter" (Giraldeau 1997:47). But in the *overdispersed* environment, where all patches are thought to be of similar quality (measured as number of prey per patch), every prey encounter is thought to mean that the patch likely contains one less prey animal. The "updated estimate of the number of prey remaining in the patch

Fig. 5.8
Information-based foraging takes into consideration the perceived estimates of each food item that may be left in an environment after any encounter (marked on the graphs with X) such as a kill or a sighting of the item. The arrows at the end of each curve indicate the time at which the patches are abandoned. When foragers encounter prey that they perceive to be patchily distributed and unpredictable in the environment, they may be encouraged to keep on searching again after each encounter (as indicated in the top graph); but when foragers encounter prey they perceive to be distributed everywhere in low density, they may not expect to see such prey again very often (as the graph in the center indicates) and thus are inclined to leave the patch sooner after an encounter. (Redrawn from Giraldeau 1997.)

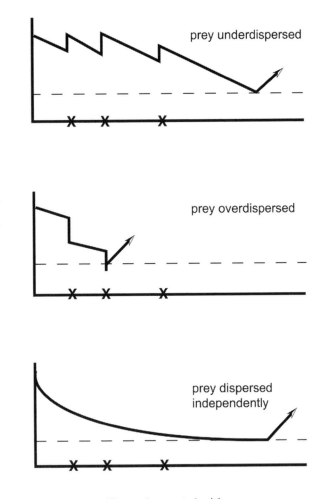

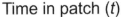

now declines with encounters" (Giraldeau 1997:47). And in the *random* environment, each prey encounter means nothing in terms of the prey remaining in the patch, and thus has no effect on the forager's estimate of remaining prey.

Bayesian modeling of forager choices in underdispersed environments – which I think describes late Pleistocene megamammal ranges in North America – suggests that the most successful forager (1) "has the highest updated estimate of the number of prey remaining in the patch"; (2) "exploits the patch more extensively"; and (3) tolerates "longer unrewarded search before [her/his] updated estimate declines to the threshold for patch abandonment (fig. 3.2a)" (Giraldeau 1997:47). The less successful foraging individuals are pessimistic about prey numbers remaining in a patch and they leave patches sooner if unrewarded. Hence, in *underdispersed* environments, foragers who encounter prey sporadically will be able to procure more prey individuals if they are patient and can tolerate unproductive periods of time spent in specially selected patches.

MARGINAL VALUE, OPTIMIZATION, AND PLEISTOCENE
FORAGING THEORY

The late Pleistocene must have been hard on mammoths and mastodonts. How did Clovis foragers respond to the changes in proboscidean vulnerability, distribution, density, and behavior? Putting together the optimization theory predictions with expectations based on paleoecological reconstructions, I now attempt to predict Clovis behavior. I propose that in general the foraging returns from any typical Pleistocene patch would have conformed to the prediction in Figure 5.5 – where returns level off and then diminish over time – but the rate of return may have varied within the limits of the graph's shape. In other words, the curve for returns may have risen more or less steeply, and dropped off more or less abruptly, but it probably always maintained the asymptotic shape.

I suggest that in the Pleistocene if the patches were increasingly isolated refuges, distant from each other and limited in number, Clovis foragers (assuming group sizes were fairly consistent) would have spent relatively more time in them, creating either larger sites, more sites, or sites containing more artifacts and more kinds of artifacts. Shorter-term visits to patches that were located closer together may have created single-occupancy sites, smaller artifact assemblages, or smaller numbers of animal bones in sites.

I can suggest variance in Clovis foraging, all of which will have archeological implications. I propose here four different sets of ecological conditions and the expected foraging tactics that may have been available to Clovis individuals and populations. My intention is to contribute to the Clovis foraging model by seeking patterns that would have been created during the Pleistocene, knowing what we know about paleoenvironments of the Clovis interval. I envision these tactics based on an appreciation of foraging rationality, which I admit has been significantly flavored by an intensive reading of the literature about megamammal behavior and my personal experiences in Africa studying elephants and other large animals.

(1) When water and animals that are considered optimal food species are dispersed patchily in any environment, I suggest that the optimal foraging tactic would be to go to the water points and the prey's feeding patches sequentially (Fig. 5.9). This does not ensure success, but it provides a better bet than sitting at one food patch and waiting for the food to arrive, while at the same time it provides access to water throughout the foraging search.

(2) When water is distributed focally but food is dispersed, the optimal tactic may be to go to the water sequentially along game trails, and if not successful in finding medium to large game, then to leave the water and travel to one food patch (along the game trail) in search of at least small game while hoping to find the larger game animals.

(3) Another alternative when water is focal and food dispersed is to move from each water point to the next nearest one along game trails and attempt to kill any game encountered.

(4) When both water and food are focal (Fig. 5.10), the optimal tactic may be to spend a short time (such as one to three days) resident in each prey feeding patch that is near water and then walk a feasible distance (from two days to two weeks for healthy adults) along game trails that lead to other water/food patches and establish a new residency for another short time (two days to two weeks or so).

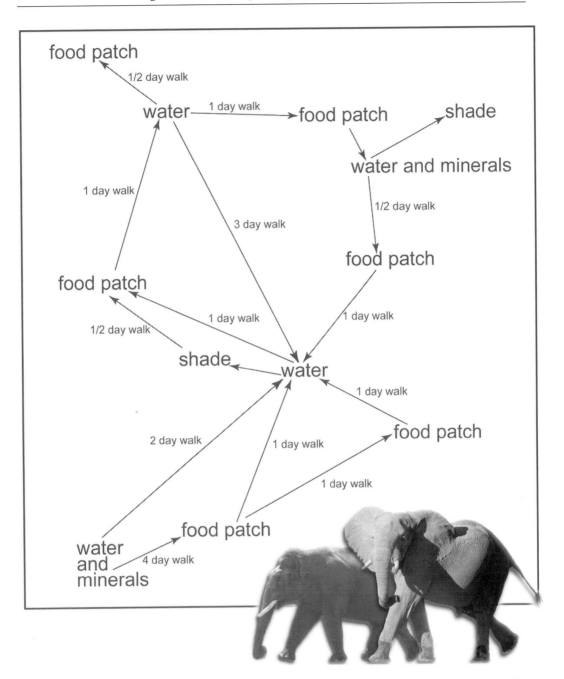

Fig. 5.9 An idealized proboscidean range in which food and water are spatially dispersed rather than clustered or "focal."

These suggested time frames are of course based on a twentieth-century archeologist's personal comfort levels, anxiety about hunger or thirst, and so on, and may bear little similarity to a Clovis forager's thoughts about foraging distances and time. However, note that the manner in which occupational debris either piles up or scatters out in individual sites should be different in the situations predicted above. Serial killing at water points is to be expected in some cases, while single encounter kills are to be expected in others. Tool maintenance or

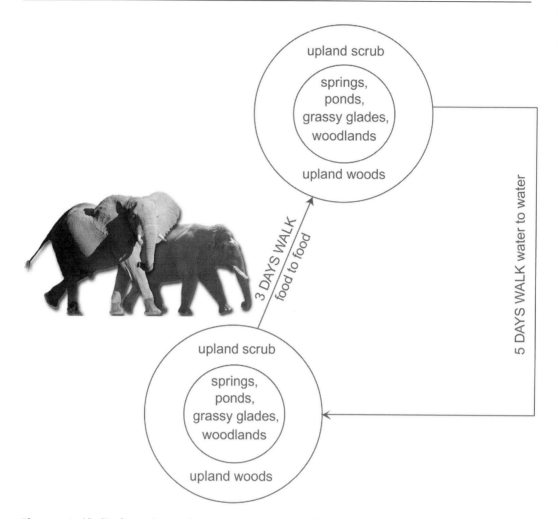

Fig. 5.10 An idealized proboscidean range in which food and water are "focal" rather than dispersed.

rejuvenation may occur at water points, along travel routes, or at raw material sources that are situated between water points. The main implication is that big-game hunting under late Pleistocene conditions may be understandable if food and water source availability can be better understood within regions or subregions, keeping in mind the increasing habitat fragmentation at the end of the Pleistocene.

Foraging models can illustrate what I perceive as a misuse of the theory to make an invalid argument in the debate about Clovis foraging behaviors. The question of relevance in this discussion is *not* "when would Clovis foragers have given up hunting mammoths" – foragers *do not consciously give up the desire to hunt their high-ranked resources*, and always try to capture them whenever they are encountered, no matter how rare or "endangered" they may be. The question that the Marginal Value Theorem (MVT) should inspire archeologists to address is: why would foragers stay in a patch longer than predicted? Why would Clovis foragers have stayed to hunt mammoths in Pleistocene patches, even when megamammals and other large species were becoming locally scarce?

Foragers, to answer this question, remain longer periods of time in patches when they are exploring them for new information and accumulating intelligence about patch quality. Different kinds of cues such as visual ones allow foragers to judge the potential quality of the patch. In classic MVT modeling, it is a forager's tracking of time spent in a patch that leads to decisions to abandon a patch. However, a forager may choose to spend extra time (beyond the consciously chosen cut-off point) whenever the perceived probability is high in a patch of finding prey at the next stopping point. And a high-quality patch will invite longer stays, as well. According to Bayesian models, in an environment where prey are not evenly dispersed (in other words, the distribution may be clumped, so that some patches are empty while others are very full), every prey encounter by foragers will raise expectations that more prey are still to be found – since the foragers know that the prey may be either very scarce or very abundant in such "underdispersed" environments. In these sorts of environments, the most successful foragers will spend much longer times in patches seeking prey, even if these search times are completely unrewarded, before abandoning patches. In environments where prey are "overdispersed," or in other words where patches are of similar quality because the prey are distributed evenly everywhere, a forager who encounters and kills one prey animal instantly knows that the chances of finding another one just went down – the patch being searched has lost one prey, and the patch's perceived quality is lowered. The patch would be abandoned relatively sooner.

What I am trying to emphasize here in the strongest possible terms is that oversimplified reading of the Marginal Value Theorem has little to say about Clovis decisions to stop hunting megamammals, whatever the densities and distributions of megamammals in the late Pleistocene environment. MVT is not some sort of biological law that forbids hunters from killing off all members of a species. MVT is a means of predicting the time to be spent in a patch, not merely the ranking and reranking of food in the patch, as based on perceived depletion of the food.

The decision by humans to persist even when unrewarded in pursuit of prey within certain patches depends on several factors (Kelly 1995). For example, if poisoned weapons are used, hunters will spend a longer time in the patch after an encounter waiting for the poison to work. If hunters are in a patch for another reason (such as toolstone acquisition or searching for water), they may choose to hunt prey that is relatively scarce everywhere else; if patch returns are perceived as "linear" – that is indefinite or unlimited in possibilities – hunters may not pay as much attention to search time; and if information about prey is perfect or dependable beyond what is normally expected, hunters may perceive the energy costs of perseverance in a patch to be minimized, even when a great deal of time is spent without an encounter.

At this point in the discussion, I concede that I have not completely bashed a badly stated line of argumentation about the "impossibility" of overkill. I recognize that of course food depletion will obviously affect a forager's perception of a patch's return rate, and will therefore affect the forager's decision about when to abandon the patch. If Clovis foragers detected that their main food items were harder to find in a patch, they should have fled the patch in search of better ones. Perhaps they did, helping to account for some of the rapidity of Clovis dispersals. Also recall that in terminal Pleistocene times, the patches that provided the optimal food prospects for hunter-gatherers also may have provided the optimal prospects to most of their prey, the large herbivores, and hence all the Pleistocene players in the extinction drama were present on the same isolated and restricted stages together, with few (and distantly separated) alternative patches to visit when the curtain began to fall. Not all of North America could provide adequate food patches for Clovis foragers or for megamammals. The patches may have been few and far between. Within the patches, as megamammal numbers declined, there were other species that could be hunted, other resources to be gathered in the refuges, so Clovis foragers may have stayed in the refugial patches right up to the bitter end for the largest herbivores (extinction) and longer, as the smaller species were moved up the food-rankings and hunted more often.

PROCUREMENT RATES AND CHANGES IN RATES?

Procurement rates: Here I offer some thoughts about how decisions regarding procurement *rates* should be factored into Clovis foraging models, in so far as Clovis hunters actively may have changed their rates of game killing owing to the climatic/environmental instability that characterized the end of the Pleistocene. I am trying to make a specific point about possible Clovis ecology, based on ideas about foraging and big-game killing, and I am not trying to propose a new theory about Clovis. These propositions are hypothetical, but they do have implications that may be testable against the archeological record.

First let us suppose that Clovis procurement rates of mammoths and mastodonts were near their rationalized maximum during the beginning of Clovis dispersal; what this means is that people killed as many megamammals as they could afford to kill per kilometer traveled or hour spent on foraging trips. The rate may have been one kill per week, or one kill per 60 km traveled, or any other sort of figure, ranging from stalks and chases per unit of time, to length of time a chase was sustained, all of which would have varied with the nature of the terrain covered, the weather, the number of mouths to feed, and so on. However, let us say that at times there was a perceived need to increase the procurement rate (owing to population increase, say, or the need to solidify social networking by acquiring a greater volume of meat to exchange). The options available to increase the rate were limited, given the late Pleistocene insularity and localization of megamammal refugia. Clovis foragers perhaps could have decided to travel farther or longer in search of game, sleeping less or relaxing less often. I would expect that this step involved more scouting and exploration preceding group movements, and a reduction in group sizes as fissioned subgroups traveled more often away from the base grouping. If this tactic did not work and the rate of procurement did not go up acceptably, the other alternative would have been to add another resource to the diet or to increase the use of lower-benefit/higher-cost resources in order to support the higher activity level of the group members. The new resource could have been another large mammal, a resource type whose return would have far exceeded that of smaller game or plant foods. And if this too did not work to increase returns adequately, and further broadening of the diet was impractical, no other new options were available. Clovis foragers therefore would have had to migrate widely, completely change their subsistence orientation, or die out.

If Clovis procurement rates were at a minimal level at the beginning of the dispersal, the option available to raise it first would have involved a degree of increase in the stalk/chase rate per kilometer traveled while foraging. If this did not work well, Clovis would have had to maximize its rate, involving the steps outlined in the paragraph above. No viable options followed – except readaptation, migration, or dying out.

The archeological traces of *rate maximization* probably would include: more toolstone curation, use of highest-quality toolstone (because of a lowered inclination to spend time away from game-procurement very often visiting quarry sites); more short-term or one-visit sites, created during wide exploratory travel; more use of lower-benefit resources and expedient extraction of these resources using tools that were not prepared especially for them; abrupt disappearances of Clovis artifacts from traditionally reused sites; more utilization of game carcasses, such as fuller butchering, and much more processing to provide meat for extended traveling; and quite possibly fewer formal tool types in sites, a result that ethnographic studies suggest arises from different groups' reduced desire to differentiate themselves socially from the neighbor groups.

I suggest that these characteristics of rate maximizing do not describe Clovis very well. For example, Clovis is often found in the eastern United States at quarry-related locales at least as often as at optimal game-attracting natural features. Clovis does not seem to have often utilized plant foods in the east or the west – there are nearly no grinding stones, for example, or plant-harvesting tools. Clovis mammoths are very lightly butchered and processed, not indicating desperation or nutritional stress among the foragers. However, many Clovis sites may have been short-term visitations, the hallmark of small bands, highly mobile foraging, and perhaps a very short "life" of the culture in time. In the end, the evidence about procurement rates – at least when it comes to megamammals – is that no changes occurred, no pressures were felt to increase the rates, and Clovis procurement of mammoths and mastodonts always may have been optimal.

METAPOPULATIONS AND VARIANCE IN CLOVIS DIETS

The word metapopulation refers to a "population of populations" (Levins 1969). Specifically it is a population that is discontinuous in space, or, in other words, one that is found in "disjunct patches of suitable habitat . . . separated by intervening unsuitable habitat" in which the animals cannot survive (McCullough 1996:1–2). Movements between patches are not routine, and local extinction in separate patches may be rather common. The rate of recolonization must exceed the rate of local extinctions for the metapopulation to persist. Under certain conditions, while each patch is potentially chaotic, the overall population system maintains stability or growth.

Clear examples of metapopulation dynamics in nature are marmots in mountain meadows in the western United States, separated from other mountain meadows by very different habitats, or klipspringers on isolated rock outcrops in Africa – animals living in disjunct habitats and in relatively small populations separated from other small populations. The opposite of a metapopulation is called either a "panmictic" or a continuous population, where genetic mixing is unrestricted by geography.

The concepts which make metapopulation theories so useful to understanding late Pleistocene foraging are: (1) corridors and edges, (2) connectivity and dispersal, and (3) landscape structure.

During the late Pleistocene, under the stressful conditions of Late Glacial climatic and biotic change, scattered populations of mammoths and people were undoubtedly out of touch with each other over great distances and long periods of time. However, as with modern disjunct animal populations, some sort of connectivity along corridors or during migratory movements must have brought the separate populations near enough to each other to maintain gene flow and exchange, else the populations (and the greater metapopulation) would have died out for good. Thus it is probable that megamammal populations did exchange genes, in spite of distances, and human populations did exchange ideas and thoughts. The corridors connecting habitats may have been along stream valleys or some other rich part of the landscape; or, if direct connections were missing, in the case of large mammals, relatively long distances can be traveled across sterile habitats. Larger animals can fast longer than can smaller-bodied taxa, and limb length and body size are fair indications of animal mobility. Late Pleistocene megamammal body size just before extinction was still large, although not as large as earlier in the Pleistocene, which may indicate a need to be mobile in Late Glacial ranges but not as mobile as in the early and middle Pleistocene.

Isotopic analyses can suggest the separation of animal ranges, if the habitats varied between ranges and animal diets provided different proportions of certain elements. Perhaps a better test of metapopulation connectivity around 11,000 rcybp would be a comprehensive genetic sampling of the many well-preserved mammoth and mastodont individuals from North American fossil sites. However, until such testing is carried out, we can do no more than guess at mega-mammal population contacts between and among the richer refugia landscapes. The corridors connecting one isolated mastodont population around the eastern Great Lakes, as one example, may have been covered with mastodont trails linking water sources, mineral licks, nut tree patches, protective cover, and other localities appealing to proboscideans and other animals, and hence attractive for Clovis foragers, too. Did mastodonts move between eastern and western Great Lakes subregions, or between north and south? Did the mastodonts of the Virginia inland river valleys ever contact the mastodonts of Virginia coastal plains? And did the coastal plain animals frequently or rarely contact members of the mastodont population in New York and New England? We may be able to answer these questions in another decade if DNA and geochemical studies are carried out.

FORAGING OUTCOMES: DISPERSAL, EXPLORATION, AND EXTINCTION

> The bones exist – the animals do not! . . . Certain we are that they existed in great abundance, from the number of their remains which are found in America. We are likewise sure that they must have been destroyed by some sudden and powerful cause . . .
>
> Rembrandt Peale 1803:9, 91

Clovis foraging in the late Pleistocene had several important outcomes beyond the feeding of Clovis individuals and groups. The tactics I imagine underlying Clovis foraging would have led to wide dispersal of people over much of North

America, which was new range that could be explored and settled without the more severe limitations that would appear later, such as the existence of ethnically distinct neighbor foragers, or the loss of so much biotic diversity. The loss of a great part of that diversity was one unwitting result of Clovis foraging.

DISPERSAL AND EXPLORATION

The foraging strategy I modeled in this chapter would have encouraged rapid exploration of new habitats and the expansion of the human foraging range. In the next chapter I further discuss range expansion and dispersal by humans, looking at these important processes from the perspective of historical ecology. So far I have suggested that Clovis foragers were interested in exploration not because they were pathological, neurotic, or obsessed, but because they were human beings with rational goals. These goals include autonomy, competency in food-procurement, reduction of competition, and the ability to reproduce one's culture. By dispersing from birth sites and exploring new ranges, Clovis foragers accomplished their goals. By focusing on megamammals, Clovis foragers found a suitable food source and a widespread prey class whose knowledge of North America could be deciphered by the foragers tracking and monitoring megamammal movements within and between late Pleistocene refugia.

EXTINCTION: MODELS AND CRITICISMS

One outcome of the model described in this chapter is megamammal extinction (G. Haynes and Eiselt 1999). My outline of the extinction process is not identical to the unfolding of events imagined in Paul Martin's blitzkrieg model of "overkill" (Martin 1967, 1984; Martin and Steadman 1999) in which rapidly dispersing human foragers kill all taxa of large animals in whatever range the people happen to pass through. My outline also differs from models that ascribe extinction mainly to changes in environment and climate.

Critics have attacked the idea that human foragers drove megafauna to extinction. Some attacks are based on insupportable opinions rather than robust theories. Native American writer Vine Deloria attacked the overkill model because of the damage he thought it did to the image of Native Americans. "Right-wing fanatics" and scholars, he wrote (Deloria 1995:112), already use the overkill model to accuse Indians of lacking moral fiber and ethical concern for the earth. In his criticisms, Deloria scorned radiometric dating, taphonomy, and archeology, and considered trans-Beringian migration to be a silly myth. After rejecting scientific explanations, he proposed that the megafauna died in geological catastrophes such as floods, volcanic explosions, or earthquakes. Or, according to some Native American folklore, a higher spirit killed the big animals relatively recently.

A more scientific critic called the idea of overkill a credo or "statement of faith rather than an appeal to scientific reason" (Grayson 2001:41) because it glosses over the disputed features of the process, such as (1) the lack of clarity in the timing of extinctions and the first arrival of humans, (2) the likelihood that climate change impacts would have killed many species with or without humans present, (3) the unexplained disappearance of certain birds and other animals that were probably never hunted by prehistoric foragers, (4) the scarcity of proboscidean killsites and the utter lack of killsites of the other extinct animals, and (5) the probable difficulties of low-density foragers actually using stone-tipped spears to kill off so many large mammals.

The problem of the timing of migrations and extinction is far from solved, but continued radiometric dating may take us much nearer an answer. The potential existence of measurable pre-Clovis human populations in North America would make the abrupt or blitzkrieg scenario of overkill less likely, especially if the pre-Clovis foragers coexisted with megafauna for thousands of years before extinction took place. However, as stated earlier, very few sites can be found anywhere that are pre-Clovis; and some of them are open to doubts about the reliability of dating or the accurate recognition of genuine artifacts. Clovis is the basal culture over the greatest part of the continent, and therefore it is apparently only Clovis foraging that affected the megafauna.

Climatic sequences from the end of the Pleistocene show that severe climate reversals occurred out of phase with the extinction events. For example, the Younger Dryas chronozone was a geological interval of cold that had abruptly reversed warm and wet conditions, beginning around 11,000 rcybp and ending just as abruptly nearly a millennium later (Alley, Meese, Shuman, Gow, and 7 others 1993; Dansgaard, White, and Johnsen 1989) (note that the duration and timing are problematical in different world areas [Moreno, Almquist-Jacobson, Denton, Grimm, Jacobson, and Watts 1998; Rutter, Weaver, Rokosh, Fanning, and Wright 2000]). This cold interval is sometimes thought to have been the last straw for larger mammals, killing them off completely after they had suffered through several cold-to-warm reversals following the Last Glacial Maximum. Yet the current best-guess chronosequence of events during the glacial to deglacial transition (for example Fiedel 1999a:fig. 6 [p. 106]) does not support this scenario of extinction based solely on climate stress. The earliest appearance of Clovis foragers was about 11,500 rcybp, followed by some extinctions possibly at 11,200 rcybp, then a return to cold conditions and a serious drought at about 10,900 rcybp, and the last extinctions afterwards when Clovis was everywhere in the continent south of the glaciers (Holliday 2000b; C. V. Haynes n.d. 1993, 1998, 1999b; see also Graham, Stafford, and Semken 1997; Stafford, Graham, Semken, and Southon 1997a, 1997b). Thus, the abrupt changes of the Younger Dryas followed the extinctions in some parts of the New World, while in others parts such as southern South America there may have been no measurable reversal into cold conditions at all (Bennett, Haberle, and Lumley 2000; Rodbell 2000).

There is simply no clear model available that explains how the extinction process tracked changes in climate and habitat at the end of the Pleistocene (see Krech 1999:38–40 for a précis of the ambiguity). There are several elegant theoretical models such as Guthrie's (e.g., 1990), King's and Saunder's (1984), and Graham's and Lundelius's (1984) which implicate climatic and vegetational changes in the great killing-off event, but the direct evidence of the progress of taxa extinctions is lacking. For example, there are no known fossil skeletons of starved or malnourished animals, no clear and unambiguous indicators of nutritionally stressed megafaunal populations, and no known finds of unusually pathological fossil bones dating to the end of the extinction event.

Adding to the uncertainty is the fact that the apparent timing of at least some of the extinctions is out of sync with the definable climatic oscillations. Until more carefully collected and prepared megafaunal bone samples are radiometrically dated, the uncertainty will remain that each and every one of thirty-three genera became extinct at different times (Grayson 1989, 1991, 2001).

Radiocarbon dates do not clearly show that all the different taxa went extinct at one and the same time interval (see Grayson 1991, 2001), which might imply that time-specific Clovis foraging is not to blame for the disappearance of every taxon. But the unfortunate fact is that the time interval of extinctions overlaps with a period of great variation in atmospheric radiocarbon, and dates falling anywhere in this interval are in effect floating without an absolute anchor in time. A date of 12,000 rcybp could come from a sample that is only 10,500 radiocarbon years old; and a date of 10,500 rcybp could be derived from a sample that is actually 12,000 radiocarbon years old.

The fuzziness in the dating makes the climate–extinction linkage much less clear. Yet even if the hazy nature of the dating is not considered too objectionable, the mechanisms of habitat changes following climatic shifts have been open to question. An example can be seen in the case of Beringia, which appears mostly depleted of megamammals before 12,000 rcybp – perhaps explaining why mammoths (in this case, the northern species, woolly mammoth [Mammuthus primigenius] rather than the southern columbian mammoth [Mammuthus columbi/jeffersonii]) were not hunted by early Alaskan cultures (although a last remnant mammoth population survived, apparently unhunted, until around 4,000 rcybp on Wrangel Island in the arctic). During the Last Glacial Maximum, all of Beringia was tundra, according to the pollen and macrofossil record (Edwards, Anderson, Brubaker and others 2000), but intergradations of tundra and steppe did exist in places, and the vegetation was a mosaic of different tundra types. A non-analogue vegetation type sometimes called "steppe-tundra" may have developed, helping to explain the high faunal diversity of the region during glacial intervals. Zimov, Chuprynin, Oreshko, Chapin, Reynolds, and Chapin (1995) hypothesized that megafauna such as mammoth and horse played at least as great a role as climate in creating more productive steppelike vegetation in late Pleistocene Beringia (also see Putschkov 1997). Megafaunal trampling and grazing transformed what would have been tundra into grass-dominated steppe. The extinction of megafauna at the end of the Pleistocene allowed vegetation to shift from dry steppe to moss-dominated tundra. In this model, human hunting caused the megafaunal extinctions, followed by the change in vegetation after the "keystone" taxa (Owen-Smith 1987) had been killed out. If this model is valid, then a mammoth-hunting human strategy must have existed in northern Eurasia after the Last Glacial Maximum and during a time of changing climate.

But Guthrie (2001) questioned the degree to which megamammals actually shaped steppe out of tundra, and proposed that less cloud cover and more aridity had a greater effect on vegetation, raising plant productivity to high enough levels to support the Pleistocene's rich and diverse large-mammal fauna. Most of the former "mammoth steppe" became taiga at the end of the Pleistocene, and Guthrie did not believe mammoth-grazing alone could have knocked back boreal forests and kept them as open steppes. Furthermore, the shift from steppe to forest also had occurred during earlier interglacials, when mammoths did not become extinct but only disappeared temporarily from the north; and equally as important, trampling grazers did not all disappear from the north at the end of the Pleistocene: bison and caribou survived yet did not expand their ranges by transforming habitats. Guthrie's (2001:570–1) most compelling arguments against the keystone status of Pleistocene mammoths involves (1) the possibly much lower density of mammoths in the north compared to modern elephants, whose higher-density feeding does transform woodlands into open lands, (2) the unpalatability of northern trees which would have prevented mammoths from seriously reducing woody vegetation patches, and (3) the mammoth's dietary avoidance of browse, as evidenced by frozen stomach contents. Hence, Guthrie's arguments do not allow for the possibility that mammoth extinction caused habitats to deteriorate from steppe to tundra and taiga. But the explanation for megamammal extinction still does not seem to be climate change alone, since dramatic changes had occurred several times before during interglacial periods and mammoths always survived to return to Beringia.

The attributing of extinction only to climate change has yet to be subjected to rigorous scrutiny. If vegetation change occurred quickly, say within twenty years of climate shifts, certainly many species of animals and plants would have responded by either changing their ranges or dying out. But not all species would have responded in identical ways. A switch from grassland to woodland would have driven away grazers such as mammoths, or killed them off, but at the same time it would have improved conditions for animals capable of browsing (such as mastodonts). Yet both mammoths and mastodonts died out. And besides, the taxa that did become extinct after the appearance of humans in North America had not gone extinct during earlier cycles of dramatic climate change when there were no humans present. This fact alone mortally weakens the case for climate change inevitably causing extinction. The earlier cycles of climate change may have been just as abrupt as the late Pleistocene reversals – but the stratigraphic record is nowhere near as detailed from the earlier times, unfortunately, and direct comparisons cannot be made. However, I do concede that if the late Pleistocene abruptness in climatic oscillations is completely unique, then the late Pleistocene extinctions may indeed be unique as well, and climate change would become a likelier culprit than it currently seems to be.

How can we explain the extinction of animal taxa that humans are less likely to have eaten, such as the ten or more genera of birds (see Anderson 1984; Harris and Jefferson 1985; Stock 1972)? Couldn't climate change account for those extinctions? Possibly yes, but possibly no. The scavenging types of birds such as condor and vulture could have died out after the megamammal carcasses disappeared; other carnivorous taxa such as an eagle and an owl are closely related to surviving forms in North or South America, and may have been races of the modern taxa. Other extinct bird taxa – such as a cowbird – may have depended on dead megafauna, so they could not survive the loss of their main food supply. The lapwing and shelduck that died out may have been hunted and eaten by humans, perhaps around migratory waterways. Bird skeletons are not easy to fossilize and preserve, and the lack of killsites or cooking areas is not unexpected.

Another point to rebut has to do with the apparent scarcity of killsites of megamammals and any other megafauna. Although the mammoth/mastodont sites are not scarce, the sites with other prey species in them are exceedingly rare, as Grayson (1991, 2001) has pointed out. But I ask, why shouldn't they be rare? Killsites are not automatic sites-in-the-making. Unless the bones in an animal's killsite are buried within a few years after its death, the chances for preservation and entry into a future fossil record are very low. Thousands of animals die every year in wild ranges around the world, and their bones never become fossils, because they weather away, are eaten by scavengers, or are fragmented completely by trampling or other natural process. The number of subtractive processes in nature is high. Animals killed and butchered where they are encountered would have left bones behind on the earth's surface only for a few decades or so before the bones became friable and eventually unidentifiable. By the time a century had passed after thousands of mammals were killed in Pleistocene ranges, their bones were no longer recognizable. In over twenty years of examining and re-examining recent animal skeletons in roadless areas, I have seen how extremely difficult it is for bones ever to enter the lithosphere. In the 13,000 calendar years after the mammoth and mastodont extinction, when Native American hunter-gatherers were regularly hunting deer in eastern North America, a fact beyond dispute, they left behind not one killsite for archeologists to find. Not a single prehistoric killsite of white-tailed deer has ever been discovered. The bones were either completely removed by weathering or scavenging animals, or the hunters fully transported or utilized every scrap. Of course deer bones are found in campsites, villages, middens, or other types of domestic locations, but these settlements were in ranges that were occupied for longer times by larger groups of people than were the Clovis ranges. Clovis settlements were created by extremely mobile and small groups within the briefest of time intervals, a very different set of conditions from later prehistoric times, and the existence of animal-bone evidence about Clovis hunting practices is understandably much scarcer.

The final point to rebut is the probable difficulty of killing mammoths and mastodonts. Megamammal-hunting foragers using stone-tipped spears or projectiles tipped with ivory and bone points would have been in great danger, if the proboscideans behaved like modern elephants. Modern African elephants are vigilant, wary, and aggressive when provoked by lions, hyenas, or human beings. But modern anti-predator behaviors may very well be specific to the modern taxa of elephants, accounting for their survival to the present day. Martin (1984) has suggested that, compared to modern elephants, American mammoths were very naïve and thus unable to defend themselves against the new predators, the Clovis hunters of 11,000 rcybp.

Mammoth populations, like most other mammalian taxa, would have had two kinds of anti-predator behavior – avoidance and response (Griffin, Blumstein, and Evans 2000). Among modern elephants, avoidance involves increasing the flight distance, keeping high levels of vigilance within mixed herds, maintaining close spatial proximity when feeding, moving, and resting, and when necessary using the hours of darkness to feed and drink. Feeding or resting sites prone to predator disturbance may be abandoned.

Taxon-specific fear may be learned quickly by naïve animals, requiring only one or two predator encounters. The fear may be learned by seeing, hearing, or smelling conspecifics showing fear or aggression towards predators. Among modern elephants, the fear may be communicated over distances much farther than elephants can directly see or hear: low-frequency vocalizations (called rumbles) and seismic waves created by foot-stomping during mock charges can communicate over extremely long distances (Payne, Langbauer, and Thomas 1986; Poole, Payne, Langbauer, and Moss 1988), and in the case of foot-stomping the range of communication is far greater than sound waves can travel – over 30 km (O'Connell-Rodwell, Arnason, and Hart 2000). If mammoths and mastodonts detected infrasound and seismic waves as well as do modern elephants, they communicated interest and fear rapidly from herd to herd within large ranges. It is possible that one frightened or angry herd responding to a Clovis attack could have stimulated distant other herds into fleeing even when the distant herds had not yet encountered the new predator.

Anti-predator responses other than fear include issuing alarm calls, bunching in defensive position, aggressively attacking the predator, and flight. Population-wide behavioral adjustments are not rapid, but may begin appearing within a single generation among some large-mammal taxa such as moose (Berger, Swenson, and Persson 2001). Yet unless the fear is reinforced in animals, it is forgotten within a short time, measured in days, weeks, or months (see Griffin et al. 2000)

The avoidance behaviors are relatively costly for modern elephants – they take time away from feeding and looking for mates and they lead to more intense feeding competition within forage patches – but they are effective and evolutionarily advantageous in ranges where predators are threats. But unlike modern elephants, mammoths and mastodonts in North America had not co-evolved with human hunters, and as a result they would not have developed the same anti-predator avoidance behaviors or responses – they were not so vigilant in herds, and they probably did not feed and move in such compact interactive groupings. They may not have reacted to threats by automatically bunching defensively, attacking the hunters, or fleeing readily as do modern elephants.

An aggressive attack that routs a threatening predator is not a behavior that can be spread throughout a population in one generation. Solitary and naïve animals would have died on their first encounter with human hunters, thus never learning avoidance or an appropriate response, and mammoths or mastodonts in small groups also may not have had chances to learn fear from chance encounters. Likewise, the behavior of compact-group feeding, affording protection to young animals, may have been difficult for naïve mammoths or mastodonts to learn when confronted with new predators, especially if forage was patchier in mammoth and mastodont ranges and animals had to scatter to find adequate nutrition (see Griffin et al. 2000 and references therein for more about animals learning anti-predator behaviors).

Elephants that live in relatively predator-free environments behave differently from harassed animals, and their behavior offers clues to the ways in which megamammals were vulnerable to human hunting. For example, in elephant populations without predators, the young males show a very early independence, wandering free from their mothers for long periods during the day. Such behavior has been seen in remote forest elephants, where even little three-year-olds move away from their mothers and explore or entertain themselves (see Mathiessen 1990, for example), sometimes confusing observers who think of these often cheeky subadults as pygmy adults. Predator-free elephants are relatively easy to approach in Africa (although still wary and dangerous when one moves too close), and individual animals may scatter widely when feeding or moving. Animals in predator-free populations may reach maturity sooner and have shorter life-spans, too, if there is less need to stay close to herds while becoming larger in order to survive on their own. Thus, being free of predators predisposes animals to be easy pickings when an efficient predator such as the human hunter does appear.

ALTERNATIVE EXPLANATIONS FOR EXTINCTIONS: HYPERDISEASE AND GRASSY KNOLL THEORIES

MacPhee and Marx (1997) proposed that a deadly "hyperdisease" spread throughout North American faunal communities around the same time as human groups were first encountering the continent. Their model is plausible because of the known instances of diseases jumping species and causing major die-offs such as the recurring global influenza pandemics, which are cases of diseases endemic in mammals or birds spreading into human populations. However, the spread of the most serious diseases has been in the direction of animal to human, not the other way around, and none has ever wiped out a whole mammalian species or large proportions of the species affected. MacPhee and associates have begun searching in cold Northeast Asia for well-preserved large-mammal carcass parts from which disease organisms or DNA can be extracted, but as of this writing no success has been reported.

Rothschild (2001) examined a sample of American mastodont skeletons of Late Glacial age (dating from about 16,000–11,000 rcybp) and found that a large proportion displayed bone pathologies he interpreted as the result of chronic tuberculosis. Such a high proportion might reflect an exceptional frequency of the disease in all of North America's mastodont populations, perhaps as high as 100 percent. Further studies are necessary to support the diagnosis, but if the hypothesis is correct it means that a sort of hyperdisease actually did exist in the past, even if it did not cause rapid mastodont extinction.

Other hypotheses to explain extinction are available in the markeplace of ideas, such as volcanic explosions or impacts by extraterrestrial objects. Many are what I consider grassy knoll theories, advanced by dissatisfied scientists not because strong new evidence has been found but mainly because they cannot bring themselves to accept the existing theories, especially climate change and overkill. The original "grassy knoll" was a grass-covered slope near which John F. Kennedy's limousine passed just as he was shot dead in Dallas, Texas, in 1963. Many conspiracy theorists who reject Lee Harvey Oswald as the lone assassin believe that an as yet undiscovered, unwitnessed (or dubiously witnessed), unsubstantiated second shooter stood on the grassy knoll and did the actual killing from there (see Posner 1993 for more discussion of the theories, eyewitness testimony, and confusion). These sorts of theories may be plausible but they do little to move the debate forward without empirical evidence or data.

Conclusions

> How vain and foolish . . . for timid untravelled man to try to comprehend aright this wondrous whale, by merely poring over his dead attenuated skeleton, stretched in this peaceful wood. No. Only in the heart of quickest perils; only when within the eddyings of his angry flukes; only on the profound unbounded seas, can the fully invested whale be truly and livingly found out.
>
> Herman Melville 1948 [orig. 1851]:449

In this chapter I have proposed a version of Clovis foraging behavior, and offered theoretical and contingent explanations for certain actions. Perhaps the most important question I have attempted to answer is: what did Clovis people eat? I have also addressed a question about what they did not eat. By using the word "eat" I refer to regularly sought food resources that Clovis people would have spent some energy preparing themselves to procure, handle, and consume. The answer to the first question is that Clovis people ate what was locally and ecologically available. They rationally decided what to search for actively, how to engineer their tools to process these foods, and what to expect to find in the future.

As for what they did not eat, I can say that Clovis people did not routinely eat plant foods that required complex preparation, such as hardshelled nuts, roots, or seeds in quantity. Milling stones are required to process seeds, grains and many nuts. Underground foods such as roots or tubers are laborious to collect, requiring burden-baskets or bags, digging equipment, skinning tools, and cooking facilities such as rock-lined pits, because many such foods contain sugars that are not digestible unless cooked. Yet grinding, cracking, or leaching technology is extremely rare or nonexistent in Clovis sites (see Table 5.4), and there are no true roasting pits, storage facilities, and processing features. Clovis-era exploitation of seeds and nuts should be reflected in settlement patterning, because Clovis vegetarians would have frequently aggregated at specific vegetational communities; yet Clovis sites are small everywhere except at quarries or water sources, and show no attraction to nut-tree-rich wooded areas or seed-rich grasslands. Clovis people also did not programmatically eat succulent fruits. There is no evidence of such plants in the pollen and macrofossil records.

Of course, the archeological inventory from Clovis times may be inadequate to reflect the actual conditions of Paleoindian life. Forager technology is in fact no more than a small part of life. As ethnologist Megan Biesele (1993:10) phrased it when discussing Kalahari Bushmen, "most of . . . technology is carried as information and technique, in fact, rather than [things] in the hands or on the back." Technology is much more than a collection of a few weapon points, water carriers, bags, ornaments, cooking tools, and so forth. As I stated before, these items are only a skim, the small bubbly bits that float on top of Clovis culture, all that is visible but only a tiny expression of the great depths of the unseen and unknowable information, techniques, knowledge, and beliefs of Clovis people.

What I have attempted to do in this part of the book is to add theoretical foundations and information to the modeling of Clovis, thus going beyond interpretations based on technological evidence and knowledge about paleoecosystems. I think the suggestions here not only explain some aspects of the Clovis archeological record (why the sites are so different, why mammoth remains are so frequently found, why the dates are tightly clustered, for example), but also explain why Clovis foraging decisions were based on rational thought. Clovis mammoths, notoriously underutilized (not fully butchered, sectioned and scattered), may be explained as the result of humans opportunistically reacting to the effects of Pleistocene stresses affecting mammoths. Clovis foragers found it easy to procure mammoths, by killing or scavenging, and did not make use of meat and byproducts the same way they would if the hunting had been more difficult. This interpretation is based on analogy with modern scavengers and predators such as lions, wolves, hyenas, and leopards. The mammoth carcasses were used to feed only the people who had been instrumental in the killing and butchering, or they provided only immediate returns to a larger group, with little or no storage or exchange of the resources through a wider social network. There was no need to think of longer-range and longer-term social bonding through complete sharing of every possible part of the carcass, which is the pattern seen among modern hunter-gatherers.

An alternative to the idea that Clovis people hunted highly vulnerable or weakened megamammals is that healthy mammoths and mastodonts were easy to kill. The degree of carcass use would also be light if killing them were unusually effortless. It is perhaps possible that Clovis hunters participated in slaying proboscideans through specialized guilds, or cooperative groups that targeted mammoths and mastodonts preferentially (see Marks 1971 for an ethnographic example from Africa).

Cashel (1997) compared the recorded behavioral strategies of foragers who hunted and gathered terrestrial mammals, birds, and fish, and found them generally well scattered in small fluid bands. Some foragers had hunting partnerships, in which men cooperated to procure game animals. Perhaps Clovis hunters cooperated when attacking megamammals. The modern foragers had no marriage residence restrictions (thus further encouraging mobility), no marked community sense (encouraging dispersal, wide exchanges of resources and mates, and foraging at the individual level or in very small groups), and no levels of distinction among kin. These patterns probably also characterized Clovis foragers.

As Cashel (1997) observed and predicted, selection pressures among such foragers encourage (1) high mobility but also high reproductive rate; (2) small foraging groupings, with less division of labor and hence less exploitation of higher-cost resources; and (3) deliberate selection of fat-rich prey and body parts.

If Clovis foragers were this type of highly mobile and small-group hunter-gatherers, the lack of bone-breakage from megamammal carcasses may have been due to the conscious choice to kill only the animals with the most body fat, whose limb-bones did not need to be broken. If Clovis foragers killed or scavenged stressed megamammals, no attempt would have been made to break limb-bones for marrow because Clovis foragers knew the fat was depleted in the long bones. But adequate small amounts of visceral fat (from around the stomach and kidneys, for example) and lean meat could be selectively taken from even starving mammoths or mastodonts.

If fat sources were abundant for foraging Clovis groups, maximum group aggregation sizes would have increased and sites would have become more permanent or been reused more often. Large-group activities would have increased (such as animal drives or enclosures). Yet only in the eastern United States are there large sites, and some of these are palimpsests of many revisits perhaps over several centuries. It would seem that fat sources were adequate but never abundant for Clovis dispersers in both the east and the west of North America.

Whatever the case may be, Clovis people killed megamammals. Mammoths and mastodonts at the end of the Pleistocene would have been the highest-ranked food resource, owing to their extremely large size, and they would have been easily found in highly predictable locations. They may have been slowly starving. Clovis people made rational decisions to hunt them, and continued to kill mammoths and mastodonts until none was left alive in the refugia, or the last survivors were demographically incapable of replenishing the population.

I acknowledge that this representation of Clovis-era subsistence is merely a best-fit model. Archeological data and biological theory are accommodated by this model very well, but I realize that it is a temporary accommodation and the model may change (or even be abandoned) someday after more sites are found, more artifacts analyzed, more food remains recovered from Clovis-era sites. As fictional LAPD detective Harry Bosch remarks, "The key [is] not to become beholden to any one theory. Theories changed and you had to change with them" (Connelly 1996 [orig. 1995]:212).

6

Colonizing foragers

> At each change of direction [in his exploration of tortuous trails in the flat, featureless scrub of the African bush] his indigenous companions would require him to point out the direction in which their camp lay, until in a day or two he was doing this quite automatically and re-orientating 'without conscious thought' at each major twist of the trail.
>
> R. Baker 1981:95, referring to how D. Lewis (1972) learned to navigate unfamiliar country

6.1 Introduction

The Clovis-era patterns of foraging and exploration appeared in the lower forty-eight United States around or just after 11,500 rcybp. The technology of biface-fluting also appeared at this time, probably inextricably linked with the subsistence and dispersal strategies I proposed in the preceding chapter. The Clovis-era foragers with fluted points and a preference for megamammals must have had a point of origin or an ancestral culture – they did not spring up in the continent like a ring of mushrooms in the night. Yet Clovis origins are entirely unknown. The pre-Clovis archeological sites in North America do not provide us with information about the development of fluting technology or the progression from general hunting-gathering to opportunistic megafauna-hunting. Most parts of the continent do not have any evidence at all of pre-Clovis human populations.

In this chapter I propose a sequence of continental entry and dispersal, starting with the early human appearances in Beringia and advancing through the widest appearance of Clovis artifacts and sites. The sequence is conjectural and supported mainly by circumstantial evidence; there are no archeological sites that indicate the route taken by Clovis precursors, the timing and rate of their movement into the continent, or their technoeconomic characteristics. To begin, I first try to establish my terms of reference and a working vocabulary to describe human population movements. Much has been written about the physical movement of prehistoric people into the Americas, but either the literature is fuzzy when it comes to definitions or the terms and concepts are used in contradictory ways.

Theories of human migration may involve ecological, demographic, or cultural factors that affect the movements of genes from one population to another, which is what evolutionary geneticists mean when they use the word "migration" (Fix 1999; Merrell 1981). Here, I do not discuss population genetics models because this field of study is new and I'm no expert (see Fix 1999 for a useful introduction).

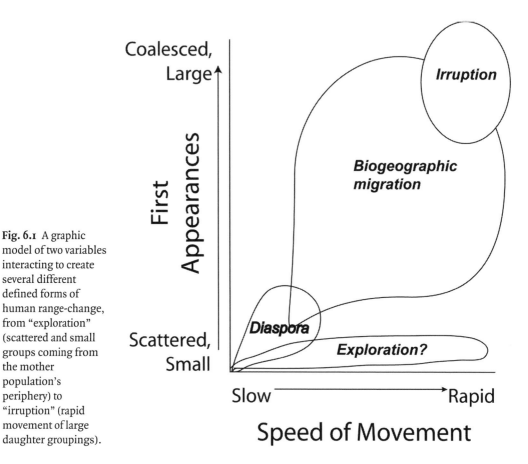

Fig. 6.1 A graphic model of two variables interacting to create several different defined forms of human range-change, from "exploration" (scattered and small groups coming from the mother population's periphery) to "irruption" (rapid movement of large daughter groupings).

6.2   Colonization theory

TOWARDS A THEORY-BASED MODELING OF HOMINID COLONIZING BEHAVIOR

The terminology chosen here is derived from the words most often used in archeological reconstructions of hominid movements, specifically the first peopling (or the repeopling) of world regions. The literature of evolutionary ecology also uses these words.

Figures 6.1 and 6.2 are idealizations of interacting variables in species or population movements. The source of groups changing their range may be wholly a border population (individuals who live near species borders), the central population, or combinations of each; the speed of movement may be rapid (and brief), or slow (and only occasional). These categories refer to behavior acted upon by natural selection. Range-change that is relatively rapid, continuous, and repetitive is a regular migratory behavior ("directed migration," rather than true range-change); species that change ranges slowly and repetitively exhibit already established adaptation to the ranges, indicating that no true range-borders exist.

Rapid movements of individuals coming mainly from the central homeland of the mother population and traveling across a species border are termed

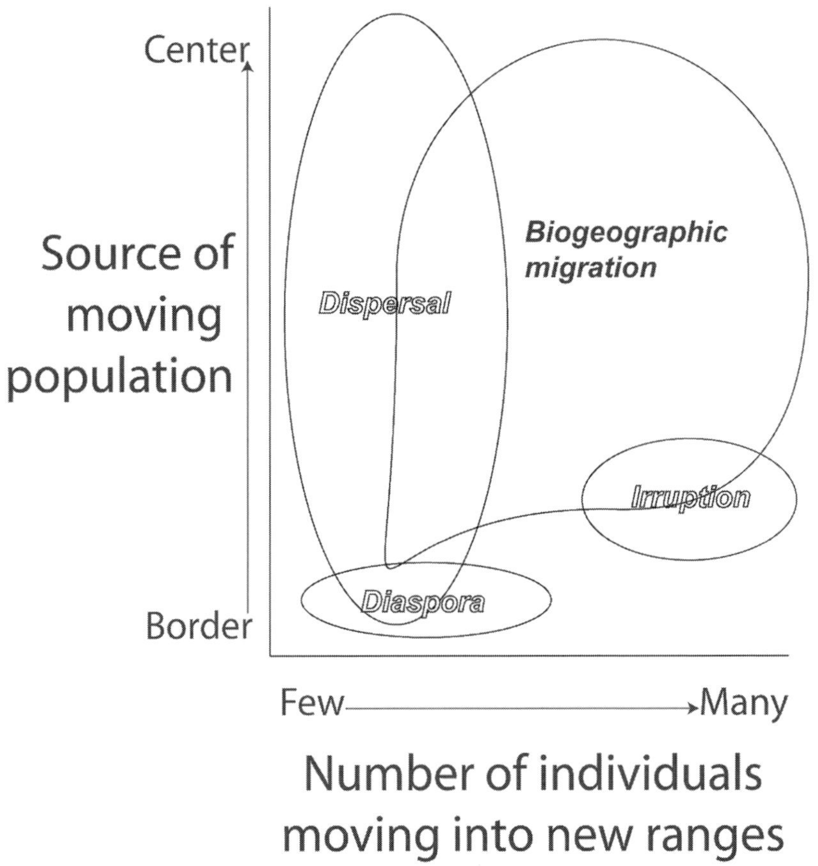

Fig. 6.2 A graphic model of two other variables interacting to create several different defined forms of human range-change, from "diaspora" (few individuals originating mainly on the peripheries of the mother population's range) to "biogeographic migration" (daughter groups in many sizes coming from both the peripheries and the central homeland of the mother population).

"Biogeographic Migrations." The movements may be *en masse* and coordinated. Border-crossing individuals who appear rapidly and *en masse*, but who come mainly from peripheral (border) populations, are involved in the process termed "irruption." When border populations slowly contribute small numbers of individuals to new ranges, the process is termed "dispersal." "Anastrophic migration" refers to the retracing of steps regularly (Wilkinson 1952). The terms used here need some discussion.

Migration

When animal populations synchronize movements seasonally or in response to environmental variation – such as the "spectacular long-distance to and fro trips of birds and butterflies" (Fix 1999:1) – they are said to "migrate." However, this word has two very different meanings in biology (Dingle 1980, 1996). Directed movements to and from feeding grounds or seasonally different ranges are here termed "anastrophic migration." Caribou in the north and wildebeeste in East Africa, to name just two examples, make this type of migration. An alternative word for movement within familiar range is "nomadism," which is based on a Greek root that means pasture; nomadism is thus the journey from pasture to pasture. The distances covered in nomadism may be huge (!Kung women in the Kalahari walk 2,400 km a year carrying a child and burdens gathered while foraging for food [Lee 1980]).

The other type of migration – a one-way movement into unfamiliar range – is called "Biogeographic Migration," and specifically refers to the process in which animals and plants spread their range into regions where they had not lived before. This latter meaning is the one most often used by archeologists when discussing the peopling of the Americas. This sort of migration – range-change – is seen more often in nature when home environments are unpredictable and organisms choose to abandon them in search of new range (Dingle 1996:61). Some of the benefits of either sort of migration are listed by Fix (1999:5), and include avoidance of inbreeeding and escape from local crowding. Some costs of migrating include energy expense while on the move, lack of familiarity with resources and reduced foraging efficiency, and susceptibility to new diseases.

During long-term climatic changes (those with periodicities of 100,000, 40,000, or 25,000 years, as predicted by Milankovitch Theory), species may slowly change their ranges in response. This is Biogeographic Migration. Even species with very low mobility or a very slim chance of surviving and reproducing when mobile in fact may be able to migrate this way. Individual survival and reproduction are favored when the individuals possess specialized abilities and behaviors that can take advantage of (or optimize returns from) changed conditions, but slow changes do not always tax species' abilities or cause major evolutionary changes in species.

Examples are range-changes in the late Pleistocene, when faunal and floral communities were quite distinct from those of the Holocene in terms of associations. Many taxa did become extinct when climates changed quickly, but many of the same species changed their ranges on an individual basis, forming very different new community associations in very different geographic ranges (changing from allopatry to sympatry) (Graham and Lundelius 1984; Guthrie 1990). Many of the taxa still existed in the Holocene, because they managed to survive terminal Pleistocene climatic changes, but once again they redistributed themselves in space and formed new sets of associations.

Shorter-term changes in atmospheric circulation patterns also cause ranges to change (see the review in Gauthreaux 1980); examples would be seasonal climate shifts, or the quasi-eighteen-year cycles of dry and wet periods in sub-Saharan Africa. The distances covered by migrating organisms may be great in both cases (long- or short-term); for example, wildebeeste in the Serengeti may travel 400 km every year on their annual migrations. Selection favors individuals with the abilities to disperse, to survive the dangers of dispersal/migration, and to find and capitalize on a welcoming new habitat, especially if the habitats outside a species' currently occupied range have higher mean favorableness (Gauthreaux 1980).

Dispersal

Dispersal is defined in biology as the movement of individuals away from their birth site (Lincoln and Boxshall 1987:118–19). This sort of movement may involve either a filling in of the available spaces located within a population's already established territory (short-distance movements made within species' ranges are here called "dispersion"), or movement into completely unoccupied space (which I term "dispersal"). Hence the word dispersal refers specifically to human movements into ranges where they did not live before.

The act of dispersal can be found in all plant and animal species; but explaining the causes or understanding the processes involved has proven very difficult, because lifetime movements can scarcely be measured in long-living organisms such as mammals. Ecologists generally postulate that competition for resources or competition for mates (CFR or CFM) and avoidance of the effects of inbreeding (IA) cause nonrandom dispersal patterns (Caley 1991; Dobson and Jones 1985; Moore and Ali 1984; Packer 1985). Methods for studying the distribution of dispersal distances are available, often using geometric probability models. Two forms of modeling are applicable: viewing dispersal as a diffusion process, or viewing it as a series of discrete steps (see, for example, Hargrove and Lange 1989). The most common form of the model is $f(x) = p(1 - p)x$, where $f(x)$ is the fraction of individuals who move distance x (which is described in units of home-range diameters) and p is the probability of stopping before moving an additional home-range diameter (Waser 1985; see also Porter and Dooley 1993 for a reassessment). In this model, individuals are described as dispersing from their birthplace in a straight line and settling in the first unoccupied territory. If unoccupied sites occur independently at random (such as in heterogeneous habitats where not all parts are equally appealing or optimal) the dispersal distances will be geometrically distributed. Sometimes dispersal is viewed as the process of movement from the maternal birth site of one generation to the birth sites of the next (see Neigel, Ball, and Avise 1991), and is predicted using a random walk model of the process (Richardson 1970), which simulates a series of separate daily steps taken in random directions.

Biologists define species borders as the limits to dispersal into new ranges (Mayr 1970). It is a surprising empirical generalization that species colonization beyond the limits is not usually successful, even when conditions outside the old range are not significantly different from inside; this is probably because gene flow from the interior effectively interrupts the development of new gene complexes that are advantageous for the outside conditions. Organisms in isolated habitats may be genetically more similar within ranges than between ranges, even when the distance separating the ranges is much less than the distance separating individuals within them.

Occasional dispersers may cross the line and temporarily succeed in reproducing within the new range, yet hard times then lead to the dispersers' failures in the new range. "Population outbreaks" occur when the borders are crossed by large numbers of dispersers originating in the species' interior range, rather than exclusively from the outer-edge populations.

Human exploratory behavior and decisions about risks can cause deviations from the geometric model's predictions. An example can be seen in archeological reconstructions of the peopling of Polynesia; G. Irwin (1989, 1990) argued that the human colonization of the remote Pacific islands proceeded by "pragmatic strategies of exploration which allowed not the fastest rate of advance but certainly the greatest chance of survival." The search for new ranges was done by long-distance sailors choosing directions (upwind) that allowed easy return in the event of failure to discover suitable new lands. Pleistocene people making terrestrial movements used pragmatic strategies to disperse into unfamiliar territory. They may have followed drainage networks, working from watershed to watershed; or they may have followed weather fronts and other meteorological phenomena.

The costs and benefits of dispersal vary from environment to environment and from species to species. Recent research in evolutionary ecology indicates that dispersal of individuals in populations is caused by a "multiplicity of ultimate factors" (Ferriere, Belthoff, Olivieri, and Krackow 2000:5). Selective pressures operate to encourage the avoidance of kin competition and inbreeding, of course, but also there are benefits to be gained from finding empty territories. Among *Homo sapiens*, dispersal is a condition-dependent behavior – that is, it is related to such linked internal and external factors as population density, resource competition, habitat quality, presence of predators, and so forth. Two major factors – poor habitat quality and crowding – may inspire human individuals to disperse farther than simple inbreeding avoidance or kin competition, as is also seen with other mammals (Ferriere *et al.* 2000). Other factors may exert a "pull" to disperse as opposed to the "push" factors – for example, individuals may leave their home ranges to explore in order to gain prestige, perhaps by discovering exotic resources and goods or by gaining unfamiliar and special knowledge. The urge to disperse need not always result from actual resource competition in the homeland, although individuals may hope to avoid such competition in the future by dispersing into unoccupied ranges.

One important component of my definition of human dispersal is that the individuals and groups who move away from homelands may live either at the edges of the pre-existing population or within the center of the population itself. In other words, dispersing individuals are not always derived only from the marginal members of populations (either the spatial or the social margins). Dispersers may thus carry with themselves the central beliefs and knowledge of their cultures (and also the genes from isolable groups).

Diaspora

I use this word to refer to a very widely scattered dispersal, in which small numbers of individuals move away from populations in different directions in search of new ranges and territories. This distinction is necessary because the scale of the *unit of migration* makes a difference in the outcome of the process of the peopling the New World. The units of migration may be single individuals, families, or larger groups. If the smaller units are involved in the migration event, the resultant gene frequencies may be quite different from the averages in the source population (Fix 1999), and similarly the cultural content of the migrants' archeological assemblages may appear divergent. Kin-structured migration, which involves the movement of relatives who share similar genetic ancestry *and* perhaps idiosyncratic beliefs or abilities, increases the stochasticity of migration (Fix 1999:35, and chapter 4), even resulting in the establishment of colonizing populations that are located far apart in their new geographic ranges but appear very similar genetically and culturally (or vice versa! – near each other geographically but very dissimilar culturally and genetically). A diaspora is a very small-group type of migration into ranges that are far apart; but if the groups originated from one source population, they could carry similar very biased samples of genes and similar technology, beliefs, values, and knowledge to distantly separated regions, producing uniform archeological assemblages.

Irruption

Animals or plants that already possess migratory abilities – such as tolerance of fasting, fat storage on the body, navigational talents, economical means of locomotion, etc. – may take advantage of unpredictable events such as unusual weather to cross otherwise respected barriers into new ranges very quickly and in relatively high numbers. Favorable conditions such as mild winters may allow irruptive dispersals over high mountains into new ranges. The numbers of dispersing individuals moving may be especially high if the home range is perceived as crowded, if food is seen as scarce, if habitats are fragmenting, or if competitive disturbances make the population restive (see, for example, Scott 1994). Such larger-scale dispersals are transitory or temporary bursts of movement. In conservation biology, an irruption is usually considered to be a form of an "invasion," or the movement of organisms into territory where competing organisms already exist, but here I use the word to mean only a rapid and temporary movement of numbers of individuals into new ranges.

There are no insurmountable physiological problems involved in the survival of rapidly irrupting humans. Humans have evolved none of the special metabolic/physiological needs and adaptations that migrating insects, birds, and other mammals possess, but culturally all humans could have exercised the same optimizing strategies of shifting to high-energy foods, storing foods by smoking, freezing, or drying, and using carry-bags to transport reserves. Finding water need not have been a problem, especially if the rapidly moving humans were expert foragers who knew how to search for several resources at the same time; one of the most effective ways to do this is to seek the signs of water-dependent animals (such as mammoths or doves), and follow their trails or their movements.

Directed regular migrations (anastrophic) are often resource-driven. Migration serves to take advantage of changing resource productivity. Yet with irruptive migrants, survival and reproduction in the homeland do not have to change to inspire outward movements. Conditions may or may not remain constant in the homeland. Organisms may gain selective advantage by changing habitats, even when their survival in the homeland does not change (the literature is reviewed in Dingle 1980). In other words, even in stable habitats, irruptive dispersal outward may confer selective advantages.

Superabundant but sporadic resources may be exploited by organisms that develop a high degree of exploratory mobility. These are said to be "fugitive" species or populations. The distances that migrants move, the direction of their movements, and so forth, are the results of particular cost-benefit ratios that may be unique for each population. No single model of migratory strategies can adequately describe the selective factors at work in each case.

Mass movements may be a function of current conditions, but they also may be unpredictable and result from intrinsic factors. Heightened competition in a homeland may lead to irruptive migration; or, it may lead to a dispersal of only some members into marginal habitats, where migration then must develop for the population to survive. The marginal occupiers may become fugitive populations. They become very mobile, very opportunistic, very flexible in adopting different strategies, such as continuing to move, settling in, changing diet breadth, or changing foraging patch sizes.

Colonization

The word "colony" is derived from Latin, *colos*, meaning a farm or estate that has been settled for cultivation (*cultus*). The literal meaning of the word "colonize" is to settle down for the purpose of tilling the soil. Pleistocene people entering new habitats for the first time had no intention of finding estates to till, and in fact the founding population never actually "settled" anywhere, in the sense that farmers settle, because they remained nomadic and highly mobile, as were their descendants for millennia. Modern biologists now use the word to refer to the process of species successfully establishing themselves in new but not necessarily different habitats (Lincoln and Boxshall 1987:89). In dealing with population movements and speciations, the word is often used to refer to permanent range expansions. "Colonization" is perhaps the most convenient term available for the end results of prehistoric global dispersals and radiations, and archeologists cannot afford to dispense with it. Nonetheless, the word has many undertones that are economic (suggesting fixed positioning, hence nonmobile subsistence strategies) as well as geographic (suggesting range expansion).

The concept of colonization is extremely foggy in archeological writing. I want to make a distinction between (1) the very first appearance by humans, and (2) the subsequent establishment of "lasting" settlement. Such a distinction has been made in studies of human occupations in northern Europe following the Last Glacial Maximum, when large parts of the continent were under glaciers or unlivable (see the papers in Kobusiewicz and Kozłowski 1999a, for example).

In section 4.1, I briefly described recent research on the post-glacial colonization of Europe and some possible similarities to Clovis colonization and settlement. Here I want to make a point about the words we use to refer to culture spread in the Old and New Worlds. R. Barton (1999:83) interpreted the first reoccupation of Great Britain as a very "short-lived pulse of activity" that is different from an actual "re-settlement" that occurred later. The traces of the earliest humans may have been left by a single group of hunter-gatherers seasonally moving through recently deglaciated landscapes. The radiocarbon dates on this earliest occupation cluster tightly, the sites are scattered and low density in distribution, the assemblages are similar and lack much diversity in each find-spot, and the toolstone used for flintknapping is similar over a large area, in some sites indicating long-distance transport (up to 160 km) from point of origin.

Similarly, the first appearance of humans after the Last Glacial Maximum elsewhere in northern Europe seems to be an "initial pioneering phase" (Rensink 1999:98, specifically referring to the southern Netherlands) characterized by infrequent or strictly seasonal trips into new lands to forage and find toolstone; generally the sites from this sort of phase were not occupied year-round, artwork is lacking in assemblages, and there are few or no large accumulations of lithics around hearths and dwellings, as would be expected in camps made by locally "resident" people. The pioneering phase not only is distinct in terms of sites and assemblages, but began quickly following deglaciation. The first humans appeared surprisingly soon after glaciation in much of central and eastern Europe – for example, the northern half of Poland was under an ice sheet as late as 18,000–17,000 rcybp, yet the Mirkowice site in northwestern Poland shows a repeated Hamburgian occupation starting early in the Bølling interstadial, no

later than 12,500 rcybp, as soon as possible after plant and animal communities started to establish themselves on the young and harsh morainic landscape
(Kabaciński, Bratlund, Kubiak, Makowiecki, Schild, and Tobolski 1999). The
sources of the foragers dispersing into lowland Poland and elsewhere in central
and eastern Europe were Epigravettian people (in the east) and Magdalénian
people (in the west), who were in place from about 16,000–15,000 rcybp around
the European lowlands, following the divergence of uniform Gravettian technocomplexes into those two patterns after the Last Glacial Maximum (Kozłowski
1990, 1999; Kobusiewicz and Kozłowski 1999b).

What would be an appropriate word that unambiguously refers only to this
sort of brief pulse of activity that appears quickly in the archeological record?
I don't think our old standby term "colonization" is that word. Aside from the
tilling and cultivation implied in the Latin root, the word *colonize* specifically
means permanent settlement on the land. If we agree to continue using the
word colonization in discussing the peopling of the New World, we must use
it carefully to refer to long-term settlement, rather than fleeting or pioneering
visits to different regions. What would be a better word to use when we refer to
short-term exploration, temporary visits, and pioneering but transient foraging
in new ranges?

I use the term "dispersal" to refer not only to human range-expansion, but
also to the processes occurring during the earliest pioneering phases when new
ranges begin to be "colonized." The very first appearances of humans in new
range is evidence of dispersal, which may or may not be followed by evidence
of colonization as populations establish themselves locally. The evidence for
colonization – the settling in – would be (1) repeated site occupations over an
extended time interval (arbitrarily set at more than 200 years, admittedly a rather
long spread of time, but unfortunately a high-resolution temporal measure is
not attainable from the use of radiocarbon dating alone), and if the dating is not
available the occupations are stacked stratigraphically, (2) diversity of tools in
the regional toolkit (no one site need contain all tool types), and (3) increasing
density of sites later in time.

This sort of operationalized definition leads to the observation that while
Clovis left ample evidence of rapid dispersal in the western United States, it
left little evidence of "colonizing" behavior – certainly not at the single-event
Clovis–mammoth sites such as Dent (CO) or Domebo (OK), nor at the Clovis
cache sites such as East Wenatchee (WA) or Simon (ID). However, the larger
fluted-point sites in the eastern United States do provide evidence of settling-in
over the long term, because repeated site occupations span several centuries
and typological change can be seen in projectile points (Anderson 1990, 1995;
Anderson and Faught 2000; see Gardner 1975, 1977 for discussion of cultural
trends in the Middle Atlantic states, for example).

The first appearers are pioneers or explorers, but they may become colonizers
in time. Once the evidence has been accepted for true "colonization" – the settling into new ranges following initial entry – there are several more processes
associated with the term and these also must be clarified and operationalized.
Note that all terms are here defined on a relative scale. The source of the border-
crossing individuals must be considered in light of the relative numbers of
individuals who move (either collectively or separately but always contempora-
neously) in similar directions. The source may be a continuum from "all-border"

to "all-center." The number of individuals that move is also a continuum from few to many.

In Fig. 6.1, the relationships possible between two variables are illustrated. One variable is an archeologically detectable characteristic called "First Appearances," which ranges from "Scattered and Small" to "Coalesced and Large" traces, referring to the degree of concentration of remains (artifacts or bones) in discrete localities. This parameter is suggested by inferring the potential contributions of different numbers of moving individuals (Fig. 6.2).

The exact terms of any particular situation are flexible: for example, placement into the upper half of Fig. 6.1 could mean either that many people leave many remains in a few sites over a short interval of time, or that a few people leave many remains in a few sites by repeated reuse of the sites. Both these different kinds of archeological detectability show a pattern here termed "Coalesced," referring to restrictions imposed either by conscious decision-making factors or the constraints of the local environments. The bottom half of the graph refers to either small groups leaving small numbers of remains found in few places, or large groups leaving the same archeological signature, here called "Scattered." Diaspora, Biogeographic Migration, and Irruption are marked on the figure where I think they fall, along relatively defined dimensions. Environmental variations along different routes may slow down movements or cause changes in the focusing or diffusion of remains, so that the categories (Diaspora, Irruption, Migration) are shown as almost a gradient.

In the simple stepping-stone or diffusion model of initial colonization, each geographic region is considered more likely colonized by founders who moved from nearer rather than farther sources. This most parsimonious model of colonization is stepwise, with founders moving from established sites to the nearby new sites (for examples of models based on genetics and biogeography, see Juan, Emerson, Oromí, and Hewitt 2000, or Thorpe, McGregor, Cumming, and Jordan 1994). Dixon (1999, 2001) has proposed this sort of spread of people into the New World around 14,000–13,000 rcybp, starting from their original beachhead on the western coast of North America. Within each region of the continent over time a cultural founder effect operated, as well as localized readaptation to changing habitats, to cause divergence from the first ancestor culture. Geographic isolation could have led to rather rapidly developing distinct adaptations to different habitats, contributing quickly to divergence reinforced by cultural preferences for exchanging ideas and mates with the most similar neighboring cultures first. Even temporary isolation – for only a few generations – may have been long enough to allow the development of considerable variability within what appear to be continuous geographic ranges (for a discussion of a genetic corollary of this cultural process, see Barton's [2000] review of recent literature).

Another possible type of colonization is the "jump-dispersal" model, in which the pattern of post-establishment spread is very distinct from budding or wavefront movement (see Lewis 1998). Jump dispersals allow populations to spread and colonize new ranges much more quickly than diffusion-front dispersals (Holway and Suarez 1999, and references therein).

A third and distinct model of dispersal and colonization must be created by archeologists who believe pre-existing human populations were already present in the New World earlier than 13,000 rcybp – this new model must be one of "invasion." Invasion biology deals with the processes of colonization, establishment, and spread of organisms that outcompete indigenous taxa and thus either displace or replace the native forms (Weiss 1988; recent work on the subject is reviewed in Holway and Suarez 1999). Invasions may succeed owing to the invaders' superior abilities to exploit resources, or to their superior interference competition with the resident peoples, expectably expressed through pronounced intercultural aggression. However, there is no known archeological evidence of warfare or interpersonal violence from late Pleistocene North America. If a series of early human migrations succeeded each other starting 35,000 years ago, but the different ethnic or cultural populations did not fight each other, they must have either (1) outcompeted each other passively, through more efficient resource exploitation, or (2) intermarried, or (3) simply never came into contact. The implications of intercultural competition during an invasion cannot be ignored out of hand, if numerous waves of migration actually did take place in the Pleistocene.

ANTHROPOLOGY, ARCHEOLOGY, AND COLONIZING BEHAVIOR

Much of the paleoanthropological literature about hominid invasions of new ranges (a process usually called colonization) depends more on abstracted game plans and site-accommodating reconstructions than on general migration/ dispersal theory. The expressions of different archeologists' points of view are informed not so much by a coherent body of dispersal theory, apparently, but by anthropological guesswork, archeological induction, and perhaps some accommodative theorizing about paleoenvironments and artifact assemblages. What is lacking in the myriad schemes, scenarios, models, and simulations is an explicit migration theory, or set of theoretical frameworks about dispersal and migration by social organisms. This is an epistemological flaw, one result of a current emphasis on learned behavior as a hominid capacity that makes natural selection seem virtually irrelevant to many anthropologists.

A productive approach to explaining dispersals is to model them as information-based (Steele, Adams, and Sluckin 1998); that is, to examine dispersing populations as inclined to fission based not only on population pressure but also on the desire to explore and survey ranges and resources. Population growth is not always the only stimulus for dispersal over long distances (Beaton 1991b; Meltzer 1995). Information-based dispersers do not randomly enter new ranges or move regular distances in all directions, as dispersal-theorists often presume in biology. Instead, information-based dispersers may have a high-velocity spread that is usually patchy and asymmetrical, such as along rivers or refugia corridors. There is no equal probability of any direction being followed from the original source areas, and no symmetry of dispersal distances (Steele, Adams, and Sluckin 1998:300–1). Source populations need not expand in a continuous wave or along radial fronts. Beaton's (1991b) Transient Explorer Model proposed that dispersers can leap over large regions without settling into them while dispersing, although "return" dispersals may eventually fill in the uninhabited lands. Transient explorers may move great distances very quickly because of the desire to acquire geographic knowledge or some other information.

Kelly and Todd (1988) modeled an information-based dispersal into North America by foragers learning to cope with seasonally and spatially patchy resources; these foragers used high-quality lithic materials, relied on bifacial technology, and preferred to hunt large mammals rather than collect plant foods for most of their diet. These tactics allowed wide exploratory journeys and rapid dispersals throughout the continent, because a knowledge of animal behavior and biology could have been transferred from one geographic region to another more easily and more effectively than knowledge of plant phenology, which probably differed from region to region.

The first foragers in North America were information-based dispersers whose movements and explorations were not forced on them by the traditionally invoked trigger of population pressure. Foragers entering a continent with so few (if any) co-foraging cultures would have reacted very differently from populations in the ethnographic present who expand or change their ranges when pressured, but who resist doing so. The first foragers in North America selected where to go, how quickly to explore and colonize, and they were capable of backtracking if necessary when resources were locally scarce in new ranges.

Young and Bettinger (1995:91) designed a model of global dispersal based on population spread at a relatively constant speed, with population pressure being the driving force. In their model, a relentless wave of human movement resulted from a steadily increasing human population. This is a theoretically sound way to explain general hominid expansion on a large scale, but on smaller temporal and spatial scales the idea that expansion is inevitable and directional (hence, not cyclic) cannot be supported empirically (Butzer 1991).

The costs and benefits of migration differ from situation to situation. The movement may be self-activated, or it may be *necessary* because home conditions are unreliable, or crowded, or too few mates are available. Conversely, an advantageous range-change may not be a necessary one. Would fluctuating climate make species movements out of their habitat dangerous or favorable? Would the motivation for movement actually make the movement itself risky, such as when habitats become fragmented? The species can stay in its old range under changing climatic conditions and become extinct, or disperse and become extinct, or evolve new behaviors and survive, if there is enough time and genetic diversity. Many interpreters of hominid migration assume that populations will not change their ranges except in response to climatic changes, especially the sharp and abrupt ones; however, another perspective (see Gamble 1986, 1994) is that environments by themselves never fully limited hominid dispersal worldwide. Instead, it was the slow process of evolving integration of complex behavior (especially social behavior) that bottlenecked population movements and colonization.

The study of hominid invasions may be reduced to little more than the search for first appearances, followed by thick descriptions of subsequent changes attributable to either climatic factors, gene flow, or social developments. The lack of a coherent body of theory and a globally applicable set of guidelines for data collection are tough enough intellectual hurdles for an archeologist to vault, but the problems are made to appear worse by the nature of archeological visibility from the earliest stratigraphic horizons. Not all parts of North America yield early archeological remains; even the regions with a record also have monstrous gaps in that record. The gaps are usually understood to be representative of a discontinuous human presence.

OTHER TERMS AND CONCEPTS

Besides the basic lexicon of terms, several shorthand phrases that stand for recognized ecological or anthropological concepts come in handy when discussing the peopling process. These phrases are information-rich and help illuminate what otherwise may remain only a very poorly lit series of events in the distant past.

Hunter-gatherer local group structure

Where resources are not uniformly distributed and are widely scattered, hunter-gatherers may structure their social groups very loosely and flexibly, as is the case with the !Kung Bushmen of the Kalahari (Lee and DeVore 1976; Marshall 1976; Yellen and Harpending 1972). Instead of living and traveling in unilineal bands, !Kung individuals choose to stay in a "temporarily unstable aggregation of families with links of kinship or friendship" (Yellen and Harpending 1972:247). Food resources can be shared within the aggregation, as is information about foraging strategies and range conditions. The lack of kin-based rules associated with unilineal band social structure means that disputes could arise without an easy way to achieve simple resolution in the !Kung situation, and thus the freedom to split off from groups and come together again later is essential. Yellen and Harpending (1972) call this loose organization "anucleate," in which society is flexibly networked through kinship, friendship, and contacts via trading. High mobility and the use of large home ranges characterize anucleate groups. Studies of the !Kung show that relatively few fathers and mothers still live in the same area where they were born (only about 57 percent), and the distance between birthplaces of spouses is rather great (70 km) (see Fix 1999 for discussion of these and other societies).

During the initial peopling of the New World, extremely mobile and loosely organized groups viewed themselves as culturally "affiliated" with each other and with an overarching social/technological/ethnic entity – a "people," a "tribe," or a "culture," whatever term may be appropriate – but they also broke off contact from other groups to travel long distances, both to find mates and to explore surrounding regions so the resources could be exploited and information about them could be shared.

Synchronous metapopulations

Global disturbances at the end of the Pleistocene – namely climate change leading to vegetation changes – would have affected scattered human populations in the New World in certain similar ways, even if the local expressions of the disturbances were not identical. The "Moran effect" is the name given the synchrony seen in separated populations that have a common density-dependent structure and that experience global random disturbance (see Ranta, Kaitala, and Lundberg 1999, and references). The demographic effects of local disturbances are linked to global disturbances because of "distance-dependent spatially autocorrelated effects" (Ranta et al. 1999:400). This means that while climate change may be similar continent-wide, and while regional vegetational dynamics in response may not be at all universal, the overall effects on widely scattered human populations very well may appear similar during sequences of change. Dispersal of individuals from affected human populations is one mechanism that acts to couple population subunits together, so they begin acting synchronously. Specifically, periods of population growth and reduction may seem to be synchronized over huge expanses, sometimes almost locked in phase and sometimes drifting in and out of phase. Such dynamic effects have been seen in populations of several mammalian taxa, such as Canadian lynx in eight Canadian provinces, for example (Ranta et al. 1997). The synchrony between regional populations does vary with the distance separating them, so that nearer populations are more often in close phase, and farther populations are more and more out of phase. There is also a tendency for the synchrony to vary over time, because the cycles slide in and out of phase. Hence, if only one part of a time sequence is studied, the synchrony may not appear, and such synchrony may be underappreciated (Ranta et al. 1997).

What makes this phenomenon so important in terms of late Pleistocene prehistory is the mechanism that links populations across great distances – the dispersal of individuals out of one population and into a neighboring population. This sort of linkage triggers in-phase demographic responses to changes; it should also trigger in-phase cultural responses. Populations may grow and crash locked in phase the closer together they are located, and cultural developments also may seem to change the same ways, with the nearest neighbors synchronized in phase and farther populations seemingly out of phase until the long view is taken, revealing the swings in and out of phase over space and time.

THE FIRST APPEARANCE OF THE CLOVIS WAY OF LIFE

Clovis people were the first to inhabit most of North America. Their point of origin may be Beringia, but it was not originally in Beringia that the distinctive features of Clovis "culture" first appeared – the fluting, the mobility, the targeting of megamammals, the leapfrog movements into unoccupied ranges. In this short section I want to sketch what I think is a reasonable summary of how the process of rapid dispersal took place in North America, and how the transition occurred from generalized hunting and gathering to unique, opportunistically specialized megafaunal hunting.

The pre-Clovis foragers who lived in Beringia subsisted in ranges where woolly mammoths were rare or extinct, and a megamammal-oriented and opportunistic targeting of mammoths did not accompany the earliest human immigrations from western Beringia (Northeast Asia). The first migrants arrived in eastern Beringia rather quickly anyway, perhaps, as suggested by Hoffecker, Powers, and Goebel (1993), drawn into Alaska by the growing abundance of woody plants spreading over former tundra and steppe; wood may have been essential for fuel and tool raw material at this time. The spread out of Northeast Asia began after 14,000 rcybp (Goebel 1999) and possibly as late as 12,700 rcybp, when abrupt climatic warming would have increased Beringian productivity. By around 11,800 rcybp, Nenana culture had become established in eastern Beringia (Goebel 1999), and this archeological tradition seems similar enough to Clovis to be the immediate ancestor of its technology and lithic organization.

By this time, the Cordilleran and Laurentide ice sheets had separated for the entire length of the northern continent, and the biotic appeal of the corridor was rapidly increasing. The newly deglaciated corridor was cold and sparsely vegetated at first, with ice-blocked lakes and wetlands covering most of it, but waterfowl and possibly many other migratory birds followed the wetlands and lakes on their seasonal flights to the south and north. Archeological evidence shows that both western and eastern Beringian foragers were already partly subsisting on ducks, geese, and swans (Fiedel 2000c, and see references there); as well, migrating birds may have been considered "scouts" beckoning humans to follow their movements south of Beringia, where one could predict that there were good ranges awaiting discovery (since the birds returned every year from the long-distance flights).

The alternate route into the rest of North and South America, the western Pacific coastal route championed by Fladmark (1979), Dixon (1993, 1999) and others, may have been biotically productive sooner than the inland corridor, and could have been covered by boat or on foot; yet Surovell (2000b) has shown through simulation modeling that foragers traveling from Beringia to South America by the coastal route would have been spread very thin and could not have maintained viable populations. The inland "ice-free corridor" is therefore the most plausible route taken by the first pioneer foragers in the New World.

Whatever the stimulus to explore southward, human groups moved out of Beringia and reached the temperate latitudes of the United States within a very short period of time. C. V. Haynes (1999b) speculated that foragers could have followed inland routes in and around deglaciated mountains until they reached the wider expanses of today's Montana, where biotic conditions were richer. C. V. Haynes (n.d.) has imagined the trek from the Tanana Valley of Alaska to Anzick in Montana – about 5,700 km – could have been fully accomplished in six to twelve years, or even less time. A few tentative or exploratory treks may have been made in previous summer months before foragers permanently moved southwards. After the more productive prairies, steppes, and plains were reached, and the never-hunted megafauna were encountered for the first time – perhaps somewhere between 60 and 50 degrees North latitude in Alberta (Burns 1996; C. V. Haynes n.d.; Jackson and Duk-Rodkin 1996; Morlan, Dyke, and Mc-Neely 1999) – human foragers developed the fugitive and opportunistic economy of the Clovis era, which took advantage of large-mammal behavior to explore, procure animals, learn about toolstone sources, disperse, and keep in touch with each other over extremely long distances.

Where this specifically Clovis set of strategies first appeared will never be clearly known. Wilson and Burns (1999) suggest that foragers making fluted points already may have been spread through the ice-free corridor between 11,500 and 11,200 rcybp, implying that Clovis adaptations appeared everywhere in North America at nearly the same time; thus, a point of origin south of the ice sheets will probably never be identified. Other researchers have suggested other points of origin, such as the Gulf of Mexico or the High Plains. I suggest the Clovis way of life most fully developed near the present-day Mexican border, in prime mammoth habitat, and its main ideas rapidly spread from there in all directions. Earlier (proto-Clovis) foragers who had passed through the northern and central Plains left nearly no known signs of their initial passing, but by the time of the Clovis florescence after 11,200 rcybp, all the features of Clovis-era behavior were in place across much of the continent. By then the people were paying especially close attention to the mammoths and mastodonts in the continent, the animals which created the clearest and most complete trail networks linking the best foraging patches (and other species of large mammals using those patches). The human exploration along megamammal trails led foragers to refugia patches, to water sources, and to pockets of highest biotic richness. Each perturbation of climate in the period 11,500–10,500 rcybp increased the stresses on megafaunal taxa, leading to better and better foraging conditions for human groups. Within a few hundred years the entire continent was occupied or in the process of being "settled." Soon the largest ungulates were dead and gone, along with many carnivores and scavengers that had fed on them. Only in the widest grasslands, where fewer taxa of large mammals lived together, and fewer Clovis groups spent time, did any relatively large animals survive, specifically migratory grazers – bison.

THE PEOPLING OF NORTH AMERICA: IRRUPTION, DIASPORA, EXPLORATION, COLONIZATION?

No theory is at hand powerful enough to mandate a slow rate of entry by all first people into all new ranges. The first people may have dispersed widely and over long distances in very little time without running at full speed, without stumbling stupidly through unfamiliar landscapes, or any of the other fantasized objections raised to a rapid migration, under certain conditions.

The model of Young and Bettinger (1995) simulates rapid continental colonization under biologically reasonable conditions; in other words, using known or possible variables such as reproductive rates, mortality, linear distances dispersed, and so forth, the model allows humans to have invaded the New World rapidly.

If hominid invasions fit the general patterns of other biological invasions (see, for example, Richardson, Williams, and Hobbs 1994), we may expect to find evidence of high reproductive rates, reduced juvenile periods (translated perhaps into younger ages for individuals to leave their birth-families or natal sites), abilities to persist in habitats subject to frequent disturbances, and abilities to disperse long distances. Young and Bettinger (1995) factored these sorts of hominid abilities into their model. Time, which is often emphasized over other variables in archeology, does correlate positively with many biological invasions; the longer the residence period an invading species can manage, the greater its chances of survival and the greater the spatial extent of its successful colonization. Yet successes will occur even over very short time intervals; colonizers with the capacities to invade new ranges will quickly be able to survive at microsites; after the passage of more and more time, macrosites will become established, as satellite foci enlarge and coalesce. Thus, the first invaders may create scattered and diffuse archeological signatures, followed over time by increasing evidence for more people in more places.

Land areas ripe for invasion are often characterized by natural cycles that become heightened (such as greater frequencies of fires, population outbreaks, temporary droughts, or other processes that are called perturbations); as well, invadable lands may be those that undergo real changes, rather than perturbations of cycles. North America at the end of the Pleistocene was clearly undergoing both perturbations and real changes (see Porter 1988; Wright 1991).

Invasions occur often when the invading taxon encounters no competition, or reduced competition outside its normal ranges. The first human dispersers into North America may have encountered some predatory competitors, and hence worked their way into the continent very slowly; but if the continent was actually "invaded" by a rapidly dispersing hominid presence, then it seems consistent with biological principles to expect the first colonizers found very reduced competition when they moved into the new range.

The way that small mammals or pine trees invade new ranges need not provide a perfect formula for hominid invasion of the New World (see Richardson *et al.* 1994), but the biological patterns emerging from these sorts of invasions should be able to serve as a prototype for understanding what occurred when *Homo sapiens sapiens* first entered North America. Invasion seems to be a two-phase process, consisting first of the initial immigration and establishment of small, successful foci where the immigrants survive, followed by the enlarging of some foci by population growth and territorial expansion. The process is stepwise and if it occurs rapidly it qualifies to be called an *irruption*.

In the "very-slow" version of the current peopling-of-the-Americas scenarios, such as that favored by some linguists and advocates of a deep-time presence of Pleistocene cultures, the New World is viewed as peopled over a lengthy period either by time-transgressive dispersals (MacNeish 1976; Rogers, Rogers, and Martin 1992; Whitley and Dorn 1993), or by punctuated Biogeographic Migrations, most likely taking place during periods of favorable climates (as argued by Butzer 1988). In the polar-opposite "very-fast" version, which is also an example of a postulated Biogeographic Migration, Clovis may be an irruption (see Martin 1973; Mosimann and Martin 1975), with other consequences (specifically, megafaunal overkill).

There are other types of polemic about human movements into the New World, some of which do not worry so much about the ultimate causation or biological correlates of dispersal, but rather attempt to describe the foraging realities of the ongoing movement process (for example, Kelly and Todd's [1988] and Anderson's [1990] sketches of Paleoindian decision-making). Perhaps somewhere in between the two extremes are Gamble's (1986) and Beaton's (1991b) musings about different frequencies and magnitudes of movement, archeological visibility, and assemblage varieties when new ranges are invaded by Estate settlers versus Explorers. The concerns are less with evolutionary ecology or population ecology than with technology, spatial distributions of artifacts, and growth and change in material culture over time.

But taken as a whole, the literature about New World colonization is dominated by three views. (1) Entry and subsequent colonization proceeded very slowly. In this view, the first peoples are considered to have been either trickle-in dispersers who had to work their way across major barriers and reproduce at risk in new habitats, or they were pioneers who entered in low densities and slowly developed new adaptations to different environments, very gradually increasing their archeological visibility. This view is a form of the conservative geometric modeling of organism dispersal, in which individuals move away from their birth-site and settle in the first unoccupied territory (Caley 1991; Waser 1985). If the new territories are heterogeneous, not all of them will be appealing or optimal, and either they will be left empty or human groups will slowly readapt in order to settle them. (2) Another view is the fast-colonizing one, which has two distinct sub-versions. In the first variant (2A), people enter the New World as irruptions that take place during abrupt climatic changes; their numbers are soon depleted as more climatic changes occur, but eventually with continued dispersal within the new borders their archeological visibility again increases. In a second sub-version (2B), migration occurs *en masse* from a central population that seems to have leapfrogged border populations to enter new range; large numbers of people create relatively high archeological visibility from the start, but a continuation of changes in technology, subsistence, settlement, and style distinguishes the moving populations from those of the homeland. (3) Perhaps a third view is a compromise; a slow start (low numbers, low visibility) builds to a rapid conclusion of the pioneer phase and an explosive settling or colonization phase.

In theory, any of these may have been possible. The process involved in the second view, that the Americas were first populated very quickly, requires a bit more discussion about the concept of *irruption* as it is defined here. Irruptions are rapid invasions by border populations, spilling out of homeland ranges into new, uninhabited ranges, and usually resulting from an abrupt change in climate that facilitates mass movements. If the population center does not move, and if the homeland range remains unchanged, the irrupters may not move a great distance; the original irruption may not travel farther beyond the old border than the diameter of the old homeland range. Farther travel may lead to the irrupters losing touch with gene flow from their parent population.

Yet the second view of the New World's first peopling demands not only that irrupters move great distances, but that the irruptions continue *as the population centers also continue to shift*. To accommodate this situation, a new dimension must be added to the simplified defining of migrations, dispersals, and irruptions: this is the idea that as Time passes the other variables listed in this chapter's graphs change. The most important new concept is that moving centers can shift their positions over time, and that as a result irruptions may appear from many new centers after the initial irruption has first allowed a new population to enter uninhabited land.

In fact, this seems to be an appropriate way of describing what does happen during the rapid entry of a species into large new territory. For example, the first European starlings (*Sternus vulgaris*) established themselves very quickly this way in North America (Cabe 1993; Kessel 1953; Wing 1943). Starlings were introduced into the United States by one man in 1890 and 1891, and soon established a breeding population (a "center") in New York City's Central Park. As the population expanded within the center (1891–1900), a border population began to disperse outward, in the absence of major predators and serious competition. The starlings spread at least 20–50 km a year in what appears to be a wave-front, when viewed historically, based on first sightings and observations of breeding populations. The spread was achieved by centers of population establishing themselves in different areas, sending out dispersers sometimes in a slowly expanding front, and other times in rapid irruptions during harsh winters and springs when indigenous bird taxa were at a disadvantage. In other words, there was not one huge population that expanded its single center as outward boundaries ballooned; instead, there were numerous smaller centers that seemed to follow the irruptions and dispersals into new territory.

The pattern is similar for North America's Clovis cultures of about 11,000 years ago. D. Anderson (1990, 1996; Anderson and Faught 2000) has concluded that there were Clovis centers in the eastern United States ("staging centers" in his terminology) with empty or underutilized areas located in between them during the late Pleistocene. Similarly, Dincauze (1993b) terms the larger Northeastern sites "marshaling" centers, where Clovis foragers met regularly or prepared to explore or forage in distant ranges. These centers are where Clovis-age artifacts and sites are most visible. Perhaps they were located in resource-rich zones, contained ample raw material for lithic-tool manufacture, featured prominent landscape characteristics, or were hubs of natural travel corridors. Maybe some of them were the newly established population centers from which irruptions could occur, spreading into much larger land areas.

The available archeological, cultural, and ecological models of human abilities to colonize therefore support a rapid but not necessarily linearly directed dispersal of a Clovis population through the interior of the New World. The dispersal may have been a wave rather than a branching line of outward movement. The precise chronological relationships among the different centers will probably never be established, so we will not be able to trace the coalescence of different centers, or define the borders from which irruptions emerged, but at present there is little reason to doubt that this complex process could have occurred. The locations of the centers, whatever the reasons for their placement in North American geography, mark population foci from which irruptions moved into the unpopulated areas around them.

CO-TRADITIONS: IMPLICATIONS AND PREDICTIONS

As mentioned above in several places, some archeologists believe that Clovis is one of several contemporary traditions existing at around 11,000 rcybp in North America (for example, see Bryan 1988, 1991). In post-Clovis times the simultaneous existence of different traditions – such as Folsom, Midland, Agate Basin, and Plainview at around 10,200 rcybp – is clear from the archeological record. But the chronostratigraphy of projectile-point types existing around 11,000 rcybp is still unclear. Some archeologists are not convinced that several different types coexisted. If indeed Clovis was one of several contemporary types, potentially recognizable patterns distinguishing the traditions should be detected in subsistence and settlement, site distributions, and typology wherever such traditions coexisted. (See the "Key" towards the end of this chapter for suggestions about expected differences between Clovis and the putative co-traditions.)

Fluted points have been dated to an interval of time that stretches and bulges when data from region to region are examined. Eastern fluted points – those thought to be the most "Clovis-like" – have been dated from about 11,000 rcybp to 10,500 rcybp (Table 1.1). Plains Folsom fluted points are dated to a time interval the same as the later eastern fluted points, 10,900 to 10,100 rcybp (see Holliday 2000b). Other point types also have ranges of ages that differ from region to region. Goshen type projectile points pre-date Folsom at the Hell Gap site (C. V. Haynes 1992; also see Sellet 1999), but how much older the type is than Folsom is very uncertain. Radiocarbon dates from the Mill Iron (MT) site (Frison 1996) cluster at two different times, 11,360 rcybp and 10,840 rcybp (C. V. Haynes 1992), which could mean Goshen has a Clovis and a Folsom age. Goshen is very similar to the southern Plains' Plainview type, which is post-Clovis in age (see discussion in Holliday 2000a), and the type's age range may be late Clovis to early Folsom (Frison, Haynes, and Larson 1996).

A final example of possible typological coexistence is the case of western stemmed points that may date as early as Clovis fluted points elsewhere in the West (Bryan 1980, 1988, 1991; Bryan and Tuohy 1999). A continued critical examination of the overlaps in dating weakens the case for cultural "co-traditions," however. For example, the dates on Great Basin stemmed projectile points place them in the early Holocene; Beck and Jones (1997:table II) show that the date range is 11,200 to 7,080 rcybp, but only two dates out of sixty-three on record actually overlap with classic Clovis dates (11,200–10,900 rcybp). About 70 percent of the stemmed-point dates cluster within the range 10,000–7,500 rcybp. The earliest dates on stemmed points very well may be statistical outliers – certainly the tiny number of Clovis-era dates is flimsy evidence for contemporaneity with Clovis.

Clovis-like fluted points may date as late as 10,500 rcybp in the Great Basin, just as they seem to in the eastern United States and possibly in Canada and Alaska. Their use may have overlapped with the use of the earliest stemmed points. Perhaps these Clovis-like points were manufactured *after* what I call the Clovis era, at a time when megamammal-hunting opportunists were readapting to life without mammoths and mastodonts, and were exploring the very last unoccupied ranges they had leapfrogged over while dispersing into the continent the past several centuries.

We do not know for certain whether or not Clovis coexisted with other cultures – the evidence is still scant and questionable, but more study is clearly needed. Bryan and Tuohy (1999) suggested that the Clovis and stemmed-point cultures in the Great Basin were able and willing to co-occupy one region for so long because they were both non-territorial, and thus moved without restrictions from resources to resources; "food sharing," in Bryan and Tuohy's words, "actually promoted widespread movement" in a pattern that was "cyclic wandering by small family groups exploiting seasonal resources with a simple technology" (Bryan and Tuohy 1999:258). This pattern is also the Holocene adaptation in the Great Basin.

But I think we need to explain far more than the peaceful coexistence of foraging groups, if co-traditions were present during the Clovis era. We need to understand how different cultures could co-exist while only one was actively dispersing supra-regionally. Perhaps Clovis was a fugitive culture capable of invading and abandoning regions where other cultures were in place; Clovis succeeded visibly in many of these regions, creating sites with large inventories in the east and easily recognized technology virtually everywhere, whereas the earlier cultures had had extremely low visibility.

The success of Clovis as a fugitive and invasive culture can be viewed as an economic process. To understand economic success, sometimes it helps to think in terms of modern business practices (my discussion is inspired by Fisher 2000 and Christensen 1999). Highly successful businesses that abruptly up-end the competition share certain key characteristics, such as radical innovation that "disrupts" the more expensive technologies, specifically the technologies that squander energy and time on inefficient operations and unnecessary overheads. Pre-Clovis technologies may have been all-purpose foraging set-ups with versatile toolkits and lightly engineered lithic implements, unlike the highly engineered Clovis tools and risk-minimizing strategies such as caching tool stock and making huge bifaces. Nowadays we can see that cheaper, better technologies displace older ones in the process of disruption, and it is possible to envision a similar replacement in Clovis times. One part of the process today involves a reduction of time spent in such time-burning duties as hunting, or the documenting and clarifying of resources that are available, where they are located, and how much can be harvested. The process can be illustrated in this way: if there were pre-Clovis foragers who generalized, they were no doubt constantly on the move in search of multiple resources, whereas Clovis foragers trekked immediately to optimal resource patches, scheduled trips to quarries and planned to cache toolstone and tool stock.

Another major part of the disruption process today involves the improvement of efficiency at the low end of the economy – for instance, to put the example in the Clovis era, instead of requiring storage facilities and grinding technology, which generalist foragers do require, the Clovis innovators cut out the expenses by targeting only the resources that could be utilized with minimal preparation, particularly meat and fat. Anyone in Clovis culture could either kill a mammoth or find one that was vulnerable to persistent harrying and eventually death, perhaps by blocking access to water sources.

The best disrupters in modern businesses are those that solve "small problems quickly, using as little technology as possible" (Fisher 2000:186). Clovis did these things too, solving the problems of eating, exploring, dispersing, mapping resources, and competing with other human groups by opportunistically specializing in megamammal-hunting but using a technology suited to solving many subsistence problems. Meanwhile, the problems of society – maintaining linguistic and social coherence over large geographic ranges, teaching offspring to recreate the culture, ensuring long-term survival – could then be addressed with more energy and creativity, after the widest possible range of day-to-day problems were efficiently dealt with.

Disruptive technologies nowadays tend to be modular. Modularity drives down costs in businesses, just as in cultures. Clovis seems to have been a "modular" tradition: as in the modular industries of today, Clovis technology emphasized "low inventory, a high degree of flexibility and zero defects" (Fisher 2000:184), which can be seen in the Clovis sites with relatively few artifacts (away from quarry-related loci), the bifacial technology which allowed many different uses of a single tool type, and the superbly engineered thin-biface reduction strategies. In the less modular societies that may have preceded Clovis, special-purpose subgroups procured or prepared the major technological items and foods needed in the economy, and social subgroups (such as microbands) were probably tethered to macrobands by the regular perceived need for rituals, by requirements for mate exchange processes, and other types of social ties. Pre-Clovis people were not as "modular" as Clovis if they owed allegiance through kinship and cultural loyalty to greater "tribal" groupings, or they divided foraging and economic labor within the subgroups by means of sex and age. But perhaps Clovis foragers were much more independent small groups containing males and females who contributed equally to gathering and hunting, who freely dispersed, and who carried out other processes with far less dependence on the larger macrogroups such as "tribes." Each member of a Clovis group may have been capable of carrying out critical tasks completely on her or his own. Each group was a self-contained "module," thus cutting the social costs associated with migration of whole cultures and tribes that attempt to maintain tighter social coherency.

These and other features of disruptive technologies may well sum up how Clovis outcompeted its co-traditions (if such co-traditions indeed actually existed) and spread so widely and rapidly. Clovis appeared as a cheaper and more efficient way of life in late Pleistocene North America, and older technologies and economies were swallowed up or died out quickly in the face of the Clovis cost-cutting. However, as time passed and Clovis groups encountered the results of late Pleistocene climate changes, in addition to growing human populations and the persistent, radical rearrangement of food and water resources, another disruptive improvement in technology and subsistence may have appeared, replacing Clovis with other, more regionally distinct patterns of adaptations. In some regions, Clovis may have logically developed into Folsom, carrying on certain parts of the original cultural patterning such as extreme mobility and extraordinarily fine lithic craftsmanship, in response to habitat and resource continuities. But in most regions of North America, the superiority of the Clovis way of life was eclipsed by very new and different adaptations in mobility, social organization, technology, and subsistence.

A KEY for defining how "co-traditions" and lineal traditions may appear archeologically

1. Who was first (chronostratigraphically)? Clovis?	IF YES, GO TO 2
Other?	IF YES, GO TO 3
2. Clovis preceded Stemmed and other traditions, then disappeared.	IF YES, GO TO A
Clovis preceded Stemmed, then evolved into them.	IF YES, GO TO B
3. First culture not Clovis, but ancestral to it and all others.	IF YES, GO TO C
First culture not Clovis, but one of the "co-traditions" such as Stemmed	IF YES, GO TO D

A. Clovis did not evolve into Stemmed and others, but did precede them.
   Predictions: Disjunctions in site distributions.
                  Technology and resource bases distinct.
                  Radiometric dating discontinuities and stratigraphic separation.

B. Clovis and Stemmed are similar ages, but Clovis is ancestral to Stemmed and others.
   Predictions: Technology and distributions similar.
                  Resources bases similar but differing more and more over time.

C. First sites pre-date Clovis, but are ancestral to Clovis and Stemmed and others.
   Predictions: Generalized, diffuse occupational debris, widespread distribution.
                  Broad technological repertory, developing in different ways.
                  Resource base = "Pleistocene Archaic."

D. Clovis is late, post-dating Stemmed and others.
   Predictions: No resident Clovis exists in certain regions, except as ephemeral visitors.
                  Stemmed point culture is widespread and sites are distinct from Clovis.
                  Different technology and distributions, no close parallels between Clovis and Stemmed (otherwise they would have been competitors).

Conclusions

Once the first sites had been created and Clovis foragers appeared in new ranges, the continent was no longer unpeopled; yet Clovis foragers did abandon some ranges over time and depopulated large parts of the continent. At each moment the system was changing and different, but the dispersion was not irreversible. Clovis dispersals were like drops of ink falling into clear water – even as the ink disappears and the water clears up again, seemingly returning to its original state, the ink actually has changed the water in a profound way. The presence of Clovis in North America changed North America forever – the landscape had a new species introduced – yet like the water whose ink drop disappears, no permanent signs of the first dispersers necessarily remained in the long-term everywhere after the initial entry.

Clovis dispersals were not a free-for-all of human waves pushing into the continent. Certain biological and physical "rules" did affect Clovis demography, dispersal, and evolution, but the behavior of people represented at each different Clovis site is still almost unpredictable; each person at each site can be thought of as a point moving within multi-dimensional space, affected by variables such as weather, history, time, resources, and other people. Although the dispersing behavior of Clovis people therefore may seem unpredictable and almost chaotic, it was not random. Clovis dispersal and individual human behaviors did follow social trends, foraging tendencies, biological rules, rationality, cultural prescriptions, and so forth. Yet no algorithm can be used to predict Clovis human behavior at each site, because sequences of human actions cannot be that easily predicted. Clovis behavioral "paths" were flexible and could reach a limitless number of states.

During the terminal Pleistocene, dispersing behavior in general was probably "aperiodic" – with few or no regular repetitions in local variables such as resources, seasonality, technology, mating, or whatever. Dispersal behavior therefore must be considered complex and never fully repeating itself, because Pleistocene environments were constantly changing and the flow of Clovis dispersers into unoccupied and previously occupied ranges changed the physical and social stage. Such unpredictable behavior can be strongly affected by even small perturbations. Initial conditions have tremendous effects. Clovis is unique from locale to locale because resources were different, or seasonality varied, or demography changed, or any of a number of variables was different, even if only slightly.

However, broad patterns did occur, appearing almost periodic, although perfect repetitions did not truly appear. For example, some eastern Clovis sites show evidence of regular return visits to quarries or other landscape feature, when different families camped and carried out similar tasks at each separate visit. Yet there are noticeable differences from visit to visit and site to site (see Carr 1986, for example). Each Clovis site and each component in multiply revisited sites tell different stories.

A final point about an archeological dispute is in order. Some interpreters of Clovis dispersals and settlement do not agree on whether regional populations were territorial or free-wandering (Storck and Tomenchuk 1990). The existence of stone-tool caches may imply a "repetitive land-use" or the existence of true home ranges for some Clovis groups (Storck and Tomenchuk

1990:81). The caching may have been a method of evening out the patchy distribution of toolstone in some regions. Meltzer (1989b) has proposed that exotic cherts were more likely obtained in person by eastern Clovis groups rather than through trade with neighboring groups, meaning that some Clovis groups traveled 200 km or more to acquire the stone they preferred to use. Repetitive movements to obtain cherts may very well define "core areas" for specific groups well larger than modern Arctic foraging groups have, and indicate that Clovis populations were truly landscape-attached rather than freely nomadic throughout the continent (an early view that is no longer pervasive in the literature – see Storck and Tomenchuk's [1990:88–9] discussion and Beardsley, Holder, Krieger, Meggers, Rinaldo, and Kutsche 1956; Mason 1962, 1981; Ritchie and Funk 1973; Snow 1980). Little hard evidence exists to support the idea that Clovis groups were range-oriented, or that they restricted their movements to defined ranges; however, little evidence exists for any alternative land-use, either. Storck and Tomenchuk (1990) suggest that future studies may support the idea of range loyalty, but the possible data so far have not been well analyzed.

My modeling of Clovis dispersals and foraging does not imply that free-wandering was a norm in the later Pleistocene. Even the most "transient explorers" (Beaton 1991b) may seem to be without "ranges" or territories, but they probably do not walk all their lives without returning to some familiar landscapes. The existence of Clovis caches surely indicates landscape-attachment for western and eastern Clovis groups, but it is an attachment quite distinct from the clear territoriality we see today among modern hunter-gatherers. We will never know whether Clovis foragers felt loyalty or affection for features in the landscape, but we certainly have enough clues to conclude that certain landscapes were familiar and comfortable. The lack of rock art, cumulative burial grounds, and unmistakably symbolic artifacts means that Clovis groups were ephemeral and always just passing through. But however Clovis people emotionally defined themselves in the landscape, they were the discoverers and pioneers in most of the continent, and they knew it.

7 Unified conclusions about the Clovis era

One already knows the ending; one moves the story toward it.

J. Irving 1999:156

7.1 Introduction

To us, so far removed in time and so different in our orientation to landscape-use and footborne exploration, Clovis-era archeological sites provide a series of disconnected views of life. The sites are freeze-frames of one-time subsistence or technological events in the lives of very foreign people. These scattered events of artifact and social history do not often enough provide clear patterns repeated over time in different sites and subregions to give us visions of their lives. We see moments in the lives of artifacts too, such as bifaces that come to rest many kilometers away from where they were shaped, after they had been used or resharpened in another site. We find flakes from bifaces that had been shaped somewhere else, reshaped at the site, then carried away to be deposited or lost for ever someplace else. Episodes of human behavior are lit briefly by these bits of discarded artifacts and bone refuse, but a coherent synthesis of life in the Clovis era does not come into focus out of them. We witness only isolated moments of action but never encounter the actors again, apparently, from site to site across the continent. Where were the people who made the site at Domebo, Oklahoma (Leonhardy 1966), one week before they killed the mammoth, or one year before? Where did they go after they lightly butchered the mammoth? Where had the Clovis points been used or manufactured before they were abandoned in the bonebed? What thoughts did people have about these sharp bifaces before plunging them into the Domebo mammoth? And where did the people go between their visits to the large Debert, Shoop, or Bull Brook sites in the eastern United States? Did families congregate seasonally at these sites where discrete clusters of diverse tool classes are found, then go on their different ways to forage widely scattered and out of touch with each other on the landscape the rest of the year?

The Clovis way of life will never be easy to explain or decode. What I have tried to do in this book is to understand how a way of life like Clovis could come into being, disperse so far and rapidly, and affect the largest animals sharing the foragers' ranges. I have done this using principles and theories and facts that I think make the reconstructions plausible and strong. This model of Clovis life may strike some readers as unlikely, based on preconceptions about late Pleistocene habitats and foraging, but I hope the model will be fairly tested and not simply rejected out of hand. Perhaps some readers will find the model reasonable and acceptable; maybe some readers will discover a new way of thinking about Clovis.

There is a viewpoint among many prehistorians that if you don't know everything, then you know nothing (paraphrased from R. J. Mason's response to a critic [Mason 1962]). Since no one knows "everything" about the Clovis era, owing to inadequate sampling or other reasons, does this mean that nothing should be said about it?

This book has been a synthesizing study of a distant time period in American prehistory. In the 1990s, such synthesizing studies of the late Pleistocene almost went out of style, possibly following in the spirit of larger sociological trends such as decentralization of authority in business and government, in the context of recognizing regional diversity. A specialized regionalism had taken over in Paleoindian studies, producing effects similar to what regionalism wrought in European Upper Paleolithic research (Otte and Keeley 1990), where it had been a reaction against too many continent-wide generalizations based mainly on a specific sequence – such as the Dordogne in France – or a key site. The earlier syntheses of Paleoindian lifeways often focused very heavily on isolated or local events and emphasized *in situ* development of culture without regard for outside influences, such as migration or diffusion (which may be virtually indistinguishable when seen from a single site without occupational interruption). Maybe local traditions were thought to lose importance if they were interpreted as introduced from outside or profoundly altered by migrations and diffusion – perhaps suggestive of an archeological racism or imperialism. Any hint of population movement, cultural replacement, and diffusion of ideas may have been perceived as almost demeaning to local traditions. There is still great resistance to the concept that technology or beliefs often originate outside local cultural sequences. Yet, text-supported history in Europe clearly shows numerous population movements and diffusions of ideas, even if prehistory is not allowed to contain similar trends (Otte and Keeley 1990:578).

THE CLOVIS DISPERSAL

Two different views of dispersal are found in the debates about the peopling of the New World. One point of view is that whenever humans encounter new habitats they abruptly stop dispersing into them. That is to say, when different conditions are discovered by dispersing people, the people must stop range-expansion so they can conquer, overcome, or adapt to the new habitats through radical new behaviors. A second point of view is that dispersal is directed movement into new habitats that need not be identical to those of the existing home range. Dispersers are urged forward or drawn ahead by smoke seen from afar, by the intriguing similarities that opportunistic foragers can find in new lands, or by the strong need to escape high costs incurred if they stay in the old ranges. Dispersers into new ranges may need to behave in a special way to get to the new lands – they may need to build a bigger boat, for example, or sail in a new direction, but otherwise radical new behavior is not always displayed. This second point of view accommodates the initial human entry into the islands of the South Pacific or the Australasian continental mass of Sunda-Sahul. It also accommodates the initial entry of the New World.

Outward dispersal may be necessary because home ranges are too cold, too dry, too unreliable, or too crowded; but dispersal out of a changing or unpredictable range is usually dangerous. The movement may be risky because resources up ahead are unpredictable or depleted. On the other hand, dispersal also may result from positive forces, such as the perception that new ranges are available and favorable, in which case the ability and willingness to move is advantageous. The species most at risk of dying out anywhere in the world are those with poor abilities to disperse, especially if they also have narrow geographic ranges, highly specific habitat requirements, and low fecundity. Habitat fragmentation or the loss of even small patches of prime habitat is very hard on such species. Clearly, however, humans were not at risk during any time in the late Pleistocene, judging from their success at colonizing new ranges worldwide so quickly after the first appearance of modern *Homo sapiens sapiens*; their adaptive qualifications must have included the ability to disperse rapidly into new and different habitats whenever the pull or push was felt.

Clovis was a fugitive culture that spread throughout North America and points south in a very brief time interval. It was "fugitive" because no clearly established homeland or point of origin can be identified, and as a way of life its spread did register in the archeological record but is not traceable from moment of birth through moment of evolution into something else. It was a "culture" unlike any ever seen since in the New World.

Clovis was fugitive in many other ways, too. Although there is a possibility that beehive shelters were built at some sites, such as Thunderbird in Virginia (Gardner 1974), Clovis people did not build structures meant to be permanent or long-lasting. The potential implications of this sort of behavior may be decipherable by looking deeply at the ethnographic record of mobile people who also do not construct permanent features or monuments. Such people constantly redefine their place in the world every day when they choose new living and sleeping spaces within older camping areas, or when they reselect their camping areas within larger landscapes. They do not create the kinds of anchor points modern people take for granted such as houses and solid dwellings; all Clovis shelters were temporary and their locations could be shifted according to needs, whims, or some other rationale. The very act of selecting the same camping spot chosen weeks before would have been a creative statement of attachment to points and places, while the act of selecting new and different camps would have been a statement of cultural or individual control of one's past and future. Like the behavior of highly mobile foragers who relate to their landscape in shifting and evanescent ways, Clovis behavior was extremely light upon the landscape of the Pleistocene. Over a large part of the continent, Clovis fire-hearths were not often reused, even within revisited campsites such as those near quarry sites. Lithic activity areas in quarry-related camps may have been reused by necessity (chipping features littered the ground), yet frequently reused activity areas for sleeping or food preparation are nearly impossible to find over most of the continent.

CLOVIS DISPERSAL AND MEGAMAMMAL EXTINCTION

As presented here, a contingent-series model of causality explains fluted-point subsistence, settlement, and biogeographic migration in the context of late Pleistocene climatic change, paleoenvironmental developments, megamammal behavioral patterns, and rational foraging decisions. Each event in the model was contingent upon the earlier event(s). The necessary and sufficient causes were serial in occurrence (Table 7.1).

The first event A in the series was the changing of late Pleistocene habitats, creating isolated refugium patches for megamammal populations; this shifting of habitats took place after the Last Glacial Maximum, an interval lasting from about 19,500 to 16,100 rcybp (Mix, Bard, and Schneider 2001:639–40). Climatic changes between 16,000 and 11,500 rcybp were not uniform everywhere, but generally followed a trend from slow warming with occasional interludes of cold to abrupt reversals and oscillations. During this interval of time, if there were human populations in North America, technologies and subsistence tactics were developing in response to the climatic and biotic shifts. But at the end of this interval, around 11,500 rcybp, the major elements of Clovis technology were appearing – blades, bifaces, and fluting. Foragers targeted larger mammals, and found them easier to locate and probably easier to kill than before, since habitats were fragmenting and large mammals were changing their ranges in response. Ecological stresses were heavy on large mammals.

Event B was the exploratory dispersal of fluted-point-makers into ranges where signs of stress on mammoths and mastodons could be found; the largest mammals were especially easy to track and kill during the difficult time of the Younger Dryas chronozone, and the Clovis drought of this interval created isolated refugial patches.

Event C was the intensified hunting and scavenging of mammoths and mastodons, especially in the refugia, along with wider exploration and dispersal between such patches. The dispersals and exploration were facilitated by the probable membership of Late Pleistocene people in what can be considered concentric series of groups, eccentric clusters of groups, and ephemeral groups, all at the same time. Clovis or fluted-point culture in general through the continent may have been a sort of very loose community, characterized by a sense of identity and historical traditions, while local fluted-point-makers comprised bands of companions – the formally organized groups that had far fewer traditional or sentimental attachments to historical norms. The bands of companions were autonomous and mobile, but they contacted their larger communities from time to time. Overall, the foraging ecology of fluted-point-makers thus could remain superficially uniform across the continent, but the uniformity also was overlain by regional and local variability.

CLOVIS MIGRATION

Biogeographic migration was a significant part of the intergenerational cultural strategy of Upper Paleolithic peoples. Many habitats at the end of the Pleistocene were ephemeral, unstable, or oscillating between different states, especially during the last 10 millennia (21,000–11,000 rcybp). During this interval, the human ability to migrate or disperse widely was a cultural strategy that allowed people to track or locate optimal if ephemeral habitats. Yet although such habitats attracted Upper Paleolithic people towards them, they also were not ideal for keeping the people in them for long, since they were changing. Over time, more migrating people may have arrived than remained resident in such habitats, even when arrivals were infrequent, and food would not have been

TABLE 7.1 Chronosequence of climate and hypothesized human responses after the Last Glacial Maximum.

¹⁴C YEARS BP	CLIMATE	CHRONOZONE OR EVENT	FAUNAL EVENT	CULTURAL EVENT
19,500–16,100	Very cold, dry	Last Glacial Maximum	No extinctions	Archeological remains rare to nonexistent anywhere in continent
13,000	Warm	Bølling	No extinctions; patchiness increases as zonal habitats replace high-diversity mosaics	Archeological remains rare to nonexistent anywhere in continent
12,000	Warm	Allerød	No extinctions; isolated refugia are biotic oases	Archeological remains rare to nonexistent anywhere in continent
11,500	Cold	Intra-Allerød cold period	No extinctions	Earliest Clovis radiocarbon dates, very restricted range; animal trails explored
11,200	Warm	Unnamed warm interval	Possibly some large-mammal extinctions	Clovis present in wide area of continent
10,900	Cold, drier	Younger Dryas begins abruptly		Clovis becoming locally more variable, spending longer times in certain places
10,800	Cold continues		All megafauna extinctions complete, including mammoths and mastodonts	Clovis-like materials distributed continent-wide; foragers switch patches and prey
10,200	Warm, wetter	Younger Dryas ends abruptly		Fluted points no longer made

adequate over the long run. Climatic changes created unfavorable conditions, and the offspring of immigrants were encouraged to emigrate.

A large proportion of the human population in any region 11,000 rcybp may have stayed as "residents" in defined ranges, intending to have children and settle into the territories for the long-term. As with other taxa of dispersing animals (see, for example Kessel 1953 and Wing 1943 on European starlings), the human groups electing to settle were probably most attracted to the edges of ranges, because populations would have been relatively less dense there.

However, some Clovis foragers were always only temporary visitors to regions, and they returned to other ranges or moved through vast areas as explorers rather than colonizers. Overall the explorations by transient Clovis foragers, who did not "settle" or intend to settle in the new ranges, enormously expanded the Clovis presence – and the archeological record – into many distant new lands. Some of these fugitive visitors later in their lives may have returned to certain ranges they had once passed through or explored temporarily, to become colonists and longer-term settlers. They may have joined others who had settled earlier or they may have finally established the very first local populations in these new ranges.

Thus the nature of the fluted-point presence was regionally and locally variable. Some ranges were settled early; other ranges were occupied only temporarily. Some ranges saw human populations established rapidly; other ranges were given a once-over and then abandoned, perhaps several times during the Clovis era. The existence of local populations settling into new ranges grew denser and denser over time, but "drift" (both genetic and cultural) would have been minimal because the dispersal happened so quickly. At the same time, the high mobility of a part of the population would have blended the continent's populations both genetically and culturally.

Advancing Clovis populations would have spread more rapidly into habitats that offered ample resources and space, of course, as opposed to marginal habitats. Judging on the basis of richness and diversity of resources, one could predict the southeast and south-central regions of the continent were settled more quickly than any other part. Yet marginal areas would have seen even more rapid movement into and through them by dispersers who did not stay in them for very long. The very earliest period of dispersal would have been the most rapid, because population levels – and competition for resources – were at their lowest; as well, newcomers without local knowledge had to explore widely and quickly to learn about local possibilities.

In cases when the immigrants did not have offspring in the new habitats, or did not bring any to them, residency times would have been relatively brief and limited. It is possible that women with children may not have been as extraordinarily mobile as were unattached men (but see Surovell 2000a). Unfortunately, the concrete archeological evidence of the absence of offspring is very tricky to isolate; among other possibilities is the lack of skeletons in locales where human populations did not truly become "established," or a lack of hearths and sleeping areas in sites where children were never present. The Anzick (MT) site did contain Clovis artifacts with the bones of at least one young child (Owsley and Hunt 2001), and therefore we know that children were clearly part of the Clovis dispersal. Perhaps they were valued because of their rarity, and perhaps they enjoyed an unusual social status as the future inheritors of a completely new landscape.

THE CLOVIS INDIVIDUAL

We know next to nothing about each Clovis woman and man. Some fluted points are so alike as to appear the handiwork of one and the same individual; but how much farther can we go in recognizing behavioral individuality or the daily experiences of Clovis-era people? Were the flintknappers who created the Drake (CO) cache also present at the Dent (CO) mammoth kills? Did the Lehner (AZ) foragers also witness the death of the Naco and Escapule (AZ) mammoths? These seem to be unknowable facts about Clovis individuals.

We are also nearly clueless about Clovis people's biology. The bits of human skeleton that may be Clovis age – such as from Anzick (MT) or other sites – make up a very small sample to be generalizing from. But some characteristics do stand out, such as relatively small stature. Among some modern foragers, small stature and slow growth rates are "adaptive" because "small babies are easier to carry" when "people have to walk a lot"; and as a result smallness "makes sense in terms of the nomadic foraging way of life" (Lee 1980:331; also see Sealy and Pfeiffer 2000). Lee noted how among adult !Kung foragers, "shorter men are more successful hunters than are taller men," all of which might suggest that Clovis people were probably short-statured. Indeed, the oldest known human skeletal remains from the Americas (see Table 1.2) have provided evidence for short stature, unfortunately all derived from post-Clovis specimens (summarized in Dixon 1999:143, and table 5.1). A man from Warm Mineral Springs (FL) dating to 10,300 rcybp stood about 163 cm tall (~5 feet 4 inches); another man from Kennewick (WA) dating to about 8,400 rcybp stood 176 cm (~5 feet 9 inches). Not only were these post-Clovis foragers not tall, but they had suffered accidents, dietary stress, disease, and brief lives – few lived beyond thirty years of age. Did these characteristics also apply to Clovis? Only a sampling of older skeletons that someone may discover in the future will allow us to answer that question.

CLOVIS MOBILITY AND GENDER ROLES

The gender-related implications of high mobility are difficult to identify. If the primary subsistence activities of each group were carried out by men, then women may have been relatively "sedentarized," to use a term from anthropological studies. Fertility would have been high under sedentarized conditions (Ripley 1980) – if women were less mobile than men, did not gather as much food, and did not carry burdens of food and children for long distances. However, if Clovis women were not sedentarized, and were mobile, food-gathering, and burden-bearing – like most modern forager women – they were not capable of having high reproductive rates (Lee 1980; Ripley 1980:353), and mobile late Pleistocene foragers must be imagined traveling with few children.

A large number of factors suggest that Clovis groups made residential or fission-group moves much more frequently than once a month – for example, the lack of substantial housing in archeological sites, the evidence indicating movements of consumers to resources such as quarries and megamammal carcasses, the absence of evidence for logistical movements (or "collecting" *sensu* Binford [1980]), the possibly great sizes of ranges (up to 2,000–5,000 km²), and the apparent unimportance of plant exploitation (Binford 1980). Moving more than once a month is an unusually high frequency, but the relatively high costs of searching for terrestrial mammals in biomes that were not floristically productive were traded off against high exploratory returns and high energy returns from megamammals. Meat could be easily stored as an overwintering buffer, either in caches such as Frison (1976, 1991; Frison and Todd 1986) proposed were present at the Colby (WY) Clovis mammoth site, or as dried or frozen deboned meat-stores in earth-pits, which would have been fairly impossible ever to fossilize. Perhaps the semiarticulated mammoth skeletons at some Clovis sites were the frozen storage sites themselves.

Extremely mobile men and women divided their work to accommodate maintenance needs, subsistence requirements, child-raising, and other activities. Women with children could carry them or lead them to foraging patches, but were probably restricted in the speed and distances they could travel day to day. But women did participate in making the executive decisions about when camps should be moved, because they were the most sensitive to the exhaustion of resources that were within reasonable walking distance of camp.

The Clovis-era foraging I envision in this book involved both gathering and hunting by men and women whenever possible, and perhaps even communal hunting of megamammals regularly.

CLOVIS "RESOURCE MANAGEMENT"

"Landscapes" are places with a symbolic and often totemic meaning layered over the ecogeological values and meanings. Subsistence resources are almost always the basis upon which the ideational meanings are organized; for example, Australian Aboriginals make totemic maps of resources and regulate access rights to them (Layton 1999) based on social and biological relationships. Kin-based (or ancestral-based) "estates" are country where kin ties allow people to have access to clustered sacred sites; certain features mark the edges of estates, which are often aligned with watersheds or watercourses. People spend most of their time inside the estate's heart closer to water than on the edges. Because plants and animals are often perceived as being unpredictable inside and out of estates, people willingly grant reciprocal rights to neighbors in other estates to exploit temporary abundances of resources in anyone's estates, although sacred sites and water sources may be indirectly "guarded" (Layton 1995).

Clovis group-relationships with other groups also probably centered around the regulation of access to critical resources. But Clovis groups were estate settlers only towards the latter part of their existence in North America, just before the radiation of variance in technology, subsistence, and settlement that marks the post-Clovis period, and their attachment to resources may have been very adjustable. I suggest that the earliest Clovis foragers were not inclined to behave territorially or defensively, and would have allowed each other unusually free access to late Pleistocene resources (although I doubt that direct face-to-face competition was invited or tolerated). One line of evidence for this easygoing attitude is the absence of rock art or other kinds of permanent symbol-rich records which function to advertise a social presence and ownership of country.

I see another possible support for the suggested Clovis trait of free access: there is little or no archeological, palynological, or stratigraphic evidence of direct human involvement in managing ecosystems. While the Clovis removal of megafauna did have measurable effects on late Pleistocene/early Holocene habitats, it was probably unpremeditated and does not count as an example of aboriginal "resource management" (Blackburn and Anderson 1993; Williams and Hunn 1982), a term which means such practices as bush-burning or pruning (to clear vegetation and to encourage specific kinds of new growth). Of course, much of the potential evidence about selective burning or other kinds of deliberate resource management may not be preserved this far removed in time – such as, for example, the cutting of spears or bow-staves out of living trees in such a way as to shape the regrowth of the wood (see Wilke 1988 for a study of late prehistoric bow-stave removals from juniper trees). Thus the absence of such evidence in the archeological record may be a taphonomic problem.

The most influential type of resource management practice available to Clovis foragers would have been the setting of fires. Fires had many uses to later American aboriginal people (summarized in Krech 1999: 101–22), and these include: clearing brush to make animals easier to find; clearing dead vegetation to make new growth green up and attract animals; driving and encircling animals; changing the habitat (encouraging edge effects and disturbed-ground taxa such as deer) or allowing the spread of fruit bushes or other plants on the edges of tree stands; visual communication; protection against trespassers; and making travel easier. Fires set by foragers may get out of hand, or after being set they may be ignored to burn far more area than originally expected, so that even modest burns often have big consequences. Thus in ecosystems where Clovis foragers did set fires, if ever they did, we should see signs of "fire-driven dynamic mosaics" of vegetation (Haydon, Friar, and Pianka 2000) overlaying the climate-driven and megamammal-driven patch-scale mosaics; we should also be able to find relatively large and abundant pieces of charcoal in buried sediments where the fires burned (Blackford 2000; Clark 1988).

But we have not detected such evidence. Except in parts of South America where the incidence of charcoal from the time interval of interest may be related to the habitat and climate changes of the Younger Dryas rather than to human activity, the post-glacial vegetational histories of large regions do not reflect the influences of fire. Fires set by Clovis people were rare or minimal, and resource management by fire was therefore not done in Clovis times.

My conclusions are these:

1. The people who made Clovis and Clovis-like projectile points were exploratory and pioneering over most of their range. If there were pre-existing human populations in North America, the archeological record provides only extremely scanty evidence of pre-Clovis technology, and even less evidence of subsistence and social organization.
2. The unique Clovis strategies of mobility, technology, social organization, subsistence, and risk management spread through the continent not by diffusion but by rapid dispersal (grading into the process called "biogeographic

migration"). If there were any pre-existing populations before this dispersal event, the archeological record provides no evidence about competition for resources, exchange, or other interactions.

3. Clovis mobility involved cyclic movements layered over serial movements.
4. Clovis populations were broad-spectrum foragers, of course, but they also rationally narrowed their range of preferred food items during a very specific time interval of the late Pleistocene.
5. Terminal Pleistocene megamammal sites with human behavioral association are abundant – in fact they are outstandingly abundant – and some sites appear to be short-term kills, even the largest ones such as Lehner (AZ) or Dent (CO). Clovis hunters killed megamammals far more often than modern foragers would choose to do – for rational, understandable reasons – and finished off the mammoths and mastodons. They also may have killed off other large mammal taxa.
6. Clovis populations were not universally stressed by change in climate and biota in the last 1,000 years of the Pleistocene, but they did rationally change mobility and subsistence strategies towards the end of the Clovis era.

7.2   The end

Journalist Roger Downey (2000) bemoaned the apparent callowness of American archeologists who, he thought, still dwell on an American frontier where they pretend to be conquerors of American wildness and discoverers of its secret past – a past that Native Americans know all about. The frontier mentality, in this view, is a template of the nineteenth-century pioneers-versus-Indians story.

Yet a hostile attitude towards archeological models of discovery may contain a wilful misunderstanding of the more appropriate meaning of the word "frontier" in archeology. The western frontier that Frederick Turner thought had passed in 1890 was a state of mind where violence against the natives was fated and ineluctable. But the frontier in Clovis studies is a constantly shifting zone of questioning, where the archeologists themselves are a fluid population of foreigners who encounter perils and strangeness on a quest for knowledge. The frontier always moves forward and new foreigners enter the zone every year, seeking fame and fortune in high-profile research. The trail-blazing strangeness of life in the zone is what attracts the pioneers, but some of them cannot survive. New prehistoric sites are found, new interpretations are put on offer, and the most appealing may be accepted for a time. But what ultimately shapes the direction and speed of this shifting frontier is the testing and questioning done by archeologists who trail behind the pioneers. No one can be considered a conquerer in this twenty-first-century frontier, yet every archeologist dispossesses the original settlers. Each generation of scholars explores the field, contributes to it, and then must welcome the next generation of questioners and doubters.

During the last fifty years, we as archeological frontiersmen have probably deluded ourselves over and over again with each saga-du-jour about the peopling of the Americas. But within the relentless rebirthing of the field of study, some ideas persist because they have made sense. The idea that Clovis-era foragers foraged rationally and opportunistically in late Pleistocene landscapes – with large mammals as their preferred prey – is not merely one more déclassé story about America's past. It is an enduring and sound account of prehistory that does the best job of explaining the archeological record. Clovis groups dispersed very far and very quickly not because they were chasing mammoths, but because they were experts at finding patches where high-ranked food resources were to be found. These patches were stepping stones to continental colonization by Clovis people, and they were also the last refugia of mammoths and mastodonts.

Appendix

TABLE A.1 Radiocarbon ages (rcybp) calibrated (roughly) to mid-points of likeliest calendar-year ages. Note that this chart is deliberately simplified and rough, because calibration itself is not simple. Several calibration programs are available, and may vary because of different interpretations of data; the main sources for this table are Fiedel (1999a) and Stuiver, Reimer, Bard, Beck, Burr, Hughen, Kromer, McCormac, van den Plicht, and Spurk (1998).

RADIOCARBON AGE (RCYBP)	CALENDAR-YEAR AGE (YR BP)	YR BC
20,000	23,950	22,000
19,500	22,950	21,000
19,000	22,450	20,500
18,500	21,950	20,000
18,000	21,450	19,500
17,500	20,950	19,000
17,000	20,200	18,250
16,500	19,950	18,000
16,000	19,150	17,200
15,500	18,450	16,500
15,000	17,950	16,000
14,500	17,450	15,500
14,000	16,950	15,000
13,500	16,200	14,250
13,000	15,350	13,400
12,500	15,085	13,135
12,000	14,065	12,115
11,500	13,350	11,400
11,000	13,000	11,050
10,500	12,620	10,670
10,000	11,350	9,400
9,500	11,030	9,080
9,000	10,200	8,250

References

Aaris-Sørinsen, K., and Erik Brinch Petersen. 1986. The Prejlerup aurochs – an archaeozoological discovery from boreal Denmark. *Striae* 24:111–17.

Abraczinskas, Laura Marie. 1992. The distribution of Pleistocene proboscidean sites in Michigan: an update of records and a co-occurrence analysis of their relation to surface saline water. Unpublished M.Sc. thesis, Michigan State University.

Absolon, K. 1945a. *Die Erforschung der diluvialen Mammutjägerstation von Unter-Wisternitz an den Pollauer Bergen in Mähren. Arbeitsbericht über das erste Grabungsjahr 1924.* Brno.

    1945b. *Die Erforschung der diluvialen Mammutjägerstation von Unter-Wisternitz an den Pollauer Bergen in Mähren. Arbeitsbericht über das dritte Jahr 1926.* Brno.

Absolon, K., and Bohuslav Klíma. 1977. *Předmostí: ein Mammutjägerplatz in Mähren. Archaeologiae Moravieae* 8.

Adams, Jonathan M. 1996. New palaeovegetation maps of the Americas at 1 kyr intervals, 15,000–9,000 C14 years B.P. Website dated 20/3/1996 http://www.soton.ac.uk/~tjms/nerc.html accessed December 2000.

Adams, Jonathan M., and H. Faure. 1995. Review and atlas of palaeovegetation: preliminary land ecosystem maps of the world since the Last Glacial Maximum. Website dated 25/10/1995 http://www.soton.ac.uk/~tjms/adams1.html accessed December 2000.

Adams, Robert McCormick. 1941. Archaeological investigations in Jefferson County, Missouri. *Transactions of the Academy of Science of St. Louis* 30(5).

    1949. Archaeological investigations in Jefferson County, Missouri. *The Missouri Archaeologist* 11:1–72.

Adovasio, J. M. 1983. The AENA compilation of fluted points in eastern North America: a perspective from Meadowcroft Rockshelter. *Archaeology of Eastern North America* 11:6–12.

    1999. Paradigm-death and gunfights. *Scientific American Discovering Archaeology* [1(6)] Special Report: Monte Verde Revisited, p. 20.

Adovasio, J. M., J. D. Gunn, J. Donahue, and R. Stuckenrath. 1975. Excavations at Meadowcroft Rockshelter, 1973–1974: a progress report. *Pennsylvania Archaeologist* 45:1–30.

    1977. Meadowcroft Rockshelter: retrospect 1976. *Pennsylvania Archaeologist* 47:1–93.

    1978. Meadowcroft Rockshelter, 1977: an overview. *American Antiquity* 43:632–51.

Adovasio, J. M., and D. R. Pedler. 1997. Monte Verde and the antiquity of humankind in the Americas. *Antiquity* 71:573–80.

Adovasio, J. M., and O. Soffer. 1992. Flotation samples from Mezhirich, Ukraine: a microview of macroissues. Paper presented at the 57th Annual Meeting of the Society for American Archaeology, Pittsburgh, Pennsylvania.

Adovasio, J. M., O. Soffer, D. C. Hyland, B. Klíma, and J. Svoboda. 1998. Perishable technologies and the genesis of the eastern Gravettian. *Anthropologie* 36:43–68.

Agenbroad, Larry D. 1984. New World mammoth distribution. In P. S. Martin and R. G. Klein (eds.), *Quaternary Extinctions: A Prehistoric Revolution*, pp. 90–112. Tucson, University of Arizona Press.

Agenbroad, Larry D., and Jim I. Mead. 1987. Late Pleistocene alluvium and megafauna dung deposits of the central Colorado Plateau. In G. Davis and E. VandenDolder (eds.), *Geologic Diversity of Arizona and Its Margins: Excursions to Choice Area*, pp. 68–85. Arizona Bureau of Geology and Mineral Technology Special Paper No. 5. Tucson, Arizona Bureau of Geology and Mining Technology.

Ahler, Stanley A., and Phil R. Geib. 2000. Why flute? Folsom point design and adaptation. *Journal of Archaeological Science* 27:799–820.

Allee, W. C., A. E. Emerson, O. Park, T. Park, and K. P. Schmidt. 1949. *Principles of Animal Ecology*. Philadelphia, PA, Saunders.

Alley, R. B., D. A. Meese, A. J. Shuman, A. J. Gow, K. C. Taylor, P. M. Grootes, J. W. C. White, M. Ram, E. D. Waddington, P. A. Mayewski, and G. A. Zielinski. 1993. Abrupt accumulation increase at the Younger Dryas termination in the GISP2 ice core. *Nature* 362:527–9.

Alroy, John. 1999. Putting North America's end-Pleistocene megafaunal extinction in context: large-scale analyses of spatial patterns, extinction rates, and size distributions. In R. D. E. MacPhee (ed.), *Extinctions in Near Time: Causes, Contexts, and Consequences*, pp. 105–43. New York, Kluwer Academic/Plenum Publishers.

2001. A multispecies overkill simulation of the end-Pleistocene megafaunal mass extinction. *Science* 292:1,893–6.

Alsoszatai-Petheo, John. 1986. An alternative paradigm for the study of early man in the New World. In A. L. Bryan (ed.), *New Evidence for the Pleistocene Peopling of the Americas*, pp. 15–26. Orono, Center for the Study of Early Man and University of Maine.

Alvard, M. 1995. Intraspecific prey choice by Amazonian hunters. *Current Anthropology* 36:789–818.

Ammann, Brigitta, H. J. B. Birks, Stephen J. Brooks, Ulrich Eicher, Ulrich von Grafenstein, Wolfgang Hofmann, Geoffrey Lemdahl, Jakob Schwander, Kazimierz Tobolski, and Lucia Wick. 2000. Quantification of biotic responses to rapid climatic changes around the Younger Dryas – a synthesis. *Palaeogeography, Palaeoclimatology, Palaeoecology* 159:313–47.

Anderson, Adrian D. 1962. The Cooperton mammoth: a preliminary report. *Plains Anthropologist* 7.

(general editor). 1975. The Cooperton mammoth: an early man bone quarry. *Great Plains Journal* 14:130–73.

Anderson, Adrian D., and Joseph A. Tiffany. 1972. Rummells-Maske: a Clovis find-spot in Iowa. *Plains Anthropologist* 17:55–8.

Anderson, David G. 1990. The Paleoindian colonization of eastern North America: a view from the Southeastern United States. *Research in Economic Anthropology*, Supplement 5:163–216.

1995. Paleoindian interaction networks in the eastern woodlands. In M. S. Nassaney and K. E. Sassaman (eds.), *Native American Interaction: Multiscalar Analyses and Interpretations in the Eastern Woodlands*, pp. 1–26. Knoxville, University of Tennessee Press.

1996. Models of Paleoindian and Early Archaic settlement in the Lower Southeast. In D. G. Anderson and K. E. Sassaman (eds.), *The Paleoindian and Early Archaic Southeast*, pp. 29–57. Tuscaloosa, University of Alabama Press.

Anderson, David G., and Michael K. Faught. 1998a. Downloadable database on website "A North American Paleoindian Projectile Point Database", dated 8 May 1998, http://www.fsu.edu/special/paleo/paleoind.html accessed November 2000.

1998b. The distribution of fluted Paleoindian projectile points: update 1998. *Archaeology of Eastern North America* 26:163–87.

2000. Paleoindian artefact distributions: evidence and implications. *Antiquity* 74:507–13.

Anderson, David G., Michael K. Faught, and Christopher Gillam. 1998. Paleoindian site/artifact distributions viewed from a very large scale: evidence and implications. Paper presented at the 63rd Annual Meeting of the Society for American Archaeology, Seattle, Washington.

Anderson, David G., and J. Christopher Gillam. 2000. Paleoindian colonization of the Americas. Implications from an examination of physiography, demography, and artifact distribution. *American Antiquity* 65:43–66.

Anderson, Elaine. 1984. Who's who in the Pleistocene: a mammalian bestiary. In P. S. Martin and R. G. Klein (eds.), *Quaternary Extinctions: A Prehistoric Revolution*, pp. 40–89. Tucson, University of Arizona Press.

Anonymous [*Scientific Monthly*]. 1935. The Moab mastodon pictograph. *Scientific Monthly* (October 1935):378–9.

Anonymous [*Japan Times*]. 2000. Further doubts dug up on archaeologist's "finds." *The Japan Times Online*, 20 November 2000. http://www.japantimes.co.jp/cgi-bin/getarticle.pl5?nn20001120a2.htm accessed November 2000.

Anonymous [*Mainichi News*]. 2000. Dirty diggers dealt another credibility blow. *Mainichi Daily News*, 11 November 2000. http://www.mainichi.co.jp/english/news/archive/200011/11/news08.html accessed November 2000.

Anthony, D. W. 1990. Migration in archaeology: the baby and the bathwater. *American Anthropologist* 92:895–914.

1997. Prehistoric migration as a social process. In J. Chapman and H. Hamerow (eds.), *Migrations and Invasions in Archaeological Explanation*, pp. 21–32. BAR International Series 664. Oxford.

Anuskiewicz, R. J. 1988. Preliminary archaeological investigations at Ray Hole Spring in the eastern Gulf of Mexico. *Florida Anthropologist* 41:181–5.

Anuskiewicz, R. J., P. R. Gerrell, J. S. Dunbar, and J. F. Donoghue. 1994. Evidence of prehistoric man on the North American Continental Shelf from a sinkhole located 32 km offshore in 12 m seawater. Paper presented at the 59th Annual Meeting of the Society for American Archaeology, Anaheim, California.

Arroyo-Cabrales, Joaquín, Silvia Gonzalez, Luis Morett A., Oscar J. Polaca, and Graham Sherwood. 1999. Tocuila and its contribution to paleoenvironmental reconstruction of the Basin of Mexico. Paper presented at the 2nd International Mammoth Conference, 16–20 May, Rotterdam, The Netherlands.

Arroyo-Cabrales, Joaquín, Oscar J. Polaco, and Felisa J. Aguilar-Arellano. 1999. Taxonomy and distribution of the mammoth of Mexico (genus *Mammuthus*): a review of the collections of the National Institute of Anthropology and History. Poster presented at the 2nd International Mammoth Conference, 16–20 May, Rotterdam, The Netherlands.

Arroyo-Cabrales, Joaquín, Oscar J. Polaco, Eileen Johnson, and A. Fabiola Guzman. 1999. Distribution of the genus *Mammuthus* in Mexico. Paper presented at the 2nd International Mammoth Conference, 16–20 May, Rotterdam, The Netherlands.

Arslanov, K. A., G. T. Cook, Steinar Gulliksen, D. D. Harkness, Tuovi Kankainen, E. M. Scott, Sergey Vartanyan, and Ganna I. Zaitseva. 1998. Consensus dating of mammoth remains from Wrangel Island. *Radiocarbon* 40:289–94.

Ashcroft, Bill, Gareth Griffiths, and Helen Tiffin. 1998. *Key Concepts in Post-Colonial Studies*. London, Routledge.

Austerlitz, Robert. 1980. Language-family density in America and North Eurasia. *Ural-Altaische Jahrbücher* 52:1–10.

Aveleyra A. de Anda, Luis. 1955. *El segundo mamut fósil de Santa Isabel Iztapan, Mexico, y artefactos asociados*. Instituto Nacional de Antropologia e Historia, Direccion de Prehistoria Publ. No. I.

Aveleyra A. de Anda, Luis, and Manuel Maldonado-K. 1953. Association of artifacts with mammoth in the Valley of Mexico. *American Antiquity* 18:332–40.

Bahn, Paul G. 1998. *The Cambridge Illustrated History of Prehistoric Art*. New York, Cambridge University Press.

Bahn, Paul G., and Jean Vertut. 1997. *Journey through the Ice Age*. Berkeley, University of California Press.

Baker, R. Robin. 1981. *Human Navigation and the Sixth Sense*. London, Hodder and Stoughton.

Baker, Tony. 2000. Paleoindian & Other Archaeological Stuff [active website]. http://www.ele.net accessed January 2001.

Baldini, J. Marina, Antonio Vita, Massimo C. Mauri, Vincenzina Amodei, Massimiliano Carrisi, Silvia Bravin, and Luigi Cantalamessa. 1997. Psychopathological and cognitive features in subclinical hypothyroidism. *Progress in Neuro-Psychopharmacology and Biological Psychiatry* 21:925–35.

Balter, Michael. 2000. Paintings in Italian cave may be oldest yet. *Science* 290:419–21.

Barnes, S. Alfred. 1939. The difference between natural and human flaking on prehistoric flint implements. *American Anthropologist* 41:99–112.

Barnes, R. F. W., and K. L. Jensen. 1987. How to count elephants in forests. *IUCN African Elephant and Rhino Specialist Group Technical Bulletin* 1:1–6.

Barrett, S. A. 1911. *The Material Culture of the Klamath Lake and Modoc Indians of Northeastern California and Southern Oregon*. University of California Publications in American Archaeology and Ethnology 5(4).

Barrish, Barbara L. 1995. The Paleo Crossing Site: fluted point typology and chronology. Unpublished M.A. thesis, Kent State University, Ohio.

Barton, Nick. 2000. The rapid origin of reproductive isolation. *Science* 290:462–3.

Barton, R. N. E. 1999. Colonisation and resettlement of Europe in the Late Glacial: a view from the western periphery. In M. Kobusiewicz and J. K. Kozłowski (eds.), *Post-Pleniglacial Re-Colonisation of the Great European Lowland*, pp. 71–86. Folia Quaternaria 70. Krakow, Polska Akademia Umiejętności.

Basgall, Mark E., and M. C. Hall. 1991. Relationships between fluted and stemmed points in the Mojave Desert. *Current Research in the Pleistocene* 8:61–4.

Beardsley, Richard K., Preston Holder, Alex D. Krieger, Betty J. Meggers, John B. Rinaldo, and Paul Kutsche. 1956. Functional and evolutionary implications of community patterning. In R. Wauchope (ed.), *Seminars in Archaeology*, pp. 130–57. Society for American Archaeology Memoir No. 11. Salt Lake City.

Beaton, John M. 1991a. Paleoindian occupation greater than 11,000 yr B.P. at Tule Lake, northern California. *Current Research in the Pleistocene* 8:5–7.

1991b. Colonizing continents: some problems from Australia and the Americas. In T. D. Dillehay and D. J. Meltzer (eds.), *The First Americans: Search and Research*, pp. 209–30. Boca Raton, FL, CRC Press.

Beck, Charlotte, and George T. Jones. 1997. The terminal Pleistocene/early Holocene archaeology of the Great Basin. *Journal of World Prehistory* 11:161–236.

Beck, Curt W. 1996. Comments on a supposed Clovis "mastic." *Journal of Archaeological Science* 23:459–60.

Becker, E. 1973. *The Denial of Death*. New York, The Free Press.

Begley, Sharon, and Andrew Murr. 1999. The first Americans. *Newsweek* 133(17):50–7.

Bement, Leland C. 1999. *Bison Hunting at Cooper Site: Where Lightning Bolts Drew Thundering Herds*. Norman, University of Oklahoma Press.

Benedict, F. G. 1936. *The Physiology of the Elephant*. Carnegie Institution of Washington Publication No. 474. Washington, DC, Carnegie Institution.

Bennett, K. D., S. G. Haberle, and S. H. Lumley. 2000. The Last Glacial–Holocene transition in southern Chile. *Science* 290:325–8.

Berger, Joel, Jon E. Swenson, and Inga-Lill Persson. 2001. Recolonizing carnivores and naïve prey: conservation lessons from Pleistocene extinctions. *Science* 291:1,036–9.

Berger, Rainer. 1975. Advances and results in radiocarbon dating: early man in America. *World Archaeology* 7:174–84.

Bettinger, Robert L. 1991. *Hunter-Gatherers: Archaeological and Evolutionary Theory*. New York, Plenum Press.

Biberson, P., and E. Aguirre. 1965. Expériences de taille d'outils préhistoriques dans des os d'éléphant. *Quaternaria* 7:165–83.

Biesele, Megan. 1993. *Women Like Meat: The Folklore and Foraging Ideology of the Kalahari Ju/'hoan*. Bloomington, Indiana University Press.

Binford, Lewis R. 1967. Smudge pits and hide-smoking: the use of analogy in archaeological reasoning. *American Antiquity* 32:1–12.

1979. Organization and formation processes: looking at curated technologies. *Journal of Anthropological Research* 35:172–97.

1980. Willow smoke and dogs' tails: hunter-gatherer settlement systems and archaeological site formation. *American Antiquity* 45:4–20.

1982. The archaeology of place. *Journal of Anthropological Archaeology* 1:5–31.

1983. *In Pursuit of the Past: Decoding the Archaeological Record*. London, Thames and Hudson.

Blackburn, Thomas C., and Kat Anderson. 1993. *Before the Wilderness: Environmental Management by Native Californians*. Menlo Park, CA, Ballena Press.

Blackford, J. J. 2000. Charcoal fragments in surface samples following a fire and the implications for interpretation of subfossil charcoal data. *Palaeogeography, Palaeoclimatology, Palaeoecology* 164:33–42.

Bleed, Peter. 1986. The optimal design of hunting weapons: maintainability or reliability? *American Antiquity* 51:737–47.

2000. Special report: Digging out of the scandal. On website http://www.eastasianarchaeology.org/special/japanarchscandal2.htm accessed December 2000.

Bobrowsky, Peter T., and Nat Rutter. 1990. Geologic evidence for an ice-free corridor in northeastern British Columbia, Canada. *Current Research in the Pleistocene* 7:133–5.

Bocquet-Appel, Jean-Pierre, and Pierre-Yves Demars. 2000. Population kinetics in the Upper Paleolithic in western Europe. *Journal of Archaeological Science* 27:551–70.

Boldurian, Anthony T. 1985. Variability in flintworking technology at the Krajacic Site: possible relationships to the pre-Clovis Paleoindian occupation of the Cross Creek drainage in southwestern Pennsylvania. Unpublished Ph.D. dissertation, University of Pittsburgh.

Bonnichsen, Robson. 1979. *Pleistocene Bone Technology in the Beringian Refugium*. National Museum of Man [Canada] Mercury Series, Archaeological Survey of Canada Paper No. 89.

1991. Clovis origins. In R. Bonnichsen and K. L. Turnmire (eds.), *Clovis: Origins and Adaptations*, pp. 309–30. Corvallis, OR, Center for the Study of the First Americans.

1997. An introduction to "Who were the first Americans." Paper presented at the 58th Annual Biology Colloquium, Oregon State University, Corvallis, Oregon.

Bonnichsen, Rob A., and Alan L. Schneider. 1999. Breaking the impasse on the peopling of the Americas. In R. A. Bonnichsen and K. L. Turnmire (eds.), *Ice-Age Peoples of North America: Environments, Origins, and Adaptations of the First Americans*, pp. 497–519. Corvallis, OR, Center for the Study of the First Americans.

Bordes, François. 1961. *Typologie du Paléolithique ancien et moyen*. Publications de l'Institut de Préhistoire de l'Université de Bordeaux, Mémoire no. 1. Bordeaux.

Bosinski, Gerhard. 1994. Menschendarstellungen der Altsteinzeit. In K. Wehrberger (ed.), *Der Löwenmensch: Tier und Mensch in der Kunst der Eiszeit*, pp. 77–99. Ulm, Ulmer Museum and Jan Thorbecke Verlag.

Bradley, Bruce A. 1982. Flaked stone technology and typology. In G. Frison and D. Stanford (eds.), *The Agate Basin Site: A Record of the Paleoindian Occupation of the Northwestern High Plains*, pp. 181–212. New York, Academic Press.

    1991. Flaked stone technology in the Northern High Plains. In G. Frison (ed.), *Prehistoric Hunters of the High Plains*, 2nd edition, pp. 365–95. San Diego, CA, Academic Press.

    1993. Paleo-Indian flaked stone technology in the North American High Plains. In O. Soffer and N. D. Praslov (eds.), *From Kostenki to Clovis: Upper Paleolithic–Paleo-Indian Adaptations*, pp. 251–62. New York, Plenum Press.

    1997. Bifacial thinning in the early Upper Paleolithic of eastern Europe. *Chips* 9(2):8–9.

    1999. Clovis ivory and bone tools. [Reprinted from J. Hahn, M. Menu, Y. Taborin, P. Walter, and F. Widemann (eds.), *La Travail et l'usage de l'ivoire au Paléolithique supérieur*. Ravello, Instituto Poligrafico e Zecca dello Stato Libreria dello Stato, Centro Universtario Europeo per I Beni Culturali] on website http://www.primtech.net/ivory/ivory.html accessed December 2000.

Bratlund, B. 1996. Archaeozoological comments on Final Paleolithic frontiers in south Scandinavia. In L. Larsson (ed.), *The Earliest Settlement of Scandinavia and Its Relationship with Neighboring Areas*, pp. 23–33. Acta Archaeologica Ludensia, series 8, 24, Lund.

Breitburg, Emanuel, John B. Broster, Arthur L. Reesman, and Richard G. Strearns. 1996. The Coats-Hines site: Tennessee's first Paleoindian–mastodon association. *Current Research in the Pleistocene* 13:6–8.

Breternitz, D. A., A. C. Swedlund, and D. C. Anderson. 1971. An early burial from Gordon Creek, Colorado. *American Antiquity* 36:170–82.

Brose, David S. 1994. Archaeological investigations at the Paleo Crossing site, a Paleoindian occupation in Medina County, Ohio. In W. Dancey (ed.), *The First Discovery of America: Archaeological Evidence of the Early Inhabitants of the Ohio Area*, pp. 61–76. Columbus, Ohio Archaeological Council.

Brose, David S., and B. Barrish. 1992. Investigations at Ohio site push back dates for Clovis. *Mammoth Trumpet* 7(4):1, 3.

Brown, James H., and Mark V. Lomolino. 1998. *Biogeography*, 2nd edition. Sunderland, MA, Sinauer Associates.

Brunswig, Robert H., Jr., and D. C. Fisher. 1993. Research on the Dent mammoth site. *Current Research in the Pleistocene* 10:63–5.

Brush, Nigel, Margaret Newman, and F. Smith. 1994. Immunological analysis of flint flakes from the Martins Creek mastodon site. *Current Research in the Pleistocene* 11:16–18.

Brush, Nigel, and F. Smith. 1994. The Martins Creek mastodon: a Paleoindian butchery site in Holmes County, Ohio. *Current Research in the Pleistocene* 11:14–15.

Brush, Nigel, and Richard W. Yerkes. 1996. Microwear analysis of chipped stone tools from the Martins Creek mastodon site, Holmes County, Ohio. *Current Research in the Pleistocene* 13:55–7.

Bryan, Alan L. 1968. Early man in western Canada: a critical review. In
C. Irwin-Williams (ed.), *Early Man in Western North America: Symposium of the Southwestern Anthropological Association, San Diego, 1968*, pp. 70–7. Eastern New Mexico University Contributions in Anthropology 1(4). Portalas, NM.

1969. Early man in America and the late Pleistocene chronology of western Canada and Alaska. *Current Anthropology* 10(4):339–65.

1979. Smith Creek Cave. In D. R. Tuohy and D. Rendall (eds.), *The Archaeology of Smith Creek Canyon, Eastern Nevada*, pp. 162–251. Nevada State Museum Anthropological Papers No. 17. Carson City, NV.

1980. The stemmed-point tradition: an early technological tradition in western North America. In L. B. Harten, C. N. Warren, and D. R. Tuohy (eds.), *Anthropological Papers in Memory of Earl H. Swanson*, pp. 77–107. Idaho State Museum of Natural History Special Publication. Pocatello, ID.

1988. The relationship of the stemmed and fluted point traditions in the Great Basin. In J. A. Willig, C. M. Aikens, and J. L. Fagan (eds.), *Early Human Occupation in Far Western North America: The Clovis–Archaic Interface*, pp. 53–74. Nevada State Museum Anthropological Papers No. 21. Carson City, NV.

1991. The fluted-point tradition in the Americas – one of several adaptations to late Pleistocene American environments. In R. Bonnichsen and K. L. Turnmire (eds.), *Clovis: Origins and Adaptations*, pp. 15–33. Corvallis, OR, Center for the Study of the First Americans.

Bryan, Alan L., and Donald R. Tuohy. 1999. Prehistory of the Great Basin/Snake River Plain to about 8,500 years ago. In R. Bonnichsen and K. L. Turnmire (eds.), *Ice Age Peoples of North America: Environments, Origins, and Adaptations*, pp. 249–80. Corvallis, OR, Center for the Study of the First Americans.

Budinger, Fred E., Jr. 1999. Pleistocene archaeology of the Manix Basin, central Mojave Desert, California. Poster presented at the "Clovis and Beyond" conference, 28–30 October 1999, Santa Fe, New Mexico.

2000. Thermoluminescence sediment dates on two distinct artifact-bearing units at the Calico site, central Mojave Desert, California: 135 ka b.p. and 14.4 b.p. [sic]. *27th Great Basin Anthropological Conference Program and Abstracts*, p. 38. Ogden, UT.

Bullen, Ripley P., S. David Webb, and Benjamin I. Waller. 1970. A worked mammoth bone from Florida. *American Antiquity* 35:203–5.

Bulmer, Ralph. 1953. Review of book *Culture: A Critical Review of Concepts and Definitions* by A. L. Kroeber and Clyde Kluckhohn. *Man* (September 1953):136–7.

Bulsara, Adi R., and Luca Gammaitoni. 1996. Tuning in to noise. *Physics Today* 49(3):39–45.

Burdukiewicz, Jan Michał. 1999. Concerning chronology of the Hamburgian culture. In M. Kobusiewicz and J. K. Kozłowski (eds.), *Post-Pleniglacial Re-colonisation of the Great European Lowland*, pp. 127–46. Folia Quaternaria 70. Krakow, Polska Akademia Umiejętności.

Burns, James A. 1996. Vertebrate paleontology and the alleged ice-free corridor: the meat of the matter. *Quaternary International* 32:107–12.

Butler, B. R. 1963. An early man site at Big Camas Prairie, south-central Idaho. *Tebiwa* 6(1):22–3.

1978. *A Guide to Understanding Idaho Archaeology, 3rd edition: The Upper Snake and Salmon River Country*. Pocatello, Idaho Museum of Natural History.

Butler, B. R., and R. J. Fitzwater. 1965. A further note on the Clovis site at Big Camas Prairie, south-central Idaho. *Tebiwa* 8(1):38–40.

Butzer, K. W. 1988. A "marginality" model to explain major spatial and temporal gaps in the Old and New World Pleistocene settlement records. *Geoarchaeology* 3:193–203.

1991. An Old World perspective on potential Mid-Wisconsinan settlement of the Americas. In T. D. Dillehay and D. J. Meltzer (eds.), *The First Americans: Search and Research*, pp. 137–56. Boca Raton, FL, CRC Press.

Byers, Douglas S. 1962. Comments on "The Paleo-Indian tradition in eastern North America" by R. J. Mason. *Current Anthropology* 3:247–50.

Cabe, Paul R. 1993. European starling (*Sturnus vulgaris*). In A. Poole and F. Gill (eds.), *The Birds of North America, Number 48*. Philadelphia, The Academy of Natural Sciences, and Washington, D.C., American Ornithologists' Union.

Caley, M. J. 1991. A null model for testing distributions of dispersal distances. *The American Naturalist* 138(2):524–32.

Callahan, Errett. 1979. The basics of biface knapping in the eastern fluted point tradition: a manual for flintknappers and lithic analysts. *Archaeology of Eastern North America* 7:1–180.

Cann, Rebecca L., Mark Stoneking, and Allan C. Wilson. 1987. Mitochondrial DNA and human evolution. *Nature* 325:31–6.

Carlotto, Mark J. 1997. *The Martian Enigmas: A Closer Look*, 2nd edition. Berkeley, CA, North Atlantic Books.

Carlson, David L., and D. Gentry Steele. 1992. Human–mammoth sites: problems and prospects. In J. W. Fox, C. B. Smith, and K. T. Wilkins (eds.), *Proboscidean and Paleoindian Interactions*, pp. 149–69. Waco, TX, Baylor University Press.

Carlson, Roy L. 1991. Clovis from the perspective of the ice-free corridor. In R. Bonnichsen and K. L. Turnmire (eds.), *Clovis: Origins and Adaptations*, pp. 81–90. Corvallis, OR, Center for the Study of the First Americans.

Carr, Kurt W. 1975. The Fifty site: a Flint Run Paleoindian complex processing station. Unpublished M.A. thesis, Catholic University of America.

1986. Core reconstructions and community patterning at the Fifty site. *Journal of Middle Atlantic Archaeology* 2:79–92.

1988. Lithic reduction sequences and quarry utilization at the Shoop and "50" Paleoindian sites. Paper presented at the 53rd Annual Meeting of the Society for American Archaeology, Toronto, Ontario.

Carter, George F. 1980. *Earlier Than You Think: A Personal View of Man in America*. College Station, Texas A&M University Press.

Cashel, Susan. 1997. Dietary shifts and the European Upper Paleolithic transition. *Current Anthropology* 38:579–603.

Cassells, E. S. 1983. *The Archaeology of Colorado*. Boulder, CO, Johnson Publishing.

Cavalli-Sforza, Luigi Luca. 1991. Genes, peoples and languages. *Scientific American* 265(5):72–8.

1997. Genes, peoples, and languages. *Proceedings of the National Academy of Sciences (USA)* 94:7,719–24.

Charnov, E. L. 1976. Optimal foraging: the marginal value theorem. *Theoretical Population Biology* 9:129–36.

Chatters, James C. 1999. The Paleoamerican skeleton known as Kennewick man. Paper presented at the "Clovis and Beyond" conference, 28–30 October 1999, Santa Fe, New Mexico.

Chatters, James C., Walter A. Neves, and Max Blum. 1999. The Kennewick man: a first multivariate analysis. *Current Research in the Pleistocene* 16:87–90.

Childers, W. M., and H. L. Minshall. 1980. Evidence of early man exposed at Yuha Pinto Wash. *American Antiquity* 42:297–308.

Chlachula, J., and R. LeBlanc. 1996. Some artifact-diagnostic criteria of quartzite-cobble tool industries from Alberta. *Canadian Journal of Archaeology* 20:61–73.

Chlachula, J., and L. Leslie. 1998. Preglacial archaeological evidence at Grimshaw, the Peace River area, Alberta. *Canadian Journal of Earth Sciences* 35:871–84.

Chrisman, Donald, Richard S. MacNeish, and Geoffrey Cunnar. 1998. Human modification of animal bones in pre-Clovis zones of Pendejo Cave in Orograngе, NM. Poster presented at Society for American Archaeology 63rd Annual Meeting, Seattle, Washington.

Chrisman, Donald, Richard S. MacNeish, Jamshed Mavahwalla, and Howard Savage. 1996. Late Pleistocene human friction skin prints from Pendejo Cave, New Mexico. *American Antiquity* 61:357–76.

Christensen, Clayton. 1999. *The Innovator's Dilemma: When New Technologies Cause Great Firms to Fail.* Boston, MA, Harvard Business School Press.

Clark, Donald W. 1991. The northern (Alaska-Yukon) fluted points. In R. Bonnichsen and K. L. Turnmire (eds.), *Clovis: Origins and Adaptations*, pp. 35–48. Corvallis, OR, Center for the Study of the First Americans.

Clark, Donald W., and A. M. Clark. 1993. *Batza Téna: Trail to Obsidian (Archaeology at an Alaskan Obsidian Source).* Archaeological Survey of Canada, Mercury Series Paper 147.

Clark, G. 1994. Migration as an explanatory concept in Paleolithic archaeology. *Journal of Archaeological Method and Theory* 1:305–43.

Clark, J. Desmond. 1974. *Kalambo Falls Prehistoric Site*, Vol. II. Cambridge, Cambridge University Press.

2001. *Kalambo Falls Prehistoric Site*, Vol. I. Cambridge, Cambridge University Press.

Clark, J. S. 1988. Particle motion and the theory of charcoal analysis: source area, transport, deposition and sampling. *Quaternary Research* 20:67–80.

Clausen, C. J., H. K. Brooks, and A. B. Wesolowsky. 1975. The early man site at Warm Mineral Springs, Florida. *Journal of Field Archaeology* 2:191–213.

Clausen, C. J., A. D. Cohen, C. Emiliani, J. A. Holman, and J. J. Stipp. 1979. Little Salt Spring, Florida: a unique underwater site. *Science* 203:609–14.

Clemens, Elisabeth S. 1994. The impact hypothesis and popular science: conditions and consequences of interdisciplinary debate. In W. Glen (ed.), *The Mass-Extinction Debates: How Science Works in a Crisis*, pp. 92–120. Stanford, CA, Stanford University Press.

Close, Frank. 1991. *Too Hot to Handle: The Race for Cold Fusion.* Princeton, NJ, Princeton University Press.

Clotte, Jean (ed.). 1995. *La Grotte Chauvet.* Paris, Seuil "Arts rupestres."

Cohen, Jon. 1999. The march of paradigms. *Science* 283:1,998–9.

Collins, Michael B. 1999a. *Clovis Blade Technology: A Comparative Study of the Kevin Davis Cache, Texas.* Austin, University of Texas Press.

1999b. Reply to Fiedel, Part II. *Scientific American Discovering Archaeology* [1(6)] *Special Report: Monte Verde Revisited*, pp. 14–15.

1999c. Stratigraphic, chronometric, and lithic technological evidence for pre-Clovis at Wilson-Leonard, Texas. *Current Research in the Pleistocene* 16:21–2.

1999d. The Gault Site, Kincaid Rockshelter, and Keven Davis Cache. Collection and exhibit number 71 at the "Clovis and Beyond" conference, 28–30 October, Santa Fe, New Mexico.

2001. TAS field school – archeological survey, testing, and excavations. TAS Field School 2001 page on website of Texas Archeological Society http://www.txarch.org/fieldschool/fs2001/fs2001.htm#TASFieldSchool2001 accessed 25 January 2001.

Collins, Michael B., Glen L. Evans, T. N. Campbell, M. C. Winans, and C. E. Mear. 1989. Clovis occupation at Kincaid Shelter, Texas. *Current Research in the Pleistocene* 6:3–6.

Collins, Michael B., Thomas R. Hester, and Pamela J. Headrick. 1992. Engraved cobbles from the Gault site, central Texas. *Current Research in the Pleistocene* 9:3–4.

Collins, Michael B., Thomas R. Hester, David Olmstead, and Pamela J. Headrick. 1991. Engraved cobbles from early archaeological contexts in central Texas. *Current Research in the Pleistocene* 8:13–15.

Conan Doyle, Arthur. 1918. *The New Revelation.* New York, George H. Doran Co. 1924. The adventure of the Sussex vampire. *The Strand Magazine,* January 1924.

Connelly, Michael. 1996 [orig. 1995]. *The Last Coyote.* New York, St. Martins Press.

Conybeare, A., and G. Haynes. 1984. Observations on elephant mortality and bones in water holes. *Quaternary Research* 22:189–200.

Copeland, James M., and Richard E. Fike. 1988. Fluted projectile points in Utah. *Utah Archaeology* 1:5–28.

Cotter, John L. 1938. The occurrence of flints and extinct animals in pluvial deposits near Clovis, New Mexico, part VI: report on the field season of 1937. *Proceedings of the Philadelphia Academy of Natural Sciences* 90:113–17.
1954. Implications of a Paleoindian co-tradition for North America. *American Antiquity* 20:54–7.

Cotterell, B., and J. Kaminga. 1990. *Mechanics of Pre-Industrial Technology.* Cambridge, Cambridge University Press.

Cowan, I. McT., and V. C. Brink. 1949. Natural game licks in the Rocky Mountain National Parks of Canada. *Journal of Mammalogy* 30:379–87.

Cox, Steven L. 1986. A re-analysis of the Shoop site. *Archaeology of Eastern North America* 14:101–70.

Crader, D. C. 1983. Recent single-carcass bone scatters and the problem of "butchery" sites in the archaeological record. In J. Clutton-Brock and C. Grigson (eds.), *Animals and Archaeology, Vol. I: Hunters and Their Prey,* pp. 107–41. BAR International Series No. 163. Oxford.

Cremo, Michael A., and Richard L. Thompson. 1998. (Revised edition; originally published 1993). *Forbidden Archeology: The Hidden History of the Human Race.* Los Angeles, CA, Bhaktivedanta Book Publishing, Inc.

Cressman, Luther S. 1942. *Archaeological Researches in the Northern Great Basin.* Carnegie Institution of Washington Publication 538. Washington, DC.
1956. Klamath prehistory. *Transactions of the American Philosophical Society* 46:374–513.

Crook, W. W., and R. K. Harris. 1962. A Pleistocene campsite near Lewisville, Texas. *American Antiquity* 23:233–46.

Curran, Mary Lou. 1999. Exploration, colonization, and settling in: the Bull Brook phase, antecedents, and descendants. In M. A. Levine, K. E. Sassaman, and M. S. Nassaney (eds.), *The Archaeological Northeast,* pp. 3–24. Westport, CT, Bergin and Harvey.

Curran, Mary Lou, and John R. Grimes. 1989. Ecological implications for Paleoindian lithic procurement economy in New England. In C. Ellis and J. Lothrop (eds.), *Eastern Paleoindian Lithic Resource Use,* pp. 41–74. Boulder, CO, Westview Press.

Currey, J. D. 1979. Mechanical properties of bone tissues with greatly differing functions. *Journal of Biomechanics* 12:313–19.

Custer, Jay F., John A. Cavallo, and R. Michael Stewart. 1983. Lithic procurement and Paleo-Indian settlement patterns on the Middle Atlantic coastal plain. *North American Archaeologist* 4:263–76.

Custer, Jay F., and R. Michael Stewart. 1990. Environment, analogy, and early Paleoindian economies in northeastern North America. In K. B. Tankersley and B. L. Isaac (eds.), *Early Paleoindian Economies of Eastern North America,* pp. 303–22. Research in Economic Anthropology, Supplement 5. Greenwich, CT, JAI Press.

Dansgaard, W., J. W. C. White, and S. J. Johnsen. 1989. The abrupt termination of the Younger Dryas climate event. *Nature* 339:532–3.

Dansie, Amy. 1997. Early Holocene burials in Nevada: overview of localities, research and legal issues. *Nevada Historical Society Quarterly* 40(1):4–14.

Dansie, Amy J., and William Jerry Jerrems. 1999. Lahontan chronology and early human occupation in the western Great Basin: a new look at old collections. Poster presented at the "Clovis and Beyond" conference, 28–30 October, Santa Fe, New Mexico.

   2000. More bits and pieces: a new look at Lahontan chronology and human occupation. Manuscript submitted 12/2000 to the "Clovis and Beyond" conference Proceedings volume.

Darnell, Regna. 1987. Comments on J. H. Greenberg book *Language in the Americas*, appearing in "Language in the Americas: A CA Book Review." *Current Anthropology* 28:653–6.

Darwin, Charles. 1872. *On the Origin of Species by Means of Natural Selection*, 6th edition. London, Murray.

Davidsson, L. 1999. Are vegetarians an "at risk group" for iodine deficiency? *The British Journal of Nutrition* 81(1):3–4.

Davis, Emma Lou (ed.). 1978. *The Ancient Californians: Rancholabrean Hunters of the Mojave Lakes Country*. Natural History Museum of Los Angeles County, Science Series 29. Los Angeles.

Davis, Emma Lou, and C. Panlaqui. 1978. Chapters 1–5. In E. L. Davis (ed.), *The Ancient Californians: Rancholabrean Hunters of the Mojave Lakes Country*. Natural History Museum of Los Angeles County, Science Series 29. Los Angeles.

Davis, Owen K., Larry D. Agenbroad, Paul S. Martin, and Jim I. Mead. 1984. The Pleistocene dung blanket of Bechan Cave, Utah. In H. H. Genoways and M. R. Dawson (eds.), *Contributions in Quaternary Vertebrate Paleontology: A Volume in Memorial to John E. Guilday*, pp. 267–82. Carnegie Museum of Natural History Publication No. 8. Pittsburgh, PA.

Davis, William E., Winston B. Hurst, and Deborah A. Westfall. 1993. Cultural resource inventory of the Utah Department of Transportation's SR 6/50 Improvement Project: Marjum Pass Road to Crystal Peak Road, Millard County, Utah. Unpublished report submitted to Utah Department of Transportation.

Dawkins, Richard. 1989. *The Selfish Gene*. New York, Oxford University Press.

Débénath, André, and Harold L. Dibble. 1994. *Handbook of Paleolithic Typology. Vol. I: Lower and Middle Paleolithic of Europe*. Philadelphia, University of Pennsylvania University Museum.

de Garine, Igor. 1996. Food and the status quest in five African cultures. In P. Wiessner and W. Schiefenhövel (eds.), *Food and the Status Quest: An Interdisciplinary Perspective*, pp. 193–217. Providence, RI, Berghahn Books.

Delcourt, Paul A. 1985. The influence of late-Quaternary climate and vegetational change on paleohydrology in unglaciated eastern North America. *Ecologia Mediterranea* 11(1):17–26.

Deller, D. B. 1988. The Paleo-Indian occupation of southwestern Ontario: distribution, technology, and social organization. Unpublished Ph.D. dissertation, McGill University.

Deller, D. B., and C. J. Ellis. 1988. Early Paleo-Indian complexes in southwestern Ontario. In R. S. Laub, N. G. Miller, and D. W. Steadman (eds.), *Late Pleistocene and Early Holocene Paleoecology of the Eastern Great Lakes Region*, pp. 251–63. Bulletin of the Buffalo Society of Natural Sciences Volume No. 33. Buffalo.

1990. Paleo-Indians. In C. J. Ellis and N. Ferris (eds.), *The Archaeology of Southern Ontario to A.D. 1650*, pp. 37–63. Occasional Publication No. 5, London Chapter, Ontario Archaeological Society. London, Ontario.

1992. *Thedford II: A Paleo-Indian Site in the Ausable River Watershed of Southwestern Ontario*. University of Michigan Museum of Anthropology Memoir 25. Ann Arbor, MI.

2001. Evidence for Late Paleoindian ritual from the Caradoc site (AfHj–104), southwestern Ontario, Canada. *American Antiquity* 66:267–84.

Deloria, Vine, Jr. 1995. *Red Earth, White Lies: Native Americans and the Myth of Scientific Fact*. New York, Scribner.

Delporte, H., J. Hahn, L. Mons, G. Pinçon, and D. de Sonneville-Bordes. 1988. *Fiches typologiques de l'industrie osseuse préhistorique, cahiers I: Sagaies*. Commission de Nomenclature sur l'Industrie de l'Os Préhistorique, Aix-en-Provence, Université de Provence.

Dent, Richard J. 1985. Amerinds and the environment: myth, reality, and the Upper Delaware Valley. In C. W. McNett, Jr. (ed.), *Shawnee Minisink: A Stratified Paleoindian–Archaic Site in the Upper Delaware Valley of Pennsylvania*, pp. 123–63. Orlando, FL, Academic Press.

1999. Shawnee Minisink: new dates on the Paleoindian component. Poster presented at the 64th Annual Meeting of the Society for American Archaeology, Chicago, Illinois.

Dent, Richard J., and Barbara E. Kauffman. 1985. Aboriginal subsistence and site ecology as interpreted from microfloral and faunal remains. In C. W. McNett, Jr. (ed.), *Shawnee Minisink: A Stratified Paleoindian–Archaic Site in the Upper Delaware Valley of Pennsylvania*, pp. 55–79. Orlando, FL, Academic Press.

Derenko, Miroslava, Tomasz Grzybowski, Boris A. Malyarchuk, Jakub Czarny, Danuta Miścicka-Śliwka, and Ilia Z. Zakharov. 2001. The presence of mitochondrial haplogroup X in Altaians from South Siberia. *American Journal of Human Genetics* 69:237–41.

Derevianko, A. P., V. N. Zenin, S. V. Leshchinskiy, and E. N. Mashchenko. 2000. Peculiarities of mammoth accumulation at Shestakovo site in west Siberia. *Archaeology, Ethnology & Anthropology of Eurasia* 3(3):42–55.

de Sonneville-Bordes, D. 1974. The Upper Palaeolithic. In S. Piggott, G. Daniel, and C. McBurney (eds.), *France Before the Romans*, pp. 30–60. Park Ridge, NJ, Noyes Press.

Diamond, Jared. 2000. Enhanced: Blitzkrieg against the Moas. Website version of article from *Science* 287:2,170–1, http://www.sciencemag.org/cgi/content/full/ 287/5461/2170?maxtoshow=&HITS=20 . . ./200 accessed November 2000.

Dikov, N. N. 1996. The Ushki sites, Kamchatka Peninsula. In F. H. West (ed.), *American Beginnings*, pp. 144–250. Chicago, IL, University of Chicago Press.

Dillehay, Tom D. 1997. *Monte Verde: A Late Pleistocene Settlement in Chile. Vol. II: The Archaeological Context and Interpretation*. Washington, DC, Smithsonian Institution Press.

2000. *The Settlement of the Americas: A New Prehistory*. New York, Basic Books.

Dillehay, Tom D., Michael B. Collins, Mario Pino, Jack Rossen, Jim Adovasio, Carlos Ocampo, Ximena Navarro, Pilar Rivas, David Pollack, A. Gwynn Henderson, Jose Saavedra, Patricio Sanzana, Pat Shipman, Marvin Kay, Gaston Múñoz, Anastasios Karathanasis, Donald Ugent, Michael Cibull, and Richard Geisler. 1999a. On Monte Verde: Fiedel's confusions and misrepresentations. Website http://www.uky.edu/Projects/MonteVerde/monteverde.pdf accessed November 2000 .

Dillehay, Tom D., Mario Pino, Jack Rossen, Carlos Ocampo, Pilar Rivas, David Pollack, and Gwynn Henderson. 1999b. Reply to Fiedel, Part I. *Scientific*

American Discovering Archaeology [1(6)] *Special Report: Monte Verde Revisited*, pp. 12–14.

Dincauze, Dena F. 1981. The Meadowcroft papers. *Quarterly Review of Archaeology* 2(1):3–4.

1993a. Fluted points in the eastern forests. In O. Soffer and N. D. Praslov (eds.), *From Kostenki to Clovis: Upper Paleolithic – Paleo-Indian Adaptations*, pp. 279–92. New York, Plenum Press.

1993b. Pioneering in the Pleistocene: large Paleoindian sites in the Northeast. In J. B. Stoltman (ed.), *Archaeology of Eastern North America: Papers in Honor of Stephen Williams*, pp. 43–60. Mississippi Department of Archives and History, Archaeological Report No. 25. Jackson, MS.

Dincauze, Dena F., and Mary Ann Curran. 1983. Paleoindians as generalists: an ecological perspective. Paper presented at the 48th Annual Meeting of the Society for American Archaeology, Pittsburgh, Pennsylvania.

Dingle, H. 1980. Ecology and evolution of migration. In S. A. Gauthreaux, Jr. (ed.), *Animal Migration, Orientation, and Navigation*, pp. 2–101. New York, Academic Press.

1996. *Migration: The Biology of Life on the Move.* Oxford, Oxford University Press.

Dixon, E. James. 1993. *Quest for the Origins of the First Americans.* Albuquerque, University of New Mexico Press.

1999. *Bones, Boats and Bison: Archeology and the First Colonization of Western North America.* Albuquerque, University of New Mexico Press.

2001. Human colonization of the Americas: timing, technology and process. *Quaternary Science Reviews* 20:277–99.

Dobson, S. F., and W. T. Jones. 1985. Multiple causes of dispersal. *American Naturalist* 126:855–8.

Dolukhanov, Pavel M. 1997. The Pleistocene–Holocene transition in northern Eurasia: environmental changes and human adaptations. *Quaternary International* 41–2:181–91.

Douglas-Hamilton, Iain. 1972. On the ecology and behaviour of the African elephant. Unpublished D.Phil. thesis, University of Oxford.

Downey, Roger. 2000. *Riddle of the Bones: Politics, Science, Race, and the Story of Kennewick Man.* New York, Springer-Verlag.

Dreimanis, A. 1967. Mastodons, their geologic age and extinction in Ontario, Canada. *Canadian Journal of Earth Sciences* 4:663–75.

Driver, Jonathan C. 1988. Late Pleistocene and Holocene vertebrates and paleoenvironments from Charlie Lake Cave, northeast British Columbia. *Canadian Journal of Earth Sciences* 25:1,545–53.

1995. Social hunting and multiple predation. *MASCA Research Papers in Science and Archaeology* 12 Supplement:23–38.

1998. Human adaptation at the Pleistocene/Holocene boundary in western Canada, 11,000 to 9000 BP. *Quaternary International* 49/50:141–50.

1999. Raven skeletons from Paleoindian contexts, Charlie Lake Cave, British Columbia. *American Antiquity* 64:289–98.

Driver, Jonathan C., M. Handly, K. R. Fladmark, D. E. Nelson, G. M. Sullivan, and R. Preston. 1996. Stratigraphy, radiocarbon dating, and culture history of Charlie Lake Cave, British Columbia. *Arctic* 49(3):265–77.

Drumm, J. 1963. *Mammoths and Mastodons: Ice-Age Elephants of New York.* University of New York, State Education Department, State Museum and Science Service Educational Leaflet No. 13.

Dudley, Joseph P. 1999. Seed dispersal of *Acacia erioloba* by African bush elephants in Hwange National Park, Zimbabwe. *African Journal of Ecology* 37:375–85.

2000. Seed dispersal by elephants in semiarid woodland habitats of Hwange National Park, Zimbabwe. *Biotropica* 32(3):556–61.

Dunbar, James S. 1991. The resource orientation of Clovis and Suwanee age Paleoindian sites in Florida. In R. Bonnichsen and K. L. Turnmire (eds.), *Clovis: Origins and Adaptations*, pp. 185–213. Corvallis, OR, Center for the Study of the First Americans.

Dunbar, James S., Michael K. Faught, and S. David Webb. 1988. Page/Ladsen (8JE591): an underwater Paleo-Indian site in northwestern Florida. *The Florida Anthropologist* 41:442–52.

Dunbar, James S., and S. David Webb. 1996. Bone and ivory tools from submerged Paleoindian sites in Florida. In D. G. Anderson and K. E. Sassaman (eds.), *The Paleoindian and Early Archaic Southeast*, pp. 331–53. Tuscaloosa, University of Alabama Press.

Dunbar, James S., S. D. Webb, and Michael K. Faught. 1992. Archaeological sites in the drowned Tertiary Karst Region of the Eastern Gulf of Mexico. In L. Johnson and M. Stright (eds.), *Paleo-Shorelines and Prehistory: An Investigation in Method*, pp. 117–46. Boca Raton, FL, CRC Press.

Edgar, Heather Joy Hecht. 1997. Paleopathology of the Wizards Beach Man (AHUR 2023) and the Spirit Cave Mummy (AHUR 2064). *Nevada Historical Society Quarterly* 40(1):57–61.

Edwards, M. E., P. M. Anderson, L. B. Brubaker, T. A. Ager, A. A. Andreev, N. H. Bigelow, L. C. Cwynar, W. R. Eisner, S. P. Harrison, F.-S. Hu, D. Jolly, A. V. Lozhkin, G. M. MacDonald, C. J. Mock, J. C. Ritchie, A. V. Sher, R. W. Spear, J. W. Williams, and G. Yu. 2000. Pollen-based biomes for Beringia 18,000, 6000 and 0 ^{14}C yr BP. *Journal of Biogeography* 27(3):521–54.

Eisele, J., D. D. Fowler, G. Haynes, and R. A. Lewis. 1995. Survival and detection of blood residues on stone tools. *Antiquity* 69:36–46.

Eiseley, Loren C. 1943. Archaeological observations on the problem of post-glacial extinctions. *American Antiquity* 8:209–17.

1946. The fire-drive and the extinction of the terminal Pleistocene fauna. *American Anthropologist* 48:54–9.

Ellis, Christopher J., and D. Brian Deller. 1988. Some distinctive Paleo-Indian tool types from the Lower Great Lakes Region. *Midcontinental Journal of Archaeology* 13:111–58.

1997. Variability in the archaeological record of northeastern Early Paleoindians: a view from southern Ontario. *Archaeology of Eastern North America* 25:1–30.

Ellis, Christopher J., and J. Lothrop (eds.). 1989. *Eastern Paleoindian Lithic Resource Use.* Boulder, CO, Westview Press.

Elston, Robert G., and P. Jeffrey Brantingham. In press. Microlithic technology in northern Asia: a risk minimizing strategy of the Late Paleolithic and Early Holocene. In Steven Kuhn and Robert G. Elston (eds.), *Thinking Small: Global Perspectives on Microlithization.* American Anthropological Association Archaeological Papers 12. Arlington, VA.

Erlandson, Jon M., and Madonna L. Moss. 1996. The Pleistocene–Holocene transition along the Pacific Coast of North America. In L. G. Straus, B. V. Eriksen, J. M. Erlandson, and D. R. Yesner (eds.), *Humans at the End of the Ice Age: The Archaeology of the Pleistocene–Holocene Transition*, pp. 277–301. New York, Plenum Press.

Escutenair, Catherine, Janusz K. Kozłowski, Valéry Sitlivy, and Krzystof Sobczyk. 1999. *Les Chasseurs de mammouths de la vallée de la Vistule: Kraków-Spadzista B, un site gravettien à amas d'ossement de mammouths.* Brussels, Musées Royaux d'Art et d'Histoire and Jagellonian University of Kraków.

Fagan, Brian M. 1997. The first Americans: a brilliant new work documents the antiquity of Monte Verde, Chile. *Archaeology* 50(2):60–3.

Faught, Michael K. 1996. Clovis origins and underwater prehistoric archaeology in northwestern Florida. Unpublished Ph.D. dissertation, University of Arizona, Tucson.

Faught, Michael K., and David G. Anderson. 1996. Across the straits, down the corridor, around the bend, and off the shelf: an evaluation of Paleoindian colonization models. Paper presented at the 61st Annual Meeting of the Society for American Archaeology, New Orleans, Louisiana.

Faught, Michael, and Brinnen Carter. 1998. Early human occupation and environmental change in northwestern Florida. *Quaternary International* 49/50:167–76.

Faught, Michael K., J. S. Dunbar, and S. D. Webb. 1992. New evidence for Paleoindians on the Continental Shelf of Northwestern Florida. *Current Research in the Pleistocene* 9:11–12.

Faunmap Working Group. 1994. *Faunmap: A Database Documenting Late Quaternary Distributions of Mammal Species in the United States.* Illinois State Museum Scientific Papers Vol. XXV, Nos. 1 and 2. Springfield, IL.

Fedje, Daryl W., and Heiner Josenhans. 2000. Drowned forests and archaeology on the continental shelf of British Columbia, Canada. *Geology* 28(2): 99–102.

Ferriere, R., J. R. Belthoff, I. Olivieri, and S. Krackow. 2000. Evolving dispersal: where to go next? *Trends in Ecology and Evolution* 15:5–7.

Ferring, C. Reid. 1989. The Aubrey Clovis site: a Paleoindian locality in the Upper Trinity River Basin, Texas. *Current Research in the Pleistocene* 6:9–11.

    1990. The 1989 investigations at the Aubrey Clovis site, Texas. *Current Research in the Pleistocene* 7:10–12.

    1995. The late Quaternary geology and archaeology of the Aubrey Clovis site, Texas: a preliminary report. In E. Johnson (ed.), *Ancient Peoples and Landscapes,* pp. 227–81. Lubbock, Museum of Texas Technical University.

Fiedel, Stuart J. 1996. Blood from stones? Some methodological and interpretive problems in blood residue analysis. *Journal of Archaeological Science* 23:139–47.

    1999a. Older than we thought: implications of corrected dates for Paleoindians. *American Antiquity* 64:95–116.

    1999b. Artifact provenience at Monte Verde: confusion and contradictions. *Scientific American Discovering Archaeology* [1(6)] *Special Report: Monte Verde Revisited,* pp. 1–14.

    2000a. The peopling of the New World: present evidence, new theories, and future directions. *Journal of Archaeological Research* 8:39–103.

    2000b. Response to Dillehay. Published electronically on "About archaeology" website http://archaeology.about.com/science/archaeology/library/weekly/ aa070200c.htm accessed December 2000.

    2000c. Quacks in the ice: waterfowl, Paleoindians, and the discovery of America. Paper presented at the Society for American Archaeology 65th Annual Meeting, Philadelphia, Pennsylvania.

Figgins, Jesse D. 1933. A further contribution to the antiquity of man in America. *Proceedings of the Colorado Museum of Natural History* 12(2):4–10.

Fisher, Daniel. 2000. The man who would save health care. *Forbes* 167(1):180–2, 184, 186, 188.

Fisher, Daniel C. 1984a. Taphonomic analysis of late Pleistocene mastodon occurrences: evidence of butchery by North American Paleo-Indians. *Paleobiology* 10:338–57.

    1984b. Mastodon butchery by North American Paleo-Indians. *Nature* 308:271–2.

1987. Mastodont procurement by Paleoindians of the Great Lakes region: hunting or scavenging? In M. H. Nitecki and D. V. Nitecki (eds.), *The Evolution of Human Hunting*, pp. 309–421. New York, Plenum.

1996. Extinction of proboscideans in North America. In J. Shoshani and P. Tassy (eds.), *The Proboscidea: Evolution and Palaeoecology of Elephants and Their Relatives*, pp. 296–315. Oxford, Oxford University Press.

1999. Mastodons, mammoths, and humans in the North American mid-continent. Paper presented at the "Clovis and Beyond" conference, 28–31 October, Santa Fe, New Mexico.

Fisher, Daniel C., Bradley T. Lepper, and Paul E. Hooge. 1994. Evidence for butchery of the Burning Tree mastodon. In W. S. Dancey (ed.), *The First Discovery of America: Archaeological Evidence of the Early Inhabitants of the Ohio Area*, pp. 43–57. Columbus, The Ohio Archaeological Council.

Fisher, John W., Jr. 1987. Shadows in the forest: ethnoarchaeology among the Efe Pygmies. Unpublished Ph.D. dissertation, University of California, Berkeley.

1992. Observations on the late Pleistocene bone assemblage from the Lamb Spring site, Colorado. In D. J. Stanford and J. S. Day (eds.), *Ice Age Hunters of the Rockies*, pp. 51–81. Niwot, University Press of Colorado and Denver Museum of Natural History.

Fitting, James E. 1977. Social dimensions of the Paleoindian adaptation in the Northeast. In W. S. Newman and B. Salwen (eds.), *Amerinds and Their Paleoenvironments in Northeastern North America*, pp. 369–74. Annals of the New York Academy of Sciences 288. New York.

Fitting, James E., D. DeVisscher, and E. Wahla. 1966. *The Paleo-Indian Occupation of the Holcombe Beach*. University of Michigan Museum of Anthropology Anthropological Papers No. 27. Ann Arbor, MI.

Fix, Alan. 1999. *Migration and Colonization in Human Microevolution*. New York, Cambridge University Press.

Fladmark, Knut R. 1979. Routes: alternate migration corridors for early man in North America. *American Antiquity* 44:55–69.

1983. Times and places: environmental correlates of mid-to-late Wisconsinan human population expansion in North America. In R. Shutler (ed.), *Early Man in the New World*, pp. 13–42. Beverly Hills, CA, Sage Publications.

Fladmark, K. R., J. C. Driver, and D. Alexander. 1988. The Paleoindian component at Charlie Lake Cave (HbRf39). *American Antiquity* 53:371–84.

Flannery, Tim. 2001. *The Eternal Frontier: An Ecological History of North America and Its Peoples*. New York, Atlantic Monthly Press.

Flesch, Rudolf (ed.). 1957. *The Book of Unusual Quotations*. New York, Harper and Brothers.

Foley, Robert. 1982. A reconsideration of the role of predation on large mammals in tropical hunter-gatherer adaptation. *Man* (N.S.) 17:393–402.

Fredrickson, David A. 1973. Early cultures of the North Coast Ranges, California. Unpublished Ph.D. dissertation, University of California, Davis.

Frison, George C. 1976. Cultural activity associated with prehistoric mammoth butchering and processing. *Science* 194:728–30.

1978. *Prehistoric Hunters of the High Plains*, 1st edition. San Diego, CA, Academic Press.

1982. The Sheaman site: a Clovis component. In G. C. Frison and D. J. Stanford, *The Agate Basin Site: A Record of the Paleoindian Occupation of the Northwestern High Plains*, pp. 143–57. New York, Academic Press.

1986a. Mammoth hunting and butchering from a perspective of African elephant culling. In G. C. Frison and L. C. Todd, *The Colby Mammoth Site: Taphonomy and Archaeology of a Clovis Kill in Northern Wyoming*, pp. 115–34. Albuquerque, University of New Mexico Press.

1986b. Summary and conclusions. In G. C. Frison and L. C. Todd, *The Colby Mammoth Site: Taphonomy and Archaeology of a Clovis Kill in Northern Wyoming*, pp. 135–41. Albuquerque, University of New Mexico Press.

1991. *Prehistoric Hunters of the High Plains*, 2nd edition. San Diego, Academic Press.

(ed.). 1996. *The Mill Iron Site*. Albuquerque, University of New Mexico Press.

1998. Paleoindian large mammal hunters on the plains of North America. *Proceedings of the National Academy of Sciences (USA)* 95:14,576–83.

1999. The late Pleistocene prehistory of the northwestern Plains, the adjacent mountains, and intermontane basins. In R. Bonnichsen and K. L. Turnmire (eds.), *Ice Age Peoples of North America: Environments, Origins, and Adaptations*, pp. 264–80. Corvallis, Center for the Study of the First Americans and Oregon State University Press.

Frison, George C., R. L. Andrews, J. M. Adovasio, R. C. Carlisle, and Robert Edgar. 1986. A Late Paleoindian animal trapping net from northern Wyoming. *American Antiquity* 51:352–61.

Frison, George, and Bruce Bradley. 1999. *The Fenn Cache: Clovis Weapons and Tools*. Santa Fe, NM, One Horse Land & Cattle Company.

Frison, George C., and Carolyn Craig. 1982. Bone, antler, and ivory artifacts and manufacture technology. In G. C. Frison and D. J. Stanford, *The Agate Basin Site: A Record of Paleoindian Occupation of the Northwestern High Plains*, pp. 157–73. New York, Academic Press.

Frison, George C., C. Vance Haynes, Jr., and Mary Lou Larson. 1996. Discussion and conclusions. In G. C. Frison (ed.), *The Mill Iron Site*, pp. 205–16. Albuquerque, University of New Mexico Press.

Frison, George C., and Lawrence C. Todd. 1986. *The Colby Mammoth Site*. Albuquerque, University of New Mexico Press.

Fryxell, R., T. Bielicki, R. D. Daugherty, C. E. Gustafson, H. T. Irwin, and B. C. Keel. 1968. A human skeleton from sediments of mid-Pinedale age in southeastern Washington. *American Antiquity* 33:511–14.

Funk, R. E. 1983. The northeastern United States. In J. D. Jennings (ed.), *Ancient North Americans*, pp. 303–71. San Francisco, CA, W. H. Freeman and Co.

Gamble, C. 1986. *The Palaeolithic Settlement of Europe*. Cambridge, Cambridge University Press.

1994. *Timewalkers: The Prehistory of Global Colonization*. Cambridge, MA, Harvard University Press.

Gardner, Martin. 1985. The great stone face and other nonmysteries. *Skeptical Inquirer* (Fall 1985). Posted on website http://www.csicop.org/si/8512/face-on-mars.html accessed 25 May 2000.

Gardner, William M. (ed.). 1974. *The Flint Run Paleo-Indian Complex: A Preliminary Report, 1971–73 Seasons*. The Catholic University of America, Department of Anthropology, Archeology Laboratory Occasional Publication No. 1.

1975. Paleoindian to Early Archaic: continuity and change in eastern North America during the late Pleistocene and early Holocene. Paper presented at the Ninth International Congress of Prehistoric and Protohistoric Sciences, Université de Nice, France.

1977. The Flint Run Complex and its implications for eastern North American prehistory. *Proceedings of the New York Academy of Sciences* ("Amerinds and Their Early Environments in Northeastern North America" Conference) 288:257–63.

1979. Paleoindian settlement pattern and site distribution in the Middle Atlantic. Paper presented at the 10th Annual Middle Atlantic Archaeological Conference, Rehoboth Beach, Delaware.

1983. Stop me if you've heard this one before: the Flint Run Paleoindian complex revisited. *Archaeology of Eastern North America* 11:49–64.

Gardner, William M., and Robert A. Verrey. 1979. Typology and chronology of fluted points from the Flint Run area. *Pennsylvania Archaeologist* 49(1):13–46.

Gauthreaux, S. A., Jr. (ed.). 1980. *Animal Migration, Orientation, and Navigation.* New York, Academic Press.

Geelhoed, Glenn William. 1999. Metabolic maladaptation: individual and social consequences of medical intervention in correcting endemic hypothyroidism. *Nutrition* 15(11/12):908–32.

Genovés, Santiago. 1972. *Ra: una balsa de papyrus a través del Atlantico.* Cuadernos de Antropología, Universidad Nacional Autónoma de México, 25.

    1973. Papyrus rafts across the Atlantic. *Current Anthropology* 14:266–7.

Gibbons, Ann. 1993. Geneticists trace the DNA trail of the first Americans. *Science* 259:312–13.

    1996. The peopling of the Americas. *Science* 274:31–3.

    1998. Mother tongues trace steps of earliest Americans. *Science* 279:1,306–7.

    2000. Europeans trace ancestry to Paleolithic people. *Science* 290:1,080–1.

Gieryn, Thomas F. 1983. Boundary work and the demarcation of science from non-science: strains and interests in professional ideologies of scientists. *American Sociological Review* 48:781–95.

Gilbert, Claudette Marie. 1979. *Mammoth Hunters: The Domebo Site.* Prehistoric People of Oklahoma No. 4 (The University of Oklahoma Stovall Museum of Science and History, and Oklahoma Archaelogical Survey).

Giraldeau, Luc-Alain. 1997. The ecology of information use. In J. R. Krebs and N. B. Davies (eds.), *Behavioural Ecology: An Evolutionary Approach,* 4th edition, pp. 42–68. Oxford, Blackwell Science Ltd.

Glennan, W. S. 1976. The Manix Lake lithic industry: early lithic tradition or workshop refuse? *The Journal of New World Archaeology* 1(7):42–61.

Gobetz, Katrina E., and Steven R Bozarth. 2001. Implications for late Pleistocene mastodon diet from opal phytoliths in tooth calculus. *Quaternary Research* 55(2):115–22.

Goddard, Ives, and Lyle Campbell. 1994. The history and classification of American Indian languages: what are the implications for the peopling of the Americas? In R. Bonnichsen and D. G. Steele (eds.), *Method and Theory for Investigating the Peopling of the Americas,* pp. 189–207. Corvallis, OR, Center for the Study of the First Americans.

Goebel, Ted. 1999. Pleistocene human colonization of Siberia and peopling of the Americas: an ecological approach. *Evolutionary Anthropology* 8(6):208–27.

Goebel, Ted, Roger Powers, and Nancy Bigelow. 1991. The Nenana Complex of Alaska and Clovis origins. In R. Bonnichsen and K. L. Turnmire (eds.), *Clovis: Origins and Adapatations,* pp. 49–79. Corvallis, OR, Center for the Study of the First Americans.

Goebel, Ted, and Sergei B. Slobodin. 1999. The colonization of western Beringia: technology, ecology, and adaptations. In R. Bonnichsen and K. L. Turnmire (eds.), *Ice Age Peoples of North America: Environments, Origins, and Adaptations,* pp. 104–55. Corvallis, OR, Center for the Study of the First Americans and Oregon State University Press.

Goldstein, David B. 2000. The context of our genetic history. *Science* 289:62–3.

Gonzalez, Silvia, Joaquín Arroyo-Cabrales, Alan Turner, Paul Pettit, and Graham Sherwood. 1999. Late Pleistocene mammoths (*Mammuthus columbi*) in central Mexico: paleoenvironment and AMS dating. Paper presented at the 2nd International Mammoth Conference, 16–20 May, Rotterdam, The Netherlands.

González-José, Rolando, Silvia L. Dahinten, María A. Luis, Miquel Hernández, and Hector M. Pucciarelli. 2001. Craniometric variation and the settlement of the

Americas: testing hypotheses by means of R-matrix and matrix correlation analyses. *American Journal of Physical Anthropology* 116:154–65.

Goodyear, Albert C. 1979. *A Hypothesis for the Use of Cryptocrystalline Raw Materials among Paleoindian Groups of North America.* University of South Carolina Institute of Archaeology and Anthropology, Research Manuscript Series No. 156.

1999a. The early Holocene occupation of the southeastern United States: a geoarchaeological summary. In R. Bonnichsen and K. L. Turnmire (eds.), *Ice Age Peoples of North America: Environments, Origins, and Adaptations of the First Americans*, pp. 432–81. Corvallis, OR, Center for the Study of the First Americans and Oregon State University Press.

1999b. Results of the 1999 Allendale Paleoindian Expedition. *Legacy* 4(1–3):8–13.

Goodyear, Albert C., John E. Foss, and Gail Wagner. 1999. Evidence of pre-Clovis in the Savannah river basin, Allendale County, South Carolina. Paper presented at the 64th Annual Meeting of the Society for American Archaeology, Chicago, Illinois.

Goodyear, Albert C., J. L. Michie, and T. Charles. 1989. The earliest South Carolinians. In A. C. Goodyear and G. T. Hanson (eds.), *Studies in South Carolina Archaeology: Essays in Honor of Robert L. Stephenson*, pp. 19–52. Anthropological Studies 9: Occasional Papers of the South Carolina Institute of Archaeology and Anthropology. University of South Carolina, Columbia.

Gordon, Bryan C. 1976. Antler pseudo-tools made by caribou. In J. S. Raymond, B. Loveseth, C. Arnold, and G. Reardon (eds.), *Primitive Art and Technology*, pp. 121–8. Calgary, Alberta, University of Calgary Archaeological Association.

Gore, Jeffrey A., and W. Wilson Baker. 1989. Beavers residing in caves in northern Florida. *Journal of Mammalogy* 70(3):677–8.

Gosden, Chris. 2000. Comments on S. Shennan, "Population, culture history, and the dynamics of culture change." *Current Anthropology* 41:823–4.

Graham, David. 1988. Scientist sees an early mark of man. Scratches may signal presence in desert 300,000 years ago. *San Diego Union* October 1988, pp. A-1 and A-3.

Graham, Russell W., C. Vance Haynes, Jr., Donald Lee Johnson, and Marvin Kay. 1981. Kimmswick: a Clovis–mastodon association in eastern Missouri. *Science* 213:1,115–17.

Graham, Russell W., and Marvin Kay. 1988. Taphonomic comparison of cultural and noncultural faunal deposits at the Kimmswick and Barnhart sites, Jefferson County, Missouri. In R. S. Laub, N. G. Miller, and D. W. Steadman (eds.), *Late Pleistocene and Early Holocene Paleoecology and Archeology of the Eastern Great Lakes Region*, pp. 227–40. Bulletin of the Buffalo Society of Natural Sciences Volume 33. Buffalo, NY.

Graham, Russell W., and Ernest L. Lundelius. 1984. Coevolutionary disequilibrium and Pleistocene extinctions. In P. S. Martin and R. G. Klein (eds.), *Quaternary Extinctions: A Prehistoric Revolution*, pp. 223–49. Tucson, University of Arizona Press.

Graham, Russell W., Thomas W. Stafford, Jr., and Holmes A. Semken, Jr. 1997. Pleistocene extinctions: chronology, non-analog communities, and environmental change. Paper presented at the American Museum of Natural History's Center for Biodiversity and Conservation Spring Symposium, 17–18 April, "Humans and Other Catastrophes: Explaining Past Extinctions and the Extinction Process," New York.

Gramly, R. Michael. 1982. *The Vail Site: A Palaeo-Indian Encampment in Maine.* Bulletin of the Buffalo Society of Natural Sciences Volume 30. Buffalo, NY.

1988. Paleo-Indian sites south of Lake Ontario, western and central New York state. In R. S. Laub, N. G. Miller, and D. W. Steadman (eds.), *Late Pleistocene and*

Early Holocene Paleoecology and Archeology of the Eastern Great Lakes Region, pp. 265–71. Bulletin of the Buffalo Society of Natural Sciences Volume 33. Buffalo, NY.

1991. Blood residues upon tools from the East Wenatchee Clovis site, Douglas County, Washington. Ohio Archaeologist 41(4):4–9.

1992. Guide to the Palaeo-Indian Artifacts of North America. Buffalo, NY, Persimmon Press Monographs in Archaeology.

1993. The Richey Clovis Cache: Earliest Americans along the Columbia River. Buffalo, NY, Persimmon Press Monographs in Archaeology.

1996. The East Wenatchee Clovis site (Richey-Roberts site): summary of findings and current status. Current Research in the Pleistocene 13:19–21.

1998. Pit features at the East Wenatchee Clovis site and elsewhere. Current Research in the Pleistocene 15:14–16.

1999. The Lamb Site: A Pioneering Clovis Encampment. Buffalo, NY, Persimmon Press.

Gramly, R. Michael, and R. E. Funk. 1990. What is known and not known about the human occupation of the northeastern United States until 10,000 B.P. Archaeology of Eastern North America 18:5–32.

Grant, Ulysses S. 1885–6. Personal Memoirs of U. S. Grant, 2 vols. New York.

Grayson, Donald K. 1989. The chronology of North American late Pleistocene extinctions. Journal of Archaeological Science 16:153–65.

1991. Late Pleistocene mammalian extinctions in North America: taxonomy, chronology, and explanations. Journal of World Prehistory 5:193–231.

1993. The Desert's Past: A Natural Prehistory of the Great Basin. Washington, DC, Smithsonian Institution Press.

1998. Confirming antiquity in the Americas (Review of T. D. Dillehay, "Monte Verde: A Late Pleistocene Settlement in Chile, Vol. 2: The Archaeological Context and Interpretation"). Science 282:1,425–6.

2001. The archaeological record of human impacts on animal populations. Journal of World Prehistory 15(1):1–68.

Green, Thomas J., Bruce Cochran, Todd W. Fenton, James C. Woods, Gene L. Titmus, Larry Tieszen, Mary Anne Davis, and Susanne J. Miller. 1998. The Buhl burial: a Paleoindian woman from southern Idaho. American Antiquity 63:437–56.

Greenberg, Joseph H. 1987a. Language in the Americas. Stanford, CA, Stanford University Press.

1987b. Language in the Americas: A CA [Current Anthropology] Book Review. Current Anthropology 28:647–67.

1996. The linguistic evidence. In F. H. West (ed.), American Beginnings: The Prehistory and Palaeoecology of Beringia, pp. 525–36. Chicago, IL, University of Chicago Press.

Greenberg, Joseph H., Christy G. Turner, and Stephen Zegura. 1986. The settlement of the Americas: a comparison of the linguistic, dental and genetic evidence. Current Anthropology 25:477–97.

Greenman, E. F. 1963. The Upper Paleolithic and the New World. Current Anthropology 4:41–91.

Griffin, Andrea S., Daniel T. Blumstein, and Christopher S. Evans. 2000. Training captive-bred or translocated animals to avoid predators. Conservation Biology 14:1,317–26.

Griffin, James B. 1983. What's the point of the survey? Archaeology of Eastern North America 11:21–2.

Grimes, J. R., W. Eldridge, B. G. Grimes, A. Vaccaro, F. Vaccaro, J. Vaccaro, N. Vaccaro, and A. Orsini. 1984. Bull Brook II. Archaeology of Eastern North America 12:159–83.

Gruhn, Ruth. 1961. *The Archaeology of Wilson Butte Cave, South-Central Idaho.* Occasional Papers of the Idaho State College Museum No. 6. Pocatello, ID.

1995. Results of new excavations at Wilson Butte Cave, Idaho. *Current Research in the Pleistocene* 12:16–17.

Gryba, E. M. 1983. *Sibbald Creek: 11,000 Years of Human Use of the Alberta Foothills.* Archaeological Survey of Alberta Occasional Paper No. 22. Edmonton, Archaeological Survey of Canada.

Gustafson, Carl E. 1980. The Manis mastodon site: a preliminary report of progress. (Manuscript) Pullman, Washington Archaeological Research Center, Washington State University.

Gustafson, Carl E., Delbert Gilbow, and Richard D. Daugherty. 1979. The Manis mastodon site: early man on the Olympic Peninsula. *Canadian Journal of Archaeology* 3:157–64.

Guthrie, R. Dale. 1983. Paleoecology of the site and its implications for early hunters. In W. R. Powers, R. D. Guthrie, and J. F. Hoffecker (eds.), *Dry Creek: Archaeology and Paleoecology of a Late Pleistocene Alaskan Hunting Camp*, pp. 209–87. Washington, DC, National Park Service.

1990. *Frozen Fauna of the Mammoth Steppe: The Story of Blue Babe.* Chicago, IL, University of Chicago Press.

2001. Origin and causes of the mammoth steppe: a story of cloud cover, woolly mammal tooth pits, buckles, and inside-out Beringia. *Quaternary Science Reviews* 20:549–74.

Gvozdover, Mariana. 1995. *Art of the Mammoth Hunters: The Finds From Avdeevo.* Oxbow Monographs 49. Oxford

Hahn, Joachim. 1994. Menschtier- und Phantasiewesen. In K. Wehrberger (ed.), *Der Löwenmensch: Tier und Mensch in der Kunst der Eiszeit*, pp. 101–15. Ulm, Ulmer Museum and Jan Thorbecke Verlag.

Hahn, Joachim, Hansjürgen Müller-Beck, and Woldgang Taute. 1985. *Eiszeithöhlen im Lonetal: Archäologie einer Landschaft auf der Schwäbischen Alb*, 2nd revised edition. Stuttgart, Konrad Theiss Verlag.

Hall, Don Alan. 1998. New World migration research paints increasingly complex picture: physical anthropologists find conflicting clues to origins of Americans. *Mammoth Trumpet* 13(4):13–16, 20.

1999. AAPA symposium offers new analyses and varied perspectives concerning first Americans: latest human biology research shares podium with linguistic, archaeological, cultural views. *Mammoth Trumpet* 14(3):6–7, 19–20.

2000. Mastodons and mammoths: yielding clues to early Americans. *Mammoth Trumpet* 15(4):4–9.

Hamilton, T. M. 1996. The Miami mastodon, 23SA212. *The Missouri Archaeologist* 54:79–88.

Hamilton, Thomas D., and Ted Goebel. 1999. Late Pleistocene peopling of Alaska. In R. Bonnichsen and K. L. Turnmire (eds.), *Ice Age Peoples of North America: Environments, Origins, and Adaptations of the First Americans*, pp. 156–99. Corvallis, OR, Center for the Study of the First Americans and Oregon State University Press.

Handbook of Texas Online, The. 1999. Gault Site. http://www.tsha.utexas.edu/handbook/online/articles/view/GG/bbgya.html accessed 24 February 2001.

Hannus, L. Adrian. 1985. The Lange-Ferguson site – an event of Clovis mammoth butchery with associated bone tool technology: the mammoth and its track. Unpublished Ph.D. dissertation, University of Utah.

1989. Flaked mammoth bone from the Lange-Ferguson site, White River Badlands area, South Dakota. In R. Bonnichsen and M. H. Sorg (eds.), *Bone*

Modification, pp. 395–412. Orono, Center for the Study of the First Americans
and University of Maine.

1990. The Lange-Ferguson site: a case for mammoth bone-butchering tools. In
L. Agenbroad, J. Mead, and L. Nelson (eds.), Megafauna and Man: Discovery of
America's Heartland, pp. 86–99. Mammoth Site of Hot Springs, South Dakota,
Scientific Papers Volume 1. Hot Springs, SD.

Hargrove, J. W., and K. Lange. 1989. Tsetse dispersal viewed as a diffusion process.
Transactions of the Zimbabwe Scientific Association 64(1):1–8.

Harrington, Mark Raymond. 1948. An Ancient Site at Borax Lake, California. Southwest
Museum Papers No. 16.

Harris, Arthur H. 1985. Late Pleistocene Vertebrate Paleoecology of the West. Austin,
University of Texas Press.

Harris, John M., and George T. Jefferson (eds.). 1985. Rancho La Brea: Treasures of
the Tar Pits. Natural History Museum of Los Angeles County, Science Series 31.

Haury, Emil W. 1953. Artifacts with mammoth remains, Naco, Arizona. I:
Discovery of the Naco mammoth and associated projectile points. American
Antiquity 19:1–14.

Haury, Emil W., E. B. Sayles, and W. W. Wasley. 1959. The Lehner mammoth site,
southeastern Arizona. American Antiquity 25:2–30.

Hay, Oliver P. 1923. The Pleistocene of North America and Its Vertebrated Animals from the
States East of the Mississippi River and from the Canadian Provinces East of Longitude
95°. Carnegie Institution of Washington Publication No. 322. Washington,
DC.

Hayden, Daniel T., John K. Friar, and Eric R. Pianka. 2000. Fire-driven dynamic
mosaics in the Great Victoria Desert, Australia – II. A spatial and temporal
landscape model. Landscape Ecology 15(5):407–23.

Haynes, C. Vance, Jr. 1964. Fluted projectile points: their age and dispersion. Science
145:1,408–13.

1966. Elephant hunting in North America. Scientific American 214:104–12.

1967. Carbon-14 dates and Early Man in the New World. In P. S. Martin and H. E.
Wright (eds.), Pleistocene Extinctions: The Search for a Cause, pp. 267–86.
New Haven, CT, Yale University Press.

1968. Geochronology of late Quaternary alluvium. In R. B. Morrison (ed.), Means
of Correlation of Quaternary Successions, pp. 591–631. Salt Lake City, University of
Utah Press.

1969a. A scientist disagrees . . . Chicago. Encyclopaedia Britannica Yearbook of Science
and the Future 1970:76–7. New York, Praeger.

1969b. The earliest Americans. Science 166:709–15.

1970. Geochronology of man–mammoth sites and their bearing upon the origin
of the Llano complex. In W. E. Dort and E. E. Johnson (eds.), Pleistocene and
Recent Environments of the Central Plains, pp. 77–92. Lincoln, University of
Nebraska Press.

1973. The Calico site: artifacts or geofacts? Science 181(4,097):305–10.

1974. Archaeological geology of some selected Paleoindian sites. In C. C. Black
(ed.), History and Prehistory of the Lubbock Lake Site, pp. 133–9. The Museum Journal
XV (West Texas Museum Association, Lubbock).

1976. Archaeological investigations at the Murray Springs site, Arizona, 1968.
National Geographic Society Research Reports (1968):165–71.

1977. When and from where did man arrive in northeastern North America: a
discussion. In W. S. Newman and B. Salwen (eds.), Amerinds and Their
Paleoenvironments in Northeastern North America, pp. 165–6. Annals of the
New York Academy of Sciences 288. New York.

1980. The Clovis culture. Canadian Journal of Anthropology 1(1):115–21.

1981. Geochronology and paleoenvironments of the Murray Springs Clovis site, Arizona. *National Geographic Society Research Reports* 13:243–51.

1982. Were Clovis progenitors in Beringia? In D. M. Hopkins, J. V. Matthews, C. E. Schweger, and S. B. Young (eds.), *Paleoecology of Beringia*, pp. 383–98. New York, Academic Press.

1984. Stratigraphy and late Pleistocene extinction in the United States. In P. S. Martin and R. G. Klein (eds.), *Quaternary Extinctions: A Prehistoric Revolution*, pp. 345–53. Tucson, University of Arizona Press.

1987. Clovis origins update. *The Kiva* 52:83–93.

1991a. Geoarchaeological and paleohydrological evidence for a Clovis-age drought in North America and its bearing on extinction. *Quaternary Research* 35:435–50.

1991b. Murray Springs and Lehner Clovis sites miscellaneous data for field trip for the visit of Soviet archaeologists to the University of Arizona, Tucson, 21 June 1991. Photocopied manuscript.

1992. Contributions of radiocarbon dating to the geochronology of the peopling of the New World. In R. E. Taylor, A. Long, and R. S. Kra (eds.), *^{14}C Dating and the Peopling of the New World*, pp. 355–74. New York, Springer-Verlag.

1993. Clovis–Folsom geochronology and climatic change. In O. Soffer and N. D. Praslov (eds.), *From Kostenki to Clovis: Upper Paleolithic–Paleo-Indian Adaptations*, pp. 219–36. New York, Plenum Press.

1998. Geochronology of the stratigraphic manifestations of paleoclimatic events at Paleoindian sites. Paper presented at the 63rd Annual Meeting of the Society for American Archaeology, Seattle, Washington.

1999a. Monte Verde and the pre-Clovis situation in America. *Scientific American Discovering Archaeology* 1(6), *Special Report: Monte Verde Revisited*, pp. 17–19.

1999b. Clovis, climate change, and extinction. Paper presented at "Clovis and Beyond" conference, 28–31 October, Santa Fe, New Mexico.

(no date, ms). Clovis, pre-Clovis, climate change, and extinctions. Paper prepared for proceedings of "Clovis and Beyond" conference, 28–31 October, Santa Fe, New Mexico.

Haynes, C. V., Jr., and E. T. Hemmings. 1968. Mammoth-bone shaft wrench from Murray Springs, Arizona. *Science* 159:186–7.

Haynes, C. Vance, Jr., Michael McFaul, Robert H. Brunswig, and Kenneth D. Hopkins. 1998. Kersey-Kuner terrace investigations at the Dent and Bernhardt sites, Colorado. *Geoarchaeology* 13(2):201–18.

Haynes, C. Vance, Jr., Dennis J. Stanford, Margaret Jodry, Joanne Dickenson, John L. Montgomery, Philip H. Shelley, Irwin Rovner, and George Agogino. 1999. A Clovis well at the type site 11,500 B.C.: the oldest prehistoric well in America. *Geoarchaeology* 14(5):455–70.

Haynes, Gary. 1980. Prey bones and predators: potential ecologic information from analysis of bone sites. *Ossa* 7:75–97.

1981. Bone modifications and skeletal disturbances by natural agencies. Unpublished Ph.D. dissertation, Catholic University of America.

1982. Utilization and skeletal disturbances of North American prey carcasses. *Arctic* 35(2):266–81.

1983. Frequencies of spiral and green-bone fractures on ungulate limb bones in modern surface assemblages. *American Antiquity* 48:102–14.

1984. Taphonomic perspectives on late Pleistocene extinctions. *Current Research* 1(2):49–50.

1985. On watering holes, mineral licks, death, and predation. In D. Meltzer and J. I. Mead (eds.), *Environments and Extinctions in Late Glacial North America*,

pp. 53–71. Orono, ME, Center for the Study of Early Man, University of Maine
    at Orono.

1986. Spiral fractures and cutmark-mimics in noncultural elephant bone
    assemblages. *Current Research in the Pleistocene* 3:45–6.

1987. Elephant-butchering at modern mass-kill sites in Africa. *Current Research in
    the Pleistocene* 4:75–7.

1988a. Longitudinal studies of African elephant death and bone deposits. *Journal
    of Archaeological Science* 15:131–57.

1988b. Mass deaths and serial predation: comparative taphonomic studies of
    modern large mammal death sites. *Journal of Archaeological Science* 15:219–35.

1989. Late Pleistocene mammoth utilization in northern Eurasia and North
    America. *Archaeozoologia* 3(1–2):81–108.

1991. *Mammoths, Mastodonts, and Elephants: Biology, Behavior, and the Fossil Record.*
    Cambridge, Cambridge University Press.

1999. The role of mammoths in rapid Clovis dispersal. In G. Haynes,
    J. Klimowicz, and J. W. F. Reumer (eds.), *Mammoths and the Mammoth Fauna:
    Studies of an Extinct Ecosystem*, pp. 9–38. *Deinsea (Annual of the Natural History
    Museum Rotterdam)* 6.

2000a. Mammoths, measured time, and mistaken identities. *Radiocarbon*
    42(2):257–69.

2000b. Clovis-era mammoth populations and extinction in the Great Basin. Oral
    presentation at the 27th Great Basin Anthropological Conference, 5–7
    October 2000, Ogden, Utah.

2002. The catastrophic extinction of North American mammoths and
    mastodonts. *World Archaeology* 33:391–416.

(In press). Mammoth and mastodont sites: what do the differences mean?
    Deinsea (Journal of the Rotterdam Natural History Museum).

Haynes, Gary, and B. Sunday Eiselt. 1999. The power of Pleistocene
    hunter-gatherers: forward and backward searching for evidence about
    mammoth extinction. In R. D. E. MacPhee (ed.), *Extinctions in Near Time: Causes,
    Contexts, and Consequences*, pp. 71–93. New York, Kluwer Academic/Plenum
    Publishers.

Haynes, Gary, and Dennis Stanford. 1984. On the possible utilization of *Camelops*
    by Early Man in North America. *Quaternary Research* 22:216–30.

Heard, Alex. 2000. *Apocalypse Pretty Soon: Travels in End-Time America.* New York, Main
    Street Books Doubleday.

Hemmings, C. Andrew. 1999. The Paleoindian occupation of Sloth Hole (8JE121).
    Paper presented at the 64th Annual Meeting of the Society for American
    Archaeology, Chicago, Illinois.

Hemmings, E. T. 1970. Early man in the San Pedro Valley, Arizona. Unpublished
    Ph.D. dissertation, University of Arizona.

Hemmings, E. T., and C. V. Haynes, Jr. 1969. The Escapule mammoth and
    associated projectile points, San Pedro Valley, Arizona. *Journal of the Arizona
    Academy of Science* 5(3):184–8.

Hengeveld, R. 1989. *Dynamics of Biological Invasions.* London, Chapman and Hall.

Herrera, Joan. 1999. Determining the species source of prehistoric ivory. "The
    Aucilla Times" 12(1) website http://www.flmnh.ufl.edu/natsci/vertpaleo/
    aucilla12_1/ivory99.htm accessed July 2001.

Hester, James J. 1972. *Blackwater Locality No. 1: A Stratified, Early Man Site in Eastern
    New Mexico.* Fort Burgwin Research Center (Southern Methodist University)
    Publication No. 8. Ranchos de Taos, NM.

Hester, James J., and James Grady. 1977. Paleoindian social patterns of the Llano
    estacado. In E. Johnson (ed.), *Paleoindian Lifeways*, pp. 78–96. *The Museum
    Journal (Texas Technical University)* 17.

Hester, Thomas R., M. Collins, and P. J. Headrick. 1992. Notes on south Texas archaeology: Paleo-Indian engraved stones from the Gault site. *La Tierra* 19(4):3–5.

Hetzel, B. S., and J. T. Dunn. 1989. The iodine deficiency disorders: their nature and prevention. *Annual Review of Nutrition* 1989–9:21–38.

Hewlett, B., J. M. H. van de Koppel, and L. L. Cavalli-Sforza. 1982. Exploration ranges of Aka Pygmies of the Central African Republic. *Man (N.S.)* 17:418–30.

Heyerdahl, Thor. 1953. *American Indians in the Pacific: The Theory behind the Kon-Tiki Expedition*. Chicago, IL, Rand McNally.

   1971. *The Ra Expeditions* (translated by Patricia Crampton). Garden City, NY, Doubleday & Company.

Hodder, Ian. 1982. *The Present Past: An Introduction to Anthropology for Archaeologists*. London, Batsford.

Hoffecker, John F., W. Roger Powers, and Ted Goebel. 1993. The colonization of Beringia and the peopling of the New World. *Science* 259:46–53.

Hofman, Jack L. 1995. The Busse cache: a Clovis-age find in northwestern Kansas. *Current Research in the Pleistocene* 12:17–19.

Hofman, Jack L., and Don G. Wyckoff. 1991. Clovis occupation in Oklahoma. *Current Research in the Pleistocene* 8:29–32.

Holdaway, R. N., and C. Jacomb. 2000. Rapid extinction of the moas (Aves: Dinornithiformes): model, test, and implications. *Science* 287:2,250–4.

Holden, Constance. 1999. Were Spaniards among the first Americans? *Science* 286:1,467–8.

Holen, Steven R. 1995. *Evidence of the First Humans in Nebraska*. Museum Notes, University of Nebraska State Museum, No. 90.

   1999. Late Pleistocene bone technology in the North American mid-continent. Paper presented at the "Clovis and Beyond" conference, 28–30 October, Santa Fe, New Mexico.

Holen, Steven R., and Robert K. Blasing. 1991. Investigations at La Sena site, Medicine Creek Reservoir, Frontier County, Nebraska. TER-QUA '91 (abstract).

Holland, John D., and Dena F. Dincauze. 1999. A Shoop site postulation – again. Paper presented at the 64th Annual Meeting of the Society for American Archaeology, Chicago, Illinois.

Holliday, Vance T. 1997. *Paleoindian Geoarchaeology of the Southern High Plains*. Austin, University of Texas Press.

   2000a. The evolution of Paleoindian geochronology and typology on the Great Plains. *Geoarchaeology* 15(3):227–90.

   2000b. Folsom drought and episodic drying on the southern High Plains from 10,900–10,200 ^{14}C yr B.P. *Quaternary Research* 53:1–12.

Holliday, Vance T., and Adrienne B. Anderson. 1993. "Paleoindian," "Clovis," and "Folsom": A brief etymology. *Current Research in the Pleistocene* 10:79–81.

Holliday, Vance T., C. Vance Haynes, Jr., Jack L. Hofman, and David J. Meltzer. 1994. Geoarchaeology and geochronology of the Miami (Clovis) site, southern High Plains of Texas. *Quaternary Research* 41:234–44.

Holman, J. Alan. 1986. The Dansville mastodont and associated wooden specimen. *National Geographic Research* (Autumn 1986):416.

Holmes, Elizabeth Eli. 1993. Are diffusion models too simple? A comparison with telegraph models of invasion. *The American Naturalist* 142(5):779–95.

Holway, David A., and Andrew V. Suarez. 1999. Animal behavior: an essential component of invasion biology. *Trends in Evolution and Ecology* 14(8):328–30.

Hoppe, K. A., P. L. Koch, and R. W. Carlson. 1995. Strontium isotope ratios in late Pleistocene mammoths and mastodons from Florida: evidence of migration. *Geological Society of America Abstracts and Program* 27:319.

Hoppe, K. A., P. L. Koch, R. W. Carlson, and S. D. Webb. 1999. Tracking mammoths and mastodons: reconstruction of migratory behavior using strontium isotope ratios. *Geology* 27(5):439–42.

Hou, Xiaolin, Chifang Chai, Qinfang Qian, Guodong Liu, Yongbao Zhang, and Ke Wang. 1997. The study of iodine in Chinese total diets. *The Science of the Total Environment* 193:161–7.

Housley, R. A., C. S. Gamble, M. Street, and P. Pettitt. 1997. Radiocarbon evidence for the Late Glacial human recolonisation of northern Europe. *Proceedings of the Prehistoric Society* 63:25–54.

Howard, Calvin D. 1990. The Clovis point: characteristics and type description. *Plains Anthropologist* 35(129):255–62.

Howells, W. W. 1995. *Who's Who in Skulls: Ethnic Identification of Crania from Measurements.* Papers of the Peabody Museum of Archaeology and Ethnology, Harvard University, Volume 82.

Huckell, Bruce B. 1979. Of chipped stone tools, elephants, and the Clovis hunters: an experiment. *Plains Anthropologist* 24:117–89.

Hughen, Konrad A., John R. Southon, Scott J. Lehman, and Jonathan T. Overpeck. 2000. Synchronous radiocarbon and climate shifts during the last deglaciation. *Science* 290:1,951–4.

Huizenga, John. 1992. *Cold Fusion: The Scientific Fiasco of the Century.* New York, Oxford University Press.

Humphrey, John D., and C. Reid Ferring. 1994. Stable isotope evidence for latest Pleistocene and Holocene climatic change in north-central Texas. *Quaternary Research* 41:200–13.

Hutchings, Wallace Karl. 1997. The Paleoindian fluted point: dart or spear armature? The identification of Paleoindian delivery technology through the analysis of lithic fracture velocity. Unpublished Ph.D. dissertation, Simon Fraser University.

Hyland, D. C., J. M. Tersak, J. M. Adovasio, and M. I. Siegel. 1990. Identification of the species of origin of residual blood on lithic material. *American Antiquity* 55:104–12.

Iker, Sam. 1980. Learning how innovation spreads. *Mosaic* 11(1):17–22.

Irving, John. 1999. *My Movie Business: A Memoir.* New York, Ballantine Books.

Irving, William N., and C. R. Harington. 1973. Upper Pleistocene radiocarbon dated artifacts from the northern Yukon. *Science* 179:335–40.

Irving, William N., A. V. Jopling, and B. F. Beebe. 1986. Indications of pre-Sangamon humans near Old Crow, Yukon, Canada. In A. L. Bryan (ed.), *New Evidence for the Pleistocene Peopling of the Americas*, pp. 27–48. Orono, ME, Center for the Study of Early Man, University of Maine.

Irving, William N., A. V. Jopling, and I. Kritsch-Armstrong. 1989. Studies of bone technology and taphonomy, Old Crow Basin, Yukon Territory. In R. Bonnichsen and M. H. Sorg (eds.), *Bone Modification*, pp. 347–79. Orono (ME), Center for the Study of the First Americans, University of Maine, Orono.

Irwin, Cynthia, Henry T. Irwin, and George Agogino. 1962. Wyoming muck tells of battle: ice age man versus mammoth. *National Geographic* 121(6):828–37.

Irwin, G. 1989. Against, across, and down the wind: a case for the systematic colonisation of the remote Pacific Islands. *Journal of the Polynesian Society* 98:167–206.

1990. Human colonisation and change in the remote Pacific. *Current Anthropology* 31(1):90–4.

Irwin, Henry T. 1970. Archaeological investigations at the Union Pacific mammoth kill site, Wyoming, 1961. *National Geographic Society Research Reports* (1961–2):123–5.

Iwasa, Yoh, Masahiko Higashi, and Norio Yamamura. 1981. Prey distribution as a factor determining the choice of optimal foraging strategy. *The American Naturalist* 117(5):710–23.

Jackson, L. E., and A. Duk-Rodbin. 1996. Quaternary geology of the ice-free corridor: glacial controls on the peopling of the New World. In T. Akazawa and E. J. E. Szathmary (eds.), *Prehistoric Mongoloid Dispersals*, pp. 214–27. New York, Oxford University Press.

Jackson, Lawrence J. 1988. Fossil cervids and fluted point hunters: a review for southern Ontario. *Ontario Archaeology* 48:27–41.

    1997. Caribou range and early Paleo-Indian settlement disposition in southern Ontario, Canada. In L. J. Jackson and P. T. Thacker (eds.), *Caribou and Reindeer Hunters of the Northern Hemisphere*, pp. 132–64. Aldershot, Avebury.

Jackson, Lawrence J., Christopher Ellis, Alan V. Morgan, and John H. McAndrews. 2000. Glacial lake levels and eastern Great Lakes Palaeo-Indians. *Geoarchaeology* 15(5):415–40.

Jackson, Stephen T., Robert S. Webb, Katharine H. Anderson, Jonathan T. Overpeck, Thompson Webb III, John W. Williams, and Barbara C. S. Hansen. 2000. Vegetation and environment in eastern North America during the Last Glacial Maximum. *Quaternary Science Reviews* 19(6):489–508.

Jacobson, G. L., Jr., T. Webb III, and E. C. Grimm. 1987. Patterns and rates of vegetation change during the deglaciation of eastern North America. In W. F. Ruddimann and H. E. Wright, Jr. (eds.), *North America and Adjacent Oceans during the Last Deglaciation*, pp. 277–88. The Geological Society of America, The Geology of North America, Volume K-3.

Jantz, R. L., and Douglas W. Owsley. 1997. Pathology, taphonomy, and cranial morphometrics of the Spirit Cave mummy. *Nevada Historical Society Quarterly* 40(1):62–84.

    2001. Variation among early North American crania. *American Journal of Physical Anthropology* 114:146–55.

Janzen, Daniel H., and Paul S. Martin. 1982. Neotropical anachronisms: the fruits the gomphotheres ate. *Science* 215:19–27.

Jenkins, S. H., and P. E. Busher. 1979. *Castor canadensis. Mammalian Species* 120:1–8.

Jenks, A. E. 1936. *Pleistocene Man in Minnesota: A Fossil Homo sapiens.* Minneapolis, University of Minnesota Press.

    1937. *Minnesota's Browns Valley Man and Associated Burial Artifacts.* Memoirs of the American Anthropological Association No. 49.

Jenks, A. E., and Mrs. H. H. Simpson, Sr. 1941. Beveled artifacts in Florida of the same type as artifacts found near Clovis, New Mexico. *American Antiquity* 6:314–19.

Jenks, A. E., and L. A. Wilford. 1938. Sauk Valley skeleton. *Bulletin of the Texas Archaeological and Paleontological Society* 10:162–3.

Jennings, Jesse D. 1974. *Prehistory of North America*, 2nd edition. New York, McGraw-Hill Book Company.

    1983. *Ancient North Americans.* San Francisco, CA, Freeman.

    1989. *Prehistory of North America*, 3rd edition. Mountain View, CA, Mayfield Publishing Co.

Jochim, Michael, Cynthia Herhahn, and Harry Starr. 1999. The Magdalénian colonization of southern Germany. *American Anthropologist* 101:129–42.

Johnson, Eileen (ed.). 1987. *Lubbock Lake: Late Quaternary Studies on the Southern High Plains.* College Station, Texas A&M University Press.

    1991. Late Pleistocene cultural occupation on the southern Plains. In R. Bonnichsen and K. L. Turnmire (eds.), *Clovis: Origins and Adaptations*, pp. 215–36. Corvallis, OR, Center for the Study of the First Americans.

Johnson, Eileen, and Pat Shipman. 1993. Scanning electron microscope analysis of bone modifications at Pendejo Cave, New Mexico. *Current Research in the Pleistocene* 10:72–5.

Johnson, Michael F. 1997. Confirmation of McAvoy's early Cactus Hill sequence. Paper presented at the 28th Annual Middle Atlantic Archaeological Conference, Ocean City, Maryland.

Johnson, William C., and Edward J. Kost. 1988. The distribution of *Mammut americanum* (mastodon) and *Mammuthus* (mammoth) occurrences in Kansas. *Current Research in the Pleistocene* 5:75–7.

Jones, Bruce A. 1990. Paleoindians and proboscideans: ecological determinants of selectivity in the southwestern United States. In L. B. Davis and B. O. K. Reeves (eds.), *Hunters of the Recent Past*, pp. 68–86. London, Unwin Hyman.

Jones, Do-While. 1999. Academic prejudice and oppression. "Science Against Evolution" website http://www.ridgenet.net/~do_while/sage/v3i8n.htm accessed 21 November 2000.

Jones, Peter R., and A. S. Vincent. 1986. A study of bone surfaces from La Cotte de St. Brelade. In P. Callow and J. M. Cornford (eds.), *La Cotte de St. Brelade 1961–1978: Excavations by C. B. M. McBurney*, pp. 185–92. Norwich, Geo Books.

Jones, Rhys. 1979. The fifth continent: problems concerning the human colonization of Australia. *Annual Review of Anthropology* 8:445–66.

Jones, S., and R. Bonnichsen. 1994. The Anzick Clovis burial. *Current Research in the Pleistocene* 11:42–4.

Joyce, Colin. 2000. Archaeologist admits burying "new" finds. *The Electronic Telegraph* issue 1991 (Monday 6 November 2000). On website http://www.telegraph.co.uk accessed 15 November 2000.

Juan, Carlos, Brent C. Emerson, Pedro Oromí, and Godfrey M. Hewitt. 2000. Colonization and diversification: towards a phylogeographic synthesis for the Canary Islands. *Trends in Evolution and Ecology* 15(3):104–9.

Judge, W. James. 1973. *The Paleo-Indian Occupation of the Central Rio Grande Valley, New Mexico*. Albuquerque, University of New Mexico Press.

Kabaciński, Jacek, Bodil Bratlund, Lucyna Kubiak, Daniel Makowiecki, Romuald Schild, and Kazimierz Tobolski. 1999. The Hamburgian settlement at Mirkowice: recent results and research perspectives. In M. Kobusiewicz and J. K. Kozłowski (eds.), *Post-Pleniglacial Re-colonisation of the Great European Lowland*, pp. 211–38. Folia Quaternaria 70. Krakow, Polska Akademia Umiejętności.

Kalland, Arne. 1993. Management by totemization: whale symbolism and the anti-whaling campaign. *Arctic* 46(2):124–33.

Kaminer, Wendy. 1999. *Sleeping with Extra-Terrestrials: The Rise of Irrationalism and Perils of Piety*. New York, Pantheon Books.

Kaufman, T. S. 1980. Early prehistory of the Clear Lake area, Lake County, California. Unpublished Ph.D. dissertation, University of California, Los Angeles.

Kay, Charles. 1994. Aboriginal overkill: the role of Native Americans in structuring western ecosystems. *Human Nature* 5(4):359–98.

Kay, Marvin. 1986. Projectile point use inferred from microwear of Kimmswick Clovis points. Paper presented at the 51st Annual Meeting of the Society for American Archaeology, New Orleans, Louisiana.

    1996. Microwear analysis of some Clovis and experimental chipped stone tools. In G. H. Odell (ed.), *Stone Tools: Theoretical Insights into Human Prehistory*, pp. 315–44. New York, Plenum Press.

Keally, Charles T. 2000. Special Report: Japanese scandals – this time it's archaeology. A preliminary report. Posted on website http://www.eastasianarchaeology.org/special/japanarchscandal.htm accessed 15 November 2000.

Keeley, Lawrence H. 1980. *Experimental Determinations of Stone Tool Uses: A Microwear Analysis*. Chicago, IL, University of Chicago Press.

Kehoe, A. B. 1998. *The Land of Prehistory: A Critical History of American Archaeology*. New York, Routledge.

Kehoe, Thomas. 1966. The distribution and implications of fluted points in Saskatchewan. *American Antiquity* 31:530–9.

Kelley, Jane H., and Marsha P. Hanen. 1988. *Archaeology and the Methodology of Science*. Albuquerque, University of New Mexico Press.

Kelly, Robert J. 1995. *The Foraging Spectrum: Diversity in Hunter-Gatherer Lifeways*. Washington, DC, Smithsonian Institution Press.

Kelly, R. L., and L. C. Todd. 1988. Coming into the country: Early Paleoindian hunting and mobility. *American Antiquity* 53:231–44.

Kessel, Brina. 1953. Distribution and migration of the European starling in North America. *The Condor* 55(2):49–67.

Kimball, Larry R. 2000. The function of pre-Clovis blade and Clovis tools from Cactus Hill. Paper presented at the 65th Annual Meeting of the Society for American Archaeology, Philadelphia, Pennsylvania.

Kimura, Birgitta, Steven A. Brandt, Bruce L. Hardy, and William W. Hauswirth. 2001. Analysis of DNA from ethnoarchaeological stone scrapers. *Journal of Archaeological Science* 28:45–53.

King, J. E., and J. J. Saunders. 1984. Environmental insularity and the extinction of the American mastodont. In P. S. Martin and R. G. Klein (eds.), *Quaternary Extinctions: A Prehistoric Revolution*, pp. 315–44. Tucson, University of Arizona Press.

King, Maureen L., and S. B. Slobodin. 1996. A fluted point from the Uptar site, northeastern Siberia. *Science* 273:634–6.

Klein, Richard G. 1999. *The Human Career: Human Biological and Cultural Origins*, 2nd edition. Chicago, IL, University of Chicago Press.

Klíma, Bohuslav. 1963. *Dolní Věstonice: Vyzkum Taboriste Lovcu Mamutu v Letech 1947–1952*. Prague, Čekoslovenská Akademie Věd.

  1994. The bone industry, decorative objects and art. In J. Svoboda (ed.), *Pavlov I: Excavations 1952–1953*, pp. 94–159. Etudes et Recherches Archéologiques de l'Université de Liège [ERAUL] 66: The Dolní Věstonice Studies, Volume 2.

  1995. *Dolní Věstonice II: Ein Mammutjägerrastplatz und seine Bestattungen*. Etudes et Recherches Archéologiques de l'Université de Liège [ERAUL] 73: The Dolní Věstonice Studies, Volume 3.

Knecht, Heidi. 1993. Early Upper Paleolithic approaches to bone and antler projectile technology. In G. L. Peterkin, H. M. Bricker, and P. Mellars (eds.), *Hunting and Animal Exploitation in the Later Palaeolithic and Mesolithic of Eurasia*, pp. 33–47. Archaeological Papers of the American Anthropological Association No. 4. Arlington, VA.

Kobusiewicz, Michal. 1999. The final Pleistocene recolonisation of the northwestern Polish Plain. In M. Kobusiewicz and J. K. Kozłowski (eds.), *Post-Pleniglacial Re-colonisation of the Great European Lowland*, pp. 197–210. Folia Quaternaria 70. Krakow, Polska Akademia Umiejętności.

Kobusiewicz, Michal, and Janusz K. Kozłowski (eds.). 1999a. *Post-Pleniglacial Re-colonisation of the Great European Lowland*. Folia Quaternaria 70. Krakow, Polska Akademia Umiejętności.

  1999b. An overview of the conference. In M. Kobusiewicz and J. K. Kozłowski (eds.), *Post-Pleniglacial Re-colonisation of the Great European Lowland*, pp. 393–5. Folia Quaternaria 70. Krakow, Polska Akademia Umiejętności.

Koch, Paul L. 1998. Isotopic reconstruction of past continental environments. *Annual Review of Earth and Planetary Science* 26:573–613.

Koch, Paul L., Kathryn A. Hoppe, and S. David Webb. 1998. The isotopic ecology of Late Pleistocene mammals in North America, Part I: Florida. *Chemical Geology* 152(1–2):119–38.

Kooyman, Brian, Margaret E. Newman, Christine Cluney, Murray Lobb, Shayne Tolman, Paul McNeill, and L. V. Hills. 2001. Identification of horse exploitation by Clovis hunters based on protein analysis. *American Antiquity* 66:686–91.

Kooyman, Brian, Shayne Tolman, L. V. Hills, and Paul McNeil. 2000. The archaeological context of late Pleistocene remains from the Wally's Beach site, Alberta. *Society for American Archaeology Abstracts of the 65th Annual Meeting, April 5–9, 2000, Philadelphia, PA.*

Kozłowski, Janusz K. 1986. The Gravettian in central and eastern Europe. *Advances in World Archaeology* 5:131–200.

   1990. Northern central Europe ca. 18,000 BP. In O. Soffer and C. Gamble (eds.), *The World at 18 000 BP. Vol. I : High Latitudes.* London, Unwin Hyman.

   (ed.). 1998. *Complex of Upper Palaeolithic Sites Near Moravany, Western Slovakia. Vol. II: Moravany-Lopata (Excavations 1993–1996).* Kraków, Institute of Archaeology, Jagellonian University, and Nitra, Archaeological Institute, Slovak Academy of Sciences.

   1999. Les origines de la récolonisation de la partie septentrionale de l'Europe centrale après le pleniglaciaire. In M. Kobusiewicz and J. K. Kozłowski (eds.), *Post-Pleniglacial Re-colonisation of the Great European Lowland,* pp. 317–31. Folia Quaternaria 70. Krakow, Polska Akademia Umiejętności.

Kozłowski, Janusz K., H. Kubiak, E. Sachse-Kozłowska, B. Van Vliet, and G. Zakrzewska. 1974. *Upper Paleolithic Site with Dwellings of Mammoth Bones, Kraków-Spadzista Street (B).* Folia Quaternaria 44. Krakow, Polska Akademia Umiejętności.

Kozłowski, Janusz K., and Marcel Otte. 2000. The formation of the Aurignacian in Europe. *Journal of Anthropological Research* 56:513–34.

Krause, Lisa. 2001. Galilee's receding waters reveal stone age camp. On "National Geographic News" website http://news.nationalgeographic.com accessed 2 January 2001.

Krech, Shepard, III. 1999. *The Ecological Indian: Myth and History.* New York, Norton.

Krieger, Alex D. 1957. Early man. *American Antiquity* 22:434–6.

   1962. Comments on "The Paleo-Indian tradition in eastern North America" by R. J. Mason. *Current Anthropology* 3(3):256–9.

   1964. Early man in the New World. In J. D. Jennings and E. Norbeck (eds.), *Prehistoric Man in the New World,* pp. 28–81. Chicago, IL, University of Chicago Press.

Kroeber, A. L. 1962. The Rancho La Brea skull. *American Antiquity* 27:416–19.

Kroeber, A. L., and Clyde Kluckhohn. 1952. *Culture: A Critical Review of Concepts and Definitions.* Papers of the Peabody Museum of American Archaeology and Ethnology, Harvard University, Vol. 47, No. 1. Cambridge, MA.

Kuhn, Thomas. 1962. *The Structure of Scientific Revolutions.* Chicago, IL, University of Chicago Press.

Kuper, Adam. 1999. *Culture: The Anthropologists' Account.* Cambridge, MA, Harvard University Press.

Lahren, Larry, and Robson Bonnichsen. 1974. Bone foreshafts from a Clovis burial in southwestern Montana. *Science* 186:147–50.

Langmuir, Irving (transcribed and edited by Robert N. Hall). 1989. Pathological science: certain symptoms seen in studies of "N rays" and other elusive phenomena characterize "the science of things that aren't so." *Physics Today* 42(10):36–48.

Larsson, Lars. 1999. Perspectives on the colonisation of the Scandinavian peninsula. In M. Kobusiewicz and J. K. Kozłowski (eds.), *Post-Pleniglacial Re-colonisation of the Great European Lowland*, pp. 175–96. Folia Quaternaria 70. Krakow, Polska Akademia Umiejętności.

Laub, Richard S. 1990. The Hiscock site (western New York): recent developments of Pleistocene and early Holocene interest. *Current Research in the Pleistocene* 7:116–18.

　1992. On disassembling an elephant: anatomical observations bearing on Paleoindian exploitation of Proboscidea. In J. W. Fox, C. B. Smith, and K. T. Wilkins (eds.), *Proboscidean and Paleoindian Interactions*, pp. 99–109. Waco, TX, Baylor University Press.

　1994. The Pleistocene/Holocene transition in western New York state: fruits of interdisciplinary studies at the Hiscock site. In R. I. MacDonald (ed.), *Great Lakes Archaeology and Paleoecology: Exploring Interdisciplinary Initiatives for the Nineties*, pp. 155–67. Waterloo, Ontario, Quaternary Sciences Institute.

　1995. The Hiscock site (western New York): recent developments in the study of the late-Pleistocene component. *Current Research in the Pleistocene* 12:26–9.

　2000. A second dated mastodon bone artifact from Pleistocene deposits at the Hiscock site (western New York state). *Archaeology of Eastern North America* 28:141–54.

Laub, Richard S., Catherine A. Dufort, and Donna J. Christensen. 1994. Possible mastodon gastrointestinal and fecal contents from the late Pleistocene of the Hiscock site, western New York state. In E. Landing (ed.), *Studies in Stratigraphy and Paleontology in Honor of Donald W. Fisher*, pp. 135–48. New York State Museum Bulletin 418.

Laub, Richard S., and Gary Haynes. 1998. Fluted points, mastodons, and evidence of late Pleistocene drought at the Hiscock site, western New York state. *Current Research in the Pleistocene* 15:32–4.

Laub, Richard S., Norton G. Miller, and David W. Steadman (eds.). 1988. *Late Pleistocene and Early Holocene Paleoecology and Archeology of the Eastern Great Lakes Region*. Bulletin of the Buffalo Society of Natural Sciences Volume 33. Buffalo, NY.

Laub, Richard S., John Tomenchuk, and Peter L. Storck. 1996. A dated mastodon bone artifact from the late Pleistocene of New York. *Archaeology of Eastern North America* 24:1–17.

Laws, R. M., I. S. C. Parker, and R. C. B. Johnstone. 1975. *Elephants and their Habitats: The Ecology of Elephants in North Bunyoro, Uganda*. Oxford, Clarendon Press.

Layton, R. 1995. Relating to country in the Western Desert. In E. Hirsch and M. O'Hanlon (eds.), *The Anthropology of Landscape: Perspectives on Place and Space*, pp. 210–31. Oxford, Oxford University Press.

　1999. The Alawa totemic landscape: ecology, religion, and politics. In P. J. Ucko and R. Layton (eds.), *The Archaeology and Anthropology of Landscape*, pp. 219–39. New York, Routledge.

Leakey, Louis S. B., Ruth D. Simpson, and Thomas Clements. 1968. Archaeological excavations in the Calico Mountains, California: preliminary report. *Science* 160:1,022–3.

Lee, Richard B. 1968. What hunters do for a living, or, how to make out on scarce resources. In R. B. Lee and I. DeVore (eds.), *Man the Hunter*, pp. 30–48. Chicago, IL, Aldine.

　1980. Lactation, ovulation, infanticide, and women's work: a study of hunter-gatherer population regulation. In M. N. Cohen, R. S. Malpass, and

H. G. Klein (eds.), *Biosocial Mechanisms of Population Regulation*, pp. 321–48. New Haven, CT, Yale University Press.

Lee, Richard B., and Irven DeVore (eds.). 1976. *Kalahari Hunter-Gatherers: Studies of the !Kung San and Their Neighbors.* Cambridge, MA, Harvard University Press.

Lee, Thomas E. 1975. Old Crow? No, thank you! *Anthropological Journal of Canada* 13(3):20–30.

    1977. Introduction to G. F. Carter "On the Antiquity of Man in America." *Anthropological Journal of Canada* 15(1):2–4.

Leonhardy, Frank C. (ed.). 1966. *Domebo: A Paleo-Indian Mammoth Kill in the Prairie-Plains.* Contributions of the Museum of the Great Plains No. 1. Lawton, OK.

Leonhardy, Frank C., and Adrian D. Anderson. 1966. The archaeology of the Domebo site. In F. C. Leonhardy (ed.), *Domebo: A Paleo-Indian Mammoth Kill in the Prairie-Plains*, pp. 14–26. Contributions of the Museum of the Great Plains Number 1. Lawton, OK.

LePage, R. 1968. Problems of description in multilingual communities. *Transactions of the Philological Society* 1968:189–212.

Lepper, Bradley T. 1999. Pleistocene peoples of midcontinental North America. In R. Bonnichsen and K. L. Turnmire (eds.), *Ice Age Peoples of North America: Environments, Origins, and Adaptations of the First Americans*, pp. 362–94. Corvallis, OR, Center for the Study of the First Americans, Oregon State University Press.

Lepper, Bradley T., and David J. Meltzer. 1991. Late Pleistocene human occupation of the eastern United States. In R. Bonnichsen and K. L. Turnmire (eds.), *Clovis: Origins and Adaptations*, pp. 175–84. Corvallis, OR, Center for the Study of the First Americans.

Leroi-Gourhan, André. 1967. *Treasures of Prehistoric Art* (translated by Norbert Guterman). New York, Abrams.

Leschinsky, Sergei V. 1999. The connection of mammoth migrations with geochemical landscapes of Ca-, Mg-, Na-classes in the southeastern part of western Siberia. Paper presented at the 2nd International Mammoth Conference, 16–20 May, Rotterdam, The Netherlands.

Levine, Mary Ann. 1997. The tyranny continues: ethnographic analogy and eastern Paleo-Indians. In L. J. Jackson and P. T. Thacker (eds.), *Caribou and Reindeer Hunters of the Northern Hemisphere*, pp. 221–44. Aldershot, Avebury.

Levins, R. 1968. *Evolution in Changing Environments.* Princeton, NJ, Princeton University Press.

    1969. Some demographic and genetic consequences of environmental heterogeneity for biological control. *Bulletin of the Entomological Society of America* 15:237–40.

Lewis, D. 1972. *We, the Navigators.* Canberra, Australian National University Press.

Lewis, M. A. 1998. Variability, patchiness and jump dispersal in the spread of an invading population. In D. Tilman and P. Kareiva (eds.), *Spatial Ecology: The Role of Space in Population Dynamics and Interspecific Interactions*, pp. 46–69. Princeton, NJ, Princeton University Press.

Lincoln, R. J., and G. A. Boxshall. 1987. *The Cambridge Illustrated Dictionary of Natural History.* Cambridge, Cambridge University Press.

Longvah, T., and Y. G. Deosthale. 1998. Iodine content of commonly consumed foods and water from the goitre-endemic northeast region of India. *Food Chemistry* 61(3):327–31.

Lopinot, Neal H., Jack H. Ray, and Michael D. Conner. 1998. *The 1997 Excavations at the Big Eddy Site (23CE426) in Southwest Missouri.* Southwest Missouri State University Center for Archaeological Research Special Publication No. 2. Springfield, MO.

2000. *The 1999 Excavations at the Big Eddy Site (23CE426)*. Southwest Missouri State University Center for Archaeological Research Special Publication No. 3. Springfield, MO.

Loy, Thomas H. 1983. Prehistoric blood residues: detection on tool surfaces and identification of species of origin. *Science* 220(4,603):1,269–71.

Loy, Thomas H., and E. James Dixon. 1998. Blood residues on fluted points from eastern Beringia. *American Antiquity* 63:21–46.

Lundelius, Ernest L., Jr. 1972. Vertebrate remains from the gray sand. In J. J. Hester, *Blackwater Locality No. 1: A Stratified, Early Man Site in Eastern New Mexico*, pp. 148–63. Fort Burgwin Research Center (Southern Methodist University) Publication No. 8.

Lundelius, E. L., Jr., R. W. Graham, E. Anderson, J. Guilday, J. A. Holman, D. Steadman, and S. D. Webb. 1983. Terrestrial vertebrate faunas. In S. C. Porter (ed.), *Late-Quaternary Environments of the United States, Vol. I: The Late Pleistocene*, pp. 311–53. Minneapolis, University of Minnesota Press.

Lyman, R. Lee, Michael J. O'Brien, and Virgil Hayes. 1998. A mechanical and functional study of bone rods from the Richey-Roberts Clovis cache, Washington, U.S.A. *Journal of Archaeological Science* 25:887–906.

McAndrews, J. H., and L. J. Jackson. 1988. Age and environment of late Pleistocene mastodon and mammoth in southern Ontario. In R. S. Laub, N. G. Miller, and D. W. Steadman (eds.), *Late Pleistocene and Early Holocene Paleoecology of the Eastern Great Lakes Region*, pp. 161–72. Bulletin of the Buffalo Society of Natural Sciences Volume 33. Buffalo, NY.

MacArthur, R. H., and E. R. Pianka. 1966. On optimal use of a patchy environment. *American Naturalist* 100:603–9.

McAvoy, Joseph M. 1992. *Nottoway River Survey, Part I: Clovis Settlement Patterns*. Archaeological Society of Virginia Special Publication No. 28. Richmond, VA.

1997. Addendum: excavation of the Cactus Hill site, 44SX202, areas A–B, Spring 1996: summary report of activities and findings. In *Archaeological Investigations of Site 44SX202, Cactus Hill, Sussex County, Virginia*. Virginia Department of Historic Resources, Research Report Series No. 8. Richmond, VA.

2000. Radiocarbon age range and stratigraphic context of artifact clusters in pre-fluted point levels at Cactus Hill, Sussex Co., Virginia. Paper presented at 65th Annual Meeting of the Society for American Archaeology, Philadelphia, Pennsylvania.

McAvoy, Joseph M., and L. D. McAvoy. 1997. *Archaeological Investigations of Site 44SX202, Cactus Hill, Sussex County, Virginia*. Virginia Department of Historic Resources, Research Report Series No. 8. Richmond, VA.

MacCalman, H. R. 1967. The Zoo Park elephant site, Windhoek (1964–1965). *Palaeoecology of Africa* 2:102–3.

McCary, Ben C. 1986. Early man in Virginia. In J. N. McDonald and S. O. Bird (eds.), *The Quaternary of Virginia – A Symposium Volume*, pp. 71–78. Virginia Division of Mineral Resources Publication 75. Charlottesville, VA.

McCullough, Dale R. 1966. Introduction. In D. R. McCullough (ed.), *Metapopulations and Wildlife Conservation*, pp. 1–10. Washington, DC, Island Press.

MacDonald, Douglas H. 1997. Hunter-gatherer mating distance and early Paleoindian social mobility. *Current Research in the Pleistocene* 14:119–21.

1999. Modeling Folsom mobility, technological organization, and mating strategies in the northern Plains. *Plains Anthropologist* 44(168):141–61.

MacDonald, George F. 1968. *Debert: A Palaeo-Indian Site in Central Nova Scotia*. National Museums of Canada Anthropology Papers No. 16. Ottawa, Ontario.

1982. Foreword. In R. M. Gramly (author), *The Vail Site: A Palaeo-Indian Encampment in Maine*. Bulletin of the Buffalo Society of Natural Sciences Volume 30. Buffalo, NY.

McDonald, Jerry N. 1984. Paleoecological investigations at Saltville, Virginia. *Current Research* 1:77–8.

1985. Late Quaternary deposits and paleohydrology of the Saltville Valley, southwest Virginia. *Current Research* 2:123–4.

1986. On the status of Quaternary vertebrate paleontology and zooarcheology in Virginia. In J. N. McDonald and S. O. Bird (eds.), *The Quaternary of Virginia – A Symposium Volume*, pp. 89–104. Virginia Division of Mineral Resources Publication 75. Charlottesville, VA.

2000. *An Outline of the Pre-Clovis Archeology of SV-2, Saltville, Virginia, with Special Attention to a Bone Tool Dated 14,510 yr BP.* Jeffersoniana (Contributions from the Virginia Museum of Natural History) No. 9. Marlinsville, VA.

McDonald, Kim A. 1998. New evidence challenges traditional model of how the New World was settled: findings hint at arrival of humans almost 30,000 years earlier than many researchers had thought. *The Chronicle of Higher Education* 13 March:A22–A23.

McGlone, Matt S., and Janet M. Wilmshurst. 1999. Dating initial Maori environmental impact in New Zealand. *Quaternary International* 59:5–16.

MacGregor, Arthur. 1985. *Bone, Antler, Ivory, and Horn: The Technology of Skeletal Materials since the Roman Period.* London, Croom Helm.

McKay, G. M. 1973. *The Ecology and Behavior of the Asiatic Elephant in Southeastern Ceylon.* Smithsonian Contributions to Zoology 125. Washington, DC.

McNett, Charles W., Jr. 1985. Artifact morphology and chronology at the Shawnee Minisink site. In C. W. McNett, Jr. (ed.), *Shawnee Minisink: A Stratified Paleoindian–Archaic Site in the Upper Delaware Valley of Pennsylvania*, pp. 83–120. Orlando, FL, Academic Press.

McWeeney, Lucinda. 1999. Revising the Paleoindian environmental picture in northeastern North America. Paper presented at the 64th Annual Meeting of the Society for American Archaeology, Chicago, Illinois.

2001. Paleoindian settlement patterns and environmental change in northern New Hampshire. Paper presented at the 66th Annual Meeting of the Society for American Archaeology, New Orleans, Louisiana.

MacNeish, R. S. 1976. Early man in the New World. *American Scientist* 63:316–27.

1982. A late commentary on an early subject. In J. E. Ericson, R. E. Taylor, and R. Berger (eds.), *Peopling of the New World*, pp. 311–15. Ballena Press Anthropological Papers 23. Los Altos, CA, Ballena Press.

MacNeish, Richard, D. Chrisman, and Geoffrey Cunnar. 1998. Human modification of animal bones in pre-Clovis zones of Pendejo Cave, Orogrande NM. On-line version of poster by Chrisman, MacNeish, and Cunnar 1998 (which see) on website http://www.umas.edu/anthro/features/chrisman/ accessed 10 May 2001.

MacPhee, R. D. E., and P. A. Marx. 1997. The 40,000 year plague: humans, hyperdisease and first-contact extinctions. In S. Goodman and B. Patterson (eds.), *Natural Change and Human Impact in Madagascar*, pp. 169–217. Washington, DC, Smithsonian Institution Press.

Madsen, David B. 2000. A high-elevation Allerød–Younger Dryas megafauna from the west-central Rocky Mountains. In D. B. Madsen and M. D. Metcalf (eds.), *Intermountain Archaeology*, pp. 100–15. University of Utah Anthropological Papers No. 122. Salt Lake City, UT.

Mallouf, Robert J. 1994. Sailor-Helton: a Paleoindian cache from southwestern Kansas. *Current Research in the Pleistocene* 11:44–6.

Mandryk, Carole A. S. 1992. Paleoecology as contextual archaeology: human viability of the late Quaternary ice-free corridor, Alberta, Canada. Unpublished Ph.D. dissertation, University of Alberta, Edmonton.

1998. A geoarchaeological interpretation of the Lamb Spring site, Colorado. *Geoarchaeology* 13(8):819–46.

1999. Geoarchaeological analysis and interpretation of the Lamb Spring site, Colorado. Paper presented at 64th Annual Meeting of the Society for American Archaeology, Chicago, Illinois.

Manitoba Archaeological Society (web development: Brian Schwimmer). 1998. Clovis traditions. http://www.umanitoba.ca/faculties/arts/anthropology/ manarchnet/chronology/paleoindian/clovis2.html accessed December 2000.

Marks, Stuart A. 1971. *Large Mammals and a Brave People: Subsistence Hunters in Zambia.* Seattle, University of Washington Press.

Marshall, Lorna. 1976. *The !Kung of Nyae Nyae.* Cambridge, MA, Harvard University Press.

Martin, John F. 1983. Optimal foraging theory: a review of some models and their applications. *American Anthropologist* 85:612–29.

Martin, Paul S. 1967. Prehistoric overkill. In P. S. Martin and H. E. Wright, Jr. (eds.), *Pleistocene Extinctions: The Search for a Cause,* pp. 75–120. New Haven, CT, Yale University Press.

1973. The discovery of America. *Science* 179:969–74.

1984. Prehistoric overkill: the global model. In P. S. Martin and R. G. Klein (eds.), *Quaternary Extinctions: A Prehistoric Revolution,* pp. 354–403. Tucson, University of Arizona Press.

Martin, Paul S., and Richard G. Klein (eds.). 1984. *Quaternary Extinctions: A Prehistoric Revolution.* Tucson, University of Arizona Press.

Martin, Paul S., and David W. Steadman. 1999. Prehistoric extinctions on islands and continents. In R. D. E. MacPhee (ed.), *Extinctions in Near Time: Causes, Contexts, and Consequences,* pp. 17–55. New York, Kluwer Academic/Plenum Publishers.

Mason, Owen K., Peter M. Bowers, and David M. Hopkins. 2001. The early Holocene Milankovitch thermal maximum and humans: adverse conditions for the Denali complex of eastern Beringia. *Quaternary Science Reviews* 20:525–48.

Mason, Revil J. 1965. Makapansgat limeworks, fractured stone objects and natural fracture in Africa. *South African Archaeological Bulletin* 20(77):3–16.

Mason, Ronald J. 1962. The Paleo-Indian tradition in eastern North America. *Current Anthropology* 3(3):227–78.

1981. *Great Lakes Archaeology.* New York, Academic Press.

Matthiessen, Peter. 1990. *African Silences.* New York, Random House.

Mayer-Oakes, William J. 1986. Early man projectile points and lithic technology in the Ecuadorian Sierra. In A. L. Bryan (ed.), *New Evidence for the Pleistocene Peopling of the Americas,* pp. 133–56. Orono (ME), Center for the Study of Early Man, University of Maine.

Mayer-Oakes, William J., and Alice W. Portnoy. 2000. Ilalo Paleoindian complex in Highland Ecuador. Paper presented at the 65th Annual Meeting of the Society for American Archaeology, Philadelphia, Pennsylvania.

Mayr, E. 1970. *Populations, Species, and Evolution (Abridgement of 1963 Animal Species and Evolution).* Cambridge, MA, Harvard University Press.

Mead, J. I. 1980. Is it really that old? A comment about the Meadowcroft "overview." *American Antiquity* 45(3):579–82.

Mead, J. I., Larry D. Agenbroad, Owen K. Davis, and Paul S. Martin. 1986. Dung of *Mammuthus* in the arid southwest, North America. *Quaternary Research* 25:121–7.

Mead, J. I., R. S. Thompson, and T. R. Van Devender. 1982. Late Wisconsinan and Holocene fauna from Smith Creek Canyon, Snake Range, Nevada. *Transactions of the San Diego Society of Natural History* 20:1–26.

Mehl, Maurice G. 1966. The Domebo mammoth: vertebrate paleomortology. In
F. C. Leonhardy (ed.), *Domebo: A Paleo-Indian Mammoth Kill in the Prairie-Plains*,
pp. 27–30. Contributions of the Museum of the Great Plains No. 1. Lawton,
OK.

    1967. *The Grundel Mastodon*. Missouri Geological Survey and Water Resources
Report of Investigations No. 35. Jefferson City, MI.

    1975. Vertebrate paleomortology at the Cooperton site. In A. D. Anderson (ed.),
The Cooperton Mammoth: An Early Man Bone Quarry, pp. 165–8. Great Plains Journal
14(2).

Mehringer, Peter J., Jr. 1989. Of apples and archaeology. *Universe* 1(2):2–8.

Mehringer, Peter J., Jr., and Franklin F. Foit, Jr. 1990. Volcanic ash dating of the
Clovis cache at East Wenatchee, Washington. *National Geographic Research*
6(4):495–503.

Mehringer, Peter J., Jr., and Warren Morgan. 1988. Weapons cache of ancient
Americans. *National Geographic* 174(4):500–3.

Meighan, Clement W., and C. V. Haynes, Jr. 1970. The Borax Lake site revisited.
Science 167:1,213–21.

Meltzer, David J. 1988. Late Pleistocene human adaptations in eastern North
America. *Journal of World Prehistory* 2:1–53.

    1989a. Why don't we know when the first people came to North America?
American Antiquity 54(3):471–90.

    1989b. Was stone exchanged among eastern North American Paleo-Indians? In
C. Ellis and J. Lothrop (eds.), *Eastern Paleo-Indian Lithic Resource Use*, pp. 11–39.
Boulder, CO, Westview Press.

    1991. On "paradigms" and "paradigm bias" in controversies over human
antiquity in America. In T. D. Dillehay and D. J. Meltzer (eds.), *The First
Americans: Search and Research*, pp. 13–49. Boca Raton, FL, CRC Press.

    1993a. Is there a Clovis adaptation? In O. Soffer and N. D. Praslov (eds.), *From
Kostenki to Clovis: Upper Paleolithic – Paleo-Indian Adaptations*, pp. 293–310. New
York, Plenum Press.

    1993b. The Pleistocene peopling of the Americas. *Evolutionary Anthropology*
1(5):157–69.

    1995. Clocking the first Americans. *Annual Review of Anthropology* 24:21–45.

    1996. A northern perspective on the peopling of the Americas. *Fundhamentos* 1(1)
(*Proceedings of the International Meeting on the Peopling of the Americas, Sao
Raimundo Nonato, Piaui, Brasil* [1993]):241–58.

    1997. Monte Verde and the Pleistocene peopling of the Americas. *Science*
276:754–5.

    1999. On Monte Verde. *Scientific American Discovering Archaeology* [1(6)] *Special Report:
Monte Verde Revisited*, pp. 16–17.

Meltzer, David J., and Robert C. Dunnell. 1987. Fluted points from the Pacific
Northwest. *Current Research in the Pleistocene* 4:64–7.

Meltzer, David J., Donald K. Grayson, Gerardo Ardila, Alex W. Barker, Dena F.
Dincauze, C. Vance Haynes, Francisco Mena, Lautaro Nuñez, and Dennis J.
Stanford. 1997. On the Pleistocene antiquity of Monte Verde, southern Chile.
American Antiquity 62(4):659–63.

Meltzer, David J., and Bruce D. Smith. 1986. Paleoindian and Early Archaic
subsistence strategies in eastern North America. In S. W. Neusius (ed.),
*Foraging, Collecting and Harvesting: Archaic Period Subsistence and Settlement in the
Eastern Woodlands*, pp. 3–31. Center for Archaeological Investigations
Occasional Paper 6. Carbondale, Southern Illinois University.

Melville, Herman. 1948 [orig. 1851]. *Moby Dick or the Whale*. New York, Rinehart and
Co., Inc.

Merrell, D. J. 1981. *Ecological Genetics*. Minneapolis, University of Minnesota Press.

Merriwether, D. A., and R. E. Ferrell. 1996. The four founding lineage hypothesis: a critical re-evaluation. *Molecular Phylogenetics and Evolution* 5:241–6.

Merriwether, D. A., W. W. Hall, A. Vahlne, and R. E. Ferrell. 1996. MtDNA variation indicates Mongolia may have been the source for the founding population of the New World. *American Journal of Human Genetics* 59:204–12.

Merriwether, D. A., F. Rothhammer, and R. E. Ferrell. 1994. Genetic variation in the New World: ancient teeth, bone, and tissue as sources of DNA. *Experientia* 50(6):592–601.

1995. Distribution of the four-founding lineage haplotypes in Native Americans suggests a single wave of migration for the New World. *American Journal of Physical Anthropology* 98(4):411–30.

Mierendorf, Robert R. 1997. Comments on the East Wenatchee Clovis site (43DO482), Washington state, as reported on by Richard M. Gramly. *Current Research in the Pleistocene* 14:57–60.

Milewski, Antoni V. 2000. Iodine as a possible controlling nutrient for elephant populations. *Pachyderm* 28:78–90.

Milewski, Antoni V., and Roger E. Diamond. 2000. Why are very large herbivores absent from Australia? A new theory of micronutrients. *Journal of Biogeography* 27:957–78.

n.d. Ground water as an overlooked source of iodine, a megacatalyst in the nutrition of wild and domestic herbivores. Unpublished presentation/paper.

Miller, George J., Paul Remelka, Julia D. Parks, Betty Stout, and Vern Waters. 1991. *A Preliminary Report on Half-a-Million Year Old Cut Marks on Mammoth Bones from the Anza-Borrego Desert Irvingtonian*. Imperial Valley College Museum Society Occasional Paper No. 8. El Centro, CA.

Miller, Gifford H., John W. Magee, Beverly J. Johnson, Marilyn L. Fogel, Nigel A. Spooner, Malcolm T. McCulloch, and Linda K. Ayliffe. 1999. Pleistocene extinction of *Genyornis newtoni*: human impact on Australian megafauna. *Science* 283:205–8.

Miller, Susanne J. 1982. The archaeology and geology of an extinct megafauna/fluted-point association at Owl Cave, the Wasden Site: a preliminary report. In J. E. Ericson, R. E. Taylor, and R. Berger (eds.), *Peopling the New World*, pp. 81–95. Los Altos, CA, Ballena Press.

1989. Characteristics of mammoth bone reduction at Owl Cave, the Wasden Site, Idaho. In R. Bonnichsen and M. H. Sorg (eds.), *Bone Modification*, pp. 381–93. Orono, ME, Center for the Study of the First Americans, University of Maine.

Miller, Susanne J., and Wakefield Dort, Jr. 1978. Early man at Owl Cave: current investigations at the Wasden Site, eastern Snake River Plain, Idaho. In A. L. Bryan (ed.), *Early Man in America from a Circum-Pacific Perspective*, pp. 129–39. University of Alberta, Edmonton, Department of Anthropology, Occasional Papers No. 1. Edmonton, Alberta.

Milroy, L. 1980. *Language and Social Networks*. Oxford, Blackwell.

Minshall, Herb. 1988. Comments on "Mammoth rib review." *Pacific Coast Archaeological Society Newsletter* 27(10):3.

1989. *Buchanan Canyon: Ancient Human Presence in the Americas*. San Marcos, CA, Slawson Communications.

Mix, Alan C., Edouard Bard, and Ralph Schneider. 2001. Environmental processes of the ice age: land, oceans, glaciers (EPILOG). *Quaternary Science Reviews* 20:627–57.

Mochanov, Yuri A. 1977. *Drevneyshiye Etapy Zaseleniya Chelevekom Severo-Vostochnoy Azii*. Novosibirsk, Nauka.

Mol, Dick, Larry D. Agenbroad, and Jim I. Mead. 1993. *Mammoths*. Hot Springs, The Mammoth Site of Hot Springs, South Dakota, Inc.

Molyneaux, Brian L. 2000. Update on the Northern Loess Hills Clovis Point. *Newsletter of the Iowa Archaeological Society* 50(4):1–2.

Moore, J., and R. Ali. 1984. Are dispersal and inbreeding avoidance related? *Animal Behaviour* 32:94–112.

Moratto, Michael J. 1984. *California Archaeology*. Orlando, FL, Academic Press.

Morell, Virginia. 1990. Monte Verde archaeologist prevails in dispute over setllement's age. *The Scientist* 4(2):1, and "The Scientist" website http://www.the-scientist.com/yr1990/jan/morell_p1_900120.html accessed December 2000.

Moreno, Patricio I., Heather Almquist-Jacobson, George H. Denton, Eric C. Grimm, George L. Jacobson, Jr., and William A. Watts. 1998. Interhemispheric correlation of millennial scale climate changes during the termination of the last ice age: the southern Andes, peninsular Florida, and central Europe. *American Quaternary Association Program and Abstracts of the 15th Biennial Meeting, September 5–7, 1998, Puerto Vallarta, Mexico*, pp. 51–3.

Morett A., Luis, Joaquín Arroyo-Cabrales, and Oscar Polaco. 1998. Tocuila, a remarkable mammoth site in the Basin of Mexico. *Current Research in the Pleistocene* 15:118–20.

Morlan, Richard E. 1979. A stratigraphic framework for Pleistocene artifacts from Old Crow River, northern Yukon. In R. L. Humphrey and D. Stanford (eds.), *Pre-Llanao Cultures in the Americas: Paradoxes and Possibilities*, pp. 125–45. Washington DC, Anthropological Society of Washington.

1980. *Taphonomy and Archaeology in the Upper Pleistocene of the Northern Yukon Territory: A Glimpse of the Peopling of the New World*. National Museum of Man [Canada] Mercury Series, Archaeological Survey of Canada No. 94. Ottawa, Ontario.

1986. Pleistocene archaeology in Old Crow Basin: a critical appraisal. In A. L. Bryan (ed.), *New Evidence for the Pleistocene Peopling of the Americas*, pp. 27–48. Orono, ME, Center for the Study of Early Man, University of Maine.

1991. Peopling of the New World: a discussion. In R. Bonnichsen and K. L. Turnmire (eds.), *Clovis: Origins and Adaptations*, pp. 303–7. Corvallis, OR, Center for the Study of the First Americans.

Morlan, R. E., A. S. Dyke, and R. N. McNeely. 1999. Mapping ancient history. Website http://sts.gsc.nrcan.gc.ca/tsdweb/geoserv-mah.asp accessed September 2001.

Morris, E. A., and R. C. Blakeslee. 1987. Comment on the Paleoindian occurrence of spurred end scrapers as reported by Rogers. *American Antiquity* 52:830–1.

Morrow, Julie E. 1995. Clovis projectile point manufacture: a perspective from the Ready/Lincoln Hills site, 11JY46, Jersey County, Illinois. *Midcontinental Journal of Archaeology* 20(2):167–91.

1996. The organization of Clovis lithic technology in the Confluence region of the Mississippi, Illinois, and Missouri rivers. Unpublished Ph.D. dissertation, Washington University at St. Louis, Missouri.

1997. Clovis lithic technology at the Struttman Eikel site. *Current Research in the Pleistocene* 14:65–7.

2000a. Clovis in the Midwest. *American Quaternary Association Program and Abstracts of the 16th Biennial Meeting, Fayetteville, Arkansas, May 22–24, 2000*, p. 86.

2000b. A Clovis camp at the Martens site. *Central States Archaeological Journal* 47(2):84–5.

Morrow, Juliet E., and Toby A. Morrow. 1999. Geographic variation in fluted projectile points: a hemispheric perspective. *American Antiquity* 64(2):215–31.

Morrow, Toby A., and Juliet E. Morrow. 1994. A preliminary survey of Iowa fluted points. *Current Research in the Pleistocene* 11:47–8.

Morse, Dan F. 1997. *Sloan: A Paleoindian Dalton Cemetery in Arkansas*. Washington D.C., Smithsonian Institution Press.

Morse, Dan F., and Phyllis A. Morse. 1983. *Archaeology of the Central Mississippi Valley*. New York, Academic Press.

Mosimann, J. E., and P. S. Martin. 1975. Simulating overkill by Paleoindians. *American Scientist* 63:304–13.

Moss, Cynthia J. 1982. *Portraits in the Wild: Behavior Studies of East African Mammals*. Chicago, IL, University of Chicago Press.

Muniz, Mark. 1998. Clovis site distributions. Paper presented at the 31st Chacmool Conference, 14 November 1998, Calgary, Alberta, Canada. Cited on "The Aucilla Times" 12(1) website http://www.flmnh.ufl.edu/natsci/vertpaleo/aucilla12_1/clovis99.htm accessed August 2001.

Mussi, Margherita, and Wil Roebroeks. 1996. The big mosaic. *Current Anthropology* 37(4):697–9.

Myers, Thomas P., and R. George Corner. 1986. Possible evidence for a pre-Clovis bone-tool industry from the central Plains. *Transactions of the Nebraska Academy of Sciences* 14:41–5.

Myers, Thomas P., Michael R. Voorhies, and R. George Corner. 1980. Spiral fractures and bone pseudo-tools at paleontological sites. *American Antiquity* 45(3):483–90.

Nadel, Dani, and Ella Werker. 1999. The oldest ever brush hut plant remains from Ohalo II, Jordan Valley, Israel (19,000 BP). *Antiquity* 73:755–64.

National Research Council. 1968a. *Nutrient Requirements of Domestic Animals, Number 2: Nutrient Requirements of Swine, Sixth Revised Edition*. Publication 1599, National Academy of Sciences. Washington, DC.

   1968b. *Nutrient Requirements of Domestic Animals, Number 5: Nutrient Requirements of Sheep, Fourth Revised Edition*. Publication 1693, National Academy of Sciences. Washington, DC.

Neigel, J. E., R. M. Ball, Jr., and J. C. Avise. 1991. Estimation of single generation migration distances from geographic variation in animal mitochondrial DNA. *Evolution* 45(2):423–32.

Nelson, D. E., R. E. Morlan, J. S. Vogel, J. R. Southern, and C. R. Harrington. 1986. New radiocarbon dates on artifacts from the northern Yukon Territory: Holocene not upper Pleistocene in age. *Science* 232:749–51.

Nettle, Daniel. 1998. Explaining global patterns of language diversity. *Journal of Anthropological Archaeology* 17:354–74.

Neves, Walter. 2000. Luzia is not alone. *Science* 287:973.

Neves, Walter A., and H. M. Pucciarelli. 1991. Morphological affinities of the first Americans: an exploratory analysis based on early South American human remains. *Journal of Human Evolution* 21(4):261–73.

Nials, Fred. 1999. *Geomorphic Systems and Stratigraphy in Internally-Drained Watershed of the Northern Great Basin: Implications for Archaeological Studies*. Sundance Archeological Research Fund, University of Nevada, Reno, Technical Paper #5.

Nichols, Johanna. 1990. Linguistic diversity and the first settlement of the New World. *Language* 66(3):475–521.

   1997. Modeling ancient population structures and movement in lingusitics. *Annual Review of Anthropology* 26:359–84.

Norton, Mark R., John B. Broster, and Emanuel Breitburg. 1998. The Trull site (40PY276): a Paleoindian–mastodon association in Tennessee. *Current Research in the Pleistocene* 15:50–1.

O'Connell-Rodwell, C. E., B. T. Arnason, and L. A. Hart. 2000. Seismic properties of Asian elephant (Elephas maximus) vocalizations and locomotion. Journal of the Acoustical Society of America 108(6):3,066–72.

Odell, George H. (ed.). 1996. Stone Tools: Theoretical Insights into Human Prehistory. New York, Plenum Press.

2000. Stone tool research at the end of the millennium: procurement and technology. Journal of Archaeological Research 8(4):269–331.

Oreskes, Naomi. 1999. The Rejection of Continental Drift: Theory and Method in American Earth Science. New York, Oxford University Press.

Orlova, L. A., Y. V. Kuzmin, and I. D. Zolnikov. 2000. Time-space systematics for mammoths (Mammuthus primigenius Blum.) and prehistoric humans in Siberia (on the basis of radiocarbon dating). Archaeology, Ethnology & Anthropology of Eurasia 3(3):31–41.

O'Rourke, Dennis H., M. Geoffrey Hayes, and Shawn W. Carlyle. 2000. Ancient DNA studies in physical anthropology. Annual Review of Anthropology 29:217–42.

Orr, P. C. 1956. Pleistocene man in Fishbone Cave, Pershing County, Nevada. Nevada State Museum Bulletin 2:1–20.

1962. The Arlington Springs site, Santa Rosa Island. American Antiquity 27:417–19.

1974. Notes on the Archaeology of the Winnemucca Lake Caves, 1952–1958. Nevada State Museum Anthropological Papers No. 16. Carson City, NV.

Osborn, Henry Fairfield (edited by M. R. Percy). 1936. Proboscidea: A Monograph of the Discovery, Evolution, Migration and Extinction of the Mastodonts and Elephants of the World, Volume I: Moeritherioidea, Deinotherioidea, Mastodontoidea. New York, American Museum of Natural History.

1942. Proboscidea: A Monograph of the Discovery, Evolution, Migration and Extinction of the Mastodonts and Elephants of the World, Volume II: Stegondontoidea, Elephantoidea. New York, American Museum of Natural History.

Otte, Marcel. 1981. Le Gravettien en Europe centrale. Dissertationes Archaeologicae Gandenses no. 20.

1999. Civilisations du tardiglaciaire en Europe du nord-ouest. In M. Kobusiewicz and J. K. Kozłowski (eds.), Post-Pleniglacial Re-colonisation of the Great European Lowland, pp. 115–25. Folia Quaternaria 70. Krakow, Polska Akademia Umiejętności.

Otte, Marcel, and Lawrence H. Keeley. 1990. The impact of regionalism on Paleolithic studies. Current Anthropology 31(5):577–82.

Overstreet, David F. 1993. Chesrow, A Paleoindian Complex in the Southern Lake Michigan Basin. Case Studies in Great Lakes Archaeology, No. 2. Milwaukee, WI, Great Lakes Archaeological Press.

1996. Still more on cultural contexts of mammoth and mastodont in the southwestern Lake Michigan basin. Current Research in the Pleistocene 13:36–8.

Overstreet, David F., D. J. Joyce, K. Hallin, and D. Wasion. 1993. Cultural contexts of mammoth and mastodon in the southwest Lake Michigan Basin. Current Research in the Pleistocene 10:75–7.

Overstreet, David F., Daniel J. Joyce, and D. Wasion. 1995. More on cultural context of mammoth and mastodont in the southwestern Lake Michigan basin. Current Research in the Pleistocene 12:40–2.

Overstreet, David F., and Thomas W. Stafford, Jr. 1997. Additions to a revised chronology for cultural and non-cultural mammoth and mastodon fossils in the southwestern Lake Michigan basin. Current Research in the Pleistocene 14:70–1.

Owen-Smith, Norman. 1987. Pleistocene extinctions: the pivotal role of megaherbivores. Paleobiology 13:351–62.

1988. *Megaherbivores: The Influence of Very Large Body Size on Ecology.* Cambridge, Cambridge University Press.

1999. The interaction of humans, megaherbivores, and habitats in the late Pleistocene extinction event. In R. D. E. MacPhee (ed.), *Extinctions in Near Time: Causes, Contexts, and Consequences*, pp. 57–69. New York, Kluwer Academic/ Plenum Publishers.

Owsley, Douglas W., and David R. Hunt. 2001. Clovis and Early Archaic crania from the Anzick site (24PA506), Park County, Montana. *Plains Anthropologist* 46(176):115–24.

Packer, C. 1985. Dispersal and inbreeding avoidance. *Animal Behaviour* 33:676–87.

Palmer, Harris A., and James B. Stoltman. 1976. The Boaz mastodon: a possible association of man and mastodon in Wisconsin. *Midcontinental Journal of Archaeology* 1:163–77.

Parkman, Francis. 1949 [orig. 1847]. *The Oregon Trail: Sketches of Prairie and Rocky-Mountain Life.* New York, The Modern Library.

Patrusky, Ben. 1980. Pre-Clovis man: sampling the evidence. *Mosaic* Sept./Oct. 1980:2–10.

Patterson, Leland W. 1999. Popular misconceptions concerning the Calico site. *Current Research in the Pleistocene* 16:57–9.

Pavesic, Max G. 1985. Cache blades and turkey-tails: piecing together the western Idaho burial complex. In M. G. Plew, J. C. Woods, and M. G. Pavesic (eds.), *Stone Tool Analysis: Essays in Honor of Don E. Crabtree*, pp. 55–89. Albuquerque, University of New Mexico Press.

Pavlov, Pavel, John Inge Svendsen, and Svein Indrelid. 2001. Human presence in the European Arctic nearly 40,000 years ago. *Nature* 413:64–7.

Payen, Louis Arthur. 1982. The pre-Clovis of North America: temporal and artifactual evidence. Unpublished Ph.D. dissertation, University of California, Riverside.

Payne, K. B., W. R. Langbauer, Jr., and E. M. Thomas. 1986. Infrasonic calls of the Asian elephant. *Behavioral Ecology and Sociobiology* 18:297–301.

Peale, Rembrandt. 1803. *An Historical Disquisition on the Mammoth, or, Great American Incognitum, an Extinct, Immense, Carnivorous Animal, Whose Fossil Remains Have Been Found in North America.* London, E. Lawrence.

Peterkin, Gail Larsen. 1993. Lithic and organic hunting technology in the French Upper Paleolithic. In G. L. Peterkin, H. M. Bricker, and P. Mellars (eds.), *Hunting and Animal Exploitation in the Later Palaeolithic and Mesolithic of Eurasia*, pp. 49–67. Archaeological Papers of the American Anthropological Association No. 4. Arlington, VA.

Peterson, John H., Jr. 1993. Epilogue: whales and elephants as cultural symbols. In *Community-Based Whaling in the North*, pp. 172–4. *Arctic* 46(2).

Petrides, G. A., and R. G. Swank. 1966. Estimating the productivity and energy relations of an African elephant population. *Proceedings of the IX International Grasslands Congress, São Paulo, Brazil, January 1965*, pp. 831–42.

Pettipas, Leo F. 1967. Paleo-Indian manifestations in Manitoba: their spatial and temporal relationship with the Campbell Strandline. Unpublished M.A. thesis, University of Manitoba.

Peyrony, D. 1933. Les industries "aurignaciennes" dans le bassin de la Vézère. *Bulletin de la Société Préhistorique Française* 30:543–58.

Pianka, Eric R. 1994. *Evolutionary Ecology*, 5th edition. New York, HarperCollins College Publishers.

Pidoplichko, I. G. 1976. *Mezhiricheskoe zhilizche iz kostei mamonta.* Kiev, Naukova Dumka.

Pike-Tay, Anne, and Harvey M. Bricker. 1993. Hunting in the Gravettian: an examination of evidence from southwestern France. In G. L. Peterkin, H. M.

Bricker, and P. Mellars (eds.), *Hunting and Animal Exploitation in the Later Palaeolithic and Mesolithic of Eurasia*, pp. 127–43. Archeological Papers of the American Anthropological Association No. 4. Arlington, VA.

Pohorecky, Zenon S., and D. E. Anderson. 1968. Agassiz archaeology in Saskatchewan. *Na'pao* 1(1):48–70.

Poirier, Sylvie. 1992. "Nomadic" rituals: networks of ritual exchange between women of the Australian Western Desert. *Man* (N.S.) 27(4):757–76.

Poole, J. H., K. B. Payne, W. R. Langbauer, Jr., and C. J. Moss. 1988. The social context of some very low frequency calls of African elephants. *Behavioral Ecology and Sociobiology* 22:385–92.

Porter, J. H., and J. L. Dooley, Jr. 1993. Animal dispersal patterns: a reassessment of simple mathematical models. *Ecology* 74(8):2,346–443.

Porter, S. C. 1988. Landscapes of the last Ice Age in North America. In R. C. Carlisle (ed.), *Americans before Columbus: Ice-Age Origins*, pp. 1–24. University of Pittsburgh Ethnology Monograph No. 12. Pittsburgh, PA.

Posner, Gerald. 1993. *Case Closed: Lee Harvey Oswald and the Assassination of JFK*. New York, Random House.

Powers, W. Roger, and John F. Hoffecker. 1989. Late Pleistocene settlement in the Nenana Valley, central Alaska. *American Antiquity* 54:263–78.

Pozos, Randolfo Rafael. 1986. *The Face on Mars*. Chicago, IL, Chicago Review Press.

Prentice, I. Colin, Dominique Jolly, and BIOME 6000 participants. 2000. Mid-Holocene and glacial-maximum vegetation geography of the northern continents and Africa. *Journal of Biogeography* 27:507–19.

Preston, D. 1995. The mystery of Sandia Cave. *The New Yorker* 71(16):66–83.

Purdy, Barbara A. 1991. *The Art and Archaeology of Florida's Wetlands*. Boca Raton, FL, CRC Press.

Putnam, Charles E. 1886. *Elephant Pipes and Inscribed Tablets in the Museum of Academy of Natural Sciences, Davenport, Iowa*, 2nd edition, reprinted from Vol. IV, *Proceedings Davenport Academy*. Davenport, IA, Glass & Axtman.

Putschkov, P. V. 1997. Were the mammoths killed by the warming? Testing of the climatic versions of Würm extinctions. *Vestnik Zoologicheskii: Journal of the Schmalhausen Institute of Zoology*, Supplement 4:3–81.

Rachlow, Janet L. 1997. Demography, behavior, and conservation of white rhinos. Unpublished Ph.D. dissertation, University of Nevada, Reno.

Raloff, Janet. 2000. Cetacean seniors: whales that give new meaning to longevity. *Science News* 158:254–5.

Ramakrishnan, U., R. Manjrekar, J. Rivera, T. Gonzalez-Cossio, and R. Martorell. 1999. Micronutrients and pregnancy outcome: a review of the literature. *Nutrition Research* 19(1):103–59.

Rancier, James, Gary Haynes, and Dennis Stanford. 1982. 1981 investigations at Lamb Spring. *Southwestern Lore* 48(2):1–17.

Ranta, Esa, Veijo Kaitala, and Per Lundberg. 1997. The spatial dimension in population fluctuations. *Science* 278:1,621–3.

  1999. Synchronicity in population systems: cause and consequence mixed. *Trends in Evolution and Ecology* 14(10):400–1.

Raup, David M. 1994. The extinction debates: a view from the trenches. In W. Glen (ed.), *The Mass-Extinction Debates: How Science Works in a Crisis*, pp. 145–51. Stanford, CA, Stanford University Press.

Ray, Clayton E., B. N. Cooper, and W. S. Benninghoff. 1967. Fossil mammals and pollen in a late Pleistocene deposit at Saltville, Virginia. *Journal of Paleontology* 41:608–62.

Ray, Jack H., Neal H. Lopinot, and Edwin R. Hajic. 1998. The Big Eddy Site: a multicomponent Paleoindian site on the Ozark border, southwest Missouri. On website of Southwest Missouri State University, Center for Archaeological Research http://www.smsu.edu/car/BigEddy2.html accessed August 2001.

Reanier, R. E. 1995. The antiquity of Paleoindian materials in northern Alaska. Arctic Anthropology 32:31–50.

Redmond, Brian, and Kenneth B. Tankersley. 1999. Description of a Paleoindian bone point from Sheriden Pit. Paper presented at the 64th Annual Meeting of the Society for American Archaeology, Chicago, Illinois.

Remer, T., A. Neubert, and F. Manz. 1999. Increased risk of iodine deficiency with vegetarian nutrition. The British Journal of Nutrition 81(1):45–9.

Rendall, Doris L. 1966. A barbed antler point found at Pyramid Lake, Nevada. American Antiquity 31(5):740–2.

Rensink, Eelco. 1999. The Magdalénian site of Eyserheide and the Late Glacial human colonisation of the southern Netherlands. In M. Kobusiewicz and J. K. Kozłowski (eds.), Post-Pleniglacial Re-colonisation of the Great European Lowland, pp. 87–100. Folia Quaternaria 70. Krakow, Polska Akademia Umiejętności.

Richardson, D. M., P. A. Williams, and R. J. Hobbs. 1994. Pine invasions in the southern hemisphere: determinants of spread and invadability. Journal of Biogeography 21:511–27.

Richardson, R. H. 1970. Models and analyses of dispersal patterns, in K. Kolima (ed.), Mathematical Topics in Population Genetics, pp. 79–103. New York, Springer-Verlag.

Riddell, F. A. 1973. Fossilized California bone artifacts. The Masterkey 47:28–32.

Riddell, F. A., and W. H. Olsen. 1969. An early man site in the San Joaquin Valley. American Antiquity 34(2):121–30.

Ripley, Suzanne. 1980. Infanticide in langurs and man: adaptive advantage or social pathology? In M. N. Cohen, R. S. Malpass, and H. G. Klein (eds.), Biosocial Mechanisms of Population Regulation, pp. 349–90. New Haven, CT, Yale University Press.

Rippeteau, Bruce (ed.). 1979. Megafauna Punchers' Review 1(1). Office of the State Archaeologist, Denver, CO.

Ritchie, William A. 1953. A probable Paleo-Indian site in Vermont. American Antiquity 18(3):249–58.

1957. Traces of Early Man in the Northeast. New York State Museum and Science Service Bulletin 358. New York.

Ritchie, William A., and Robert E. Funk. 1973. Aboriginal Settlement Patterns in the Northeast. New York State Museum and Science Service Memoir No. 20. New York.

Roberts, Richard G., Timothy F. Flannery, Linda K. Ayliffe, Hiroyuki Yoshida, Jon M. Olley, Gavin J. Prideaux, Geoff M. Laslett, Alexander Baynes, M. A. Smith, Rhys Jones, and Barton L. Smith. 2001. New ages for the last Australian megafauna: continent-wide extinction about 46,000 years ago. Science 292:1,888–92.

Rodbell, Donald T. 2000. The Younger Dryas: cold, cold everywhere? Science 290:285–6.

Roebroeks, W., N. J. Conard, and T. van Kolfschoten. 1992. Dense forests, cold steppes, and the Palaeolithic settlement of northern Europe. Current Anthropology 33(5):551–86.

Rogers, R. A. 1986. Spurred end scrapers as diagnostic Paleoindian artifacts: a distributional analysis on stream terraces. American Antiquity 51:338–41.

Rogers, R. A., L. A. Rogers, and L. D. Martin. 1992. How the door opened: the peopling of the New World. *Human Biology* 64(3):281–301.

Roosevelt, Anna C. 2000. Who's on first? There's still no end to the controversy over when and how humans populated the New World [review of T. Dillehay's *The Settlement of the Americas* and of E. J. Dixon's *Bones, Boats, and Bison*]. *Natural History* 109(6):76–9.

Roosevelt, Anna C., John Douglas, Linda Brown, Ellen Quinn, Judy Kemp, and Susan Weld. 1998. Terminal Pleistocene occupations in North Asia and North America: another look at dating, geography, lithic styles, and subsistence. Paper presented at the 63rd Annual Meeting of the Society for American Archaeology, Seattle, Washington.

Roosevelt, Anna C., Matthew O'Donnell, Ellen Quinn, Judy Kemp, Christiane Lopes Machado, Maura Imazio da Silveira, and Marcondes Lima da Costa. 1998. Clovis clarification: a follow-up. *Mammoth Trumpet* 13(1):14–17.

Rose, Mark. 1999a. Monte Verde under fire. Archaeological Institute of America website http://www.archaeology.org/online/features/clovis/index.html accessed February 2001.

1999b. The Topper site: pre-Clovis surprise. *Archaeology* 52(4), and Archaeological Institute of America website http://www.archaeology.org/9907/newsbriefs/clovis.html accessed June 2001.

Rothschild, Bruce M. 2001. Hyper-disease at the Hiscock site: fact and theory. Paper presented at the Smith Symposium II: "The Hiscock Site: Late Pleistocene and Holocene Paleoecology and Archaeology of Western New York State," 14–15 October 2001, Buffalo, New York.

Rousseau, Dennis. 1992. Case studies in pathological science. *The American Scientist* 80:54–63.

Rowlett, Ralph M. 1981. A lithic assemblage stratified beneath a fluted point horizon in northwest Missouri. *Missouri Archaeologist* 42:7–16.

Rowlett, R. M., and E. G. Garrison. 1984. Analysis of Shriver site artifacts by thermoluminescence. *Missouri Archaeological Society Quarterly* 1(4):20–2.

Ruhlen, Merrit. 1991. The Amerind phylum and the prehistory of the New World. In S. M. Lamb and E. D. Mitchell (eds.), *Sprung from Some Common Source*, pp. 328–50. Stanford, CA, Stanford University Press.

1994. Linguistic evidence for the peopling of the Americas. In R. Bonnichsen and D. G. Steele (eds.), *Method and Theory for Investigating the Peopling of the Americas*, pp. 177–88. Corvallis, OR, Center for the Study of the First Americans.

Rutter, Nathaniel W., Andrew J. Weaver, Dean Rokosh, Augustus F. Fanning, and Daniel G. Wright. 2000. Data-model comparison of the Younger Dryas event. *Canadian Journal of Earth Sciences* 37:811–30.

Salmon, Merilee. 1982. *Philosophy and Archaeology*. New York, Academic Press.

Sanchez, Guadalupe, and John Carpenter. 2000. The El Bajío Clovis site in Sonora, Mexico. *Archaeology Southwest* 14(2). Online archive at www.cdarc.org/cdarc/pubs/arch_sw/v14_no2/el_bajio.htm accessed 16 November 2001.

Sapir, J. David. 1987. Comments on J. H. Greenberg book "Language in the Americas," appearing in "Language in the Americas: A CA Book Review." *Current Anthropology* 28(5):663–4.

Saunders, Jeffrey J. 1977. Lehner Ranch revisited. In E. Johnson (ed.), *Paleoindian Lifeways*, pp. 48–64. *The Museum Journal* (Lubbock, Texas) 17.

1980. A model for man–mammoth relationships in late Pleistocene North America. In N. W. Rutter and C. E. Schweger (eds.), *The Ice-Free Corridor and the Peopling of the New World*, pp. 87–98. *Canadian Journal of Anthropology* 1.

1992. Blackwater Draws: mammoths and mammoth hunters in the terminal Pleistocene. In J. W. Fox, C. B. Smith, and K. T. Wilkins (eds.), *Proboscidean and Paleoindian Interactions*, pp. 123–47. Waco, TX, Baylor University Press.

1996. North American Mammutidae. In J. Shoshani and P. Tassy (eds.), *The Proboscidea: Evolution and Palaeoecology of Elephants and Their Relatives*, pp. 271–9. Oxford, Oxford University Press.

(n.d.). Vertebrates of the San Pedro Valley 11,000 B.P. Contribution No. 68 of the Archaeological and Quaternary Studies Program of the Illinois State Museum. (Manuscript.)

Saunders, Jeffrey J., George A. Agogino, Anthony T. Boldurian, and C. Vance Haynes, Jr. 1991. A mammoth-ivory burnisher-billet from the Clovis level, Blackwater Locality No. 1, New Mexico. *Plains Anthropologist* 36(137):359–63.

Saunders, Jeffrey J., and Edward B. Daeschler. 1994. Descriptive analyses and taphonomical observations of culturally-modified mammoths excavated at "The Gravel Pit," near Clovis, New Mexico in 1936. *Proceedings of the Academy of Natural Sciences of Philadelphia* 145:1–28.

Saunders, Jeffrey J., C. Vance Haynes, Jr., Dennis Stanford, and George A. Agogino. 1990. A mammoth-ivory semifabricate from Blackwater Locality No. 1, New Mexico. *American Antiquity* 55:112–19.

Schurr, Theodore G. 2000. Mitochondrial DNA and the peopling of the New World. *American Scientist* 88:246–53.

Schurr, Theodore G., and Douglas C. Wallace. 1999. MtDNA variation in Native Americans and Siberians and its implications for the peopling of the New World. In R. Bonnichsen (ed.), *Who Were the First Americans? Proceedings of the 58th Annual Biology Colloquium, Oregon State University*, pp. 41–77. Corvallis, OR, Center for the Study of the First Americans, Oregon State University.

Scott, Thomas A. 1994. Irruptive dispersal of black-shouldered kites to a coastal island. *The Condor* 96(1):197–200.

Sealy, J., and S. Pfeiffer. 2000. Diet, body size, and landscape use among Holocene people in the southern Cape, South Africa. *Current Anthropology* 41(4):642–55.

Segerstråle, Ullica. 2000. *Defenders of the Truth: The Battle for Science in the Sociobiology Debate and Beyond*. Oxford, Oxford University Press.

Sellards, E. H. 1938. Artifacts associated with fossil elephant. *Bulletin of the Geological Society of America* 49:999–1,010.

1952. *Early Man in America: A Study in Prehistory*. Austin, University of Texas Press.

Sellet, F. 1999. A dynamic view of Paleoindian assemblages at the Hell Gap Site, Wyoming: reconstructing lithic technological systems. Unpublished doctoral dissertation, Southern Methodist University.

Semenov, S. A. 1976. *Prehistoric Technology: An Experimental Study of the Oldest Stone Tools and Artefacts from Traces of Manufacture and Wear*, translated by M. W. Thompson; originally published in Russian in 1957. New York, Barnes and Noble.

Semino, Ornella, Giuseppe Passarino, Peter J. Oefner, Alice A. Lin, Scetlana Arbuzova, Lars E. Beckman, Giovanna De Benedictis, Paolo Francalacci, Anastasia Kouvatsi, Svetlana Limborska, Mladen Marcikiae, Anna Mika, Barbara Mika, Dragan Primorac, A. Sivana Santachiara-Benerecetti, L. Luca Cavalli-Sforza, and Peter A. Underhill. 2000. The genetic legacy of Paleolithic *Homo sapiens sapiens* in extant Europeans: a Y chromosome perspective. *Science* 290:1,155–9.

Severin, Tim. 1978. *The Brendan Voyage*. New York, McGraw-Hill.

Sherratt, Andrew. 1997. Climatic cycles and behavioural revolutions. *Antiquity* 71:271–87.

Shipman, Pat. 2000. Doubting Dmanisi. *American Scientist* 88:491–4.

Shipman, P., D. C. Fisher, and J. J. Rose. 1984. Mastodon butchery: microscopic evidence of carcass processing and bone tool use. *Paleobiology* 10(3):358–65.

Shiraishi, K., Y. Muramatsu, I. P. Los, V. N. Korzun, N. Y. Tsigankov, and P. V. Zamostyan. 1998. Estimation of dietary iodine and bromine intakes of Ukrainians. *Journal of Radioanalytical and Nuclear Chemistry* 242(1):199–202.

Shoshani, Jeheskel. 1990. Distribution of *Mammut americanum* in the New World. *Current Research in the Pleistocene* 7:124–7.

Shott, Michael J. 1986. Settlement mobility and technological organization among Great Lakes Paleo-Indian foragers. Unpublished Ph.D. dissertation, University of Michigan, Ann Arbor.

1993. *The Leavitt Site: A Parkhill Phase Paleo-Indian Occupation in Central Michigan*, University of Michigan Museum of Anthropology Memoirs No. 25.

1995. How much is a scraper? Curation, use rates, and the formation of scraper assemblages. *Lithic Technology* 20:53–72.

1999. On bipolar reduction and splintered pieces. *North American Archaeologist* 20:217–38.

(n d.). Midwest Regional Paleoindian Synthesis. (Manuscript.)

Siebe, C., P. Schaaf, and J. Urrutia-Fucugauchi. 1999. Mammoth bones embedded in a late Pleistocene lahar from Popocatapetl volcano, near Tocuila, central Mexico. *Bulletin of the Geological Society of America* 111(10):1,550–62.

Sikes, Sylvia K. 1971. *The Natural History of the African Elephant*. London, Weidenfield and Nicolson.

Simon, Bart. 1999. Post-closure cold fusion and the survival of a research community: an hauntology for the technoscientific afterlife. Unpublished Ph.D. dissertation, University of California, San Diego.

Simons, Donald B. 1997. The Gainey and Butler sites as focal points for caribou and people. In L. J. Jackson and P. T. Thacker (eds.), *Caribou and Reindeer Hunters of the Northern Hemisphere*, pp. 105–31. Aldershot, Avebury.

Simons, Donald B., Michael J. Shott, and Henry T. Wright. 1987. Paleoindian research in Michigan: current status of the Gainey and Leavitt projects. *Current Research in the Pleistocene* 4:27–30.

Simpson, Ruth DeEtte. 1964. The archaeological survey of Pleistocene Manix Lake (an early lithic horizon). *Proceedings of the (35th) International Congress of Americanists* 35:5–9.

Simpson, Ruth DeEtte, Leland W. Patterson, and Clay A. Singer. 1986. Lithic technology of the Calico Mountains site, southern California. In A. L. Bryan (ed.), *New Evidence for the Pleistocene Peopling of the Americas*, pp. 89–105. Orono, ME, Center for the Study of Early Man, University of Maine at Orono.

Slobodin, Sergey. 1999. Northeast Asia in the late Pleistocene and early Holocene. *World Archaeology* 30(3):484–502.

Snow, Dean R. 1980. *The Archaeology of New England*. New York, Academic Press.

Soffer, Olga A. 1985. *The Upper Paleolithic of the Central Russian Plain*. New York, Academic Press.

1989. Female imagery in the Paleolithic: an introduction to the work of M. D. Gvozdover. *Soviet Anthropology and Archaeology* 27(4):3–8.

1993. Upper Paleolithic adaptations in central and eastern Europe and man–mammoth interactions. In O. Soffer and N. D. Praslov (eds.), *From Kostenki to Clovis: Upper Paleolithic – Paleo-Indian Adaptations*, pp. 31–49. New York, Plenum Press.

Soffer, Olga, J. M. Adovasio, and D. C. Hyland. 2000. The "Venus" figurines: textiles, basketry, gender, and status in the Upper Paleolithic. *Current Anthropology* 41(4):511–37.

Soffer, Olga, J. M. Adovasio, J. S. Illingworth, H. A. Amirkhanov, N. D. Praslov, and M. Street. 2000. Palaeolithic perishables made permanent. *Antiquity* 74:812–21.

Soffer, Olga, and Margaret Conkey. 1997. Studying ancient visual culture. In M. Conkey, P. Soffer, D. Stratmann, and N. Jablonski (eds.), *Beyond Art: Pleistocene Image and Symbol*, pp. 1–16. San Francisco, California Academy of Sciences.

Soffer, Olga, and Nikolai Dmitrievich Praslov. 1993. Introduction: fluted points and female figurines – understanding late Paleolithic people of the New and Old Worlds. In O. Soffer and N. D. Praslov (eds.), *From Kostenki to Clovis: Upper Paleolithic – Paleo-Indian Adaptations*, pp. 3–14. New York, Plenum Press.

Sokal, Alan, and Jean Bricmont. 1999. *Fashionable Nonsense: Postmodern Intellectuals' Abuse of Science*. New York, St. Martin's Press.

Spencer, Frank. 1990a. *Piltdown: A Scientific Forgery*. New York, Oxford University Press.

1990b. *The Piltdown Papers: 1908–1955*. New York, Oxford University Press.

Spiess, Arthur E., Mary Lou Curran, and J. Grimes. 1985. Caribou (*Rangifer tarandus* L.) bones from New England Paleoindian sites. *North American Archaeologist* 6:145–59.

Spiess, Arthur E., and Peter L. Storck. 1990. New faunal identifications from the Udora site: a Gainey-Clovis occupation site in southern Ontario. *Current Research in the Pleistocene* 7:127–8.

Spiess, Arthur E., and D. B. Wilson. 1987. *The Michaud Site: A Paleo-Indian Site in the New England Maritimes Region*. Occasional Publications in Maine Archaeology No. 6 (The Maine Historical Commission and the Maine Archaeological Society, Inc.).

Stafford, Thomas W., Jr. 1988. Accelerator ^{14}C dating of late Pleistocene megafauna. *Current Research in the Pleistocene* 5:41–3.

1994. Accelerator C-14 dating of human fossil skeletons: assessing accuracy and results on New World specimens. In R. Bonnichsen and D. G. Steele (eds.), *Method and Theory for Investigating the Peopling of the Americas*, pp. 45–55. Corvallis, OR, Center for the Study of the First Americans.

1999a. Chronologies for the oldest human skeletons in the New World. *Geological Society of America* Vol. 31, No. 7 (1999 Annual Meeting, Abstracts with Program), p. 24.

1999b. How radiocarbon dating has changed archaeological perspectives on the New World. Presentation at "A Celebration in Honor of Vance Haynes," 24 September 1999, Tucson, Arizona.

Stafford, Thomas W., Jr., Klaus Brendel, and Raymond C. Duhamel. 1988. Radiocarbon, ^{13}C and ^{15}N analysis of fossil bone: removal of humates with XAD-2 resin. *Geochimica et Cosmochimica Acta* 52:2,257–67.

Stafford, T. W., Jr., R. W. Graham, H. A. Semken, Jr., and J. Southon. 1997a. AMS ^{14}C chronologies for late Pleistocene mammal extinctions and human migrations in North America. Abstracts of 1997 CAVEPS on website http://bioscience.babs.unsw.edu.au/CAVEPS/abstrN-T.htm accessed January 2001.

1997b. Chronology and timing of the terminal Pleistocene extinction event in the mid-latitudes of North America. Paper presented at 7th International Theriological Congress, Acapulco, Mexico.

Stafford, Thomas W., Jr., P. E. Hare, Lloyd Currie, A. J. T. Jull, and Douglas Donahue. 1991. Accelerator radiocarbon dating at the molecular level. *Journal of Archaeological Science* 18:35–72.

Stafford, Thomas W., Jr., A. J. T. Jull, Klaus Brendel, Raymond C. Duhamel, and Douglas Donahue. 1987. Study of bone radiocarbon dating accuracy at the University of Arizona NSF Accelerator Facility for Radioisotope Analysis. *Radiocarbon* 29(1):24–44.

Stanford, Dennis. 1979. The Selby and Dutton sites: evidence for a possible pre-Clovis occupation of the High Plains. In R. L. Humphrey and D. Stanford (eds.), *Pre-Llano Cultures of the Americas: Paradoxes and Possibilities*, pp. 101–23. Washington, D.C., Anthropological Society of Washington.

1982. A critical review of archaeological evidence relating to the antiquity of human occupation of the New World. In D. H. Ubelaker and H. J. Viola (eds.), *Plains Indian Studies*, pp. 202–18. Smithsonian Contributions to Anthropology No. 30. Washington, DC, Smithsonian Institution.

1983. Pre-Clovis occupation south of the ice-sheets. In R. Shutler, Jr. (ed.), *Early Man in the New World*, pp. 65–72. Beverly Hills, CA, Sage Publications.

1987. The Ginsberg experiment. *Natural History* 96(9):10, 12–14.

1989. The first Americans: a new perspective. Paper presented at the 33rd Annual Symposium of the Archaeological Society of Maryland, Crownsville, Maryland.

1991. Clovis origins and adaptations: an introductory perspective. In R. Bonnichsen and K. L. Turnmire (eds.), *Clovis: Origins and Adaptations*, pp. 1–13. Corvallis, OR, Oregon State University and Center for the Study of the First Americans.

1996. Foreshaft sockets as possible Clovis hafting devices. *Current Research in the Pleistocene* 13:44–6.

1997. What does the new evidence mean? Oral presentation at "Who Were the First Americans?" 58th Annual Biology Colloquium, 24 April, Oregon State University, Corvallis, Oregon.

1999a. Alternative views on the peopling of the Americas. Banquet address at the "Clovis and Beyond" conference, 28–31 October 1999, Santa Fe, New Mexico.

1999b Paleoindian archaeology and late Pleistocene environments in the Plains and southwestern United States. In R. Bonnichsen and K. L. Turnmire (eds.), *Ice Age Peoples of North America: Environments, Origins, and Adaptations*, pp. 281–339. Corvallis, OR, Center for the Study of the First Americans and Oregon State University Press.

Stanford, Dennis, Rob Bonnichsen, and Richard E. Morlan. 1981. The Ginsberg experiment: modern and prehistoric evidence of a bone flaking technology. *Science* 212:438–40.

Stanford, Dennis, and Bruce Bradley. 2000. The Solutrean solution: did some ancient Americans come from Europe? *Discovering Archaeology* 2(1):54–5.

Stanford, Dennis, and Margaret A. Jodry. 1988. The Drake Clovis cache. *Current Research in the Pleistocene* 5:21–2.

Stanford, Dennis J., Margaret A. Jodry, and Larry Banks. 1995. Early Paleoindian diet breadth as seen from the Lewisville site, Texas: critter buffet as an alternative to mammoth barbecue. Paper presented at the 60th Annual Meeting of the Society for American Archaeology, Minneapolis, Minnesota. [Cited in Stanford 1999b.]

Steadman, David W. 1988. Vertebrates from the late Quaternary Hiscock site, Genesee County, New York. In R. S. Laub, N. G. Miller, and D. W. Steadman (eds.), *Late Pleistocene and Early Holocene Paleoecology and Archeology of the Eastern Great Lakes Region*, pp. 95–113. Bulletin of the Buffalo Society of Natural Sciences Volume 33. Buffalo, NY.

Steadman, David W., Thomas W. Stafford, Jr., and Robert E. Funk. 1997. Nonassociation of Paleoindians with AMS-dated late Pleistocene mammals from the Dutchess Quarry Caves, New York. *Quaternary Research* 47(1):105–16.

Steele, D. Gentry. 1989. Recently recovered Paleoindian skeletal remains from Texas and the Southwest. *American Journal of Physical Anthropology* 78:307 (abstract).

Steele, D. Gentry, and David L. Carlson. 1989. Excavation and taphonomy of mammoth remains from the Duewall-Newberry site, Brazos County, Texas. In R. Bonnichsen and M. H. Sorg (eds.), *Bone Modification*, pp. 413–30. Orono, ME, Center for the Study of the First Americans, University of Maine.

Steele, D. Gentry, and Joseph F. Powell. 1994. Paleobiological evidence of the peopling of the Americas: a morphometric view. In R. Bonnichsen and D. G. Steele (eds.), *Method and Theory for Investigating the Peopling of the Americas*, pp. 141–63. Corvallis, OR, Center for the Study of the First Americans, Oregon State University.

Steele, James, Jonathan Adams, and Tim Sluckin. 1998. Modelling Paleoindian dispersal. *World Archaeology* 30(2):286–305.

Stenger, Victor J. 2000. Buddy can you paradigm? *CSICOP On-Line, Skeptical Briefs* 10(3). On-Line Archive: www.csicop.org/sb/2000–09/reality-check.html, accessed 16 November 2001.

Stewart, T. D. 1946. A re-examination of the fossil human skeletal remains from Melbourne, Florida. *Smithsonian Miscellaneous Collections* 106:1–28.

Stock, Chester. 1972. *Rancho La Brea: A Record of Pleistocene Life in California*, 6th edition, 7th printing. Los Angeles County Museum of Natural History Science Series No. 20, Paleontology, No. 11. Los Angeles.

Stone, Anne. 1997. Reconstructing human societies with ancient molecules. Presentation at "Who Were the First Americans?" 58th Annual Biology Colloquium, 24 April, Oregon State University, Corvallis.

Storck, Peter L. 1983. Commentary on AENA's compilation of fluted points in eastern North America. *Archaeology of Eastern North America* 11:34–6.

1988. The early Palaeo-Indian colonization of Ontario: colonization or diffusion? In R. S. Laub, N. G. Miller, and D. W. Steadman (eds.), *Late Pleistocene and Early Holocene Paleoecology and Archeology of the Eastern Great Lakes Region*, pp. 243–50. Bulletin of the Buffalo Society of Natural Sciences Volume 33. Buffalo, NY.

1990. Excavations at the early Paleo-Indian Udora site, Georgina Township, York County. *Annual Archaeological Report, Ontario (Ontario Heritage Foundation)* 1:51–2.

1991. Imperialists without a state: the cultural dynamics of early Paleoindian colonization as seen from the Great Lakes region. In R. Bonnichsen and K. L. Turnmire (eds.), *Clovis: Origins and Adaptations*, pp. 153–62. Corvallis, OR, Center for the Study of the First Americans.

1997. *The Fisher Site: Archaeological, Geological and Paleobotanical Studies at an Early Paleo-Indian Site in Southern Ontario, Canada*. Memoirs, Museum of Anthropology, University of Michigan, No. 30. Ann Arbor, MI.

Storck, Peter L. and John Tomenchuk. 1990. An early Paleoindian cache of informal tools at the Udora site, Ontario. In K. B. Tankersley and B. L. Isaac (eds.), *Early Paleoindian Economies of Eastern North America*, pp. 45–93. Research in Economic Anthropology, Supplement 5.

Straus, Lawrence Guy. 2000. Solutréan settlement of North America? A review of reality. *American Antiquity* 65(2):219–26.

Straus, Lawrence Guy, and Marcel Otte. 1995. Stone age Wallonia (southern Belgium). *Current Anthropology* 36:851–4.

Stringer, C. B. 1994. Out of Africa – a personal history. In M. H. Nitecki and D. V. Nitecki (eds.), *Origins of Anatomically Modern Humans*, pp. 149–72. New York, Plenum Press.

Stuiver, M., P. J. Reimer, E. Bard, J. W. Beck, G. S. Burr, K. A. Hughen, B. Kromer, F. G. McCormac, J. van den Plicht, and M. Spurk. 1998. INTCAL98 radiocarbon age calibration, 24,000–0 cal BP. *Radiocarbon* 40:1,041–83.

Sukumar, R. 1989. *The Asian Elephant: Ecology and Management*. Cambridge, Cambridge University Press.

Sullivan, Walter. 1991. *Continents in Motion: The New Earth Debate*. New York, American Institute of Physics.

Surovell, Todd A. 2000a. Early Paleoindian women, children, mobility, and fertility. *American Antiquity* 65(3):493–508.

    2000b. Can a coastal migration explain Monte Verde? Paper presented at the 65th Annual Meeting of the Society for American Archaeology, Philadelphia, Pennsylvania.

Svoboda, Jiří (ed.). 1994. *Pavlov I: Excavations 1952–1953*. Etudes et Récherches Archéologiques de l'Université de Liège [ERAUL] 66: The Dolní Věstonice Studies, Vol. 2.

Tankersley, Kenneth B. 1994a. Was Clovis a colonizing population in eastern North America? In W. S. Dancey (ed.), *The First Discovery of America: Archaeological Evidence of the Early Inhabitants of the Ohio Area*, pp. 95–116. Columbus, The Ohio Archaeological Council.

    1994b. Clovis mastic and its hafting implications. *Journal of Archaeological Science* 21:117–24.

    1996. Archaeological paradigms, provincialism, and semantics: a reply to Beck's comments. *Journal of Archaeological Science* 23:455–8.

    1997. Sheriden: a Clovis cave site in eastern North America. *Geoarchaeology* 12(6):713–24.

    1998. The Crook County Clovis cache. *Current Research in the Pleistocene* 15:86–8.

    1999. Sheriden Cave, Ohio. Poster presented at the "Clovis and Beyond" conference, 28–31 October, Santa Fe, New Mexico.

    2000. Interpreting early Paleoindian subsistence strategies in late Pleistocene eastern North America. Paper presented at the 65th Annual Meeting of the Society for American Archaeology, Philadelphia, Pennsylvania.

Tankersley, Kenneth B., Kenneth M. Ford, Hugh Gregory McDonald, Robert A. Genheimer, and Richard Hendricks. 1997. Late Pleistocene archaeology of Sheriden Cave, Wyandot County, Ohio. *Current Research in the Pleistocene* 14:81–3.

Tankersley, Kenneth B., and Patrick J. Munson. 1999. The chronostratigraphy of Sheriden Pit. Paper presented at the 64th Annual Meeting of the Society for American Archaeology, Chicago, Illinois.

Tankersley, Kenneth B., and Brian G. Redmond. 1999. Radiocarbon dating of a Paleoindian projectile point from Sheriden Cave, Ohio. *Current Research in the Pleistocene* 16:76–7.

Tankersley, Kenneth B., Edward E. Smith, and Donald R. Cochran. 1990. The distribution of fluted points in Indiana: an update. *Current Research in the Pleistocene* 7:47–9.

Tarasov, P. E., V. S. Volkova, T. Webb III, J. Guiot, A. A. Andreev, L. G. Bezusko, T. V. Bezusko, G. V. Bykova, N. I. Dorofeyuk, E. V. Kvavadze, I. M. Osipova, N. K. Panova, and D. V. Sevastyanov. 2000. Last glacial maximum biomes reconstructed from pollen and plant macrofossil data from northern Eurasia. *Journal of Biogeography* 27(3):609–20.

Taubes, Gary. 1993. *Bad Science: The Short Life and Weird Times of Cold Fusion*. New York, Random House.

Taylor, D. C. 1969. The Wilsall excavations: an exercise in frustration. *Proceedings of the Montana Academy of Sciences* 29:147–50.

Taylor, J. G. 1969. William Turner's journeys to the caribou country with the Labrador Eskimos in 1780. *Ethnohistory* 16(2):141–64.

Taylor, R. E. 1991. Frameworks for dating the late Pleistocene peopling of the Americas. In T. D. Dillehay and D. J. Meltzer (eds.), *The First Americans: Search and Research*, pp. 77–111. Boca Raton, FL, CRC Press.

Taylor, R. E., C. V. Haynes, Jr., and Minze Stuiver. 1996. Clovis and Folsom age estimates: stratigraphic context and radiocarbon calibration. *Antiquity* 70(269):515–25.

Taylor, R. E., L. A. Payen, C. A. Prior, P. J. Slota, Jr., R. Gillespie, F. A. Gowlett, R. M. C. Hedges, A. J. T. Jull, T. H. Zabel, D. J. Donahue, and R. Berger. 1985. Major revisions in the Pleistocene age assignments for North American human skeletons by C-14 accelerator mass spectrometry: none older than 11,000 C-14 years B.P. *American Antiquity* 50:136–40.

Thieme, Hartmut. 1997. Lower Paleolithic hunting spears from Germany. *Nature* 385:807–10.

Thomas, David Hurst. 1999. One archaeologist's perspective on the Monte Verde controversy. Posted on Archaeological Institute of America website http://www.archaeology.org/online/features/clovis/index.html and accessed 15 January 2001.

   2000. *Skull Wars: Kennewick Man, Archaeology, and the Battle for Native American Identity*. New York, Basic Books.

Thompson, Robert S. 1985. The age and environment of the Mount Moriah (Lake Mojave) occupation at Smith Creek Cave, Nevada. In J. I. Mead and D. J. Meltzer (eds.), *Environments and Extinctions: Man in Late Glacial North America*, pp. 111–19. Orono, ME, Center for the Study of Early Man.

Thompson, Robert S., and Jim I. Mead. 1982. Late Quaternary environments and biogeography in the Great Basin. *Quaternary Research* 17:39–55.

Thoreau, Henry D. 1863. *Excursions*. Boston, MA, Ticknor and Fields.

Thorpe, Roger S., Duncan P. McGregor, Alastair M. Cumming, and William C. Jordan. 1994. DNA evolution and colonization sequence of island lizards in relation to geological history: mtDNA, RFLP, cytochrome B, cytochrome oxidase, 12s rRNA sequence, and nuclear RAPD analysis. *Evolution* 48:230–40.

Ting, Peter C. 1968. Bone points from Pyramid Lake. *The Nevada Archaeological Reporter* 2(3):4–13.

Titmus, Gene L., and James C. Woods. 1991. Fluted points from the Snake River Plain. In R. Bonnichsen and K. L. Turnmire (eds.), *Clovis: Origins and Adaptations*, pp. 119–31. Corvallis, OR, Center for the Study of the First Americans.

Tixier, J. 1974. *Glossary for the Description of Stone Tools With Special Reference to the Epipalaeolithic of the Maghreb*. Newsletter of Lithic Technology: Special Publication No. 1.

Tomenchuk, John. 1997. A parametric use-wear study of artifacts from areas C and C-east. In P. L. Storck, *The Fisher Site: Archaeological, Geological and Paleobotanical Studies at an Early Paleo-Indian Site in Southern Ontario, Canada*, pp. 95–161. University of Michigan Museum of Anthropology Memoirs No. 30. Ann Arbor, MI.

Tomenchuk, John, and Richard S. Laub. 1995. New insights into late Pleistocene bone technology at the Hiscock site, western New York state. *Current Research in the Pleistocene* 12:71–4.

Tomenchuk, John, and Peter L. Storck. 1997. Two newly recognized Paleoindian tool types: single- and double-scribe compass gravers and coring gravers. *American Antiquity* 62(3):508–22.

Torroni, A., and D. C. Wallace. 1995. MtDNA haplogroups in Native Americans. *American Journal of Human Genetics* 56:1,234–6.

Trigger, Bruce G. 2000. Book review of *The Land of Prehistory: A Critical History of American Archaeology* by Alice Beck Kehoe 1998 (q.v.). *American Antiquity* 65(4):776–7.

Truesdale, V. W., and S. D. Jones. 1996. The variation of iodate and total iodine in some UK rainwaters during 1980–1981. *Journal of Hydrology* 179:67–86.

Tuohy, Donald R. 1990. Pyramid Lake fishing: the archaeological record. In J. C. Janetski and D. B. Madsen (eds.), *Wetland Adaptations in the Great Basin*, pp. 121–58. Museum of Peoples and Cultures [Brigham Young University] Occasional Papers No. 1. Provo, UT.

Tuohy, Donald R., and Amy J. Dansie. 1997. New information regarding early Holocene manifestations in the western Great Basin. *Nevada Historical Society Quarterly* 40(1):24–53.

Turner, E. Randolph III. 2000. Archaeological investigations at the Cactus Hill site, Sussex Co., Virginia: an overview. Paper presented at the 65th Annual Meeting of the Society for American Archaeology, Philadelphia, Pennsylvania.

Tylor, Edward Burnett. 1871. *Primitive Culture* (2 vol.). London, Murray.

Underhill, P. A., P. Shen, A. A. Lin, L. Jin, G. Passarino, W. H. Yang, E. Kauffman, B. Bonné-Tamir, J. Bertranpetit, P. Francalacci, M. Ibrahim, T. Jenkins, J. R. Kidd, S. Q. Mehdi, M. T. Seielstad, R. S. Wells, A. Piazza, R. W. Davis, M. W. Feldman, L. L. Cavalli-Svorza, and P. J. Oefner. 2000. Y chromosome sequence variation and the history of human populations. *Nature Genetics* 26(3):358–61.

Vartanyan, S. L., V. E. Garutt, and A. V. Sher. 1993. Holocene dwarf mammoths from Wrangel Island in the Siberian Arctic. *Nature* 362:337–40.

Vencl, Slavomil. 1999. Late Upper and Late Palaeolithic in the Czech Republic. In M. Kobusiewicz and J. K. Kozłowski (eds.), *Post-Pleniglacial Re-colonisation of the Great European Lowland*, pp. 289–96. Folia Quaternaria 70. Krakow, Polska Akademia Umiejętności.

Vereshchagin, N. K. 1977. Berelyokhskoye "kladbische" mamontov. *Trudi Zoologicheskovo Instituta* 72:5–50.

Vesper, D., and R. Tanner. 1984. Man and mammoth in Kentucky. *Ohio Archaeologist* 34(3):18–19.

Voorhies, Michael R., and R. George Corner. 1984. The Crappie Hole site: a concentration of spirally fractured Rancholabrean mammal bones in western Nebraska. *Current Research* 1:53–4.

Wallace, D., and A. Torroni. 1992. American Indian prehistory as written in the mitochondrial DNA: a review. *Human Biology* 64(3):403–16.

Walthall, John A. 1998. Rockshelters and hunter-gatherer adaptation to the Pleistocene/Holocene transition. *American Antiquity* 63(2):223–38.

Ward, Peter. 1997. *The Call of Distant Mammoths: Why the Ice Age Mammals Disappeared.* New York, Copernicus.

Warren, E. R. 1927. *The Beaver.* Baltimore, MD, Williams and Wilkins.

Warren, S. H. 1920. Natural "eolith" factory beneath the Thanet sand. *Quarterly Journal of the Geologic Society* 76:238–53.

Waser, P. M. 1985. Does competition drive dispersal? *Ecology* 66:1,170–5.

Waters, Michael R. 1985. Early man in the New World: an evaluation of the radiocarbon-dated pre-Clovis sites in the Americas. In J. I. Mead and D. J. Meltzer (eds.), *Environments and Extinctions: Man in Late Glacial North America*, pp. 125–43. Orono, ME, Center for the Study of Early Man.

Waters, Michael D. 1986. Sulphur Springs woman: an early human skeleton from south-eastern Arizona. *American Antiquity* 51:361–5.

Webb, S. David, and James Dunbar. 1999. Ivory shafts from Florida: form, function, manufacture and art. Paper presented at the 64th Annual Meeting of the Society for American Archaeology, Chicago, Illinois.

Webb, S. David, James S. Dunbar, and Benjamin I. Waller. 1990. Ecological implications of ivory foreshafts from underwater sites in Florida. Paper presented at the Sixth International Conference for Archaeozoology, 21–25 May, Washington, D.C.

Webb, S. David, J. T. Milanich, R. Alexon, and J. S. Dunbar. 1984. A *Bison antiquus* kill site, Wacissa river, Jefferson County, Florida. *American Antiquity* 49:384–92.

Webster, D., and G. Webster. 1984. Optimal hunting and Pleistocene extinction. *Human Ecology* 12:275–89.

Wehrberger, Kurt. 1994. Raubkatzen in der Kunst des Jungpaläolithikums. In K. Wehrberger (ed.), *Der Löwenmensch: Tier und Mensch in der Kunst der Eiszeit*, pp. 53–75. Ulm, Ulmer Museum and Jan Thorbecke Verlag.

Weir, F. A. 1985. An early Holocene burial at the Wilson-Leonard site in central Texas. *Mammoth Trumpet* 2:1–3.

Weir, John S. 1969. Chemical properties and occurrence on Kalahari sand of salt licks created by elephants. *Journal of Zoology* 158:293–310.

    1972. Spatial distribution of elephants in an African national park in relation to environmental sodium. *Oikos* 23(1):1–13.

Weiss, K. M. 1988. In search of times past: gene-flow and invasion in the generation of human diversity. In C. G. N. Mascie-Taylo and G. Lasker (eds.), *Biological Aspects of Human Migration*, pp. 130–66. Cambridge, Cambridge University Press.

West, Frederick Hadleigh (ed.). 1996. *American Beginnings: The Prehistory and Palaeoecology of Beringia*. Chicago, IL, University of Chicago Press.

Wheeler, S. M. 1997. Cave burials near Fallon, Nevada. *Nevada Historical Society Quarterly* 40(1):15–23 [includes Dansie, Amy: "Note on textiles associated with the Spirit Cave burials," pp. 17–18].

Whitley, D. S., and R. I. Dorn. 1993. New perspectives on the Clovis vs. pre-Clovis controversy. *American Antiquity* 58(4):626–47.

Wiessner, Polly, and Wulf Schiefenhövel (ed.). 1996. *Food and the Status Quest: An Interdisciplinary Perspective*. Providence, RI, Berghahn Books.

Wilford, John Noble. 1998. Chilean field yields new clues to peopling Americas. *New York Times* 25 August: F1, F6.

Wilke, Philip J. 1988. Bow staves harvested from Juniper trees by Indians of Nevada. *Journal of California and Great Basin Anthropology* 10(1):3–31.

Wilke, P. J., J. J. Flenniken, and T. L. Ozbun. 1991. Clovis technology at the Anzick site, Montana. *Journal of California and Great Basin Anthropology* 13(2):242–72.

Wilkinson, D. H. 1952. The random element in bird "navigation." *Journal of Experimental Biology* 29:532–60.

Willey, Gordon R. 1966. *An Introduction to American Archaeology, Volume One: North and Middle America.*, Englewood Cliffs, NJ, Prentice-Hall.

    1974. New World prehistory: 1974. *American Journal of Archaeology* 78:321–31.

Williams, N, and E. S. Hunn (ed.). 1982. *Resource Managers: North American and Australian Hunter-Gatherers*. Boulder, CO, Westview Press.

Williamson, Basil R. 1975. Seasonal distribution of elephant in Wankie National Park. *Arnoldia Rhodesia* 11(7):1–16.

Willig, Judith A. 1988. Early human occupation and lakeside settlement pattern in the Dietz sub-basin of Alkali Lake, Oregon. In J. A. Willig, C. M. Aikens, and J. L. Fagan (eds.), *Early Human Occupation in Far Western North America: The Clovis-Archaic Interface*, pp. 417–82. Nevada State Museum Anthropological Papers No. 21. Carson City, NV.

    1989. Paleo-Archaic broad spectrum adaptations at the Pleistocene–Holocene boundary in far western North America. Unpublished Ph.D. dissertation, University of Oregon, Eugene.

    1991. Clovis technology and adaptation in far western North America: regional pattern and environmental context. In R. Bonnichsen and K. L. Turnmire (eds.), *Clovis: Origins and Adaptations*, pp. 91–118. Corvallis, OR, Center for the Study of the First Americans.

Willig, Judith A., and C. Melvin Aikens. 1988. The Clovis–Archaic interface in far western North America. In J. A. Willig, C. M. Aikens, and J. L. Fagan (eds.), *Early Human Occupation in Far Western North America: The Clovis–Archaic Interface*, pp. 1–40. Nevada State Museum Anthropological Papers No. 21. Carson City, NV.

Wilmeth, Roscoe. 1968. A fossilized bone artifact from southern Saskatchewan. *American Antiquity* 33:100–1.

Wilmsen, Edwin N., and Frank H. H. Roberts. Jr. 1984. *Lindenmeier, 1934–1974: Concluding Report on Investigations.* Smithsonian Contributions to Anthropology No. 24. Washington, DC, Smithsonian Institution.

Wilson, Michael Clayton, and James A. Burns. 1999. Searching for the earliest Canadians: wide corridors, narrow doorways, small windows. In R. Bonnichsen and K. L. Turnmire (eds.), *Ice Age Peoples of North America: Environments, Origins, and Adaptations of the First Americans*, pp. 213–48. Corvallis, OR, Oregon State University Press/Center for the Study of the First Americans.

Wilson, Michael, Lawrence C. Todd, and George C. Frison. (n.d.). Bison dentitions from the Murray Springs site, Arizona. (Manuscript submitted 1975 to C. V. Haynes for inclusion in Murray Springs publication.)

Wing, Leonard. 1943. Spread of the starling and English sparrow. *Auk* 60:74–87.

Witthoft, John. 1952. A Paleo-Indian site in eastern Pennsylvania: an early hunting culture. *Proceedings of the American Philosophical Society* 96:464–95.

Wittry, Warren L. 1965. The Institute digs a mastodon. *Cranbrook Institute of Science News Letter* 35(2):14–19.

Wobst, H. Martin. 1974. Boundary conditions for Paleolithic social systems: a simulation. *American Antiquity* 39:147–78.

   1978. The archaeo-ethnology of hunter-gatherers, or the tyranny of the ethnographic record in archaeology. *American Antiquity* 43(2):303–9.

Woods, J. C., and G. L. Titmus. 1985. A review of the Simon Clovis collection. *Idaho Archaeologist* 8(1):3–8.

World Health Organisation. 1996. *Trace Elements in Human Nutrition and Health.* Geneva, World Health Organisation.

Wormington, H. M. 1957 (orig. 1949) *Ancient Man in North America*, 4th edition. The Denver Museum of Natural History Popular Series No. 4. Denver, CO.

Wotzka, Hans-Peter. 1997. Massstabsprobleme bei der etnischen Deutung neolithischer "Kulturen." *Das Altertum* 43:163–76.

Wright, George Frederick. 1892. *Man and the Glacial Period.* New York, D. Appleton and Company.

Wright, Herbert E., Jr. 1991. Environmental conditions for Paleoindian immigration. In T. D. Dillehay and D. J. Meltzer (eds.), *The First Americans: Search and Research*, pp. 113–35. Boca Raton, FL, CRC Press.

Wyckoff, Don. 1999. The Burnham site and Pleistocene human occupations on the Southern Plains. In R. Bonnichsen and K. L. Turnmire (eds.), *Ice Age Peoples of North America: Environments, Origins, and Adaptations of the First Americans*, pp. 340–61. Corvallis, OR, Oregon State University and Center for the Study of the First Americans.

Wylie, Alison. 1985. The reaction against analogy. In M. B. Schiffer (ed.) *Advances in Archaeological Method and Theory*, Vol. 8, pp. 63–111. New York, Academic Press.

Yellen, J. E., and H. C. Harpending. 1972. Hunter-gatherer populations and archaeological inference. *World Archaeology* 4:244–53.

Yesner, David R. 1994. Subsistence diversity and hunter-gatherer strategies in late Pleistocene/early Holocene Beringia: evidence from the Broken Mammoth site, Big Delta, Alaska. *Current Research in the Pleistocene* 11:154–6.

1995. Whales, mammoths, and other big beasts: assessing their roles in prehistoric economies. In A. P. McCartnety (ed.), *Hunting the Largest Animals: Native Whaling in the Western Arctic and Subarctic*, pp. 149–64. University of Alberta, The Canadian Circumpolar Institute, Occasional Publication No. 36, Studies in Whaling No. 3. Edmonton, Alberta.

1996. Human adaptation at the Pleistocene–Holocene boundary (circa 13,000 to 8,000 BP) in eastern Beringia. In L. G. Straus, B. V. Eriksen, J. Erlandson, and D. R. Yesner (eds.), *Humans at the End of the Ice Age: The Archaeology of the Pleistocene–Holocene Transition*, pp. 255–76. New York, Plenum Press.

Yokoyama, Yusuke, Kurt Lambeck, Patrick De Deckker, Paul Johnston, and L. Kieth Fifield. 2000. Observed sea-level minima. *Nature Asia* 406:713.

Young, D. A., and R. L. Bettinger. 1995. Simulating the global human expansion in the Late Pleistocene. *Journal of Archaeological Science* 22:89–92.

1997. Computer simulations of the colonization of continents. Paper presented at the 62nd Annual Meeting of the Society for American Archaeology, Nashville, Tennessee.

Young, D. E. 1988. The double burial at Horn Shelter: an osteological analysis. *Central Texas Archaeologist* 11:11–115.

Youngson, Robert. 1998. *Scientific Blunders: A Brief History of How Wrong Scientists Can Sometimes Be*. New York, Carroll and Graf.

Yun, Miryung. 1995. Cold fusion: a case study of science reporting. Unpublished M.Sc. thesis, University of Utah.

Zimov, S. A., V. I. Chuprynin, A. P. Oreshko, F. S. Chapin III, J. F. Reynolds, and M. C. Chapin. 1995. Steppe–tundra transition: a herbivore-driven biome shift at the end of the Pleistocene. *The American Naturalist* 146(5):765–94.

Index

Note: the letter "F" following a page number indicates occurrence in a figure or figure caption; "T" following a page number indicates occurrence in a table. The letters "aka" mean "also known as."